Third Reich Dagger Reproductions

By

J.A. Bowman

Published by Imperial Publications

Printed and bound by The Cromwell Press Limited

Third Reich Dagger Reproductions

By
J.A. Bowman

First Edition

Typeset by Fast Moving Typesetting,
Kendal, Cumbria, England
Layout by Findlay Martin

Cover Design by Brian Molloy
B.M. Graphics

ISBN: 1 871498 16 3

Published by Imperial Publications
P.O. Box 5, Lancaster, LA1 1BQ England

CONTENTS

INTRODUCTION

This book came about in response to many requests from collectors who wanted a single volume work which dealt exclusively with the subject of Third Reich dagger reproductions. Whilst the previous work on the subject THIRD REICH DAGGERS 1933-1945 had an extensive reproduction section, not everyone wanted to wade through 500 pages of text to glean the information. Consequently this new book has restricted itself to the reproductions of Nazi daggers which have appeared on the market since 1945. Much of the information in THIRD REICH DAGGERS 1933-1945 is still valid today and has been expanded to include new information and photographs. Also there are many new collectors who have not had access to that publication due to its being out of print for several years.

The variety of reproductions, fakes and fantasy daggers featured in this book may give the impression that the collector has a hopeless task in determining the authenticity of a dagger - the reverse is true; for armed with these facts the dagger enthusiast can gather a collection in which he can now have confidence. Also this book's intent is not to deter the collector from his chosen hobby, but to enhance it. There are undoubtedly many reproductions and parts assembly daggers on the market, however it should be stressed that the balance is still in favour of genuine daggers with reproductions being in the minority. The area of greatest concern to the collector is not the outright reproduction but the parts assembly daggers which use a mixture of genuine parts usually allied to good quality reproduction blades. This is especially troubling with the rarer SA and SS daggers which can quite easily have their market price increased by 10 or 20 fold by the simple expedient of substituting a more desirable albeit reproduction blade.

Quite often reproduction and parts assembly daggers find their way onto the market through reputable sources: this is especially true of Auction Houses who have a vested interest in realising the highest price possible to maximise their commissions. Unfortunately for collectors many Auction Houses which catalogue Nazi daggers are often somewhat ambiguous in their descriptions using terms such as “type”, “pattern”, “model”, “as worn by” etc. rather than giving a categorical statement that the item is 100% genuine. This ambiguity is further backed up by sweeping disclaimers which state that even if the item purchased does subsequently prove to be a reproduction, that it was sold “as seen”, thus precluding any recourse for the purchaser.

While it is important to establish the provenance of an item, especially on the rarer and more expensive daggers, care should be taken that this does not take the form of some vague assertion like “my grandfather took this one off Himmler personally . . . ”! Far too often there is also an assumption by collectors that *where* they bought the dagger guarantees its authenticity. This misconception specifically applies to the small private museums scattered around Europe (and especially France). These museums are in effect family run businesses which are quite prepared to sell any of their exhibits; indeed many of these museums even have price tags on them! In most instances the militaria offered for sale is a reproduction and quite often not even of a very high quality. Just because a battle took place at a specific location or a well known Nazi personality “slept there” where a small museum now stands should not infer that the contents of the museum are necessarily genuine or contemporary with that event or personality.

Military Dagger Reproductions

The three military branches of the German Wehrmacht: Army, Navy and Airforce each adopted separate and distinctive forms of dress daggers during the mid-1930's. These three different types of dress daggers have all been extensively reproduced since the end of World War II in a variety of qualities. The Army dagger is probably the most widely reproduced of the three services with the Spanish reproductions being the most common. The quality of the Spanish reproduction has improved markedly since the first examples appeared in the 1960's. Most Spanish reproductions of the Army dagger feature a scabbard with a swirling pattern formed from the pebbling which was irregular on genuine examples not conforming to any definite pattern.

In recent years good quality reproduction Army blades have been made in Germany and have found their way into parts assemblies using various combinations of genuine and reproduction fittings. This type of practice has also extended to the Kriegsmarine and 2nd pattern Luftwaffe daggers which are also available from the extensive range of Spanish reproductions. The Spanish reproduction of the 2nd pattern Luftwaffe dagger is probably one of the best of the Nazi reproductions emanating from Spain. The detail and finish of these daggers are quite good, only being let down by the heavy pommel usually made from plated brass rather than the aluminium found on originals. The use of a mustard yellow plastic grip is a common feature of grips found on Spanish reproductions of both the Army and 2nd pattern Luftwaffe daggers. No doubt due to its more complicated design, the 1st pattern Luftwaffe dagger has not been extensively reproduced. Examples which have been encountered have invariably featured crudely made fittings with a blue plastic covering on the scabbard and grip instead of genuine leather.

The Kriegsmarine daggers produced in Spain have relatively good detail but usually feature a gaudy ornate scabbard which is exceptionally heavy. This type of scabbard design pre-dates the Nazi period: as most genuine Kriegsmarine daggers featured either a lightning bolt design or a beaten pattern scabbard - both types were of lightweight gilded brass. The blades of Spanish reproduction Kriegsmarine daggers have a photo-etched decorative panel dissimilar to that on the genuine Navy dagger. Also the reproduction blades are often a flat stiletto type with a single central spine rather than the twin fullers or grooves found on original examples. In recent years good quality reproduction Kriegsmarine blades of correct form and decorative style have been produced in Germany, many finding their way into parts assemblies using genuine fittings. The grips of most reproduction Kriegsmarine daggers tend to be of white plastic rather than the celluloid or ivory of originals.

The blades of reproduction military daggers will often be encountered bearing an RZM proofmark: these daggers should always be rejected as none of the three branches of the Wehrmacht came under the authority of the RZM, and consequently none of their daggers should bear the RZM proofmark. Another type of proofmark which will be encountered on reproductions is that of well known Makers such as F. W. Holler with the town of origin changed from "Solingen" to "Berlin": this is a feature found on many Spanish reproduction blades of the 1960's and 70's.

KRIEGSMARINE REPRODUCTIONS

RECOGNITION CHECKLIST

FIRST PATTERN

BLADE

- Blade etching too lightly applied.
- Poor definition on the Maker's proofmark.
- Spurious blade etchings of U-Boats, battleships, Kriegsmarine eagle and swastika, sailing ships, sea serpents, the Keil Memorial etc.
- No provision made on the tang for the spring steel strip which holds the blade locking button.
- Crudely shaped tang.
- Square shaped tang (the tang on genuine Navy blades was machine or hand filed when fitting the spring steel strip).
- It should be borne in mind in view of the aforementioned point that the absence of a billet clamp seam on the tang of a naval blade does not necessarily indicate that the blade is a reproduction: as the billet clamp marks were frequently erased during the spring fitting process.
- Presence of a felt blade washer instead of the correct leather type.

SCABBARD

- Reproduction scabbards are invariably the lightening bolt type.
- The current Spanish reproduction scabbards have a cheap looking gold plating instead of a gilt finish.
- Reproduction scabbard bands are manufactured as a part of one half of the scabbard: the two halves then being joined together; original bands were made as a single piece ring and then sweated onto the completed scabbard.
- The rings for the hanger loops are very poorly defined and too thick.
- The scabbard's throat screws are flat headed and screwed in flush with the side of the scabbard instead of being domed and potruding.
- Total absence of any scabbard throat screws.
- Absence of a scabbard liner.
- The use of thin wooden, plastic or tin slides usually just brazed, stapeled or glued into position.

GRIP

- Poor detail on the pommel and/or crossguard castings.
- Incorrect twist on the grip spiral i.e. running top right to bottom left instead of vice versa.
- Solid plastic grip with drilled out centre and no wooden liner.
- Reproduction grips are usually pure white plastic instead of the creamy colour of the original celluloid grips.
- The grip binding wire is too thin: this is usually a slender double twisted strand but is sometimes a single strand.
- The blade locking button is mounted too high on the crossguard.
- Oversize flaming ball pommel.
- Pommel screw thread off centre.
- Pommels made from alloys which are considerably lighter than the original brass fitting.

SECOND PATTERN

BLADE

- Modern blade bearing spurious etchings of battleships, sailing ships, sea serpents, Kriegsmarine eagle and swastika, etc.
- The Keil Memorial depicted as a blade decoration: the use of which as an engraving was not documented prior to 1945.
- U-Boats are frequently used as subjects for decoration on fake blades: the style of this decoration usually depicts a World War I type U-Boat, and the boat number will feature somewhere in the decoration; this is a blatant attempt to give the piece provenance.
- Blade etching applied too lightly to the blade: this is especially true on Spanish production pieces.
- The use of the modern technique of photo-etching rather than the acid dip technique (a quick examination with a magnifying glass will quickly expose photo-etching.
- The use of a felt blade washer instead of the genuine leather type: also sometimes a thin type of synthetic PVC imitation leather is used.
- The use of spurious Maker's proofmarks who were not known or authorised manufacturers of the Nazi naval dirk.
- The etching panels on many reproduction blades (especially Spanish) are too short and terminate at considerable distance up the fullers: these panels can be anything up to 2 inches too short.
- Etching panels which are not applied squarely to the blade or the border of the panel run off the edge of the blade.

SCABBARD

- Most reproduction scabbards are usually the lightening bolt type with the etching on the design not very deeply applied or well defined.
- Many modern reproduction scabbards are made from steel or alloys and are then given a cheap looking gold plating instead of the original brass structured scabbards which were professionally gilded by craftsmen.
- The oakleaf scabbard bands are too wide and exhibit moulding seams on the side.
- The scabbard bands on some reproductions are made as an integral part of one half of the scabbard as a single mould; original Solingen made scabbards were constructed with a one piece ring scabbard band which was first heated then sweated onto a complete scabbard, when the band cooled it shrunk into place on the scabbard.
- Reproduction scabbard liners are made of either: A. thin wooden strips, B. plastic, or C. are nonexistent.
- Scabbard throat screws are either not used or when they are present they are usually flay headed instead of domed and are usually screwed flush with the side of the scabbard: whereas the correct original domed head screws stand proud from the scabbard throat.
- The scabbard rings are frequently too thick and are not joined together correctly but are left with a tiny gap where the ring should meet.

GRIP

- Lightweight crossguard and pommel made from white metal or alloy with very bright gold plating applied over the metal: original fittings were cast from solid brass then gilded. Period gilding has a much more subdued gold colour than modern plating.
- Poor detail and definition on the eagle pommel and crossguard.
- Pommel screw socket off centre.

- White plastic grip often solid without a wooden liner: some better quality reproduction grips do feature a wooden sleeve inside the grip but this is usually of poor quality and does not fit very well. Most of the original grips had the celluloid moulded directly over the wooden shell at the time of manufacture whereas the modern reproduction grips have the wooden sleeves pushed in following the grip moulding process almost as an afterthought.
- The white plastic on the grips of most reproductions is far too bright and does not have the creamy coloured finish of the original celluloid grips.
- The blade locking button is mounted too high on the crossguard usually due to incorrectly located steel spring on the tang or a total absence of this part.
- Incorrect twist on the grip spiral running from top right to bottom left or vice versa.
- Grip binding wire is often too thin and usually consists of very thin twisted double strand wire or even a single twisted strand.

PROOFMARKS

The most frequently encountered Maker's proofmarks on reproduction Third Reich naval daggers are F W Holler, E & F Horster, Weyersberg, Alcoso, Eickhorn and Krebs. Although it has always been generally accepted that there were only 17 authorised manufacturers of Third Reich naval daggers this figure does require some qualification. The generally accepted list of these 17 manufacturers authorised to produce naval daggers were as follows: Alcoso, Clemen & Jung, Carl EIckhorn, F W Holler, E & F Horster, Robert Klaas, Carl Julius Krebs, Lauterjung, P D Luneschloss, Ernst Pack, Plumacher, Puma, Paul Seilheimer, Max Weyersberg, Paul Weyersberg, W K C, and Anton Wingen. However it should be borne in mind that there were three firms operating in Solingen with the name "Lauterjung", two of which are on this list: one under the name of "Lauterjung", and the other under its trade name of "Puma", which was actually "Lauterjung & Sohn, Puma-Werk". The first "Lauterjung", identified by name alone and cited in this and other texts was in fact "Lauterjung & Companie, Tiger Stahlwaren-Und Waffenfabrik" which also used the "Tiger" proofmark on the daggers they produced. The third "Lauterjung", "Hugo & Friedrich Lauterjung", which was not accredited as an authorised naval dagger Maker did however make component parts which were supplied to an used by the other two "Lauterjung" Makers. Due to this proliferation of "Lauterjungs" in Solingen there is obviously scope for some confusion when accrediting Makers: this was why the "Puma" and "Tiger" proofmarks were used by two of the firms.

Another name on the list of authorised Makers which requires clarification is that of "Krebs". There were two concerns operating in Solingen during the Third Reich era both of which produced edged weapons under the name of "Krebs". The firm related to in this text is that of "Carl Julius Krebs, KronenKrebs-Stahlwarenfabrik" whose proofmark was an oval with a crowned "K" in the centre and "Carl Julius Krebs, Solingen" etched around the inside edge of the oval. The second "Krebs" firm was that of Peter Daniel Krebs whose proofmark was a shield with a scorpion in the centre and "P D Krebs, Solingen" bordered around the inside edge of the shield, and although they produced a variety of Third Reich edged weapons they were not an authorised Maker of the naval dagger.

Alcoso is another firm which can cause some confusion due to their use of a wide number of different trademarks during the period 1918-1945. For it should be borne in mind that many Third Reich daggers were actually converted and modified from Imperial and Weimar Republic period daggers, and also it should be remembered that the naval dagger is the only Third Reich period dagger which actually had a history pre-dating 1933: the Prussian and later German Navy had worn a naval dirk of almost identical form since 1842, and it was only the substitution of the Nazi eagle and swastika pommel which distinguished the Third Reich naval dagger from its predeccesors. Many naval officers had served in the Imperial and Weimar Republic Navies and were still on active duty up to and during World War II: these officers were permitted to retain their original daggers and were only required to replace their crown or ball pommel with the updated Nazi eagle pommel. "Alcoso" was the most commonly used proofmark of this company in regard to their production of naval daggers. However other proofmarks will be encountered on naval blades which were produced by this company dating from earlier periods, and can be any of the following: a set of scales; scales and the initials "A C"; scales and "A C S"; or scales and "Alex Coppel, Solingen".

W K C is yet another authorised naval dagger Maker whose company production history predates the Nazi era: hence proofmarks will be encountered showing the initials "W K C"; a visored knight's head; and a visor knight's head within a hexagon with the letters "W K C" below the head. W K C were the initials adopted from the amalgamation of two famous Solingen blade Makers "Weyersberg" and "Kirschbaum": the new merged company became "Weyersberg, Kirschbaum & Companie", hence "W K C". Earlier proofmarks from this merger were a king's head; a king's head and knight's head side by side together; and a king's head and knight's head together with "W K C" below.

Another listed Maker whose proofmark also will show variations is Pack which relates to "Ernst Pack Sohne". Proofmarks for this company can range from the initials "E P & S" and the figure of Siegfreid, to the figure of Siegfreid with "Pack, Solingen", or "Ernst Pack, Solingen" in two parallel lines, or "Ernst Pack Sohne, Solingen". Other trademarks also used by Pack were: "Brocant", "Cito", "Hamlet", "Poco", "Solar" and "Siegfreid".

* See also page 200 for examples of genuine Kriegsmarine daggers.

Close up detail of the Pommel of the Kriegsmarine Honour dagger. This example is from a genuine Honour dagger - note the sharp detail of the eagle's feature especially the wing fletching. The diamonds are professionally set into the swastika arms whereas reproduction pommels utilise paste stones usually crudely set.

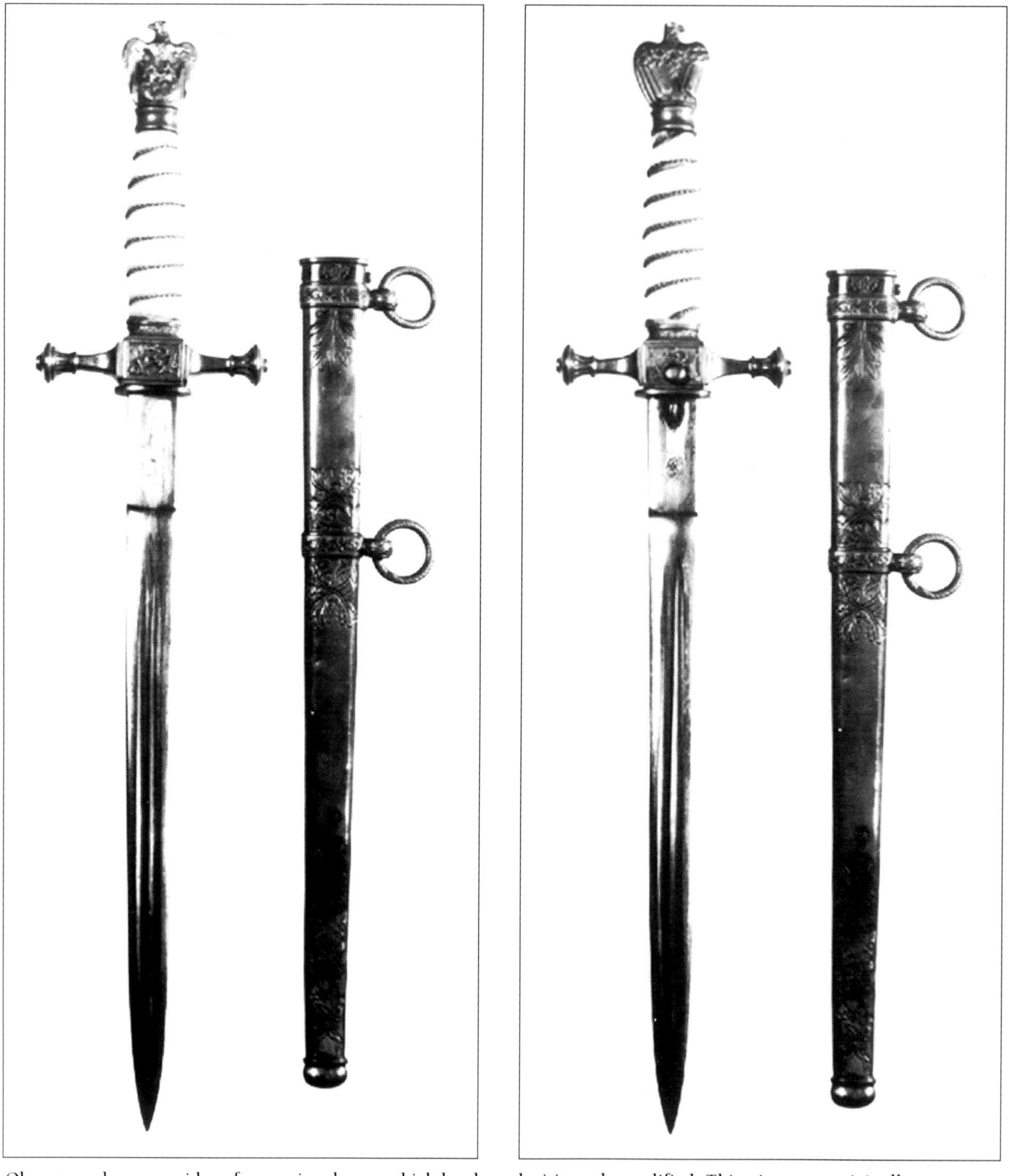

Obverse and reverse sides of a genuine dagger which has been legitimately modified. This piece was originally an Imperial Dirk of the Kaiserliche Marine period (1871-1918) which has been updated with a Nazi eagle pommel for service with the Kriegsmarine (1935-1945). This was an authorised practice for an officer who had served with honour in the Imperial Navy and continued to serve during the Nazi period. Note the maidenhair Damascus blade and the Imperial Navy crossguard and scabbard.

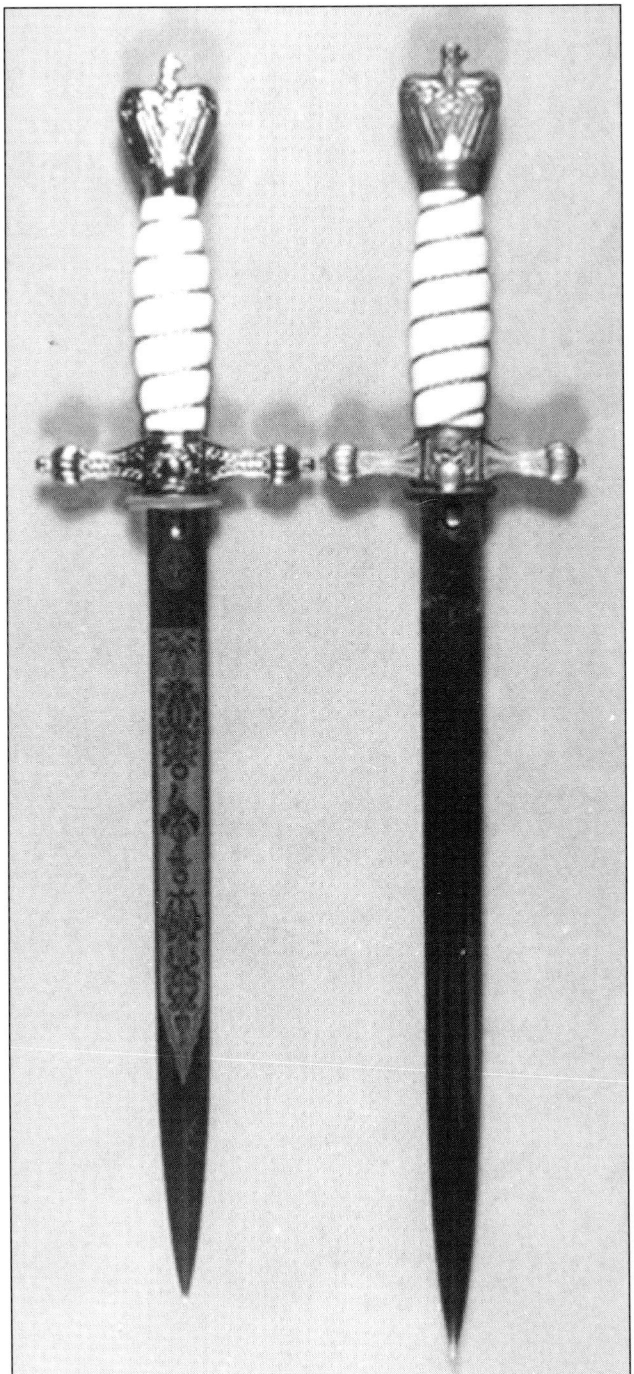

Comparison views of a genuine Kriegsmarine dagger on the right and reproduction on the left. Note the shorter blade length of the reproduction and the bright finish of the photo-etching blade decoration.

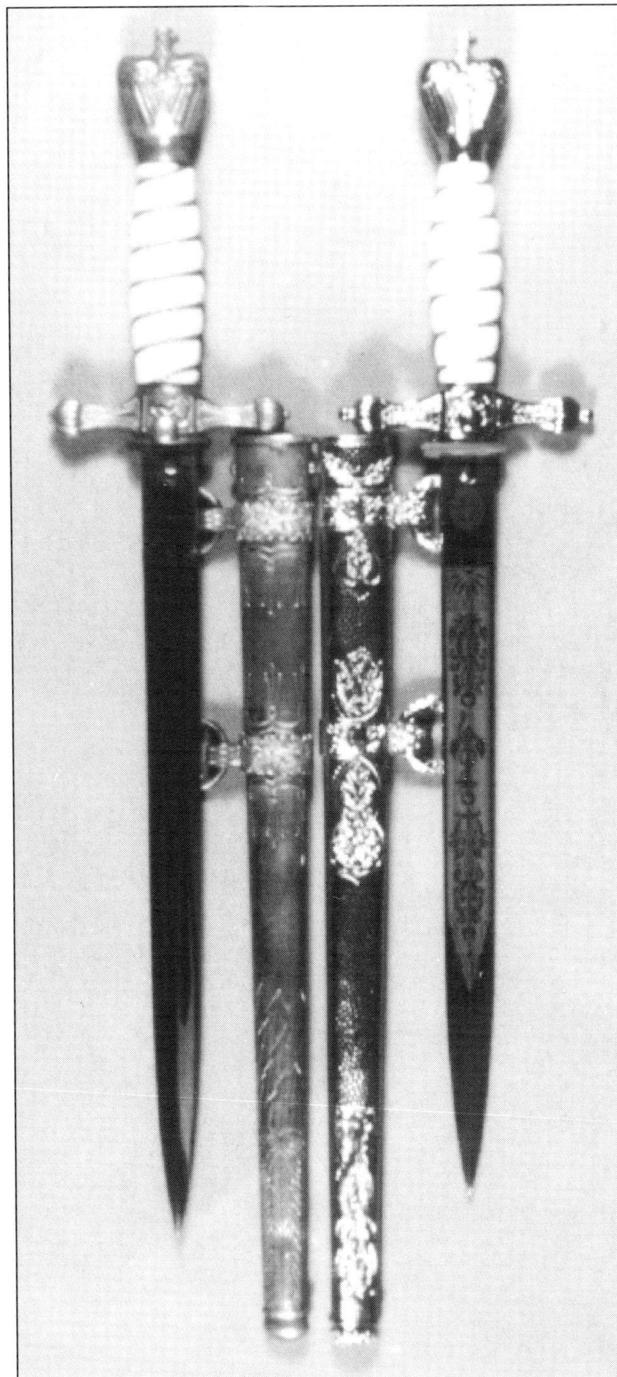

Comparison views of a genuine (left) and reproduction (right) Kriegsmarine dagger. Note the bright finish and elaborate decoration of the reproduction scabbard. Although the blade of the reproduction is shorter than that of the genuine dagger the reproduction scabbard is longer.

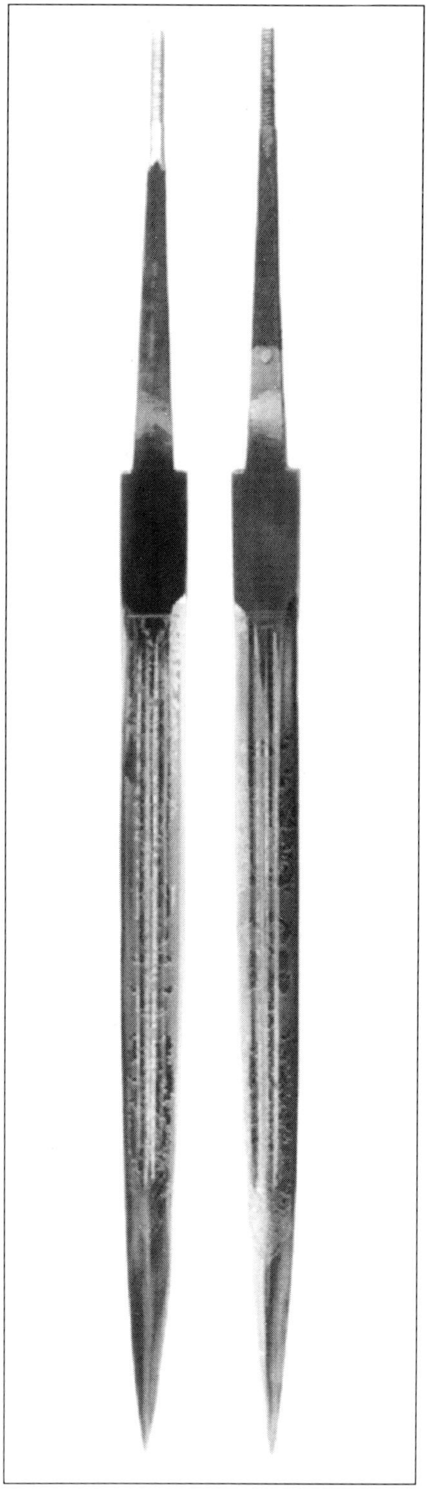

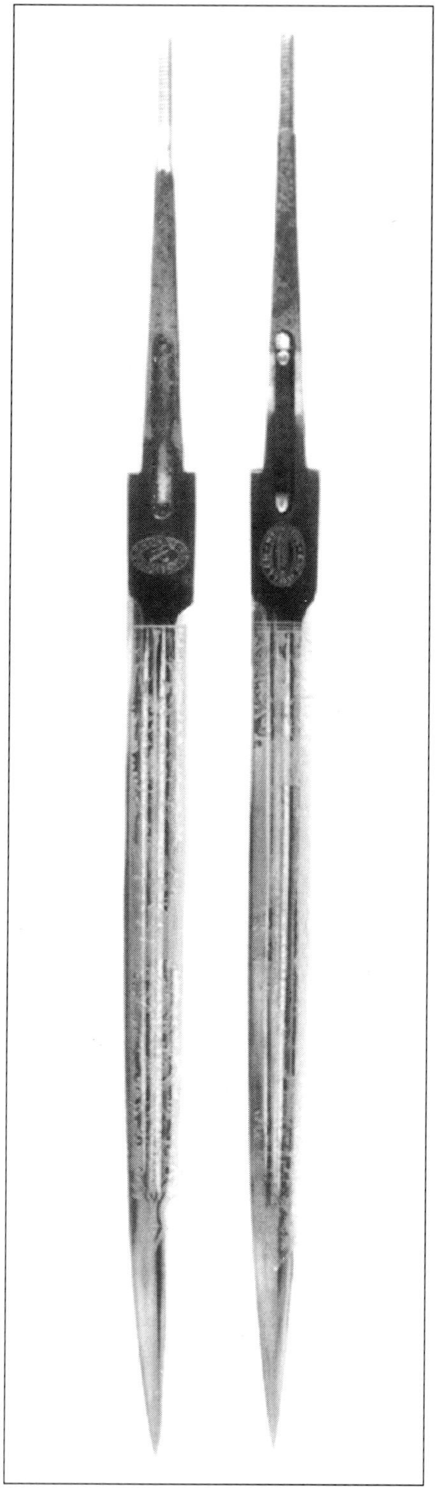

Obverse and reverse of two reproduction Naval dagger blades currently produced in Solingen, Germany. The blades are well formed and have well executed etched panels. The Maker's proofmarks of F. W. Holler and P. D. Luneschloss respectively appear on the reverse Ricassos. Note scabbard locking springs have been correctly inserted in the lower tang.

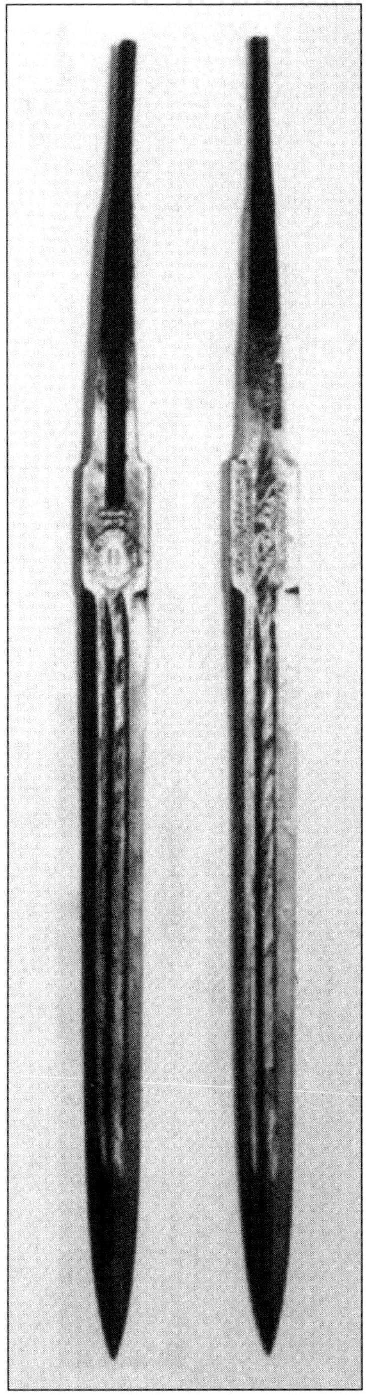

Obverse and reverse views of a reproduction Kriegsmarine Honour dagger blade. These good quality German blades bear a dedication from Grand Admiral Raeder in gold inlayed script on the ricasso. The blades are well finished and very convincing when married to other genuine parts. However this type of blade was only used in conjunction with other Honour dagger fittings such as the diamond encrusted swastika pommel.

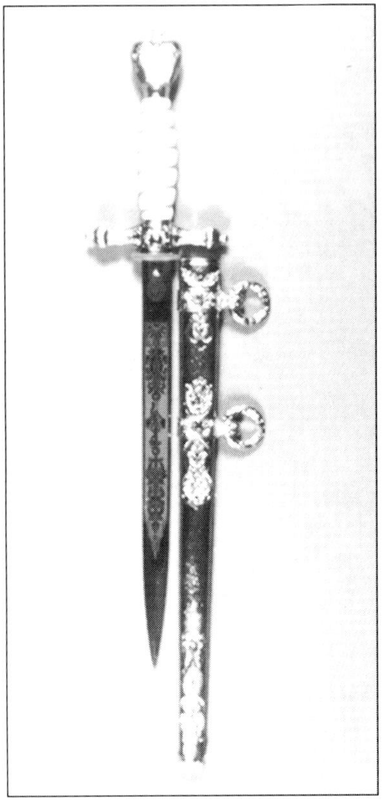
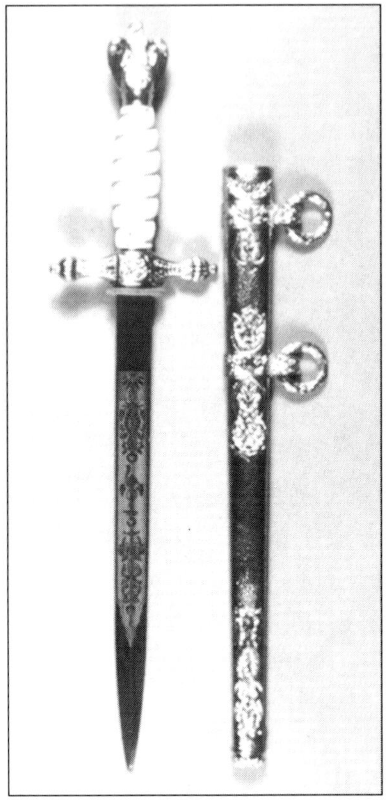
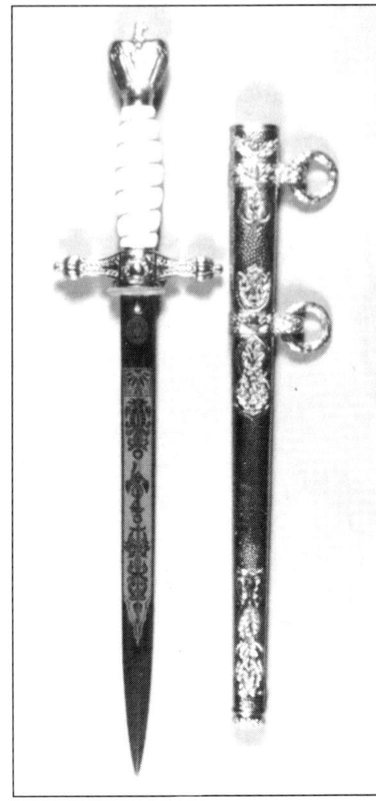
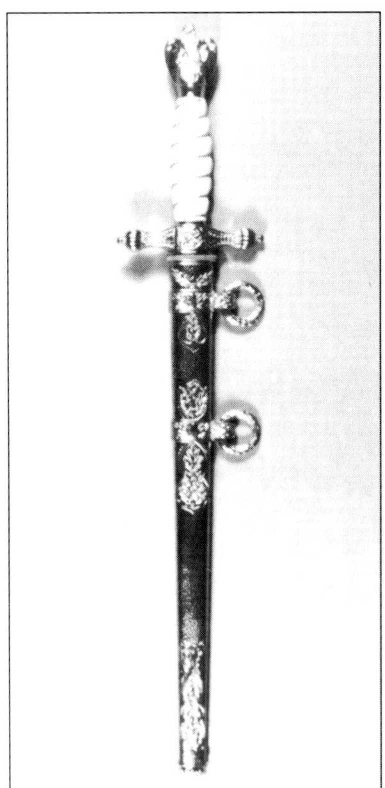
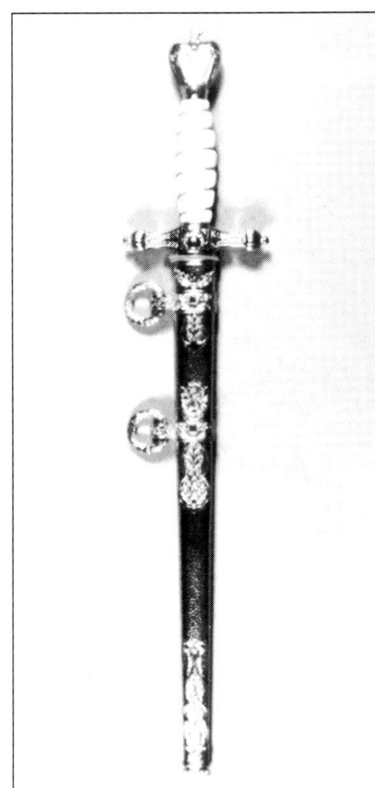

Five different views of a Spanish reproduction of the Kriegsmarine dagger. Note the photo-etched blade decoration and the gaudy decoration and finish of the scabbard. F. W. Holler is the most common Maker's mark found on these daggers.

ARMY DAGGER REPRODUCTIONS

RECOGNITION CHECKLIST

BLADE

- Proofmarks etched very lightly instead of being clear and sharp.
- Many reproduction tangs are too thick at the base and are very square in appearance all the way up the screw fitting on the tang: other later examples are oval in shape.
- Absence of any billet clamp marks is characteristic of Spanish reproduction blades.
- F W Holler is the most frequently used proofmark on Spanish reproductions with the city of manufacture erroneously stated as Berlin within the proofmark.
- Spanish blades tend to have a dull satin or grey finish rather than the high quality polish found on originals.
- Do not interpret age spotting or finger rust marks as indicators of authenticity: reproduction blades have now been made for such a long time that many exhibit normal ageing characteristics found on genuine Third Reich blades.
- The tang on reproduction blades will often have a very bright clean appearance lacking the firescale and blackening caused by the tempering process used on original blades.
- Army blades should never bear RZM proofmarks or control numbers as the Army was not subject to RZM regulations: the RZM being responsible only for NSDAP formations.
- The centre flat section is often very narrow on reproduction blades especially early Spanish types.
- The bevelled edges of the flats are often rounded on reproduction blades lacking the clearly defined lines of the original.
- There are a number of very good quality reproduction etched blades currently on the market and produced in Solingen. These blades are better observed visually.

SCABBARD

- Current production Spanish scabbards have a very distinctive pattern formed by the pebbling on the scabbard: this pattern takes the form of irregular swirls which are best observed when the scabbard is held at arms length. Genuine scabbard pebbling should have a dense appearance with no visible pattern.
- The hanger rings on the scabbard bands of Spanish reproductions are not joined and are left slightly opened: original rings were always joined together.
- Scabbard bands mounted too close together usually with the top band mounted approximately half an inch lower than on originals.
- The oakleaf decoration on reproduction scabbard bands is often very poorly defined and is also narrower than on originals.
- A very rough seam is often visible where the scabbard bands have been joined.
- Some reproduction scabbards of Spanish origin have the scabbard tip soldered on separately instead of being an integral part as on originals.
- Very thin brass scabbard liners soldered into place inside the throat of the scabbard.

GRIP

- Grip twist spiral running in wrong direction from top left to bottom right instead of vice versa.
- Some Spanish reproduction grips have a very pronounced sharp ridge on the spiral groove which is very discernible if gripped tightly.
- Two principle colours are used for reproduction grips: a very bright white and a mustardy yellow

colour - neither of which conforms to colours originally available.

- Reproduction grips are invariably solid with a hole drilled out of the centre to accommodate the tang. The hole is sometimes off centre which can be observed even without stripping the dagger down for this throws the whole shape of the hilt off the centre of the crossguard.
- Modern plastic grips are injection moulded from either nylon or polycarbonate plastics which have a high moulding temperature and tend to be quite brittle: this often causes them to chip whereas original grips made from celluloid are more likely to crack with age or mishandling.
- Poor definition on pommel and crossguard often leaving the eagle without any features or breast fletching.
- Some early reproduction crossguards had the eagle emblem added separately: this emblem is often mounted incorrectly either too high, off centre or crooked.
- The swirl on each end of the crossguard is often very poorly defined with the swirl being barely discernible.
- The hole in the top of the crossguard where the tang of the blade passes through is often very crudely formed and too large allowing the movement in the crossguard.
- The oakleaf pattern on reproduction pommels is very indistinct in some instance also with the oakleaves being too narrow.
- The dome of reproduction pommels can often taper up to a point rather than exhibiting the smooth domed appearance of originals.
- Reproduction ferrules can be considerably wider than originals and have also been observed with the oakleaf pattern running in the wrong direction.
- The pommel and ferrule should be examined for any evidence of filing which is done in an attempt to obliterate coarse moulding seams which are a feature of most Spanish reproduction pommels and ferrules.
- The pommel of some of the earlier reproductions dating from the late 1960's early 1970's were considerably taller than originals with a long screw thread socket which was longer than the thread on the tang: this often caused the pommel to be over tightened and the thread stripped from the tang causing the pommel just to rotate rather than being tight.
- Pommel screw socket threads are often off centre but this is not always discernible after the pommel has been tightened onto the grip. The centring on a pommel can be easily checked by unscrewing it then slowly screwing it back down with one finger on the edge of the pommel. If the pommel is off centre it will have a wonky motion when being tightened in this manner.
- Some fitting such as pommels, crossguards and ferrules were manufactured from brass castings and then plated: the use of these fittings give the dagger a very unbalanced feel and when weighed in the hand separately they have a very heavy feel. Spanish reproductions no longer use this alloy on the Army dagger which was only used on early reproduction pieces.

PROOFMARKS

Most Spanish reproductions use the "F W Holler, Berlin" proofmark although prior to Spain becoming a democracy in the mid-1970's and later joining the EEC the Spanish makers had very little regard for copyright laws and did at one time use the correct "F W Holler, Solingen" proofmark. However although these blades were manufactured in Toledo, Spain (a traditional centre for blade making) they are not of the same quality as the Solingen originals.

Other frequently used proofmarks on reproduction Spanish blades are E & F Horster, Alcoso, S M F and E P & S (although this proof was mainly used on the reproduction SA Rohm inscribed blades).

Proof marks on blades produced in Germany can be from any of the edged weapon manufacturing companies which survived after World War II. Some of the major proofmarks which currently appear are Eickhorn, Alcosso, Horster, Holler, Krebs, Klaas, W K C, Weyersburg, S M F, Clemen & Jung, Henckels, and Puma.

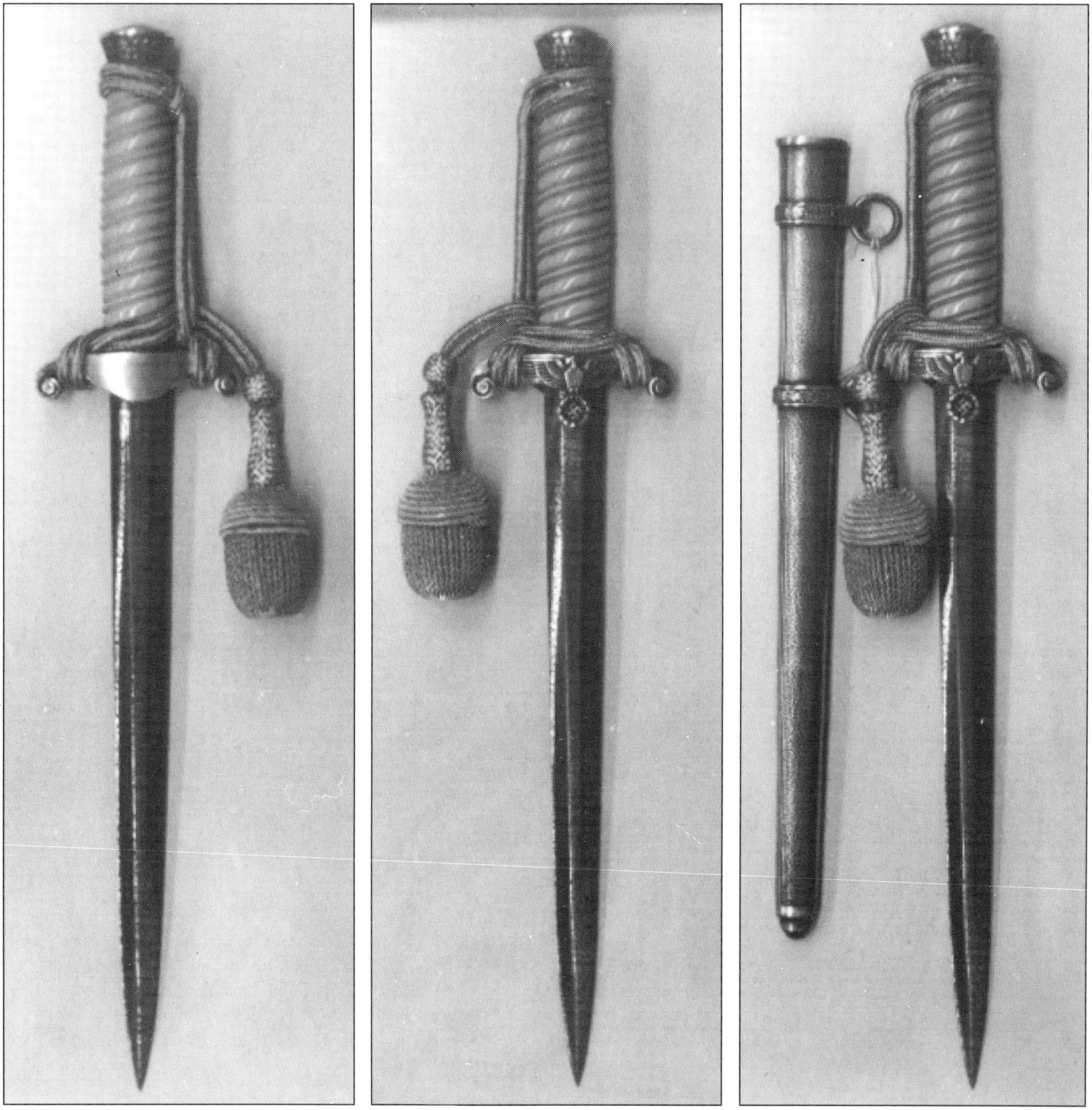

Obverse and reverse views of a parts assembly Army dagger which features a genuine pommel grip and crossguard and a reproduction blade and scabbard. The scabbard has been heavily polished to subdue the swirling pattern indicative of Spanish reproduction scabbards. The genuine portepee knot has been added as a smokescreen embellishment.

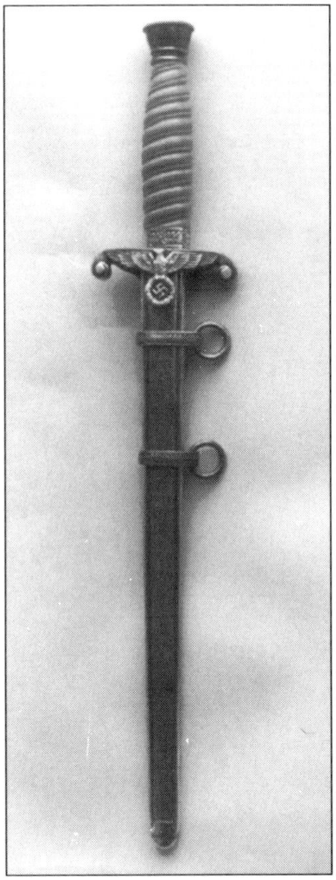

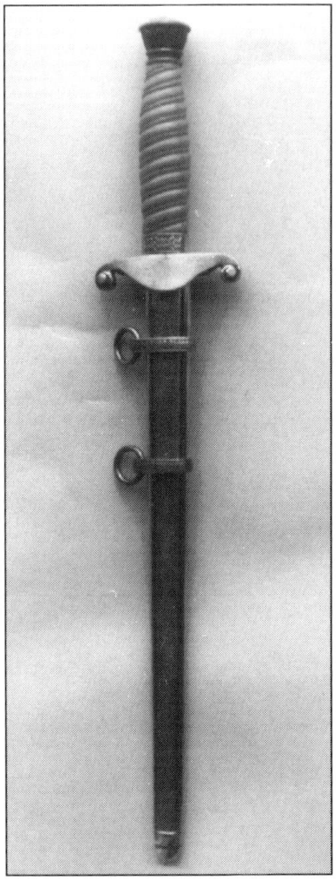

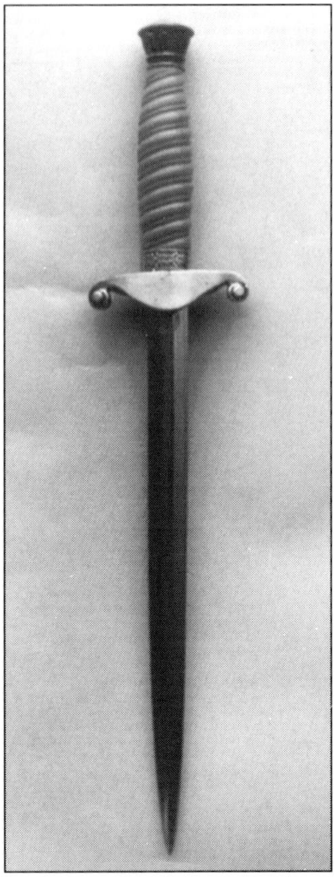

Five different views of a Spanish reproduction Army dagger. The blade bears an RZM proofmark which is inappropriate for any Military dagger. The reverse crossguard exhibits stress cracks although the detail of the obverse eagle is quite good. The scabbard has the swirling pebble effect characteristic of most Spanish reproductions. The scabbard mounts are located too close together and have poor detail on the oakleaf decoration. The grip has a bulge on the left-handside when viewed from the obverse side.

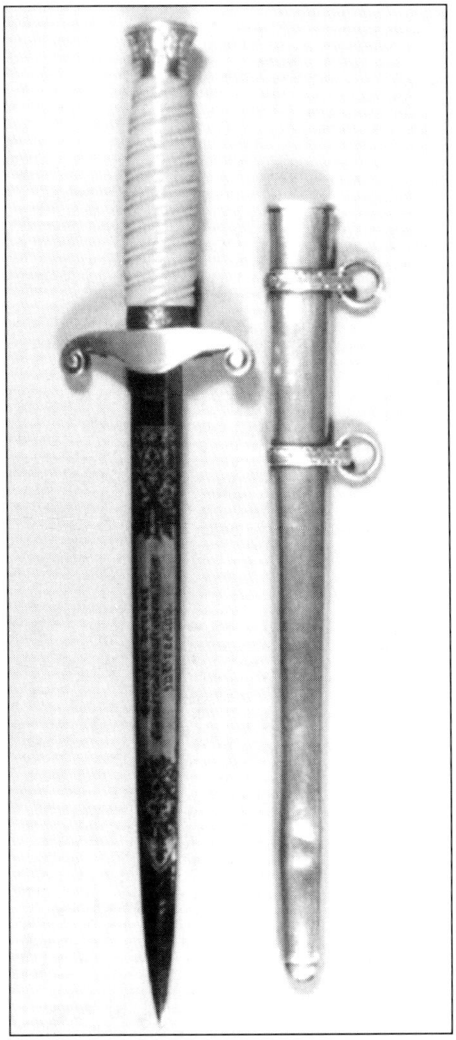
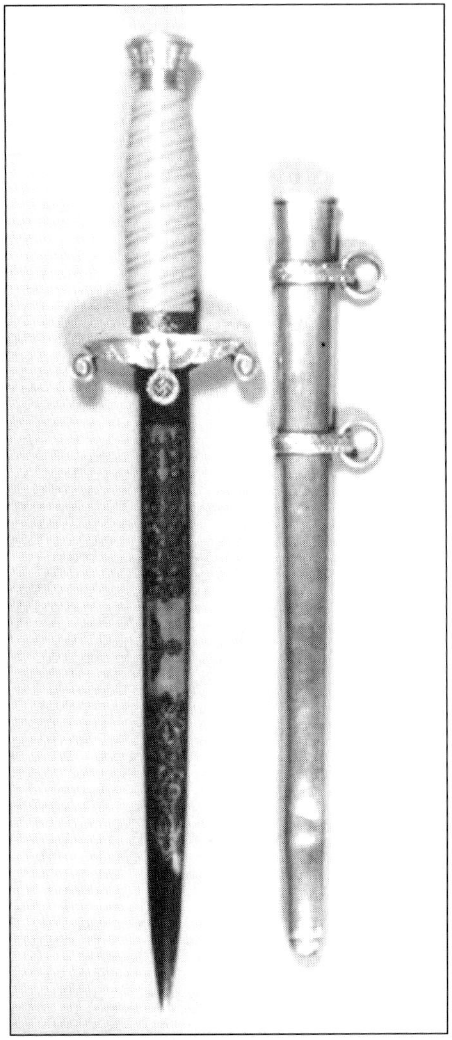

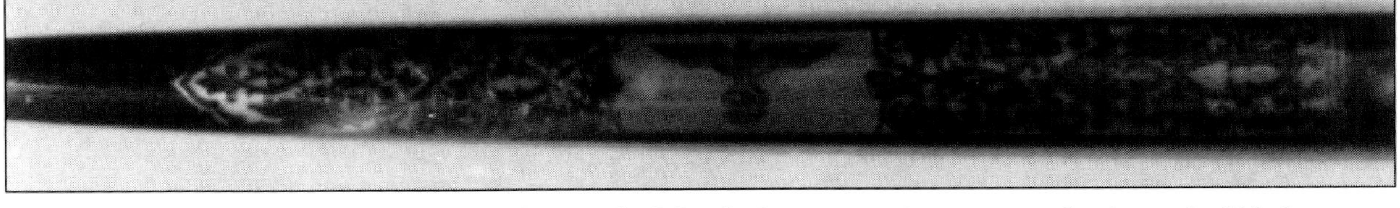

Different views of a parts assembly Army dagger which has had a current German reproduction etched blade included in its fabrication. This dagger is an amalgam of a variety of parts of different origin, as previously mentioned the blade is a modern German reproduction, the grip and pommel are from a Spanish reproduction Army dagger. The crossguard and ferrule are from a genuine Army dagger, whilst the scabbard is a Spanish reproduction which has been extensively buffed in an attempt to diminish the swirling effect characteristic of most Spanish reproduction scabbards.

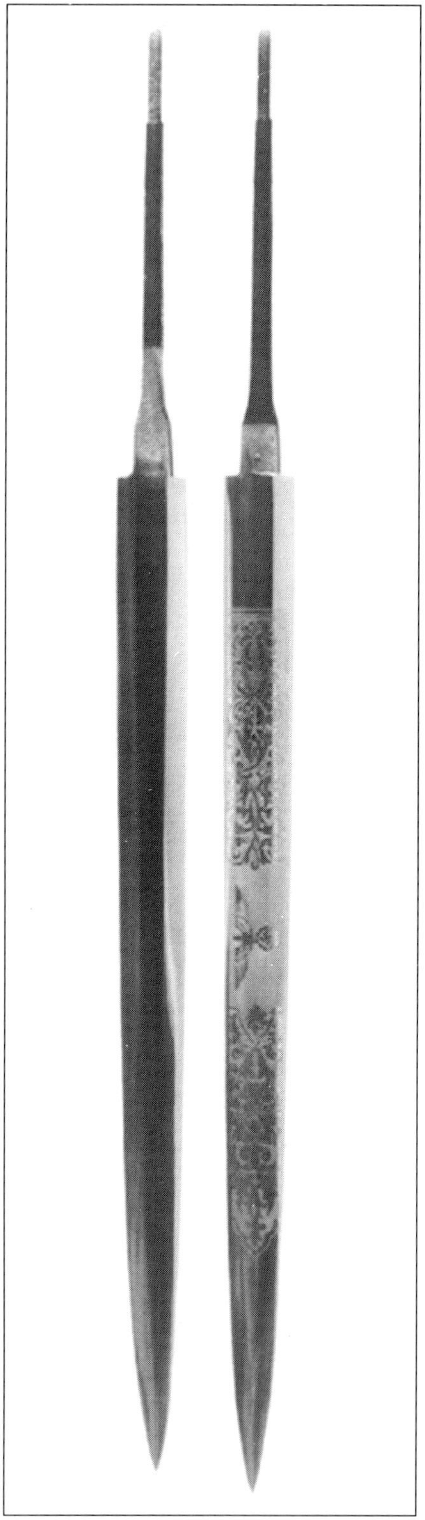

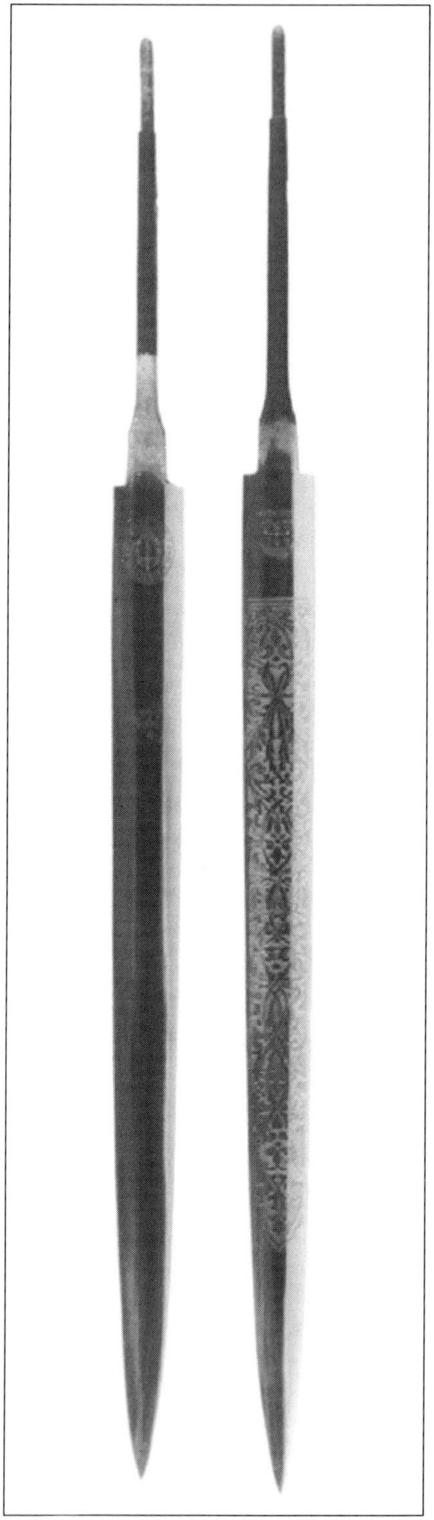

Obverse and reverse views of two reproduction Army dagger blades of current Solingen manufacture. Note the good quality etching on these blades and also the well applied Maker's proofmarks. The tangs and blades are well formed and exhibit fire scaling as a result of drop forging which was the same technique used on original blades. The example on the left is a plain Army blade whilst the righthand reproduction has a floral photo-etched design.

LUFTWAFFE DAGGER REPRODUCTIONS

RECOGNITION CHECKLIST

FIRST PATTERN

BLADE

- ➢ The spurious use of an RZM M/7 proofmark on the blade ricasso with several control numbers having been documented i.e. M/7-10, M/7-18, M/7-33, M/7-36 and M/7-66. RZM proofmarks should not appear on any Luftwaffe dagger blade or component part.
- ➢ Blade edged ground flat instead of being a tapered blunt knife edge.
- ➢ Blade made from inferior quality steel with a dull grey finish lacking any polish.
- ➢ Very narrow central flat panel on the blade, also poor definition on the bevelled edges of this section of the blade.
- ➢ Badly formed tang bearing no billet clamp seam marks.
- ➢ Screw threading on the end of the tang is too short and is very crudely machined.

SCABBARD

- ➢ The incorrect use of PVC imitation leather to wrap the scabbard: the colour of this material is often the wrong shade of blue i.e. too light.
- ➢ Some Spanish reproductions are made without suspension chains.
- ➢ Too few links in the suspension chain.
- ➢ Crudely made scabbard liners glued or soldered into the inside of the scabbard throat.
- ➢ The three scabbard mounts made from poor quality lightweight metal: making very thin fittings.
- ➢ Absence of screws to secure the scabbard fittings.
- ➢ The scabbard fittings mounted incorrectly with the middle fitting being situated in the centre of the scabbard instead of higher up.
- ➢ Oversized scabbard fittings especially the upper mount being too long.
- ➢ Scabbards made from fibreglass.
- ➢ The use of blue paint on the scabbards instead of blue leather.

GRIP

- ➢ Grip bound with PVC imitation leather instead of genuine leather.
- ➢ Grip uneven and out of proportion: some examples have a very bulbous appearance.
- ➢ Two different types of incorrect spiral twists have been observed on the grip: one has the twist running from top right to bottom left, the other has an almost lateral twist running in the opposite direction.
- ➢ Very thin wire used to bind the grip usually twisted double strand.
- ➢ Very poor detail on pommel and crossguard.
- ➢ Sunwheel swastikas very badly formed and often crudely painted with a bright gold paint.
- ➢ The grip and pommel have an ill fitting join often with the grip material sticking out the edges.

PROOFMARKS

RZM M/7-10 - 18 - 33 - 36 - 66; F W Holler, E F Horster, and Clemen & Jung are the most frequently encountered proofmarks on 1st pattern Luftwaffe reproduction daggers.

SECOND PATTERN

BLADE

- Incorrect and spurious use of RZM M/7 proofmarks on the blade ricasso. M/7-33 and M/7-36 are the most frequently encountered phoney RZM proofmarks.
- Maker's proofmarks etched very lightly instead of being clear and crisp.
- The tang is too thick at the base and has a very square appearance: other tangs will be encountered with an oval shape, and other with a very broad flat tang. All of these examples are totally different to originals.
- Absence of any billet clamp marks is a characteristic of Spanish reproduction blades.
- The F W Holler proofmark is the one most frequently found on Spanish blades with the city of manufacture changed from Solingen to Berlin.
- Many Spanish manufactured blades tend to have a dull grey satin finish rather than the high quality finish found on originals.
- Beware of tangs which have a very bight clean appearance showing no evidence of tempering.
- The centre flat section is often very narrow on reproduction blades with the bevelled section being rounded instead of having a sharp angled finish.
- There are a number of very good quality etched and presentation blades currently being produced in Solingen.

SCABBARD

- Ensure that the scabbard is constructed from the correct material. Originals were made from sheet steel whereas reproduction scabbards will be encountered made from a variety of alloys: brass, zinc, aluminium - all of which can be detected by the use of a magnet which will not adhere to these nonferrous metals.
- Ensure that the scabbard is of one piece construction and does not have separate tip soldered on. A small gap is usually evident where a tip has been added separately.
- The pebbling on the scabbard should be dense and irregular and should not show any kind of swirling patterns.
- The hanger rings on the scabbard bands of some Spanish reproductions are not joined and are left slightly opened: whereas original rings were always neatly soldered together.
- The incorrect use of large oversized hanger rings.
- Scabbard bands incorrectly mounted usually too close together.
- The oakleaf decoration is sometimes not clearly defined on reproductions.
- A rough seam is often visible where the scabbard bands have been joined together.
- Very thin brass or wooden scabbard liners soldered or riveted into place inside the throat mount or even just wedged into position.
- Poor detail and definition on the oakleaf decoration at the bottom of the scabbard.

GRIP

- The grip twist spiral running in the wrong direction from top right to bottom left instead of vice versa.
- The use of thin twisted double strand wire on the grips.
- The grips of some Spanish produced daggers have very pronounced sharp ridges on the spiral.
- The principle colours used on reproduction grips are white which has a very bright appearance and a mustardy yellow colour similar to that found on reproduction Army daggers: due to most of these examples emanating from the same source in Toledo, Spain.
- Reproduction grips are invariably solid.

- Reproduction ferrules are often too wide and lack sharp detail on the oakleaf pattern.
- A characteristic common to many Spanish reproductions, both past and present is the use of incorrect materials to produce the pommel and crossguard. Original fittings were constructed from aluminium or lightweight zinc, on later examples, whereas reproduction fittings are frequently cast from heavier alloys such as brass and then given an oxidised plating.
- The pommel on Spanish reproductions is extremely heavy to the extent of making the dagger unbalanced and also can readily be detected by weighing the pommel in one's hand whereupon the excessive weight is immediately evident.
- The crossguard can similarly be checked for excessive weight.
- The pebbling on the reverse of the crossguard is very pronounced: with each pebble being almost twice the size of those usually found on originals.
- The plain border on the reverse crossguard is often too narrow on reproductions.
- The detail on reproduction crossguard and pommels currently in production is very good; however some of the earlier examples do have a poor definition to the eagle's head, breast and wing fletching.
- Some reproduction crossguards have no decoration across the top.
- Pommels and ferrules should be examined for any evidence of moulding seams or attempts to erase them.

PROOFMARKS

The following proofmarks are those most frequently found on reproduction 2nd pattern Luftwaffe daggers: E & F Horster, F W Holler, and Alcoso, as well as RZM M/7 proofmarks which should never appear on any Luftwaffe blade or component.

Reverse view of the upper blade, crossguard, and grip of three genuine second pattern Luftwaffe daggers. Each of the three daggers is by a different Maker exhibiting different styles of background pebbling on the reverse crossguard and indeed minor variations in the crossguard itself. The grip binding also differs on each dagger, these minor variations between Makers should be taken into account before dismissing any dagger as a reproduction.

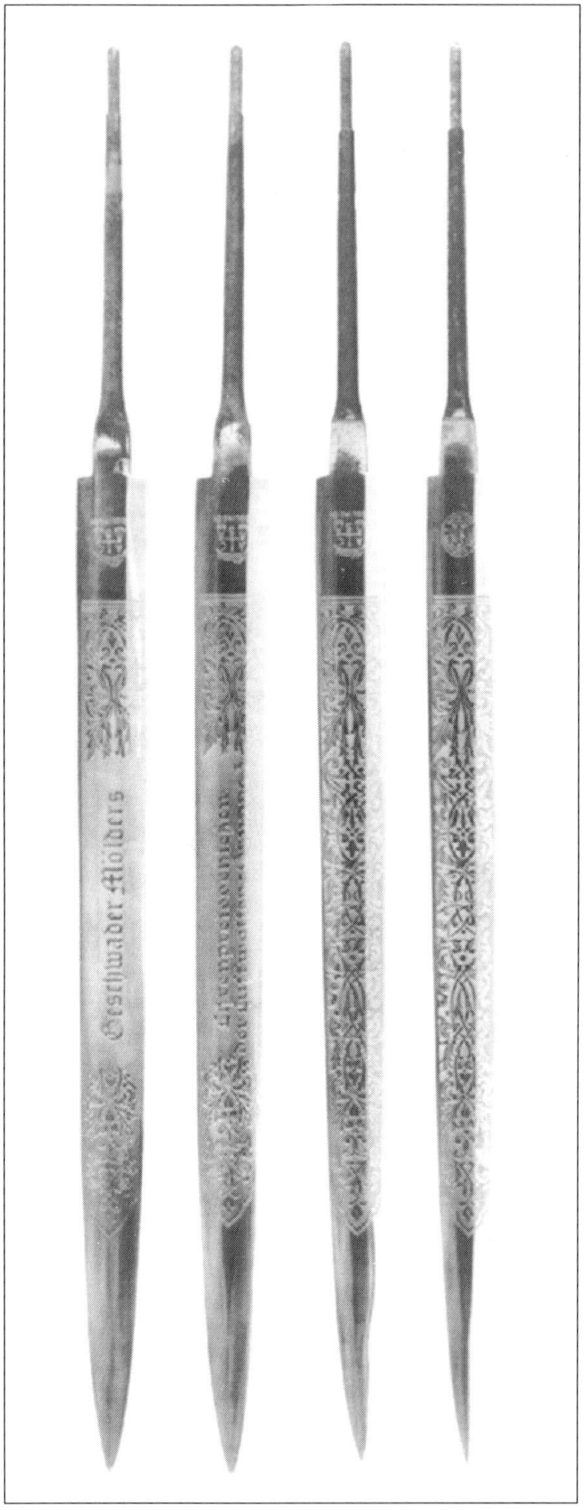
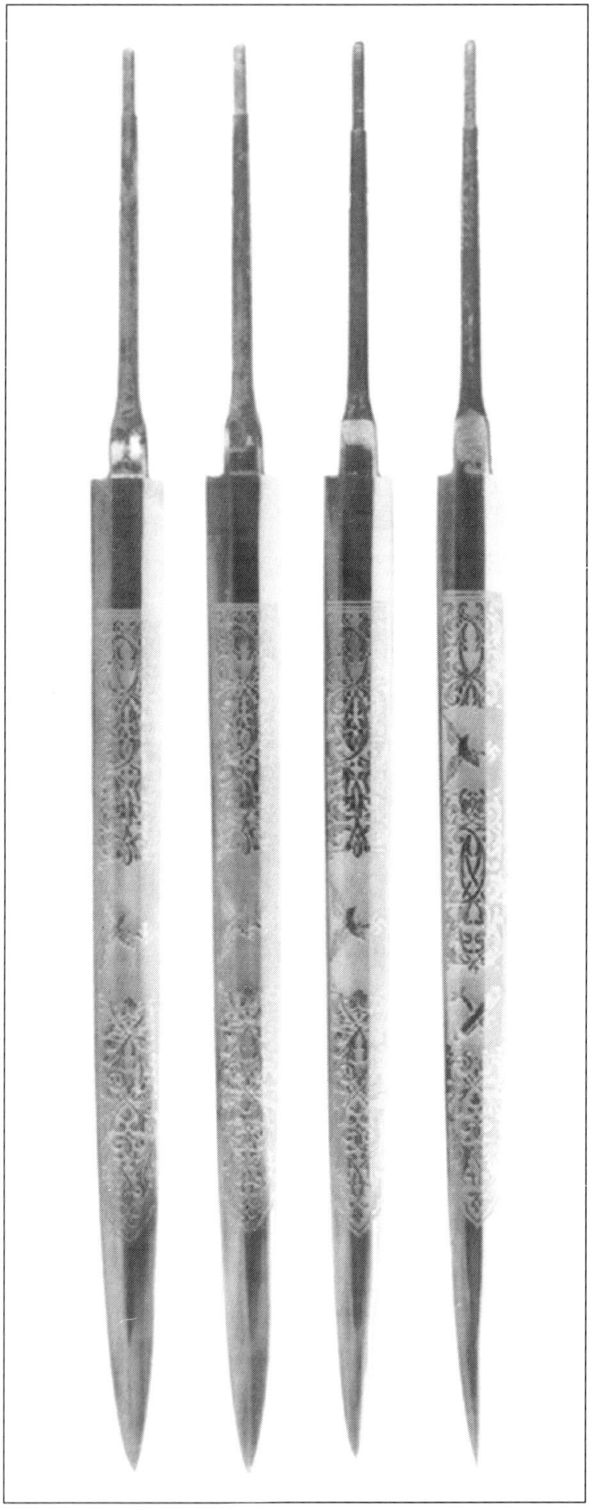

Obverse and reverse views of four different reproduction Luftwaffe second pattern dagger blades currently being produced in Solingen, Germany. The blades have etched decoration on both sides with central panels depicting Luftwaffe eagles, aircraft, and even the Geschwader Mölders legend in the centre panel of one blade. Three of the blades exhibit Alcoso proofmarks whilst the example on the left has the early Eickhorn small oval proofmark. These blades are exceptionally well made, consequently any daggers encountered having this style of blade should be very closely examined.

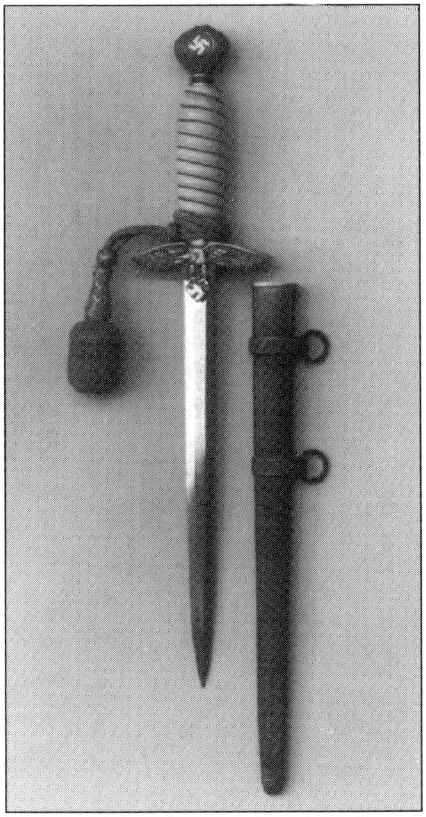

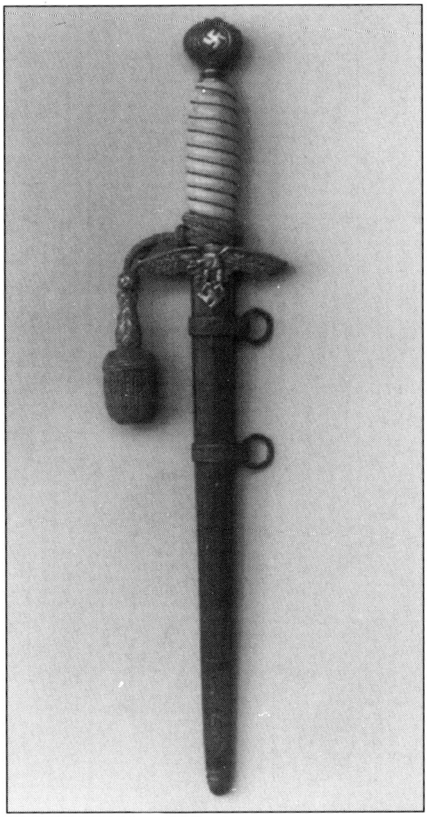

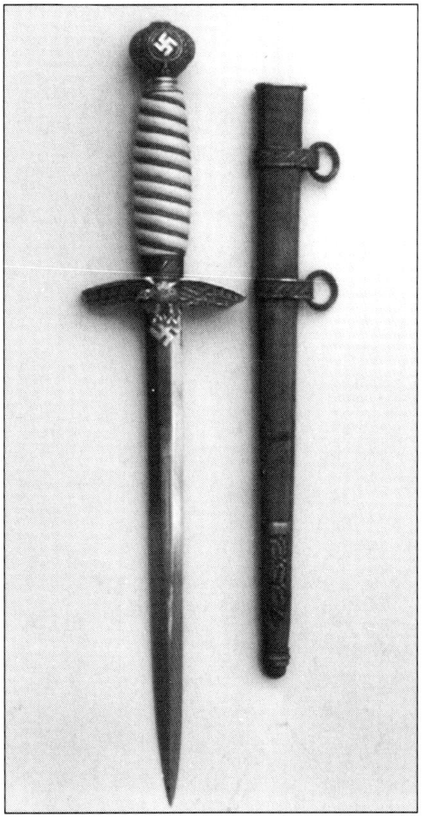

Comparison photographs of a reproduction second pattern Luftwaffe dagger illustrated above and a genuine example pictured on the right. The portepee on the reproduction is genuine and has been attached to the dagger in an attempt to disguise its true nature as a reproduction. This reproduction of German origin is of a very high quality but exhibits the following shortcomings. The white plastic grip is bound with a thin single strand wire and has a very bulbous shape. Each end of the grip tapers inwards quite dramatically, this is highlighted by the narrow neck of the pommel, beneath the portepee knot is an equally narrow ferrule. The crossguard eagle resembles an emaciated pigeon rather than the well defined shape of a genuine crossguard eagle, also the legs and talons are too elongated. The reverse of the crossguard has a thin pimply finish rather than the distinct pebbled effect of originals. The scabbard tip is elongated and has been added separately by brazing.

Paramilitary Reproductions

There were six paramilitary organisations in existence during the 12 years of the Third Reich; these were the DLV, NSFK, NPEA, RAD, RLB, and TeNo. Original daggers of the last four organisations are amongst the rarest and most expensive of the Third Reich production daggers. Consequently they have been the victim of reproductions for many years.

Many of the better quality reproduction examples of these daggers have been produced in the post-war years in Germany, often utilising some genuine elements from leftover pre-war stocks. This is especially true of the TeNo Leader's dagger which often features genuine grips allied to reproduction fittings.

Many genuine examples of the RLB daggers have parts interchanged to elevate them from the more common 2nd pattern RLB to the rarer and more expensive 1st pattern - often by the simple expedient of replacing the grip insignia.

The three types of NPEA dagger have the same basic form as the infinitely more common SA dagger, the only differences being that the lower grades of NPEA dagger have no grip insignia and carry a different blade motto. A common but otherwise genuine SA dagger can too easily be transformed into an NPEA Student's dagger by the simple expedient of replacing the blade with a good quality Solingen NPEA reproduction and a good quality plain NPEA grip. NPEA scabbards are routinely fabricated by removing the lockets from an SA dagger scabbard and soldering on a frog stud: this fabricated scabbard once painted can then be allied to a genuine bayonet frog. Unfortunately this process increases the value of the SA dagger fivefold when it is transformed by this method into an NPEA Student's dagger.

The RAD Subordinate's hewer has been reproduced in both Spain and Germany with varying degrees of success. There is also the RAD "Fat Man" hewer which first appeared in the 1960's and was marketed as a "undocumented variation", however this hewer although produced by a German Maker who had made RAD hewers during the Third Reich period was nonetheless a post-war fantasy.

The DLV 55cm long dagger was only in production for a very short period of time and bore a close similarity to the later 1st pattern Luftwaffe dagger. The DLV dagger has been the subject of parts assembly fabrications incorporating genuine parts from the 1st pattern Luftwaffe dagger. From 1934, the DLV abandoned the long dagger and adopted a short flyer's knife of a similar style to the previous DLV and 1st pattern Luftwaffe daggers (though obviously shorter).

The DLV flyer's knife has also been reproduced although not extensively as it is not one of the rarer Third Reich edged weapons. However the blade from genuine DLV knives have been misused to fabricate types of daggers which never actually existed during the Third Reich - such as the spurious Postschutz Subordinate's dagger.

The NSFK was the successor to the DLV and carried on using the same style of flyer's knife, albeit of a slightly different length. Also the composition of the dagger changed later on from a blue leather covered grip and scabbard to a blue painted crinkle finished aluminium. This second type of NSFK flyer's knife is often wrongly identified as a "reproduction" when in fact it was a perfectly legitimate descendant of this organisation's chose sidearm.

DLV AND NSFK REPRODUCTIONS

RECOGNITION CHECKLIST

BLADE

- Poorly defined Maker's proofmark.
- Narrow blade.
- Proofmarks located too far from the crossguard.
- An extremely sharp central ridge is found on many reproductions.
- A badly formed tang unusually with a rounded appearance.
- The use of an RZM proofmark which was inappropriate for the DLV/NSFK.
- The use of a felt blade washer/buffer pad instead of the blue leather type found on originals.

SCABBARD

- Scabbards with a blue painted flat finish (not to be confused with the blue painted crinkle finish of original NSFK scabbards).
- Upper scabbard fittings held in position by two screws located at the bottom of the fitting instead of the top.
- Undersized hanger loop is a feature of reproductions.
- A round ball on the end of the bottom fitting is a feature of reproductions: originals were always oval.
- The use of oversized domed screws to hold the scabbard fittings in place is a feature of many reproductions.
- The upper fitting of reproduction scabbards is marginally shorter than those found on originals.
- Reproduction scabbards do not usually feature DLV or NSFK stampings on the scabbard throat.

GRIP

- A grip with an oversize bulbous appearance is a feature of Spanish reproduction DLV/NSFK knives.
- Undersize crossguards and pommels are a consistent feature of Spanish reproductions.
- The pommel and crossguard especially on its underside exhibits casting flaws on reproduction fittings.
- The swastika inlay of reproductions is usually painted on rather than being inset in enamel.
- The lower crossguard of reproductions is smaller than the corresponding edge of the scabbard throat giving the knife an uneven appearance when in its reproduction scabbard.
- Reproductions grips are either synthetic leather with untidy pieces around the join with the pommel or have a flat blue painted finish often applied directly onto a wooden shell.

PROOFMARKS

Several Maker's proofmarks have been identified on reproductions amongst them: Carl Eickhorn, Paul Weyersberg, F W Holler and the use of the spurious RZM proofmark.

N.B. Reproduction DLV/NSFK Flyer's knives are seldom encountered with hanging straps attached, either reproduction or genuine.

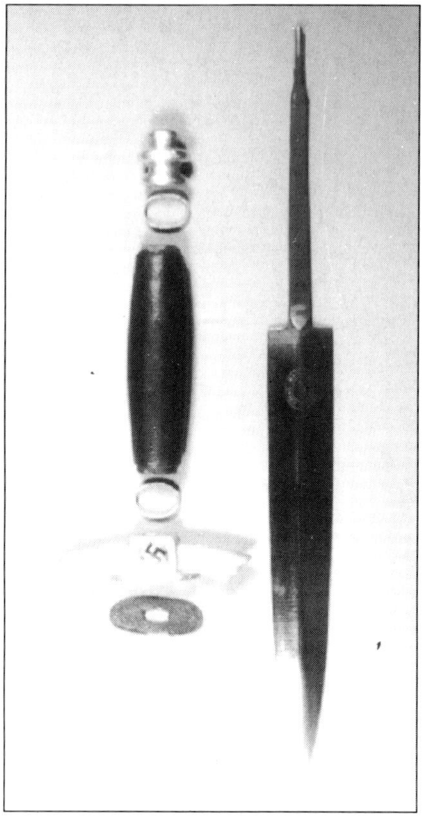

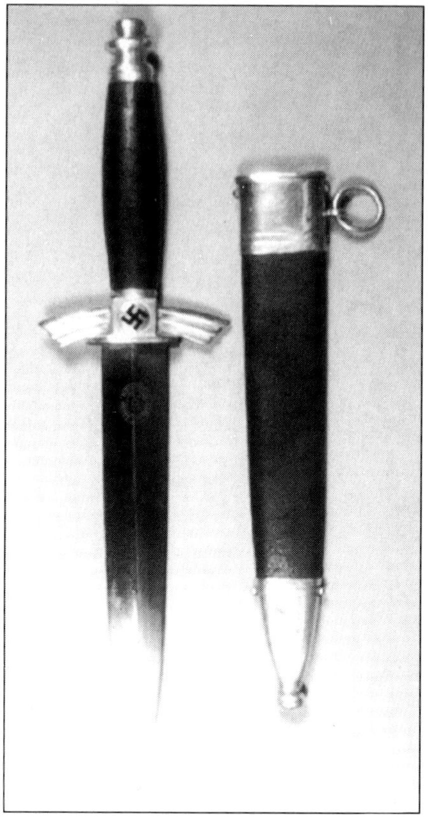

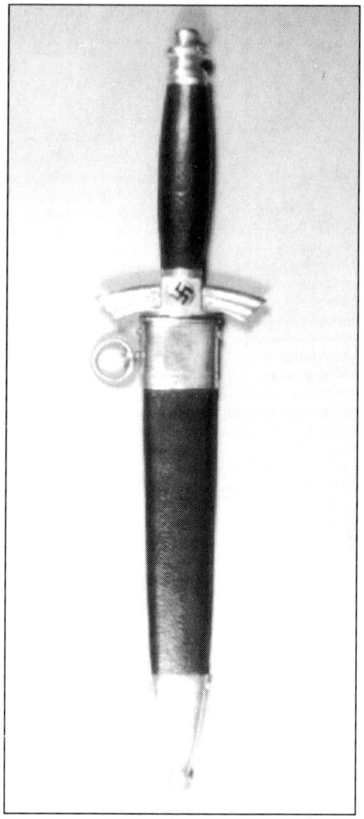

Three different views of a good quality German reproduction of a DLV/NSFK Flyer's knife which has excellent quality plating, but the fittings especially on the scabbard have a very flat appearance. The crossguard swastikas have been painted on, but are well formed. The blade is the most significant giveaway on this reproduction featuring a later Krebbs proofmark which is applied off centre; also the central ridge on the knife is not straight. Also note the flat shaped tang.

Two different examples of the Waffenamt acceptance stamps found on the scabbard throat of genuine NSFK Flyer's knives. Most reproductions do not bear the Waffenamt stamp.

NPEA REPRODUCTIONS

RECOGNITION CHECKLIST

BLADE

- ➢ Sunken NPEA motto on the blade is evidence that a former SA motto has been erased and the NPEA motto substituted over the top.
- ➢ The NPEA motto on reproduction blades is frequently photo-etched instead of the original acid etching.
- ➢ Photo-etching produces a very shallow superficial motto, lacking the depth of acid etching.
- ➢ A central blade bevel which has flattened appearance is often evidence of a motto being reapplied over another.
- ➢ Maker's proofmark appearing on the blade other than Burgsmüller or Eickhorn should not be present on genuine NPEA blades.
- ➢ RZM M/7 proofmarks should never appear on NPEA blades.
- ➢ There should always be a period (full stop) at the end of the NPEA motto: reproduction blades often omit this period.
- ➢ Blade etching starting too low down on the blade i.e. closer to the point than it should be is indicative of reproduction inscriptions.
- ➢ The letters in the NPEA motto too large often by up to 50% more than the original inscription.
- ➢ No umlaut (¨) over the "u" in the "müller" section of the "Burgsmüller" proofmark.
- ➢ No space allowed between "Karl" and "Burgsmüller" is a frequent feature of fake Burgsmüller proofmarks.
- ➢ The Burgsmüller proofmark applied too close to the crossguard.
- ➢ The Burgsmüller proofmark oversize.
- ➢ Modern reproduction blades are usually hollow ground with a dull grey satin finish.
- ➢ Reproduction NPEA blades produced in Spain often have a very sharp central ridge similar to that found on reproduction SA and SS blades.
- ➢ The tangs on reproduction blades rather than "modified" NPEA blades tend to be very badly formed being flat in appearance and bearing no billet clamp marks.

SCABBARD

- ➢ NPEA student's and Staff instructor's scabbards are often remodelled genuine SA scabbards redesigned to resemble the NPEA scabbard. Points to observe are the throat and the tip of the scabbard for evidence of the screw holes which will have been filled, and the addition of the ball fitting affixed to the scabbard tip. The ball fitting appendage is usually more spherical than on originals.
- ➢ The scabbard tip ball on redesigned scabbards is usually of brass instead of steel as on originals and is consequently not magnetic.
- ➢ Look for evidence of the ball having been soldered or brazed onto the scabbard tip.
- ➢ Repainted scabbards will normally have a shiny rather than drab finish: other forms of repainting will swing in the other direction having a matt finish which is also incorrect. The finish should be smooth and yet drab.
- ➢ NPEA Leader's scabbards are often modified 1936 pattern NSKK scabbards repainted olive green.
- ➢ The use of 1st pattern Luftwaffe suspension chains added to an NSKK scabbard.
- ➢ The use of genuine SA scabbards with the centre mount added: the upper ring on this type of

modified scabbard is usually too large being designed for a strap rather than a chain.

- Incorrect frog hook on the scabbard featuring more than two ridges on the hook.
- Look for evidence of a hook being soldered or brazed onto a scabbard.
- The use of inappropriate scabbard liners such as tin or zinc instead of the original brass which were affixed to the throat mounting.
- The absence of scabbard liners.

GRIP

- Grips incorrectly made from plastic instead of the correct original wooden type.
- Inappropriate grip inlays such as the SA symbol mounted in the upper grip. This type of inlay should not appear anywhere on any NPEA dagger.
- The use of modern reproduction eagle inlays on Staff Instructor's or Leader's daggers.
- Look for evidence in the upper grip of an SA inlay hole being filled in and then repolished.
- Crossguard with SA Gruppe letters or SS Gruppe numbers is indicative of a parts reconstruction. Markings for these two organisations should never appear on NPEA crossguards.
- Evidence of crudely engraved school or graduation marks.

FROG

- The presence of more than one rivet on the frog would indicate this was actually a Wehrmacht bayonet frog. Original NPEA frogs should only have one stud in the lower section: the rest of the frog being stitched.
- Rivets visible on the obverse edge of the frog are incorrect.
- Too large a hole for the frog hook.
- Evidence of a hole being changed or enlarged.

PROOFMARKS

- Only two firm's proofmarks should appear on NPEA blades those of Karl Burgsmüller and Carl Eickhorn.
- The appearance of any other proofmark would indicate that the blade is a remodelled SA blade.
- "Germany" appearing on the blade with the proofmark is evidence of a post-war assembled dagger intended for export outside of Germany.

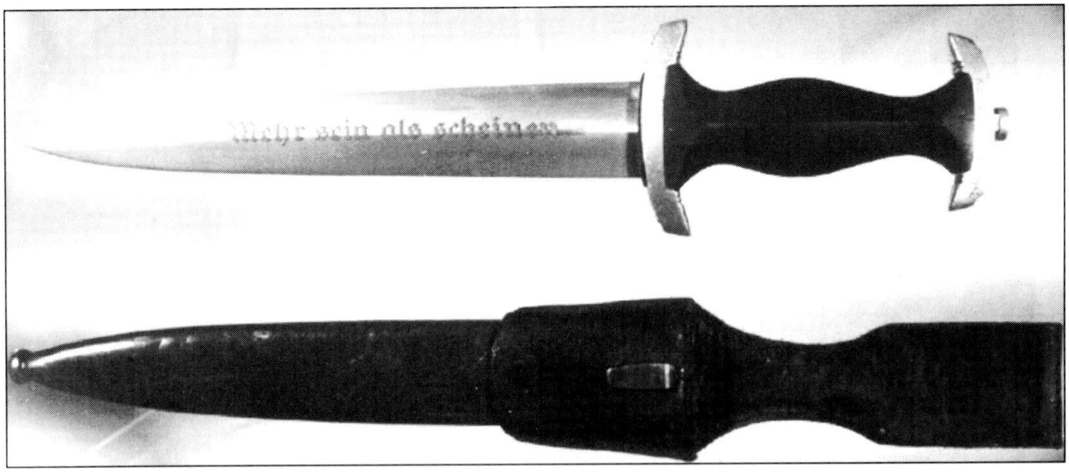

Example of a genuine NPEA student's dagger with scabbard and frog. Note the NPEA school and the award date 1942 etched into the pommel crossguard. Note the correct positioning of the blade motto and absence of any grip insignia.

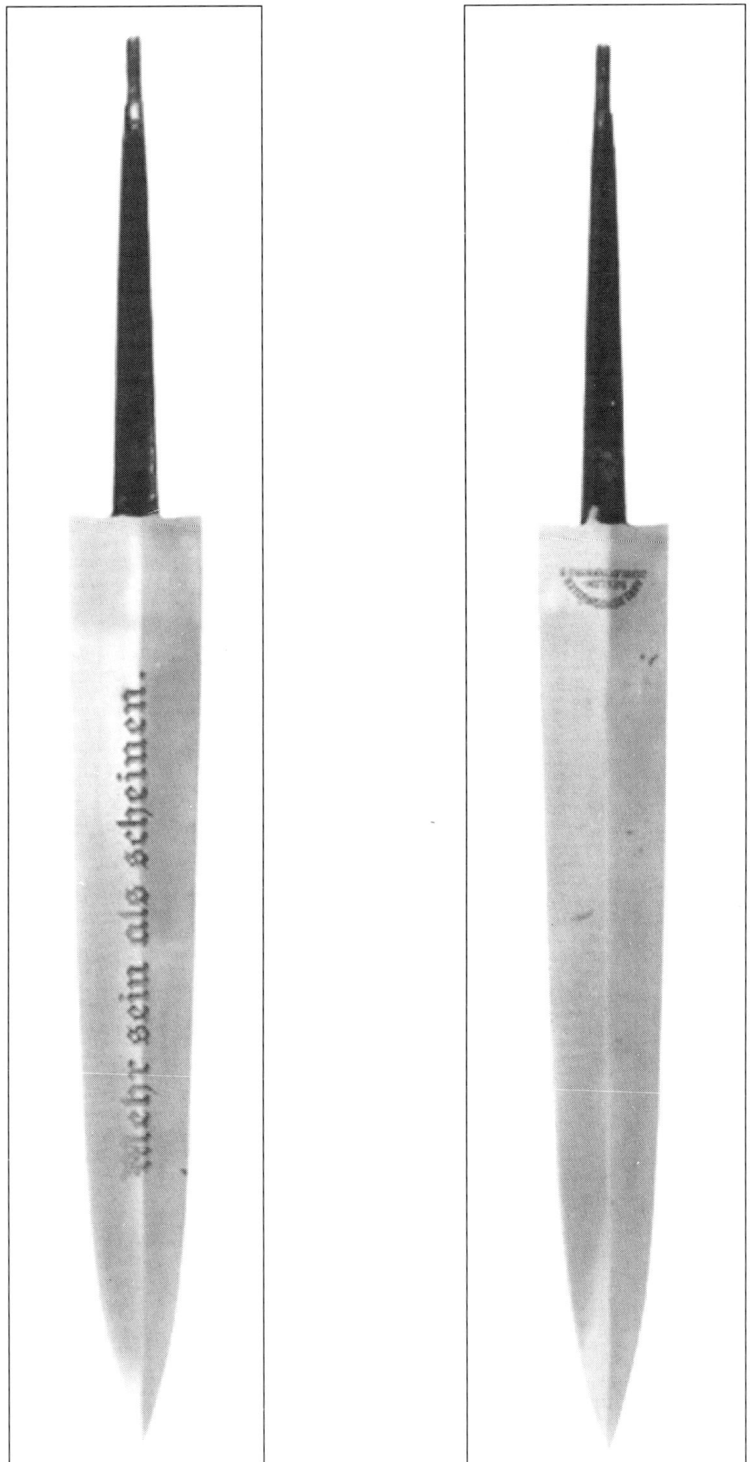

A current German made reproduction of an NPEA dagger blade. The quality is very good with tang fire scaling from the traditional drop forge processing. The central ridge is somewhat pronounced, breaking the plane of the NPEA blade motto. The obverse ricasso bears the correct style of Burgsmüller proofmark.

RAD REPRODUCTIONS

RECOGNITION CHECKLIST

SUBORDINATES HEWER

BLADE

- Poor quality plating on the blade with areas exhibiting lifting of the plate.
- Blade motto etching applied too lightly.
- Blade motto appearing out of position or applied on the wrong side of the blade i.e. the reverse side.
- A straight backed shoulder on the blade instead of the correct slightly curved scimitar style.
- Blade length excessively over size.
- Maker's or RAD proofmark applied too lightly or appearing in the wrong position.
- Use of an RZM proofmark and control numbers: RZM proofmarks were never used on the RAD hewer or Leader's dagger.
- Some blade etching is so poor it tends to break up giving a spotted effect with tiny breaks in the letters.
- The fuller on some reproduction blades is too deep with each end terminating with a rounded edge rather than a point.

GRIP

- The use of moulded plastic grips instead of genuine horn.
- The use of incorrect screws and nuts to secure the grip plates: with the nut being flat ended and/or countersunk instead of being straight and slotted as were originals.
- Evidence of filing or grinding to the beak pommel inorder to simulate a full staghorn grip.
- The use of grey alloy castings to make the ferrule and crossguard.
- Very poor quality plating ferrule, crossguard and pommel.
- Poor definition on the two horizontal lines of the crossguard giving a wavy effect rather than two straight lines.
- The use of chrome plating on the ferrule, crossguard and pommel rather than the original nickel silver or nickel plate.

SCABBARD

- Overall poor definition to both scabbard fittings top and bottom.
- Closely observe for areas where the design on each fitting "breaks up" especially in the Celtic swirl of the upper fitting.
- Spanish reproductions have the decoration on the upper fitting applied too close to the scabbard throat extending virtually to the liner insert: when on originals there should be approximately a 1/4 inch gap between the liner throat and the top of the design.
- The side hanger loop fitting on Spanish reproductions scabbards has a rounded appearance at each end: instead of being mounted at a slightly downswept angle.
- Some reproduction scabbard fittings are made from a very thin tinny ore material with the decoration being embossed from the reverse side: this is especially noticeable on the swastika on the lower fitting which has a very rounded appearance rather than the square flat appearance found on originals.
- Endeavour to judge the weight of the scabbard which is quite substantial on originals, whereas

reproductions tend to be in the extreme either too heavy or far too light.

- Scabbard paint should be closely observed for evidence of any grey primer showing through: where primer was used on originals in the 1930's red oxide was the most widely used type.
- Observe if there are any small ridges around the "V" shaped edges of the fittings which would indicate repainting: the ridges being caused by masking.

PROOFMARKS

The most commonly encountered proofmarks on Spanish reproductions are "Alcoso", F W Holler and the RZM proofmark with several different control numbers including 13, 30, 33 and 66. "Krebs" and "Puma" appear on "Fat Man" blades. The Eickhorn squirrel proofmark appears on current good quality reproductions although it is not very well acid etched on the blade ricasso and is either faint or breaking up.

HANGERS

Reproductions of RAD hewer hangers have never posed a major problem to the collector, however there is a point which should be made regarding the large 2nd type of RAD hewer hanger with the spade shaped pad. From time to time examples of these will be encountered with very wafer thin leather parts totally out of character with the more robust style generally found. This style of hanger is quite definitely *not* a reproduction, but was a wartime example produced by the Alcoso firm and is consequently nearly always found in company with an Alcoso RAD hewer. This type of hanger was a wartime expedient to save materials, and although the quality of the hanger is not very good due to the materials used the actual specifications for the item are correct.

LEADER'S DAGGER

BLADE

- Too lightly applied or poorly defined blade motto.
- Areas of spotting where the motto is breaking up.
- Motto applied on the wrong side of the blade i.e. reverse.
- Blade having little or no shoulder under the crossguard RAD insignia.
- A poor quality flat tang brazed into position inside the grip.
- The use of an RZM proofmark and control number which are totally inappropriate for this type of dagger.
- The "Alcoso" proofmark has been encountered on good quality RAD daggers with the proof being poorly etched and the scales breaking up. The letters "Alcoso" are also crudely formed.
- Poor quality plating to the blade usually exhibiting areas of lifting.

GRIP

- The use of a grey finished alloy to make the crossguard ferrule and pommel usually having a poor quality chrome plating which has not held up very well.
- Areas of pitting especially to the crossguard and the eagle head pommel.
- Poor quality definition on the crossguard RAD insignia and also to the eagle's eye and beak.
- The ribbing on the ferrule running in the wrong direction when viewed from the obverse side i.e. top left to bottom right instead of vice versa, although the ribbing appears at the correct angle on the reverse side. This effect is caused by the reproducer giving the ferrule part of the die spiral twist rather than the two diagonal sets of ferrule ribbing which appear on originals.

- The fletching on the eagle's neck on some reproduction daggers is formed from five pronounced and protruding ridges: whereas originals have four sets of fletching which are sharply indented forming an inverted "V" on the back of the eagle's neck. A simple way to test the quality of the fletching is to run thumbnail down the back of the eagle's neck: the ridges can quite easily be felt on reproductions whereas the nail will drop into the four fletching grooves on originals.
- The grip plates on most reproductions are too short by approximately 1/4 of an inch. Also the area where the grip plate rounds off under the eagle's throat is a very sharp angle on reproduction grip plates rather than slightly rounded as on genuine grips.
- Good quality reproduction RAD Leader's daggers have been encountered with a bright yellow grip and have been passed off as "variations".
- Some reproductions have the grip plates secured with the screw on the wrong side i.e. the obverse instead of the reverse. Also examples have been seen with screws visible from both sides.
- The use of "variant" insignia on the crossguard. These were never an authorised alternative and any encountered are invariably post-war fantasies.

SCABBARD

- The use of grey coloured alloys with cheap chrome plating.
- Poor definition on the scabbard decoration especially in the upper section on the Celtic swirl design. This design is also often slightly crooked in the way it has been applied to the scabbard and can be detected when held at arm's length.
- The scabbard hanger hooks are often just crudely formed semi-circular hooks rather than having the squared off shape of originals (although it should be borne in mind that variations in the shape of the hanger hooks do exist between different Makers of original daggers, though none have this pronounced rounded effect evident on the poorer quality reproductions.
- Some reproduction scabbards have the bottom sheath decoration repeated on the reverse side whereas originals were always plain on the reverse.
- A wash similar to that found on reproduction diplomatic dagger scabbards is sometimes also found on the RAD scabbard. This is to simulate the original finish found on genuine RAD scabbards.
- The two sheaths of wheat decoration on the top of the scabbard tend to just touch or are extremely close to one another on genuine scabbards: whereas there is a marked gap between the ends of each sheath on reproduction scabbard decorations.
- The tip of most reproduction scabbards tend to be more or less straight and don't have the slightly curved spade shape of originals.
- The outer lines marking the perimeter of the centre scabbard panel are very poorly defined on most reproduction scabbards with the vertical line being slightly wavy and also marginally off centre to the left when viewed upright from the obverse side.
- The pebbling on the centre panel on reproductions is much cruder than originals being somewhat larger and often forming patterns similar to those found on Army reproduction scabbards emanating from Spain.

PROOFMARKS

The most commonly encountered proofmark on reproduction RAD Leader's daggers is that of "Alcoso": although the proofmark is very badly applied having spotty appearance with the scales breaking up in places, also the letters in the word "Alcoso" are very poorly formed. Examples of RZM proofmarks have been encountered, but this is not as common an occurrence as it is on the RAD hewer. Good quality Solingen made blades are currently available for the RAD Leader's dagger with a variety of proofmarks from different Makers. Although these are currently being made they are invariably sold as "left over pre-war stock". They are extremely well made being drop forged with the acid etched motto on the blade being very well executed, and are best detected by their very new, "mint appearance".

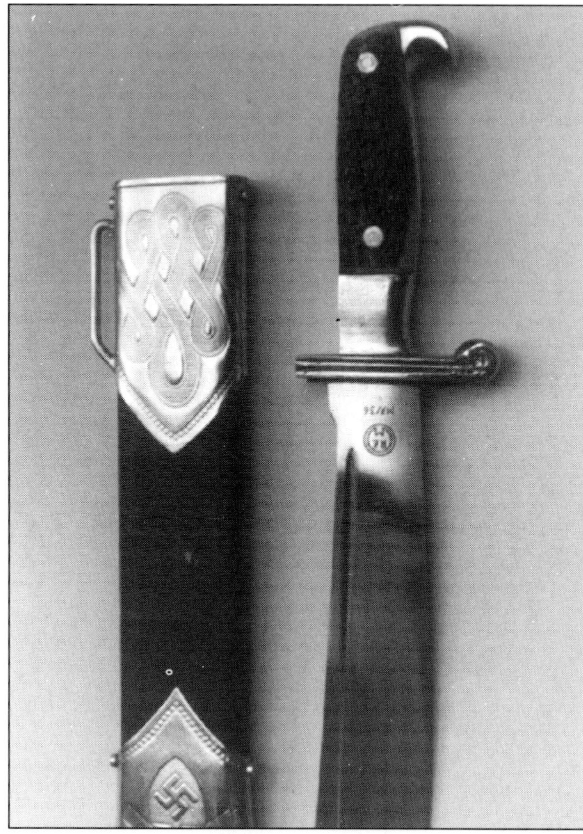

Three different views of a current Spanish reproduction RAD Subordinate's hewer. This particular piece has been in circulation for over 20 years and demonstrates a reasonable quality in both its appearance and material composition. The blade is of a better quality than earlier examples, but has a much too pronounced upward sweep to the edge of the blade giving it a scimitar style appearance. The motto is well etched but is too centrally located on the blade. Original mottos were etched considerably closer to the ricasso. Close inspection of the top and bottom fittings will show that they are thin sheet stampings which lack some of the sharper detail of originals. Also the Celtic swirl on the top scabbard fitting is actually situated marginally to the right on the fitting rather than being centrally located on the fitting as originals were. The interlocking perlring decoration around the "V" edge of each fitting is located too close to the edge on the "V" of the bottom fitting and is unevenly applied on the top fitting. The application of the perlring on originals was an equal distance from the edge on both fittings. The scabbard attachment for the hanger is incorrectly shaped and would not have had sufficient clearance to have accommodated a 1st pattern hanging strap had this been an original. On the positive side this particular reproduction has excellent dimensions, and various parts from these Spanish hewers, especially the grip plates, have been encountered in parts assemblies with genuine parts with which they seem to fit relatively well.

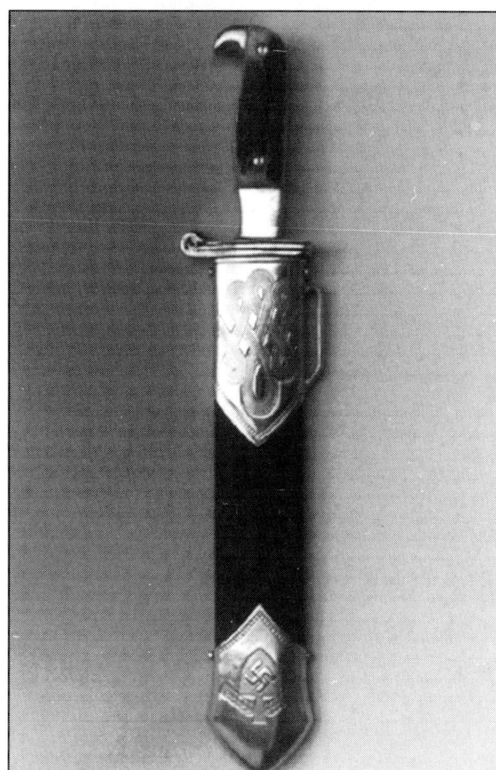

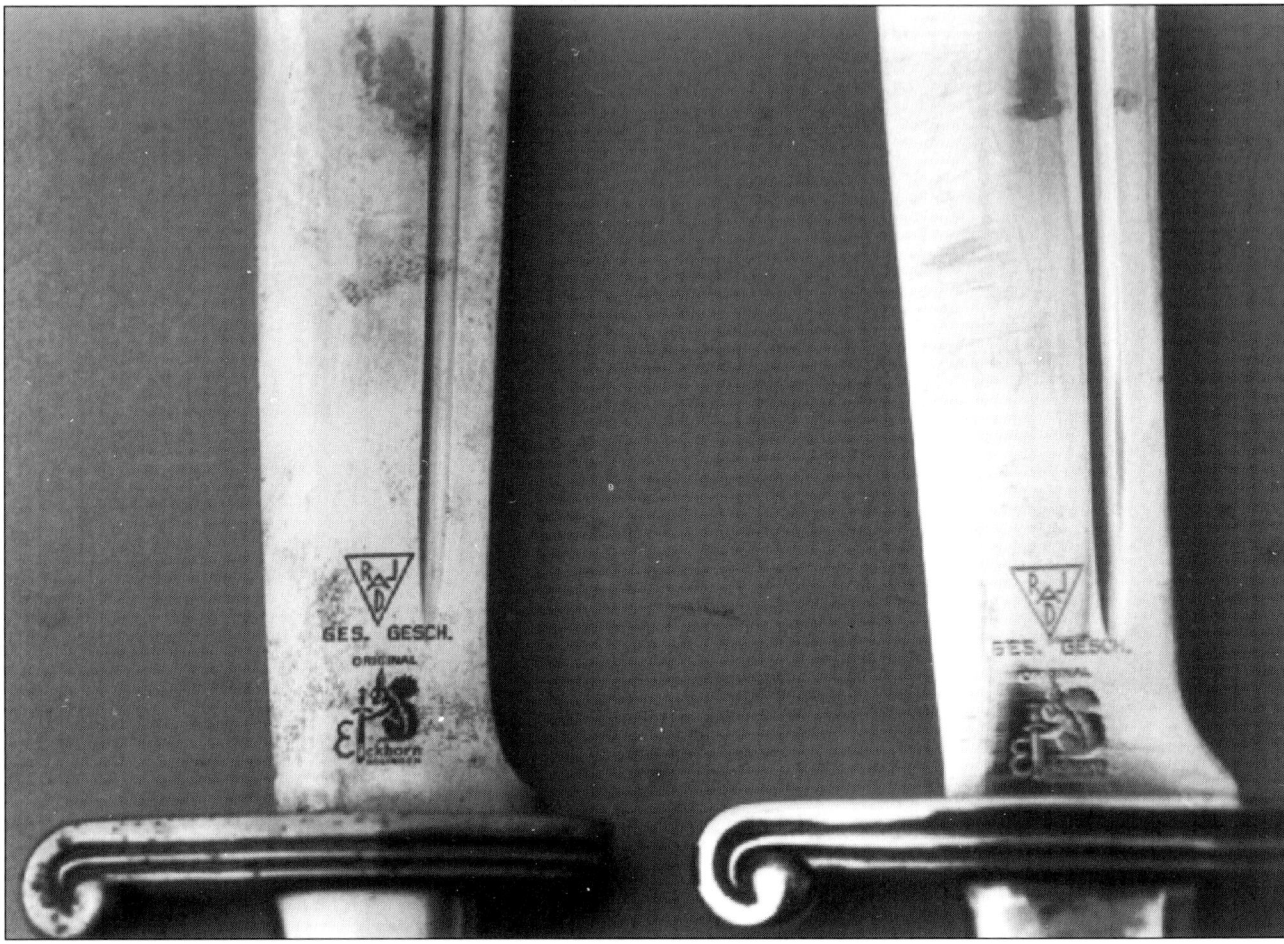

Close up view of the proofmarks on a genuine RAD hewer on the left and a 1970's reproduction on the right. On the left the genuine hewer exhibits a well executed acid etched Eickhorn proofmark with the RAD and Patent proofmark above which even after 50 years is still exceptionally sharp, even though the blade and crossguard exhibit age pitting. On the right however the "mint" Eickhorn hewer, although it has an exceptionally clean blade, has extremely poorly executed proofmarks which in some areas, mainly around the squirrel and the word "GES" are barely legible. It will also be noted that the proofmark on the right-hand reproduction has been applied far too close to the crossguard; this has obviously been done to prevent the word "GESCH" from running into the elongated fuller. The poorly applied proofmark and also the poor acid etching of the "Arbeit Adelt" motto are the only significant characteristics which distinguish these post-war produced Eickhorn hewers from genuine Third Reich era production pieces.

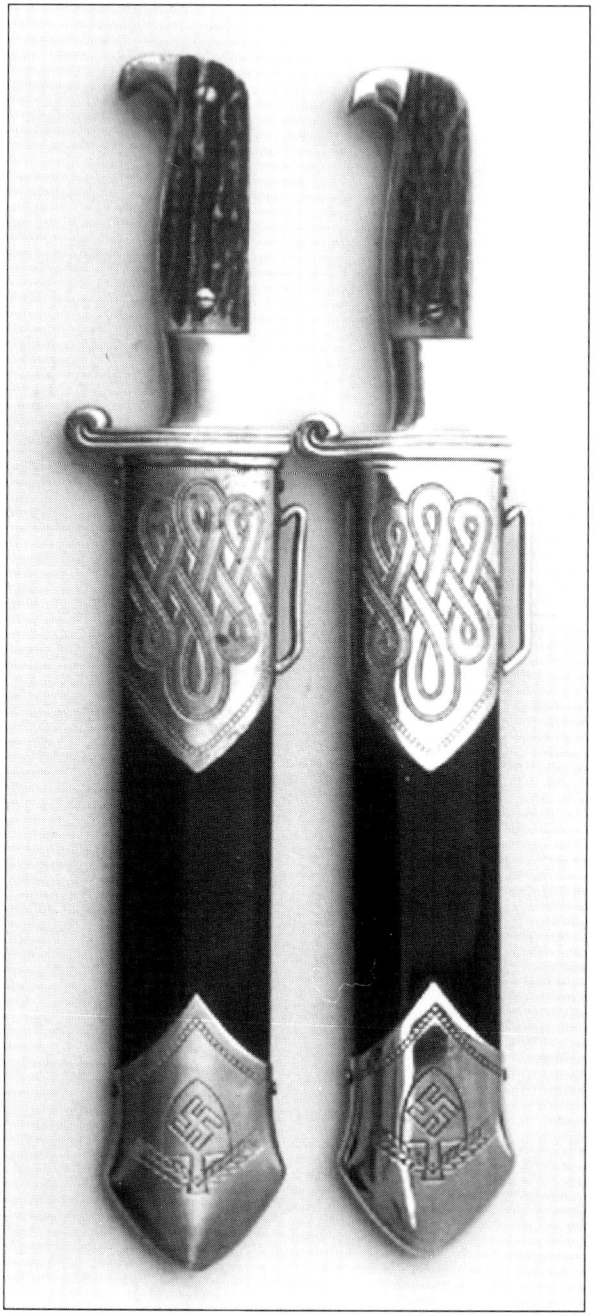

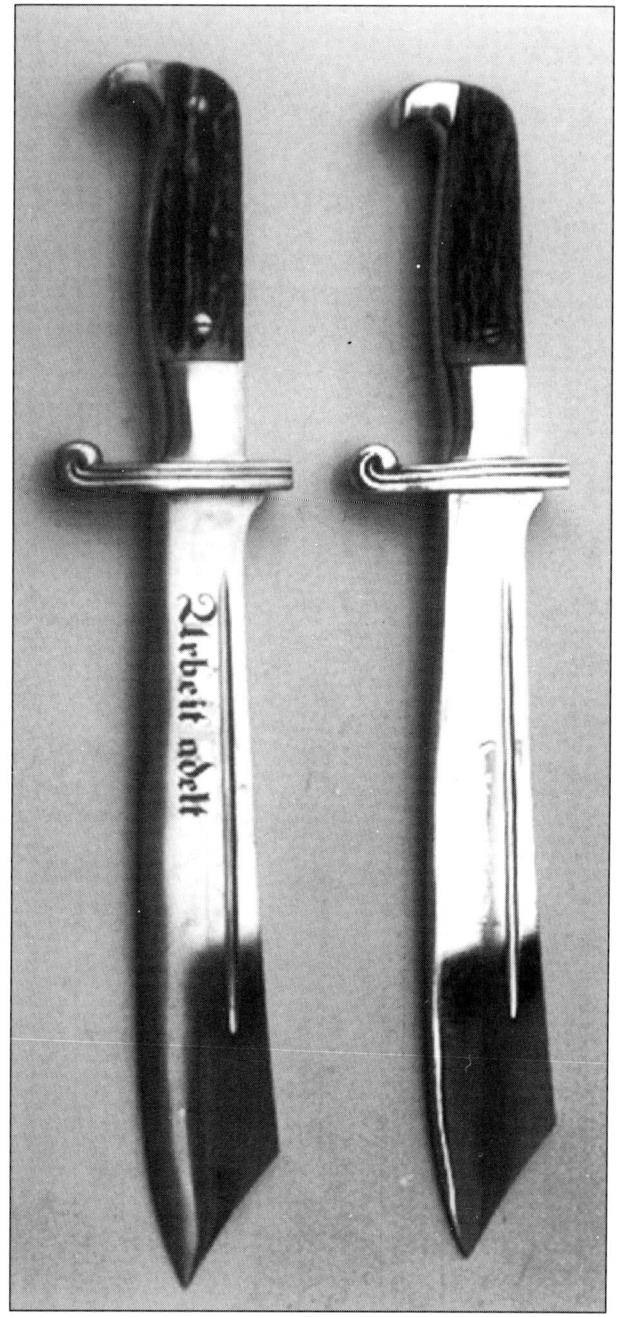

These photographs show a genuine Third Reich era RAD hewer on the left, and on the right a 1970's vintage reproduction example produced from original dies. As can be observed the technical quality of this hewer is perfect: probably having been produced from the same or similar dies but with a 40 year interval between their production. Both original and reproduction hewers bear the Carl Eickhorn proofmark and when in their scabbards are only distinguishable by the new appearance of the hewer on the right (which would appear to be a collector's dream, a "mint example") It is only when the hewer blades are examined side by side that any comparison can realistically be drawn between the genuine and reproduction. Immediately noticeable is the poorly defined blade motto on the right hand reproduction, especially when compared to the crisp detail and background toning of the original on the left.

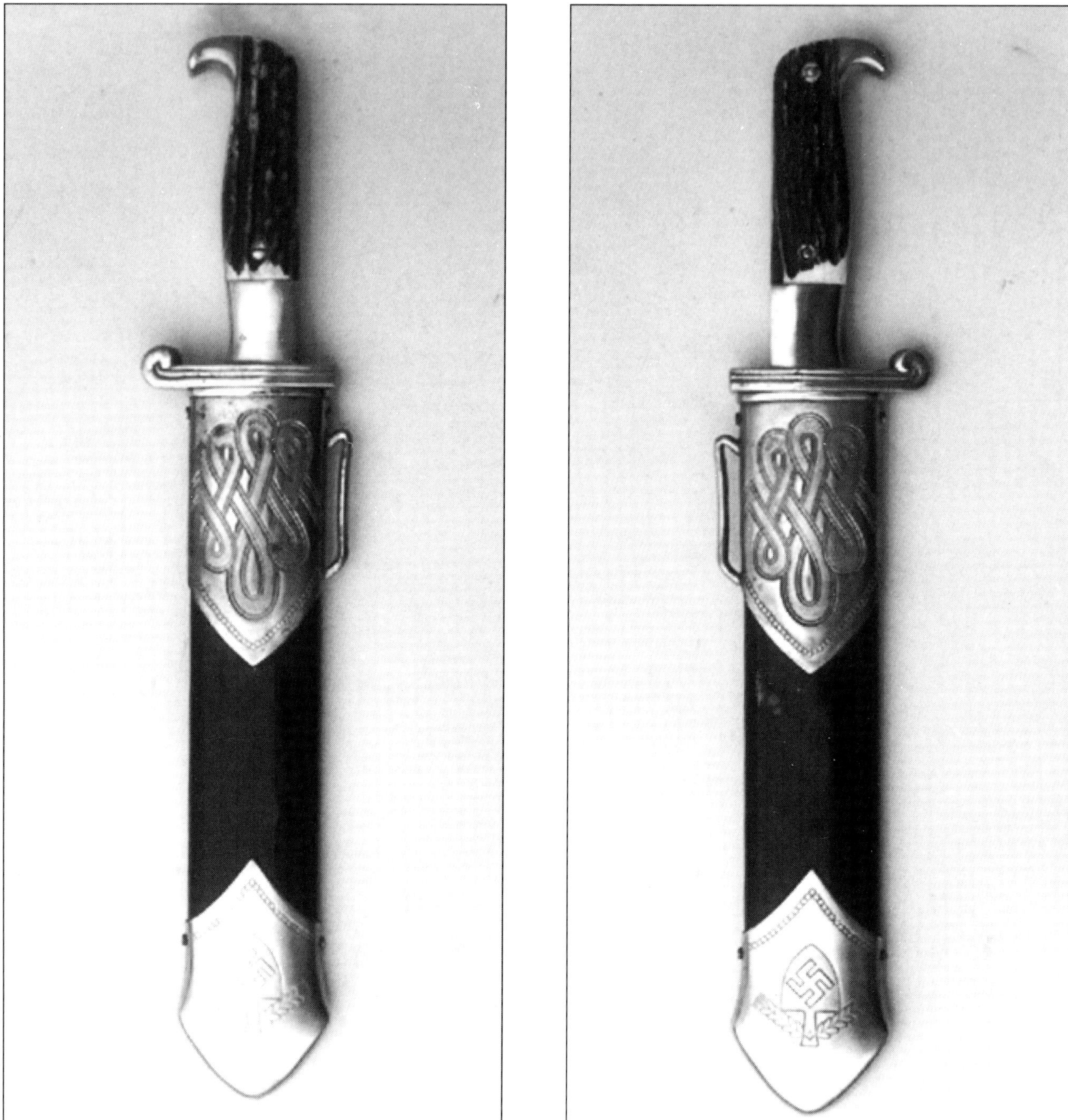

Obverse and reverse view of a genuine Third Reich era RAD hewer.

Modern reproductions of the RAD Leaders dagger (left) and the Subordinates hewer (right). Note the shiny new finish of both examples.

The RAD "Fat Man" hewer produced by Krebs in the 1960's. This hewer never existed as an authorised variation during the Third Reich era. Note that the RAD motto is applied on the reverse side of the blade, genuine hewers had the motto on the obverse side. The blade shape is also markedly different from the regulation RAD hewer.

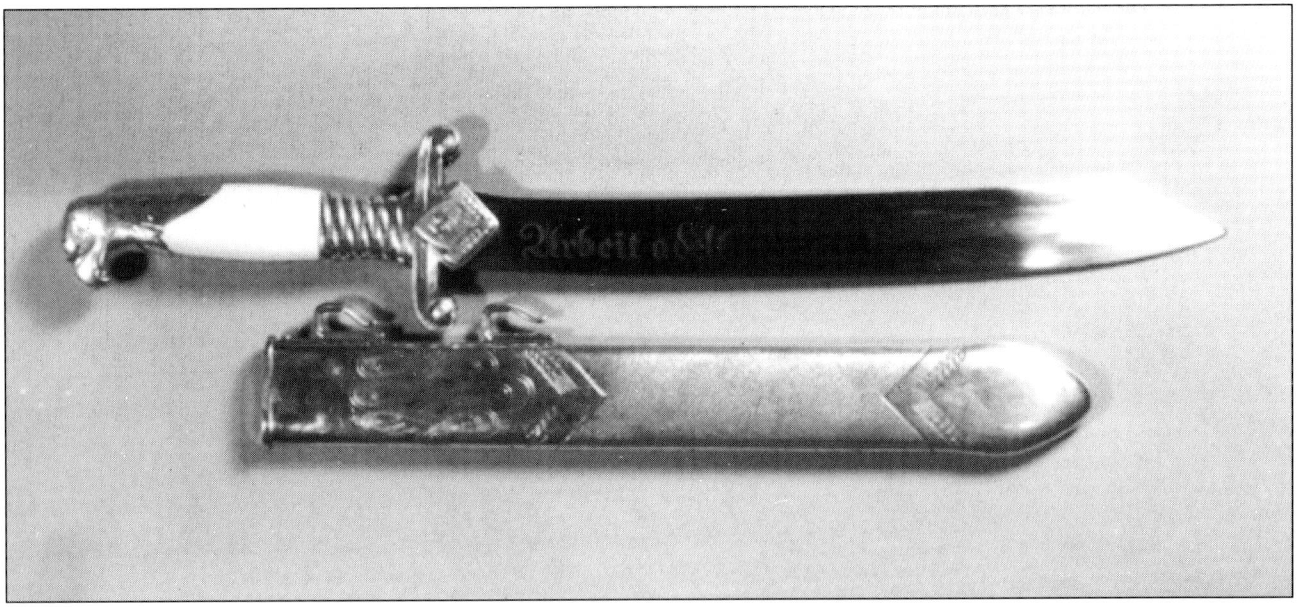

Out of scabbard view of a reproduction RAD Leaders dagger.

RLB REPRODUCTIONS

Reproductions of all patterns of the RLB daggers have been produced in both Spain and Germany since the 1960's. In most respects the daggers of the two different patterns i.e. 1936 & 1938 are identical except for the modified RLB insignia which is different on the 1938 pattern.

The RLB reproduction daggers produced in Spain feature cast brass fittings which are then lightly silver plated. This plating has a tendency to wear off quite rapidly revealing the brass underneath.

The scabbards of both the Subordinate and Leader's have a painted finish, whereas original Leader's scabbards were covered in dark blue leather. However reproduction examples of both patterns of RLB Leader's daggers will be encountered with scabbards covered in a thin imitation blue leather covering.

In most respects the scabbards used on reproduction RLB daggers are the same as those found on Postschutz reproductions originating from Spain.

The blades of Spanish reproduction RLB daggers tend to have a flat central ridge rather than the pronounced one found on originals. Unlike originals many reproductions feature proofmarks on the blade ricasso usually that of the RZM.

Good quality reproduction parts for RLB daggers have been produced in Germany since the 1960's, and quite often feature in parts assembly fabrications, using a mixture of reproduction and genuine parts.

In addition to outright blatant reproductions, there is also the practice of changing the insignia on genuine second pattern RLB daggers with good quality reproduction first pattern insignia. This minor substitution can drastically increase the value of a second pattern RLB dagger either Leader's or Subordinate's. Consequently the grip insignia of all RLB daggers whether original or reproduction require the closest inspection.

RECOGNITION CHECKLIST

BLADE

- Use of an RZM proofmark is indicative of Spanish reproduction blades.
- Paul Weyersberg is generally accepted to be the sole manufacturer of RLB daggers, consequently RLB daggers encountered bearing other makers proofmarks should be viewed with suspicion.
- Many genuine RLB daggers will be encountered bearing no makers proofmark whatsoever, consequently this type of blade is quite acceptable.
- A flat broad tang is a feature of reproduction RLB blades.
- Blades with a matt grey finish are more than likely Spanish reproductions.

SCABBARD

- Scabbards with silver plated brass fittings are reproductions.
- RLB Leaders daggers with painted scabbards are reproductions.
- RLB Leaders daggers with a thin synthetic leather covering are reproductions.

GRIP

- RLB grip fittings constructed from brass with a light silver plating are reproduction.
- Painted wooden grips are a feature of reproductions.
- Observe the grip insignia for evidence of substitution.
- Crossguard and pommel fittings with poor detail or casting pits should be viewed with suspicion.

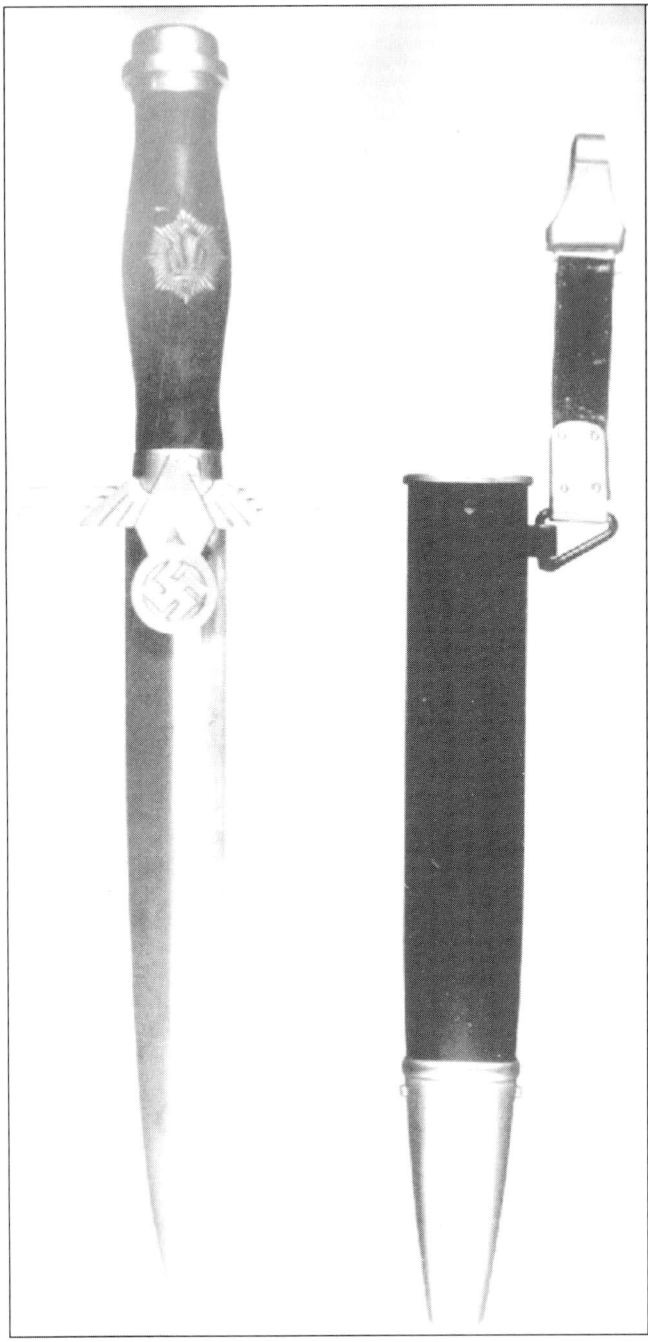

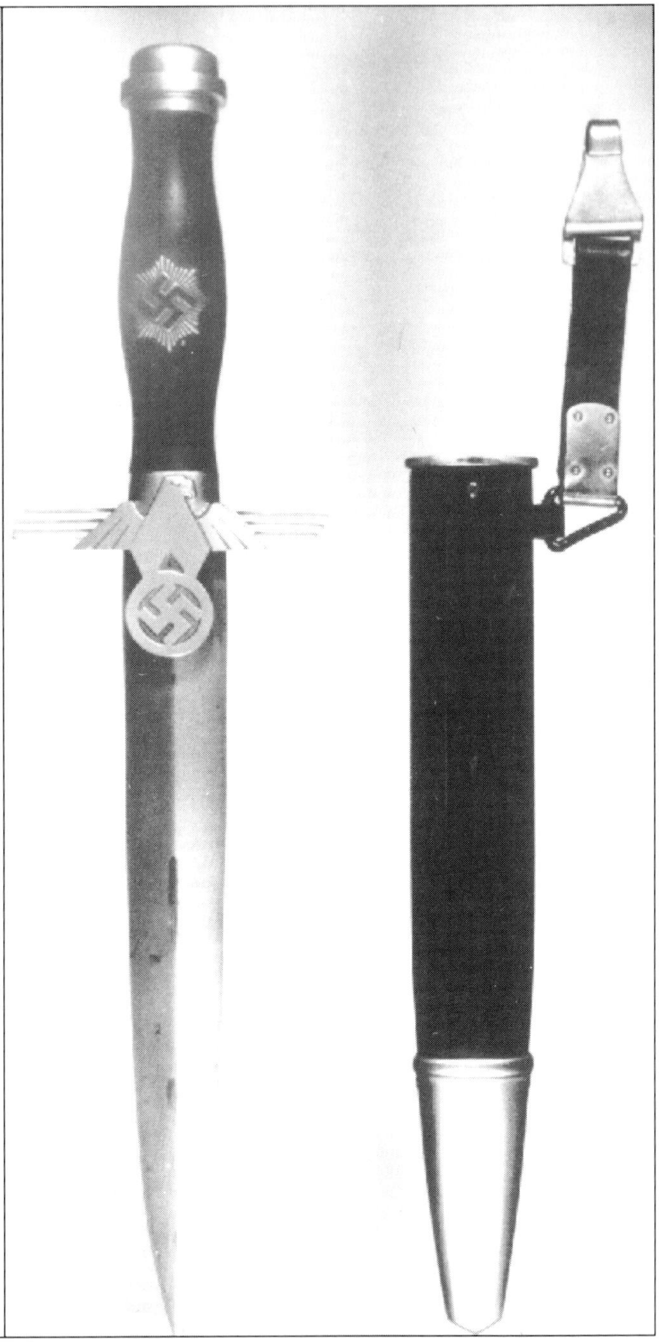

Two examples of genuine first and second pattern RLB Subordinate's daggers, both daggers are virtually identical except for the grip insignia. The dagger on the left is a first pattern with the letters RLB within the starburst, whilst the example on the right is a second pattern dagger which features the same style of starburst, but with a swastika inlay. One other minor difference is in the bottom scabbard fitting, the first pattern on the left has exposed screw retainers, whilst the second pattern scabbard on the right has the screws recessed.

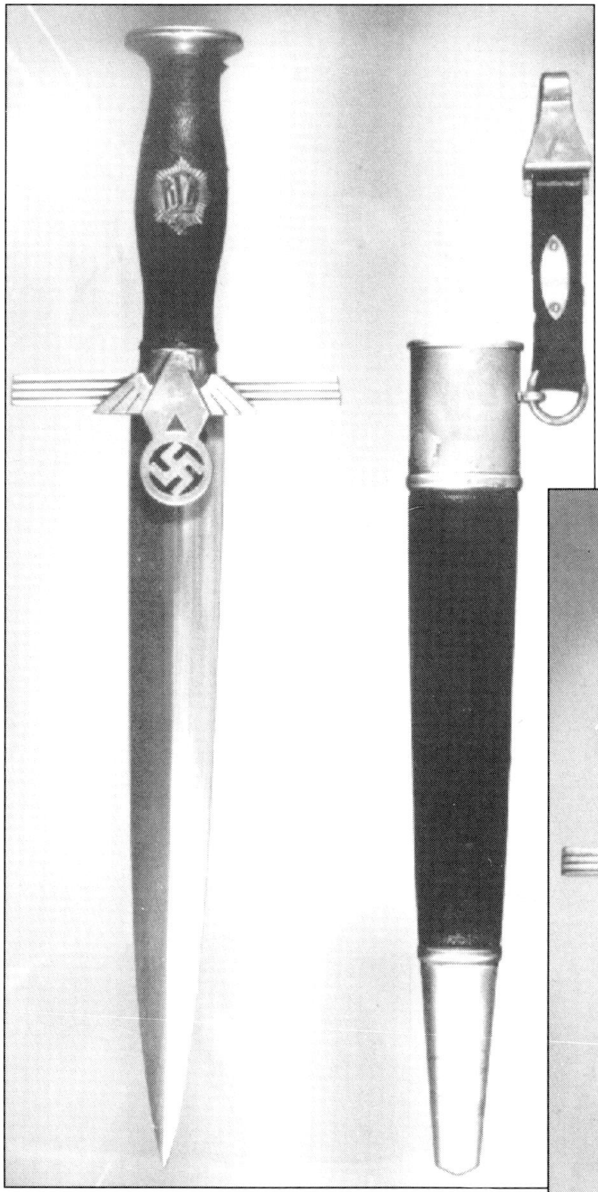

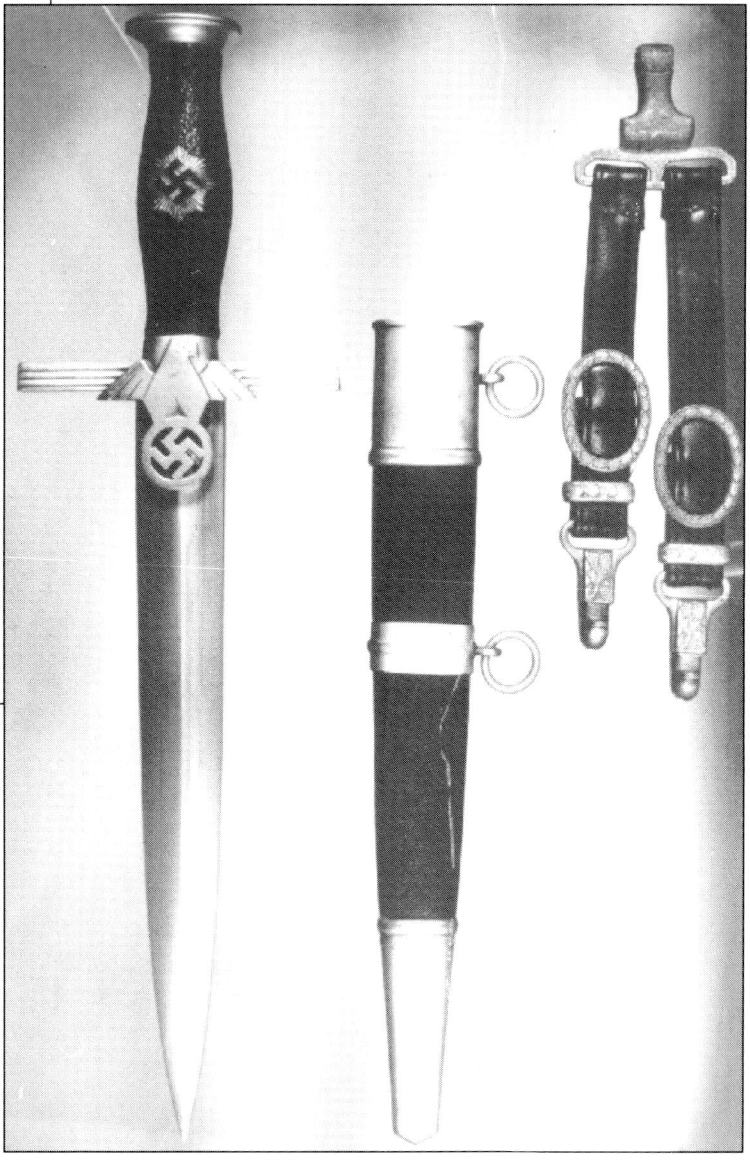

Two examples of genuine first and second pattern RLB Leader's daggers, which exhibit some minor differences between the first pattern dagger above, and the second pattern Leader's dagger below. The grip insignia has the same starburst design on both daggers, however the letters RLB on the first pattern were changed to a swastika emblem on the second pattern Leader's dagger. The other modification between the two different patterns lies in the scabbard, which has a similar style on both patterns however the second pattern scabbard has an additional centre ramp added to accommodate the newly introduced leather hanging straps.

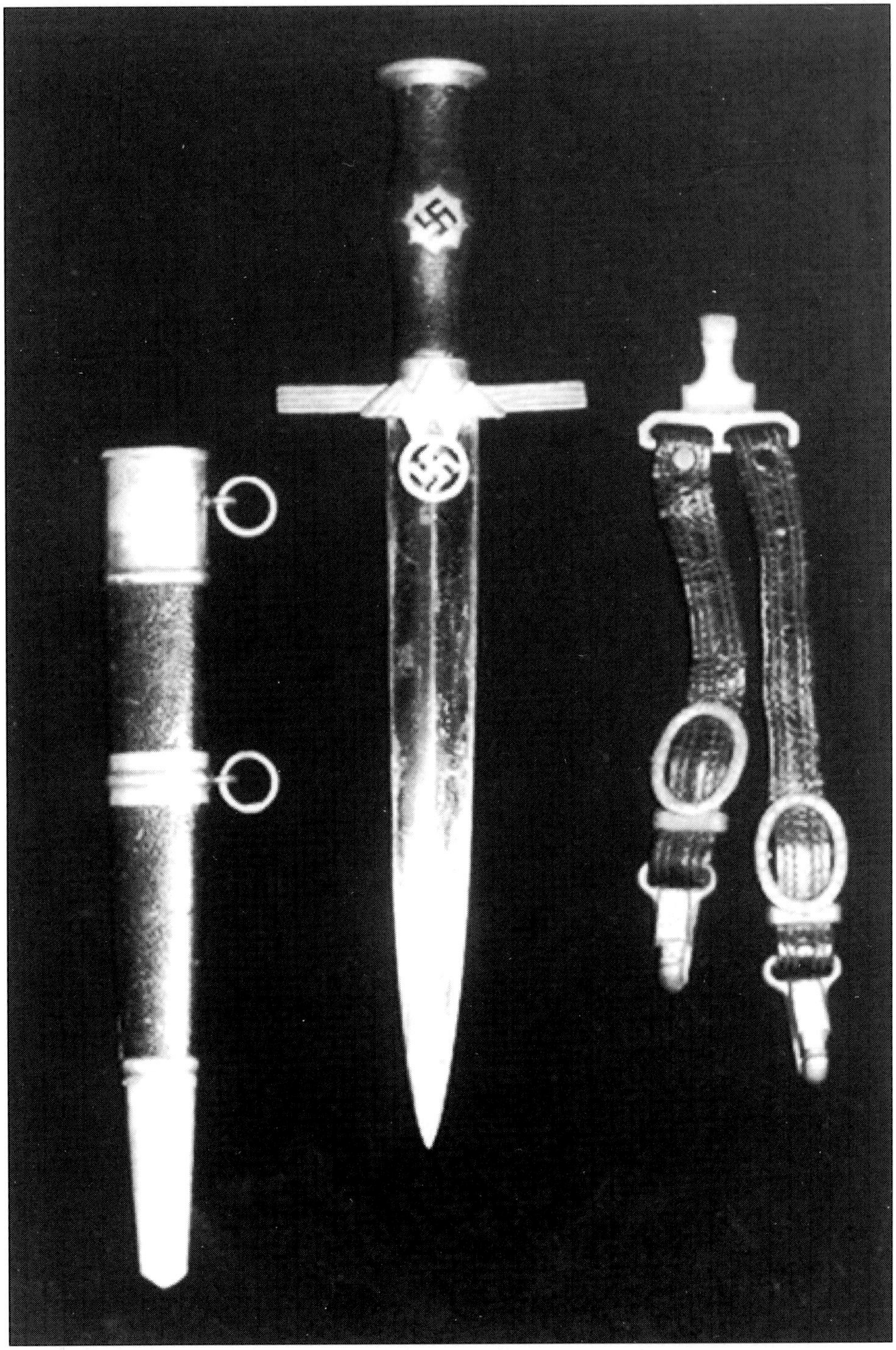

Obverse view of a reproduction 1938 2nd pattern RLB Leader's dagger which is of extremely good quality and is only let down by the poor quality alloy fittings and the badly positioned RLB insignia. The piece is accompanied by a set of genuine RLB hanging straps.

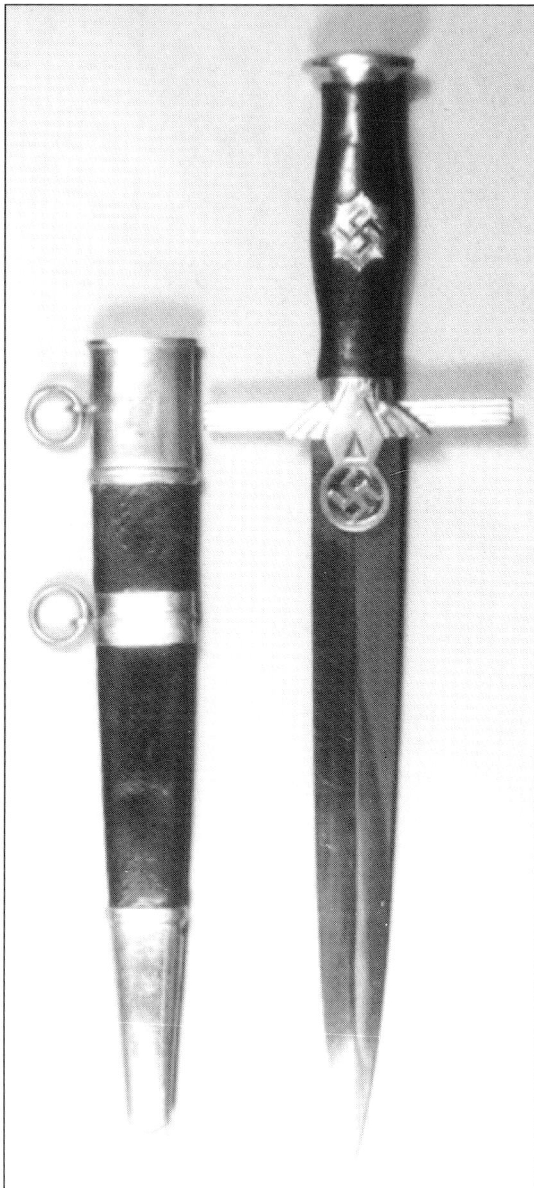

RLB Leader's parts assembly dagger. A genuine scabbard, grip, pommel and scabbard with a replacement blade.

TENO REPRODUCTIONS

The original TeNo Hewer and Leader's dagger were both Paul Casberg creations designed specifically for the Carl Eickhorn company who held the sole manufacturing rights for all TeNo daggers. This exclusivity is in some ways a positive aid to identifying reproduction TeNo daggers, as any examples bearing the proofmark of any other Maker other than Carl Eickhorn can be immediately rejected as reproductions. However one should be careful for not every example of a TeNo dagger bearing an Eickhorn proofmark is by any stretch of the imagination always genuine. It has been suggested in the past that perhaps there were other Makers of the TeNo dagger: one name suggested has been that of P D Luneschloss. However there is not a shred of evidence which would confirm that Luneschloss or any other Maker for that matter other than Eickhorn was ever authorised producers of TeNo daggers. Similarly it has also been suggested in the past that there were two types of TeNo dagger produced by Eickhorn which were used as an excuse for variations in the TeNo Leader's dagger. There is no conceivable reason why Eickhorn should have two sets of dies for the same dagger, especially since they had sole manufacturing rights. These daggers are not variant genuine Eickhorn examples but post-war parts assemblies containing a mixture of original and reproduction parts which is where the variation in component parts comes in.

Parts assembly TeNo Leader's daggers have been produced in Germany since the end of World War II, and depending on the period of assembly have varying amounts of original parts in their construction. What most of these parts have in common is that they invariably utilise original grips. The blades are usually post-war manufacture and being Solingen produced are of an excellent quality being dropped forged and bearing the correct Eickhorn and TeNo proofmarks. These German post-war produced daggers are only spoiled by the quality of the crossguard and pommel which often exhibit minor areas of pitting and are poorly finished off inside.

There are three distinct types of Spanish reproduction TeNo Leader's daggers: one use the correct Eickhorn proofmark in conjunction with the TeNo proofmark on the reverse blade; the second type has only the TeNo proofmark and no Maker's proofmark whatsoever; and the third type bears the TeNo proofmark in company with a spurious Maker's proofmark of P D Luneschloss. However the style of this proofmark is one that is not known to have been used by Luneschloss during the period of the Third Reich, or for that matter prior to that period. The Spanish applied proofmark is an amalgam of two earlier Luneschloss trademarks which were an Hellenic helmet with a sword passing through it within an oval with the words "P D Luneschloss, Solingen" around its inside edge. The probable reason for choosing P D Luneschloss by the Spanish manufacturers is that the real Luneschloss company actually went out of business in 1965, and would therefore not be in a position to object about anyone fraudulently using their name on a spurious proofmark for a reproduction dagger.

A myth often related about TeNo Subordinate's hewers is that only originals have the embossed squirrels on the inside of the grip plates. Whilst this statement has some foundation in fact it is a little too sweeping for although all genuine hewers do have the embossed grip plates so do some good quality reproductions and parts assembly hewers. Therefore it would probably be more accurate to say that daggers without the embossed squirrel grips are reproductions.

Some of the Spanish reproductions of the TeNo hewer have quite good definition but use inferior quality materials in their construction. Although the overall appearance is good, close examination should allow the collector to identify these particular examples for what they are. A consistent characteristic of Spanish reproductions of the TeNo hewer is that they seldom have a frog attached to them as apparently this provision was never allowed for by the reproducers. Although odd reproduction examples have appeared over the years being suspended from genuine frogs in an attempt to give them some credibility.

A final point regarding TeNo daggers is that whilst original daggers invariably bear issue serial numbers stamped into the blade ricasso and scabbard throat the same is also true of many good reproductions. This is done to give the reproduction more credibility as many collectors believe that only genuine TeNo daggers bear the issue numbers and that reproduction do not. A fact that should be borne in mind is that some original TeNo daggers which remained unissued and were subsequently picked up as souvenirs did not carry serial numbers. Therefore while the presence of serial numbers is no guarantee of originality the absence of them is similarly not concrete evidence of a reproduction, and that a number of different characteristics need to be taken into account before concluding a TeNo dagger is either genuine or a reproduction.

RECOGNITION CHECKLIST

LEADER'S DAGGER

BLADE

- Blades bearing a Maker's proofmark other than that of Carl Eickhorn should be viewed with suspicion.
- The absence of the Eickhorn proofmark is a characteristic of some reproductions.
- Blades with a matt grey satin finish are characteristic of Spanish reproductions.
- A broad flat tang has been observed on reproductions.
- Blades with etched dedications within decorative panels usually photoengraved are characteristic of reproductions.
- The use of the RZM proofmark which was not appropriate for any TeNo dagger.
- The absence of billet clamp marks.
- Poorly defined Eickhorn and TeNo proofmarks. Original proofmarks were always crisp and clearly defined.

SCABBARD

- Scabbards made from brass. Original scabbards were always steel with an oxidised finish. A magnet will detect brass or other alloy scabbards.
- Chrome or silver plated scabbards. Originals always had an oxidised finish.
- Scabbards with elongated ends with the bottom decoration being longer and more pointed than originals.
- Scabbard pebbling which forms a swirling pattern is indicative of Spanish reproductions.
- The presence of casting seams on the scabbard bands.
- Scabbard liners of incorrect form being long and thin and being soldered or brazed into position whereas originals were always riveted into position.

GRIP

- Crossguard and pommels cast from brass or other alloys giving the dagger a heavy feel. Original fittings were always made from aluminium.
- Chrome or silver plated crossguard and pommels are a feature of Spanish reproductions. Original fittings always had an oxidised finish.
- Poor detail on crossguard and pommel.
- Areas of pitting especially on the top edges of the pommel and crossguard.
- Poor definition on the TeNo eagle and insignia.
- Grips with a straight appearance.

PROOFMARKS

The only proofmarks which should appear on genuine TeNo Leader's daggers are Maker's proofmark of Carl Eickhorn and the inspection proofmark of the TeNo.

SUBORDINATE'S HEWER

BLADE

- The presence of any Maker's proofmark other than Carl Eickhorn should be viewed with suspicion.
- Poor quality plated blades exhibiting areas of wear or plate loss are a feature of early Spanish reproduction hewers.
- The use of the RZM proofmark which is inappropriate for any TeNo dagger
- The bottom curve on some reproduction hewers is straight instead of having a slight up turned curve.
- The blade fuller on Spanish reproductions is too short terminating approximately two inches from the crossguard whereas originals extend to within one inch of the crossguard. Also each end of the fuller is rounded on reproductions instead of tapering to a point as on originals.
- Poorly etched proofmarks lacking the crisp detail of originals
- The TeNo proofmark is applied too close to the crossguard on some reproductions.
- A thin blade washer is used on reproduction TeNo hewers.

SCABBARD

- Scabbards manufactured from brass rather than sheet steel.
- The use of silver or chrome plated alloy to make the scabbard fittings instead of nickel plating.
- Evidence of soldering on the reverse upper fitting where the frog attachment has been added.

GRIP

- Grip plates which do not have the embossed Eickhorn squirrel logo are characteristic of Spanish reproductions.
- Grip fittings with poor definition especially around the TeNo eagle and insignia.
- The eagle head shape of the pommel is rounded on what would be the beak on reproductions instead of being sharply defined as originals were.
- Grip fittings cast from brass or other alloys exhibiting minor pitting. The fittings are usually plated over the pitting which is a product of poor casting.
- The use of brass to make the fittings which is either silver or chrome plated instead of the nickel silver of originals.

PROOFMARKS

The Carl Eickhorn Maker's proofmark and the TeNo inspection proofmark are the only proofmarks which should appear on any TeNo dagger.

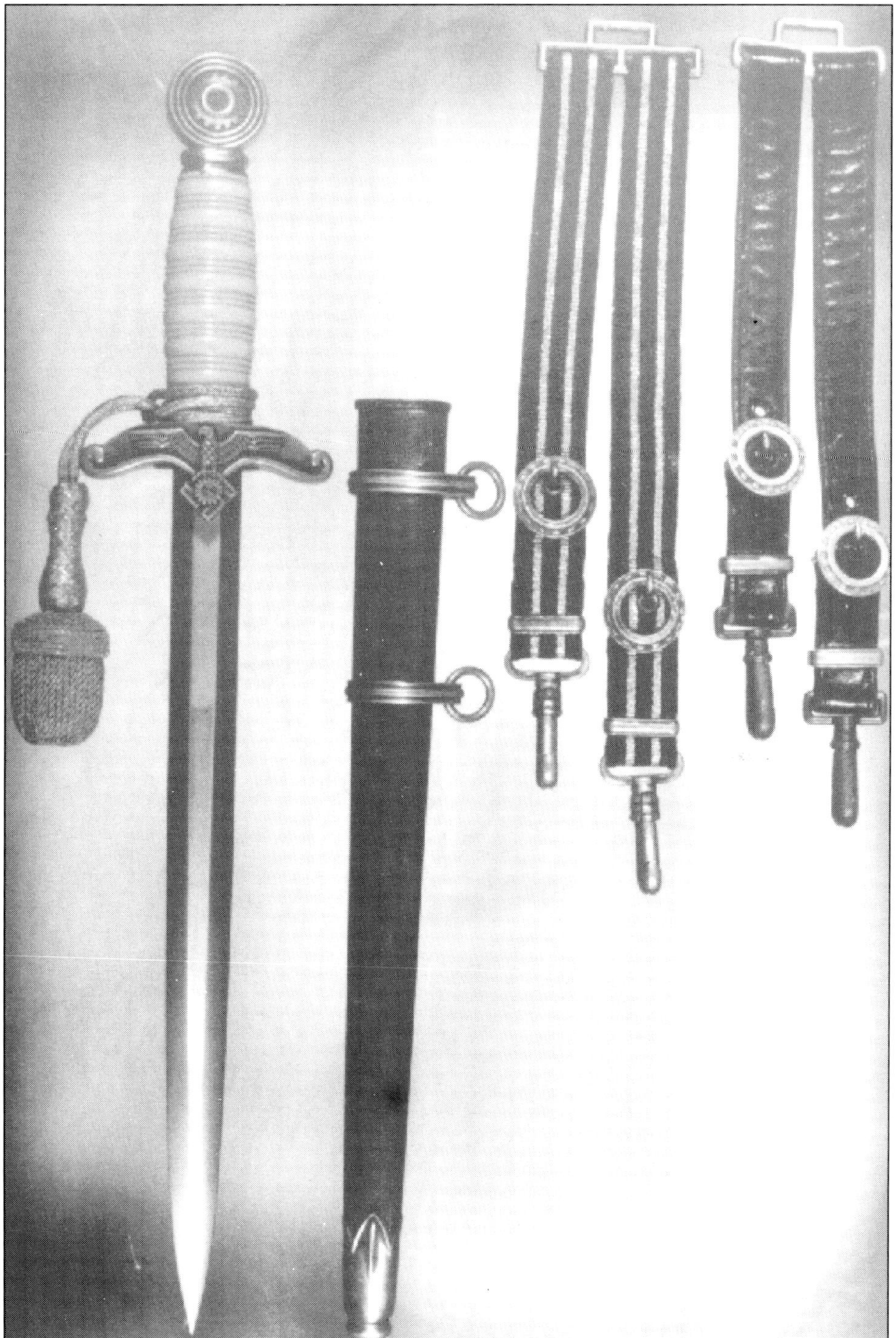

Obverse full length view of a genuine TeNo Leaders dagger. This dagger has a portepee knot wrapped in the correct TeNo fashion. Also illustrated are the two types of authorised TeNo Leader hanging straps: on the left for dress wear and on the right leather straps for service wear.

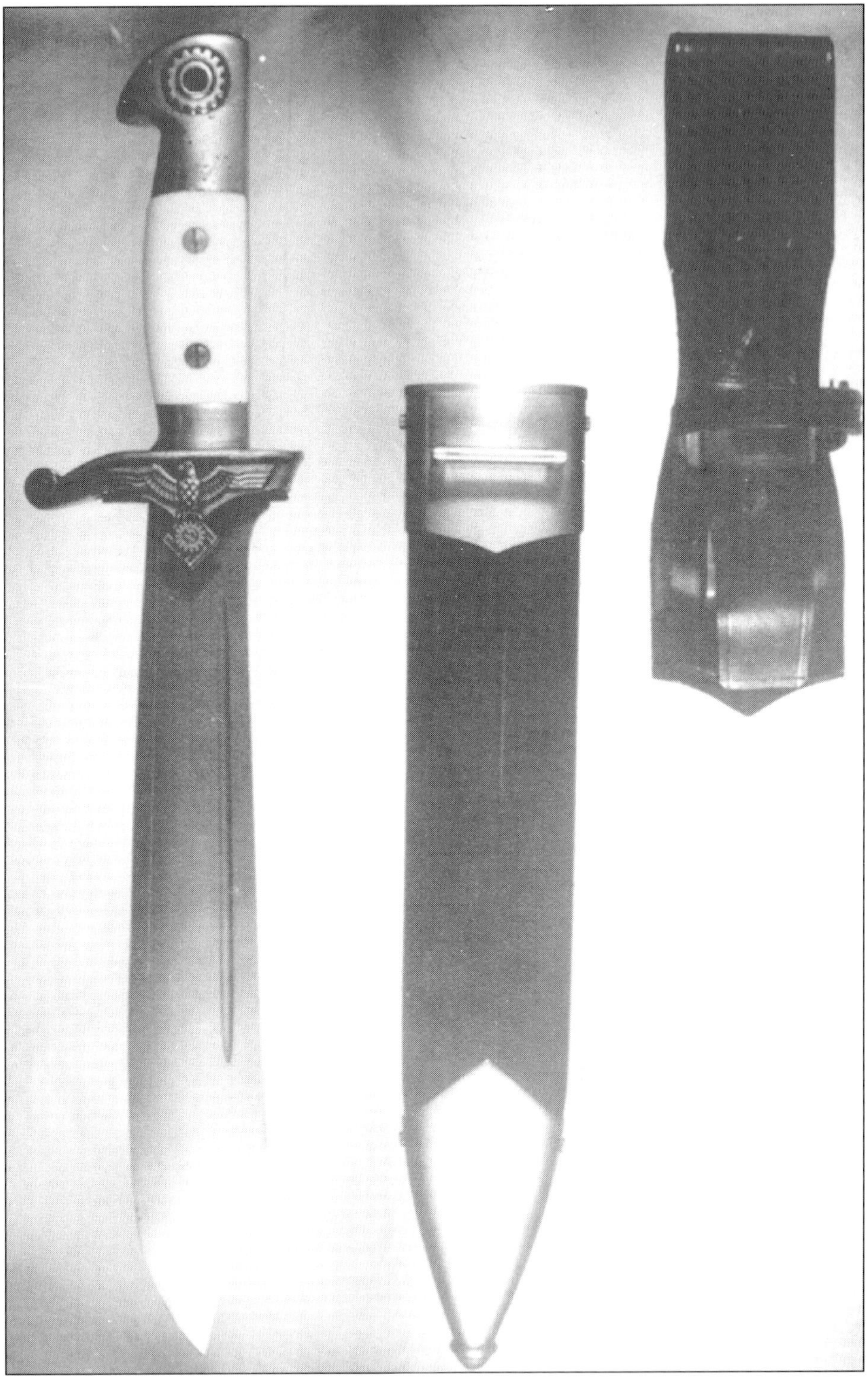

Obverse full length view of a genuine TeNo Subordinate's hewer, with the reverse of the scabbard displayed to show the method of attaching the frog. Note the sharp detail of the crossguard insignia and the quality of the scabbard fittings.

Close-up view of the reverse blade ricasso of a genuine TeNo Leaders dagger. Note the correct style of Eickhorn proofmark below and the TeNo patent proofmark above. Any TeNo Leader's blade not bearing this configuration should be viewed with suspicion.

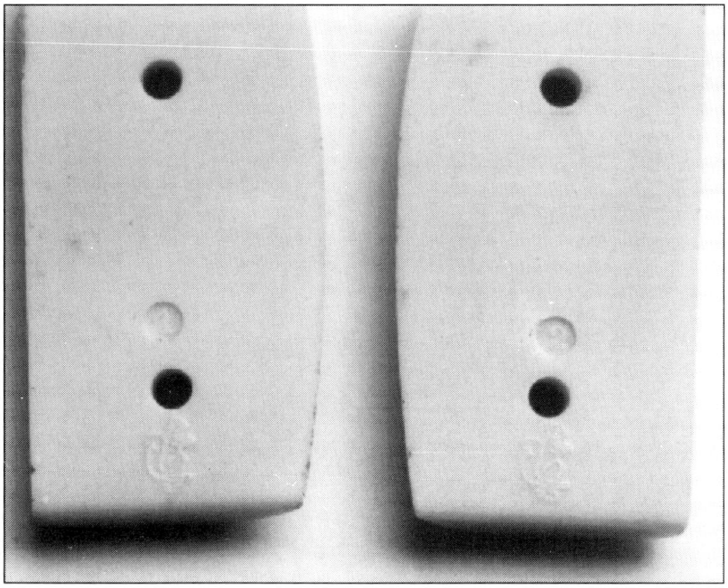

Close-up view of the inside of a genuine TeNo Subordinate's grip plates. The grip plates are numbered 1 and 2 within round recessed slots. The Eickhorn squirrel proofmark is embossed below the bottom screw hole. Grip plates without these markings or with incorrectly applied or positioned markings should be viewed with suspicion.

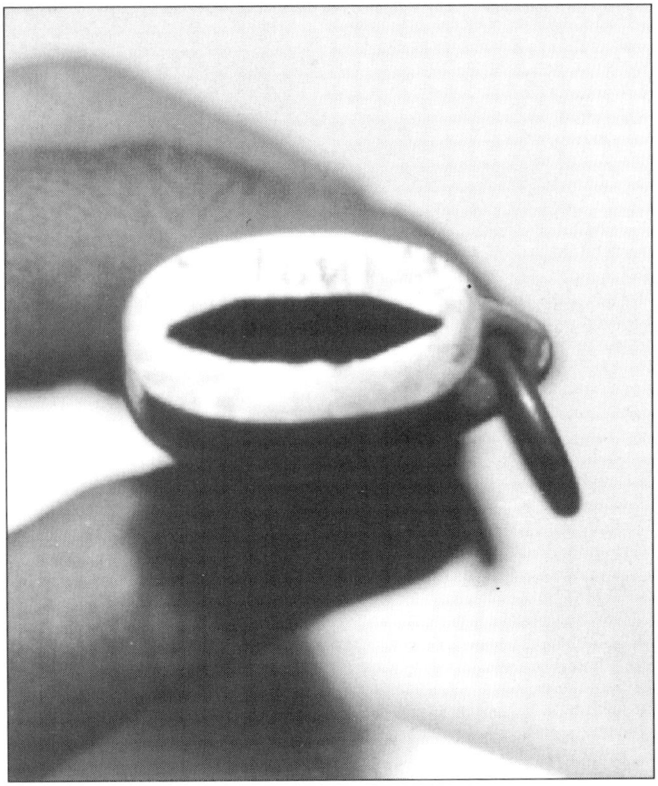

Close-up view of the scabbard throat of a genuine TeNo Leaders dagger. The serial number on the throat should correspond to the serial number on the blade. Absence of this serial number on the scabbard throat or blade should be viewed with suspicion.

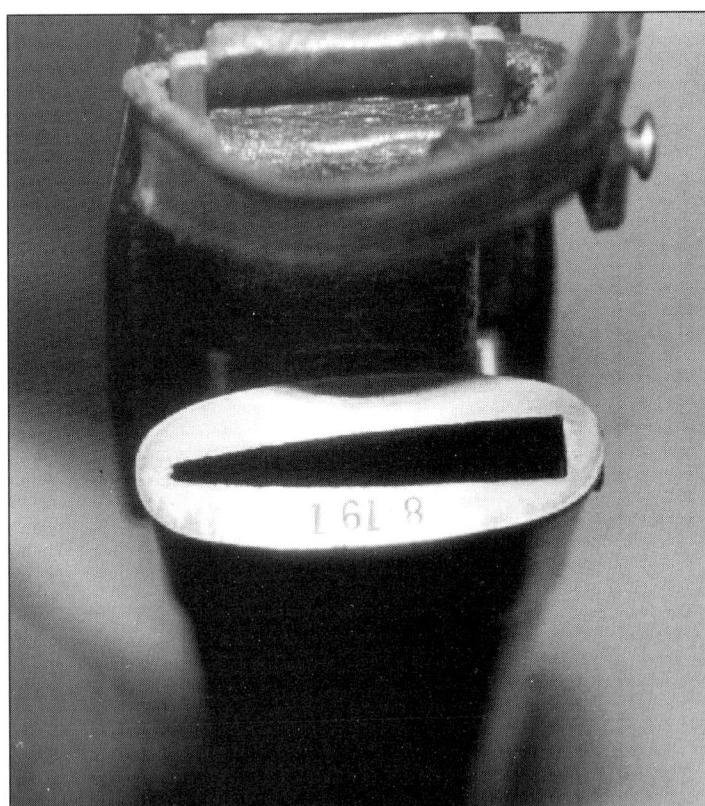

Close-up view of the frog attachment and scabbard throat of a genuine TeNo Subordinates hewer. Note the correct form of serial numbering on the scabbard throat.

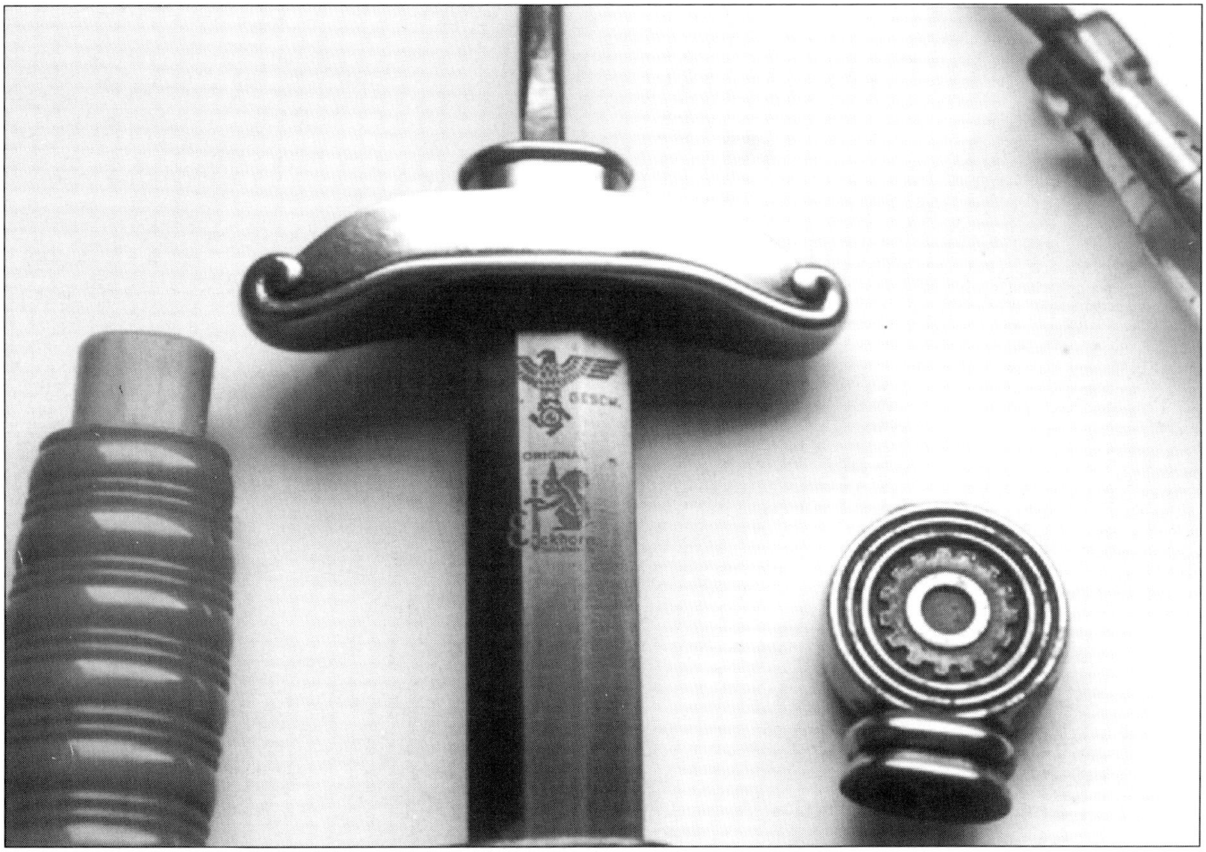

A disassembled view of the grip of a TeNo Leader's dagger. Of particular note is the pommel detail of this genuine example when compared with the reproduction pictured below.

Close-up view of a reproduction pommel from a TeNo Leaders dagger. Note the poor detail of the cogwheel design.

Close-up view of the ricasso proofmark configuration on a genuine TeNo Subordinate's hewer.

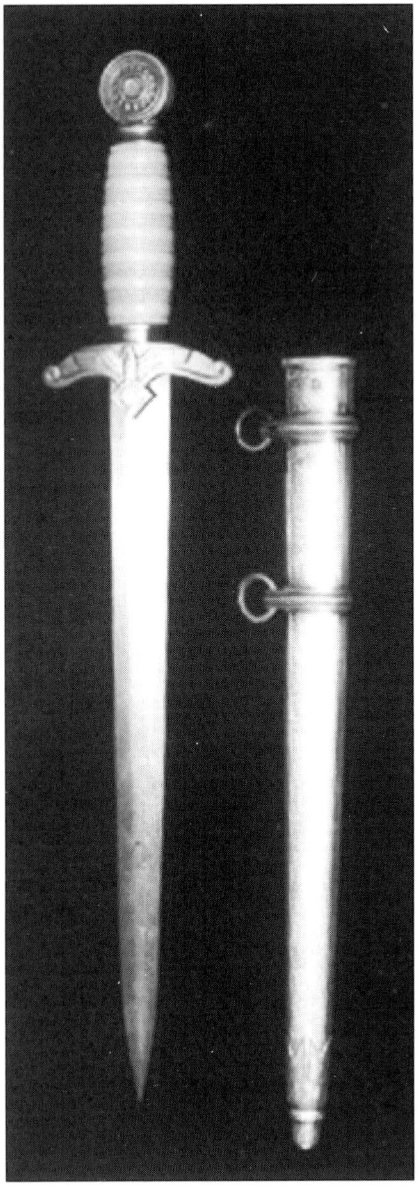

(Below) Close-up detail of a reproduction TeNo Leader's dagger crossguard, grip and blade ricasso. Note the crude detail and the casting marks. The TeNo eagle and insignia are poorly defined and lack the clarity of original fittings. The blade is too wide at the ricasso and tapers too sharply towards the tip. Note the serial numbers on the blade which are slightly oversize, also the prefix 31 has been observed on several different TeNo Leader's reproductions of German origin. The grips of this reproduction are original leftover stock and as such are difficult to fault.

(Above) Full length out of scabbard view of a reproduction TeNo Leader's dagger. Note the incorrect shape of the scabbard tip which is teardrop shaped instead of being elipitical. This type of reproduction has been produced in Germany since the 1960's.

Political Reproductions

The Political daggers of the Third Reich encompass four organisations: the SS, SA, NSKK and Hitler Youth. These four formations are categorised by the fact that each of them fell under the jurisdiction of the RZM (Reichszeugmeisterei) of the NSDAP. This body was set up in late 1934 to regulate and oversee the production and distribution of all NSDAP items which included the daggers of the four political formations. Prior to the existence of the RZM, there had been no strict regulations governing political daggers which led to innumerable variations in the dimensions of the SS, SA and NSKK daggers. This was due to the large number of Makers who were producing daggers by the million for the burgeoning NSDAP organisations. After 1934 all daggers of the NSDAP Party were required to bear the RZM proofmark in conjunction with the M/7 RZM code number denoting the article was a dagger, followed by the RZM control number which identified the Maker. Due to the strict parameters of this Ministry, the RZM proofmark should only appear on daggers of the four Party formations produced after 1934 and not to any other dagger from organisations other than the four previously mentioned.

The political daggers were produced in larger quantities than any other category of Third Reich edged weapon, especially the SA dagger and Hitler Youth Knife which were produced in millions. The SS and NSKK daggers were produced in the hundreds of thousands. However within each of the SS and SA daggers, there were specific categories of specially issued daggers which were considerably rarer, and are consequently now more desirable and more expensive. These include the SA and SS Rohm Honour daggers, the Himmler Honour dagger, the SA High Leader's dagger, SS Honour dagger and presentation daggers of both the SS and SA.

This wide variety of Party daggers makes this section of the book the largest due to the multitude of political dagger reproductions currently on the market. The coverage of these types of daggers reflects both their collectibility and the high price they consequently attract. In view of the high production numbers for the common versions of the SS, SA and NSKK daggers, the current market values for originals is somewhat inflated especially in view of the quantity of reproductions also in circulation (or possibly because of this fact).

Genuine examples of many of the political daggers are amongst the highest priced and in some instances the rarest of any of the daggers produced during the Third Reich. The daggers of the SS have a particular attraction for many collectors due to the elite status accorded to that organisation between 1933 and 1945. Collections invariably start with the most common dagger, that of the SA, however the dagger most collectors seek as soon as they start collecting is an example of the SS dagger. Unfortunately many collectors are dazzled by the mystic of the SS runes, and often end up with a reproduction. This is especially true when the collector tries to start his SS collection off with an SS dagger from the top of the range such as the Himmler Honour dagger of which there were only 200 genuine examples ever awarded. There are numerous reproductions of the Himmler Honour dagger on the market of varying qualities. When considering the purchase of one of these daggers it is worth bearing in mind the production figure of *200* and the fact they were only authorised to be made by one firm, Carl Eickhorn of Solingen. This firm produced most of the prestigious Party dagger: SA High Leader's , SS Honour, SS and SA presentation daggers etc. Proofmarks of other Makers or of the RZM should be viewed with extreme suspicion.

Every effort has been made in this section to present as many facts and examples of reproductions as is possible, however political dagger reproductions could fill a single volume in their own right.

SS DAGGER REPRODUCTIONS

The impulse and urge to buy what is one of the more expensive of the Nazi production daggers is not always tempered with the requisite measure of caution witnessed by the number of new dagger collectors who wind up with a less than perfect specimen of the much sought after and in some respects overrated SS dagger. Even if the new collector does not end up with an outright reproduction there are many other alterations and embellishments which can and have been effected on a seemingly genuine SS dagger: some only minor but others major.

Most collectors are familiar with the cheap Spanish reproductions of the SS dagger which can be bought quite inexpensively. These pieces are so badly made that they would not fool a child let alone an experienced collector. The extremely poor workmanship which is the hallmark of this type of dagger and the ease with which they can be identified is often used as a security blanket by some collectors who take the view that because they can readily identify this particular type of blatant reproduction that this single nugget of information is all they need to know about SS reproductions and that everything else in the garden is rosey. Many individuals persist in this mistaken belief and are usually the same people who consider it money wasted on a good reference book costing a tiny fraction of the price of that excellent quality reproduction they have residing in their collection.

This point has been made to emphasise the vigilance which is required in today's SS dagger market, for the quality of many of the current German reproductions is unbelievably good. This excellence of quality also extends to the SS dagger blades which are currently being forged in Solingen, and range from the standard SS blade with correctly etched motto to up market blades with superbly executed Rohm and Himmler dedications. These blades are marketed as modern produced blades by most reputable dealers: the collector's problems really start when these blades find their way into the hands of the less scrupulous individual. An indication of just how good these blades are is illustrated by the fact that one reputable U.S. dealer who sells these Solingen blades has decided to add a distinguishing mark to those blades himself to enable the unwary collector to identify them as reproductions. It is proposed that this will take the form of a tiny hook on the tail of the Eickhorn squirrel proofmark which is the proofmark that appears on most of the good quality reproduction blades. Another proposal is to have the letter "R" for reproduction stamped into the tang of the blade. This identification policy is just in the process of being formulated and further information will be furnished to the collector in the subsequent updated second edition of this book. This preparedness to identify reproduction dagger blades by a major dealer and distributor is highly commendable especially in light of the hypocrisy which surrounds the dagger market in which many of the people who publicly criticise the sale of reproduction blades are privately amongst the reproduction blade dealers' best customers!

The good quality Rohm and Himmler dedicated blades currently produced in Solingen invariably find their way into a fabrication made up with the grip, scabbard and fittings from an ordinary but otherwise genuine 1933 pattern SS dagger which will effectively more than quadruple the market value of the dagger. As well as upgrading genuine SS daggers with good quality reproduction Honour blades there is also a well established practice of converting genuine 1933 pattern SA daggers into passable examples of 1933 pattern SS daggers. In its simplest form this type of fabrication merely requires the substitution of the SA grips and blade with good quality reproductions of these two parts. The brown SA scabbard is then painted black to complete the deception: where an NSKK dagger has been used this final painting process is not even necessary due to its already black painted original scabbard.

Superficially this type of fabrication looks very convincing but is quite often exposed by minor oversights such as SA Gau markings on the crossguard instead of the correct SS group numbers in Roman numerals. A useful aid in identifying fabricated SS daggers is to pay close attention to the grip, especially at each end where the grip fits into the crossguards. Original SS grips were made from ebony which had a natural black colour which was further enhanced by staining and a very fine grain.

Reproduction and restained SA grips will exhibit brown streaks on the end grain of the wooden grip. Genuine ebony SS grips often exhibit chipping around the edges. This is due to the hardness and extremely close grain of this type of wood, and is a characteristic not found on SA grips which tend to dent and bruise rather than chip. One final point on grips is that whether they are black or otherwise, plastic was never used to make original SS or SA grips.

Spanish reproductions of the SS Honour dagger usually favour a heavily ornamented style with decoration on the scabbard as well as the dagger fittings. Even though original examples of this style are very seldom seen the Spanish reproductions of the SS Honour dagger are relatively well made, but exhibit many of the classic Spanish reproduction characteristics including excessive over embellishments such as giving their Honour dagger copies a Himmler dedicated blade and an RZM proofmark! Some fabricated SS Honour daggers feature a superb quality Solingen made artificial Damascus blades with the blade motto and proofmark finished in gold plate in high relief. These blades are known to be available in both the small and large rosebud pattern damascene and also the maidenhair pattern. The blades have been made with authentic looking and well executed Eickhorn proofmarks of the small early oval type and also the larger oval proofmark.

In summation it is no exaggeration to state that the modern German reproduction SS daggers and parts (especially the blades) are probably the finest and most convincing of any Third Reich dagger reproductions, and consequently represent an extremely serious threat to the integrity of many collections - the effect of which cannot be too strongly emphasised. The quality and proliferation of reproduction SS blades has been brought about by the increasingly exorbitant prices paid for a dagger that was in its original and genuine form a mass produced item. The price of SS daggers has been grossly inflated in recent years out of all proportion to the dagger's true rarity value, and this price is kept artificially high by hype about the SS dagger's exclusivity and the elite status of the SS. This is yet another example of the practice of "talking up" the price of a dagger.

The actual form of all the SS dagger types is the same and is also identical in form to the SA dagger. With the exception of the grip and the blade motto all the component parts of the SS and SA daggers are the same. At the time of producing the original daggers in the Third Reich era no actual distinction was made between parts for SA and SS daggers prior to assembly: the blades for both daggers were forged from the same steel. The organisational distinctions only actually came into play after the blades had their acid-etched motto applied and their different grips fitted. Therefore it is logical that in most respects the points to observe in determining the authenticity of SS daggers are the same as those for the SA dagger. The only variables being the grip, motto, Honour dedications and other SS related embellishments.

RECOGNITION CHECKLIST

1933 PATTERN SS DAGGER

BLADE

- ➢ A sharp central ridge on the blade is a consistent reproduction characteristic
- ➢ The etching of the SS motto is too shallow on many reproduction blades.
- ➢ Incorrect positioning of the SS motto either too high but usually too low on the blade.
- ➢ Most reproductions of both good and poor quality feature the RZM proofmark on the blade.
- ➢ The appearance of a proofmark of a Maker or the RZM on the obverse blade ricasso is indicative of reproductions. Proofmarks on originals were always applied to the reverse ricasso.
- ➢ The word "GERMANY" stamped into the blade ricasso or tang was only used on post World War II production or parts assembly daggers.
- ➢ A poorly executed blade motto showing areas of spotting is indicative of post-war blades.

- A badly applied RZM or Maker's proofmark should cast doubt on the authenticity of a dagger.
- A broad flat tang is indicative of modern Spanish reproductions.
- When looking down the flat surfaces of a blade most modern reproductions will almost always have a waviness in the finish of the blade - a feature very rarely seen on good quality originals.
- Some Spanish reproduction blades are extremely thin and have a very cheap looking chrome plating applied over them: this plating also extends over and into the recesses of the blade motto. This was never a feature of originals.
- The central spine on some poorer quality SS reproduction blades is slightly off centre.
- A poor blade to lower crossguard fit is a feature of many parts assembly SS daggers.
- The use of a felt or leather blade washer is usually to cover up a badly fitting blade. The only genuine Party form daggers which legitimately utilised a blade washer were those of the NPEA and some SA and SS Honour daggers where the washers were intended as a buffer pad to protect quality fittings.
- Currently produced German reproduction blades are slightly narrower at the top (ricasso) by approximately 2 millimetres.
- A seemingly genuine blade which has a sunken centre panel may be an original SA blade which has had the "Alles fur Deutschland" motto removed and the SS motto reapplied in its place.
- SS mottos applied off centre either above or below the central ridge have been observed. These blades although appearing to be completely genuine are thought to be genuine pre-1945 Party form blade blanks which have had the SS motto applied in post-war years. They are usually encountered without a Maker's or RZM proofmark.

SCABBARD

- Absence of scabbard liners is an indication of a reproduction of Spanish origin.
- Spanish reproduction SS scabbards have an oversize suspension ring which is also approximately 50% thinner than those found on originals.
- The lower scabbard fitting on some reproductions has a very rounded appearance especially around the ball tip which has a much more ovoid shape than originals.
- Long thin scabbard liners brazed into position. Original liners were wide and ribbed with a semi-circular tongue shape at the base and were riveted into position on the throat attachment.
- Most upper scabbard fittings on Spanish reproductions are of one piece construction. Original fittings were always two piece consisting of an outer locket and an inner throat sleeve to which the brass scabbard liners were riveted.
- Virtually all reproduction scabbards are devoid of the lead tip former which was positioned into the inside tip of the scabbard and acted as a counter balance and a soft blade stop on originals. It should however be mentioned that some later examples of genuine SS dagger scabbards will also be encountered without the lead inner former sleeve.
- Generally speaking the top and bottom scabbard fittings should match the dagger fittings in their material composition i.e. being either all nickel silver or all nickel plated. A mixture of different fittings on the scabbard and dagger is indicative of parts assembly daggers and/or replacement scabbards.
- Virtually all reproduction scabbards encountered have a black painted finish usually with a very bright appearance. Reproduction scabbards are not usually encountered with the early black anodised finish.
- Observe around the edges of the scabbard fittings for bare metal, paint gaps or ridges where the fittings have been masked off to repaint a brown SA scabbard black. This is sometimes done when the fittings cannot be removed for repainting. Where fittings can be removed the whole scabbard should be inspected for any evidence of repainting of a brown scabbard or even complete areas of

brown paint which may have been hidden under the fittings. Original scabbards were always painted completely before the scabbard fittings were positioned. There should be no areas of bare metal, modern grey primer or brown paint under the fittings.

GRIP

- The inside ends of the grips should be examined for evidence of any light coloured grain where a modern applied black satin has not penetrated.
- The use of black plastic to make SS dagger grips is a practice only used post-war reproducers. Original grips were always ebony.
- Examine the edges around the SS insignia button and also the eagle grip inlay for evidence of gaps or bruising where poor quality reproduction SS or genuine SA insignia have been replaced with good quality SS insignia.
- Early Spanish and German reproductions used a stained softwood to make the grips which had a very coarse grained appearance totally unlike original ebony grips which had a very fine grain.
- An incorrectly positioned eagle inlay which is usually mounted too high being in the centre of the grip of reproductions. Originals were always positioned in line with the thickest part of the grip which is slightly below centre.
- Some early Spanish reproduction SS grips had a flat SS rune which was not enamelled: originals were always enamelled.
- The SS grip runes on some reproductions are elongated and thin and lack the sharp detail of originals.
- Some reproduction eagle grip inlays feature an eagle of incorrect form having square cut wings and tapered wingtips.
- Some modern eagle inlays feature an eagle with a cone shaped head and an oversized hooked beak: this is a style of eagle never encountered on any original SS dagger.
- On the eagle inlays of some reproductions the swastika is oversize and too thick having a flat appearance; also the detail on the swastika legs is very poor.
- Some post war wooden grips produced in Germany have extremely sharp edged in the area of the central ridge and the upper and lower "V" shape of the grips. These grips are very similar in style to some of the reproduction plastic examples only in wood.
- A distinctive feature of some reproduction grips is that the upper and lower necks of the grip are of virtually the same diameter giving the grip a much too symmetrical appearance. Original grips always had a thinner upper neck with the bottom neck being considerably broader and designed to fit snugly into the contours of a clenched left hand.
- The underside of the crossguard has a gouged out trench on some parts assembly daggers to facilitate a superficially snug blade to crossguard fit.
- The appearance of Gau markings on the lower crossguard would indicate a converted SA dagger or parts replaced from an SA dagger.
- The absence of SS group markings is not conclusive proof of a reproduction, however where there is evidence on the crossguard of grinding or scrubbing this may indicate that the crossguards were originally SA and have had their Gau markings removed.

PROOFMARKS

The majority of reproduction SS daggers tend to use the RZM proofmark in conjunction with a variety of M7 Maker's control numbers. The most frequently encountered RZM M7 control numbers on reproduction SS blades are: M7/11; M7/33; M7/36; M7/66; and M7/85. The Maker's proofmarks most frequently encountered were those of Carl Eickhorn, Ernst Pack & Sohne and Robert Klaas. The proofmarks of these Makers have been observed in all their various forms which were in use during the 1930's i.e. small and large Eickhorn oval proofmark, etc.

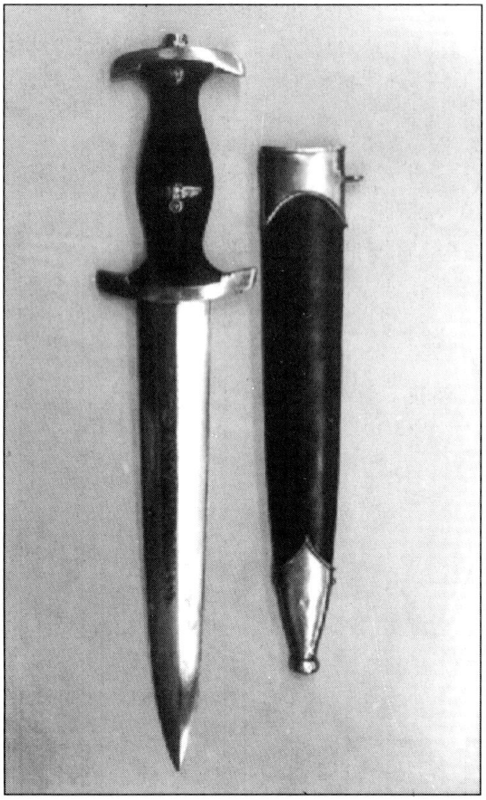

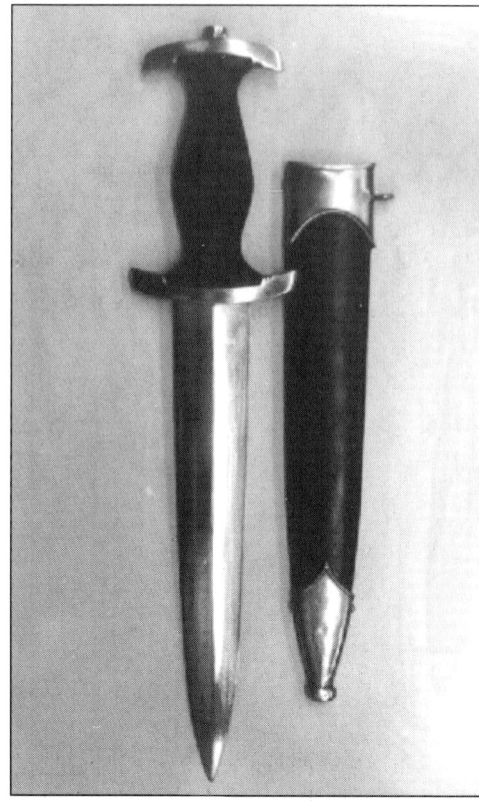

Obverse and reverse sides of a good quality German reproduction of the 1933 pattern SS dagger. The scabbard has plated zinc lockets with the bottom ball decoration being slightly oversize on the upper locket the hanging strap suspension loop is too thin and is devoid of the larger suspension ring. The grip and crossguard fittings are well formed but are devoid of any SS group markings. The badge is well made but has a pronounced central ridge. The reverse of the blade carries the RZM and SS proofmark with a 1938 issue date.

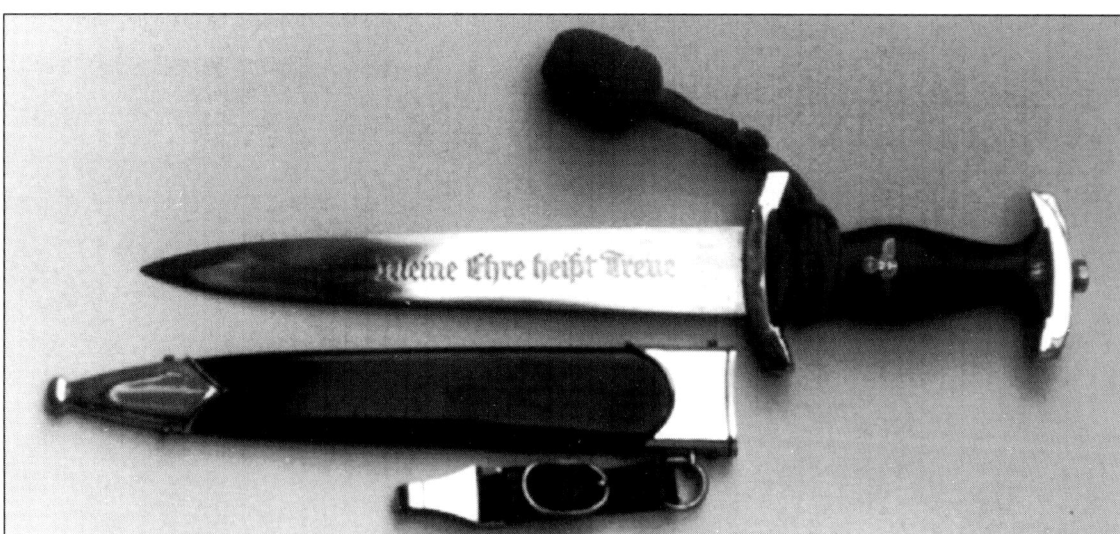

Obverse out of scabbard view of a genuine 1933 pattern SS dagger, with the correct form of portepee knot and hanging strap. This dagger is a very early example with nickel silver fittings manufactured by Carl Eickhorn of Solingen.

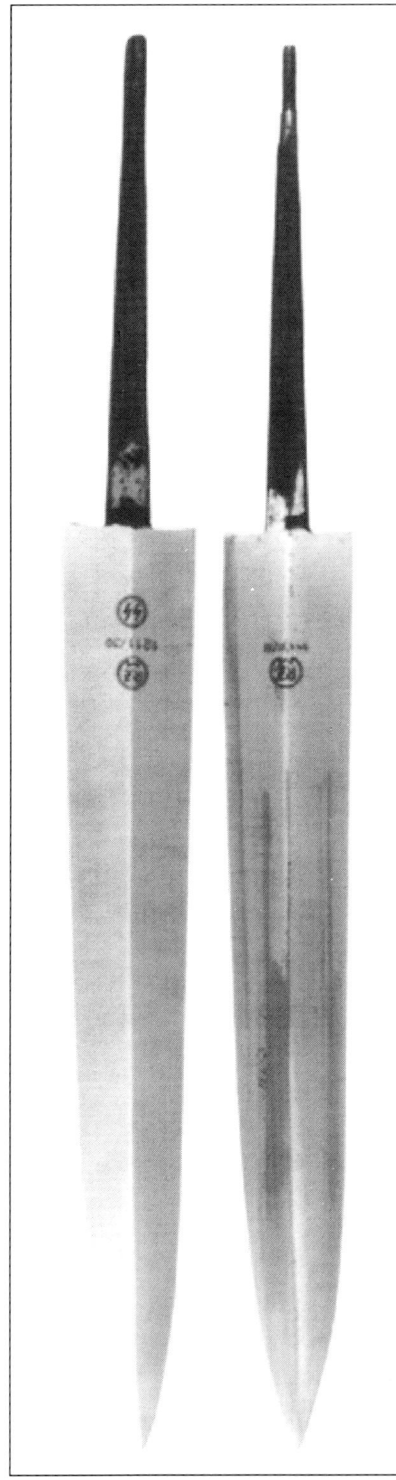

Examples of two different reproduction SS blades. These excellent quality blades are currently being produced in Solingen. Notice that the SS motto script is markedly different on the two blades, they also have different versions of the RZM proofmark.

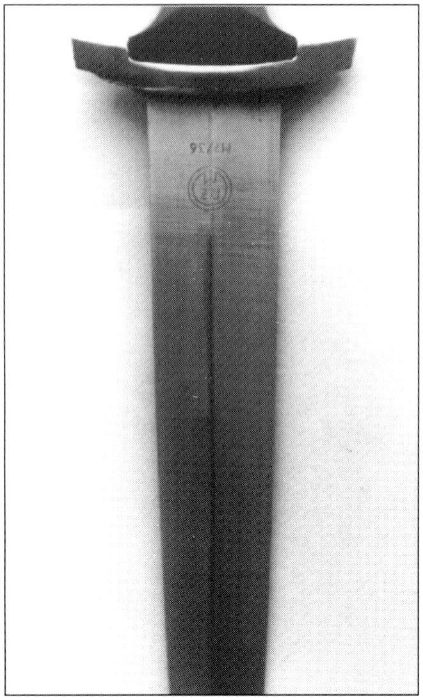

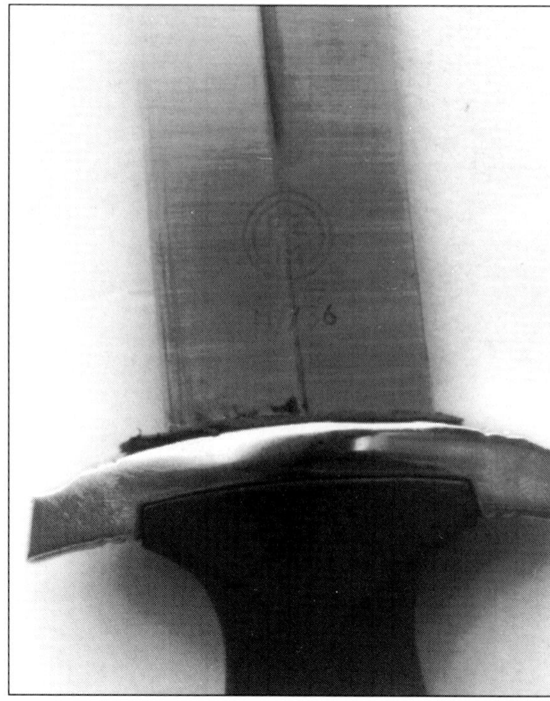

Five views of a Spanish reproduction 1933 pattern SS dagger. Note the matt grey finish to the blade which also has a sharp central spine. The black plastic grips have the eagle insignia mounted much too high. The scabbards on this particular type of SS reproduction are superficially quite good, and are often married to genuine daggers which lack a scabbard. Note the sharp central ridge, and also the very poorly executed blade motto. An RZM proofmark has been spuriously applied to this reproduction blade along with the M7/36 control number of F.W. Holler.

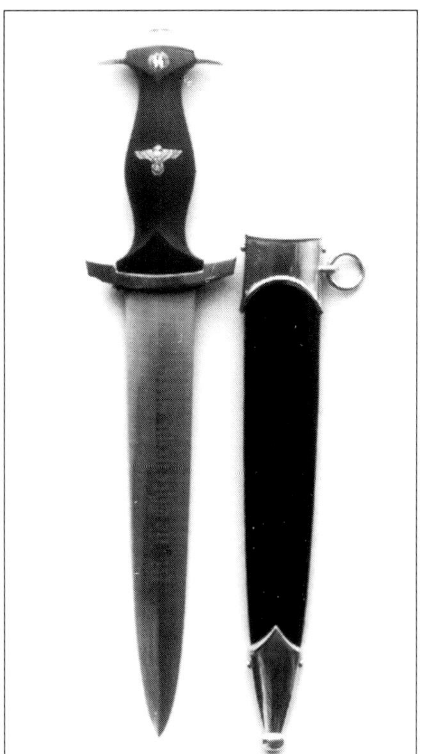

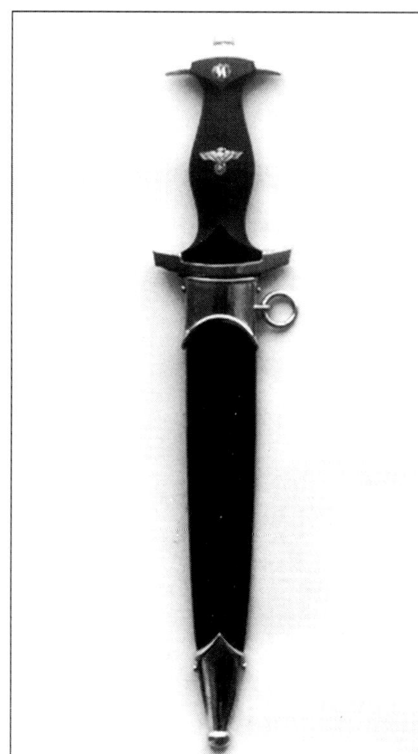

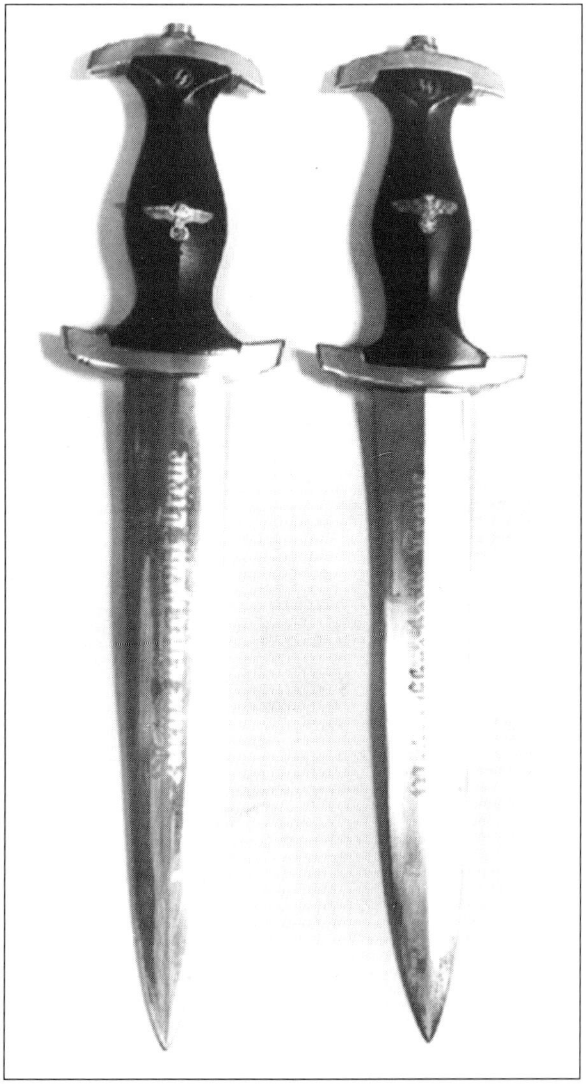

Side by side comparison of a genuine 1933 pattern SS dagger on the left and a good quality reproduction on the right. Points to note are the grip to crossguard fit and the grip eagle positioning. The reproduction on the right has a slight gap between grip and crossguard whilst the eagle is mounted too high on the grip. Also of note is the sharp central ridge on the blade of the reproduction.

Blade comparisons between a genuine SS blade at the top and a reproduction below. Note sharp central ridge and lightly etched motto on the reproduction.

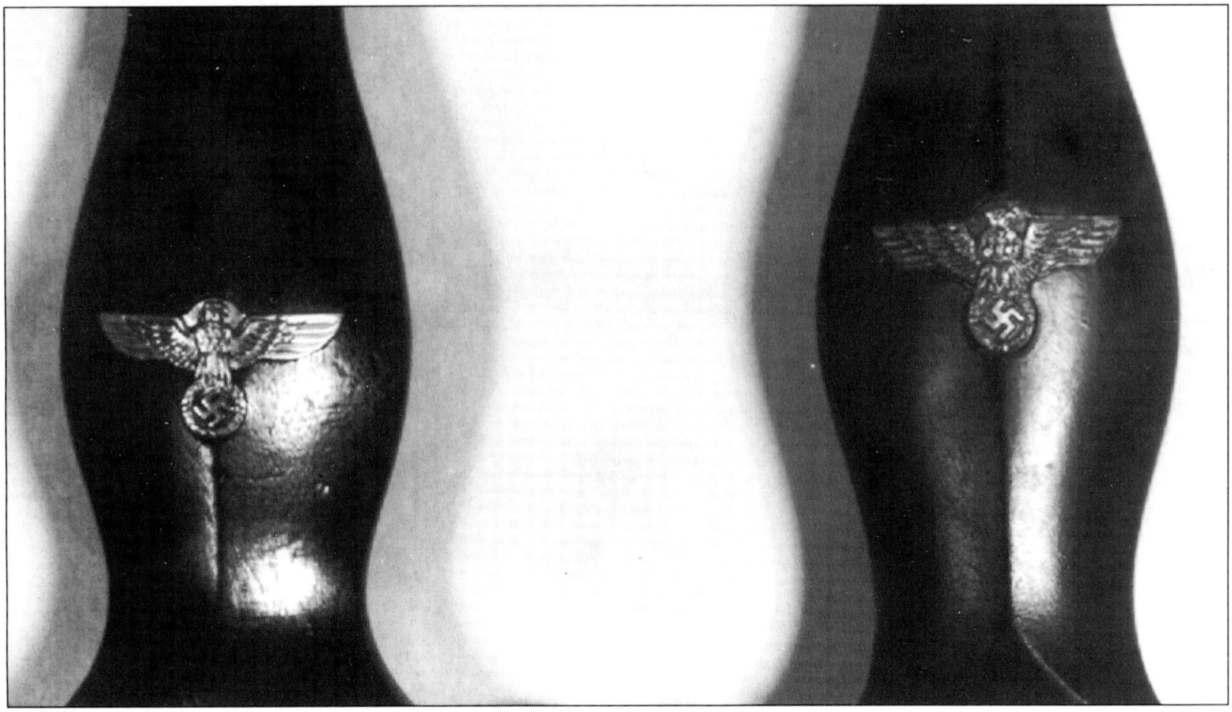

Close-up comparison photograph of the grip detail of a genuine (left) and reproduction (right) SS dagger. The overall grip shape of the reproduction is incorrect having the bulge machined too high. Consequently the grip insignia is also mounted too high. Note the square appearance of the reproduction grip insignia compared to the original on the left.

Close-up comparison of the blades of the same SS daggers as above. The genuine blade on the left speaks for itself. The reproduction on the right exhibits a sharp central ridge and poorly applied RZM proofmark and Maker's control number. This reproduction from the 1960's now has age pitting on the blade, but this should not be interpreted to imply that the blade is genuine. Any steel blade can exhibit pitting with the passage of time despite its origins.

SS ROHM HONOUR DAGGER REPRODUCTIONS

As there were only 9,900 original SS Rohm Honour daggers awarded in 1934 this would have been an extremely rare dagger even had the order to erase the Rohm inscription or remove the dagger from service not been made. A further point to take into consideration is that an SS Mann would undoubtedly have been less likely to have retained a Rohm inscription on his SS dagger than a member of the SA. This is only logical in view of the involvement of the SS in the murder of Ernst Rohm! Therefore it is relatively safe to assume that very few genuine SS Rohm Honour daggers will have survived with a partial inscription let alone a full Rohm dedication with signature.

These points have been raised to highlight a practice, namely the substitution of a genuine Rohm inscribed blade from an SA dagger into a genuine SS dagger. There is no evidence of any SS Mann being permitted to have an SA Rohm Honour dagger blade bearing the "Alles fur Deutschland" motto fitted into an SS dagger with black grips. The SA/SS Rohm Honour dagger is a post-war fantasy irrespective of whether the blade has a full, partial or erased inscription or whether the blade is a genuine SA Rohm or a post-war reproduction example of the same blade. The only acceptable form which a genuine SS Rohm Honour dagger should take is for the blade to have the "Meine Ehre heisst Treue" motto on the obverse side and the Rohm dedication on the reverse side of the blade.

A fabrication which is more commonly encountered is when the plain blade of a genuine SS dagger is replaced by a reproduction SS blade bearing a Rohm inscription. The quality of these reproduction blades varies considerably and have the same general characteristics as the reproduction SA Rohm Honour blades with the exception of the SS blade motto which reads "Meine Ehre heisst Treue" instead of the SA "Alles fur Deutschland" motto. These reproduction SS blades have been observed inserted into genuine SS daggers and can usually be identified by the poor blade to crossguard fit and also by the way the blade fits into the scabbard: being either too tight or too slack and/or having a small gap between the scabbard throat and dagger crossguard as a consequence of the parts being of different manufacture.

Original 1933 pattern SS daggers have been observed with a spurious Ernst Rohm dedication added to the reverse blade. These post-war embellishments take the same form and character as the spurious Rohm dedications which appear on SA daggers, and are subject to the same identification points as the aforementioned SA Rohm Honour dagger.

The RZM proofmark has been observed on reproduction SS Rohm Honour daggers and was completely inappropriate even for genuine examples. The Maker's proofmarks which appear on the good quality reproduction SS Rohm blades of current manufacture are the following: Ernst Pack & Sohne (E P & S) and Carl Eickhorn (with large and small oval proofmark).

In attempting to identify reproduction or fabricated SS Rohm Honour daggers the "recognition checklist" on the SA Rohm Honour dagger reproductions and 1933 pattern SS dagger reproductions should be used in conjunction with the additional points related in this section.

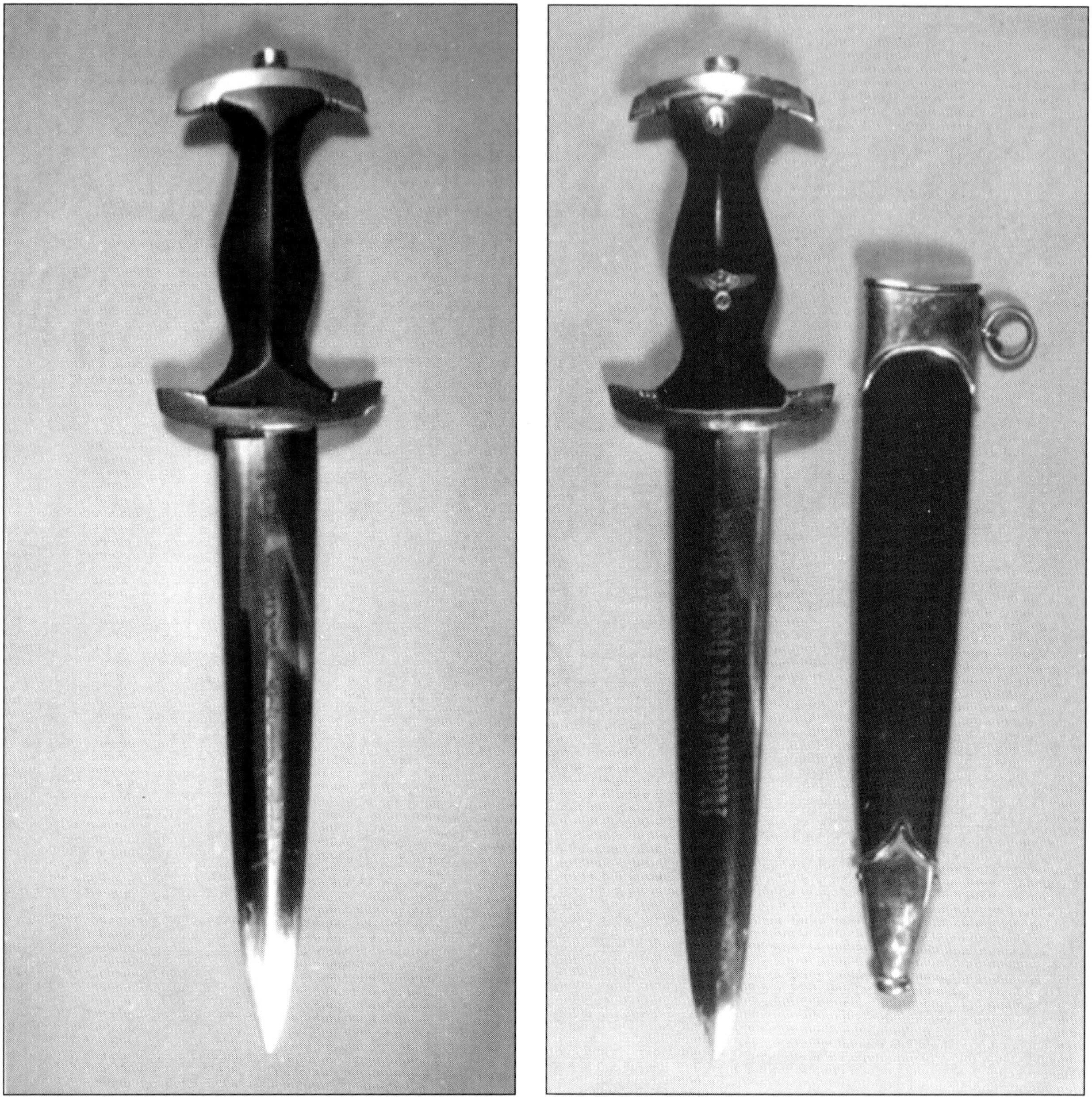

Obverse and reverse views of a genuine 1933 pattern SS dagger bearing a bogus Rohm inscription. This inscription has been quite well executed onto a genuine E P & S blade, but has been applied too close to the tip.

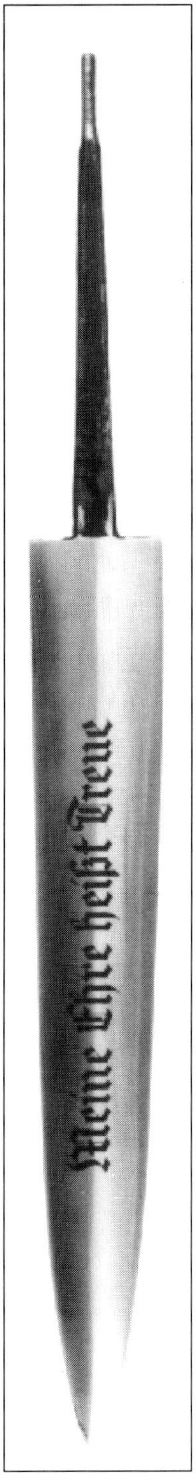

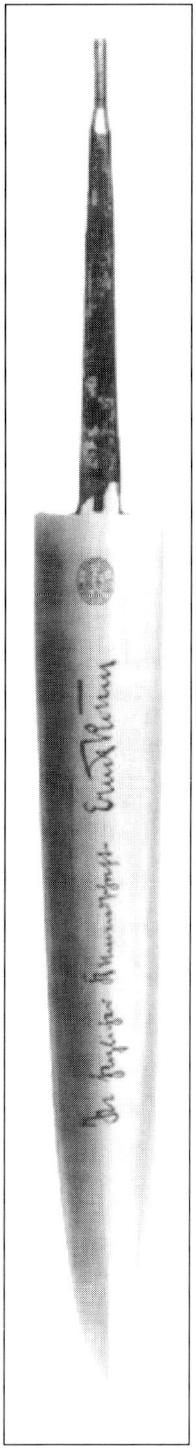

Obverse and reverse sides of a reproduction SS Rohm dagger blade. These top quality blades are currently being produced in Solingen and have a well executed SS blade motto and Rohm dedication. The reverse blade bears an Eickhorn oval proofmark. The blade inscriptions are reproduced from original templates.

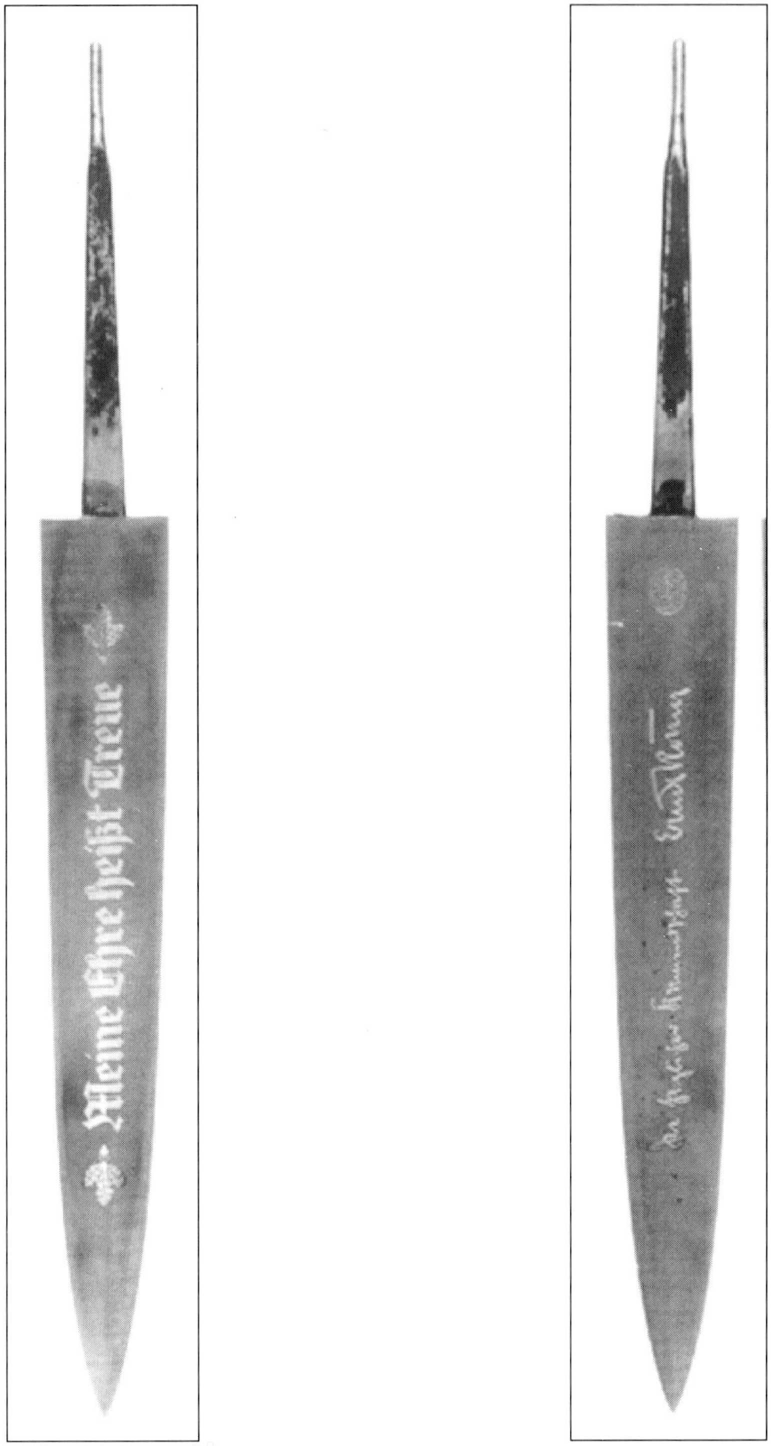

Obverse and reverse sides of a reproduction SS Rohm Honour dagger blade. This current Solingen made reproduction has an artificial Damascus blade with gold inlaid inscription and motto which have been executed using original Third Reich period templates.

SS HIMMLER HONOUR DAGGER

As only two hundred pieces were ever awarded, the Himmler Honour dagger was the rarest of any production SS dagger. The genuine Himmler dagger is only distinguished from the standard 1933 pattern SS dagger by two distinctive characteristics: first the Himmler dedication on the reverse of the blade which reads "In herzlicher Freundschaft, H. Himmler" ("In heartfelt friendship, H. Himmler"); and second the absence of any SS Group numbers which was due to the dagger being an award item rather than an issue piece. This second characteristic is a positive aid in identifying genuine SS service daggers which have been fabricated to copy the Himmler Honour dagger.

Carl Eickhorn was the sole authorised manufacturer of the SS Himmler Honour dagger, and as these daggers were for special presentation by the Reichsführer SS Heinrich Himmler each dagger was hand finished with a degree of care not lavished on most SS daggers. Consequently the original examples of these daggers are extremely well put together having an excellent grip to crossguard fit and blade to lower crossguard fit. In addition to the consistent quality of workmanship in Himmler Honour daggers they also had a consistency in the type and quality of materials used in their construction. All genuine examples featured a black anodised scabbard and superior quality solid nickel silver fittings. Additionally all 200 examples of the Himmler Honour dagger bore the 1934/35 Eickhorn proofmark on the reverse ricasso.

The underside of the lower crossguard carried a serial number which was the bench number of the craftsman who assembled and hand finished each dagger: these numbers ranged from 0 to 9. A bench number has been observed on every genuine example of the SS Himmler Honour dagger. This was no doubt done to ensure that the SS knew who to "execute" if they ever found fault with a finished dagger!

Unlike many other daggers, with the SS Himmler Honour dagger it is possible to make several emphatic statements which will be of assistance in identifying reproductions or fabrications. The use of any Maker's proofmark other than Carl Eickhorn's is a fake. Similarly any SS Himmler Honour dagger bearing an RZM proofmark is also a fake. Any dagger having poor quality plated fittings can also be regarded as a fake: fittings should always be solid nickel silver. This final point is highlighted for in some fabrications of the Himmler dagger later post-1936 plated fittings which bore no SS Group numbers have been used in post-war fabricated Himmler Honour daggers.

In common with the Rohm Honour dagger there have also been numerous reproductions of the Himmler Honour dagger and modern reproduction Himmler inscribed blades which have been used in fabricating Himmler Honour daggers in association with genuine but unrelated SS parts. Although reproduction and fabricated Himmler daggers have their own peculiar characteristics, some of which have already been stated, the points to observe for the standard 1933 pattern SS dagger can also be applied to the Himmler dagger. Consequently only the most pertinent characteristics relating directly to the Himmler Honour dagger are listed in this section, and it is recommended that these points to be observed should be viewed in conjunction with those of the 1933 pattern SS dagger and 1934 SS Rohm Honour dagger.

RECOGNITION CHECKLIST

BLADE

- Any Maker's proofmark other than Carl Eickhorn is inappropriate.
- The use of the RZM proofmark is equally inappropriate.
- A sharp central ridge on the blade is a feature of reproduction blades.
- The etching of the SS motto is shallow on many reproduction blades.
- The etching of the Himmler inscription being poorly applied and lacking the sharp definition of the

original dedication.

- ➢ Engraved Himmler dedications are incorrect. Original dedications were always executed by acid etching.
- ➢ Incorrect positioning of the Himmler dedication being applied too low or too high on the blade. Original inscriptions were always applied slightly higher than central on the reverse blade. Phoney inscriptions have been observed applied too close to the proofmark or too close to the tip.
- ➢ A characteristic of post-war blade inscribing is the use of modern photoengraving which was never a process used on originals.
- ➢ The use of an incorrect period Eickhorn proofmark usually featuring the large oval, but examples have been encountered with just the Eickhorn squirrel proofmark.
- ➢ The Eickhorn proofmark applied too low down the blade: original proofmarks were usually applied within less than 1/4 of an inch of the lower crossguard.
- ➢ Some reproduction Himmler daggers produced in Spain had a very sharp central spine which appears to split the Himmler dedication in half.
- ➢ Dedications applied to the blade either unevenly or at a slight angle: original Himmler dedications were always applied up the centre of the blade.
- ➢ The "." period (full stop) between the initial "H" and the surname "Himmler" is either missing or very indistinct on some post war reproductions.
- ➢ Some poorly etched blades will exhibit small gaps in the letters of the dedication or even parts of the letters actually missing. Original dedications were always very sharply defined.
- ➢ The good quality reproduction blades currently being manufactured in Germany and bearing the Himmler dedication have a blade approximately 1/4 of an inch shorter than originals.
- ➢ The same aforementioned blade of current German manufacture is also markedly slimmer towards the point than originals.
- ➢ A good quality German blade currently in circulation has a good overall form without a sharp central ridge and a good quality well applied dedication: however although these blades feature the correct small oval Eickhorn it is positioned too low down on the blade and is very close to the letter "r" in the terminating word "Himmler".

GRIP

With the exception of the serial numbers on the lower crossguard and the absence of SS Group numbers, all other aspects of the Himmler Honour dagger reproductions are the same as those for the 1933 pattern SS dagger. However it should also be borne in mind that the materials used in the grip construction of originals were especially selected for their superior quality and finished to a very high standard.

SCABBARD

No distinction was made on the scabbard of genuine SS Himmler Honour daggers which differed from the 1933 pattern scabbard. Genuine examples of the Himmler scabbard all had a black anodised finish with nickel silver fittings. Some modern Spanish reproductions of the Himmler dagger feature embellished scabbards with oakleaf decoration which were not appropriate for this particular Honour dagger and did not appear until much later on other SS Honour daggers. Scabbards with plated fittings should be viewed with suspicion as this type of fitting did not come into use until several years after the original award of the Himmler Honour dagger in 1934. All other points to observe in identifying reproductions or fabricated Himmler scabbards can be applied from the 1933 pattern SS reproduction scabbard points to observe.

PROOFMARKS

The only correct and appropriate proofmark which should appear on the blade of a genuine SS Himmler Honour dagger is the small oval of Carl Eickhorn. Currently produced German blades of a reasonable quality also use the large oval Eickhorn as well as the small, and also the E P & S proofmark which was appropriate for both the SS and SA Rohm dedicated blades but not for the SS Himmler. German reproduction blades of early manufacture will be encountered bearing an inappropriate RZM proofmark with a phoney Himmler dedication: this proofmark is also one favoured by most Spanish reproductions.

A parts assembly SS Himmler Honour dagger which features genuine crossguards and grip married to a reproduction blade. These blades were produced in the 1960's and have a pronounced sharp central spine, with a bogus RZM proofmark, Maker's control number and circular SS runes proofmark. The Himmler inscription is quite well executed but is marginally undersize and located too close to the tip of the blade. The RZM proofmark was not appropriate on any SS Himmler Honour dagger blades, the only proofmark which should appear is the oval squirrel of Carl Eickhorn, the sole authorised Maker of this dagger.

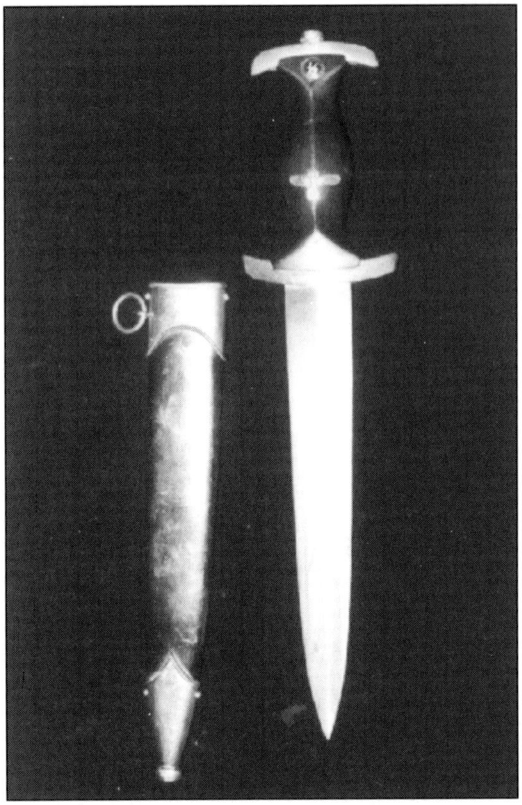

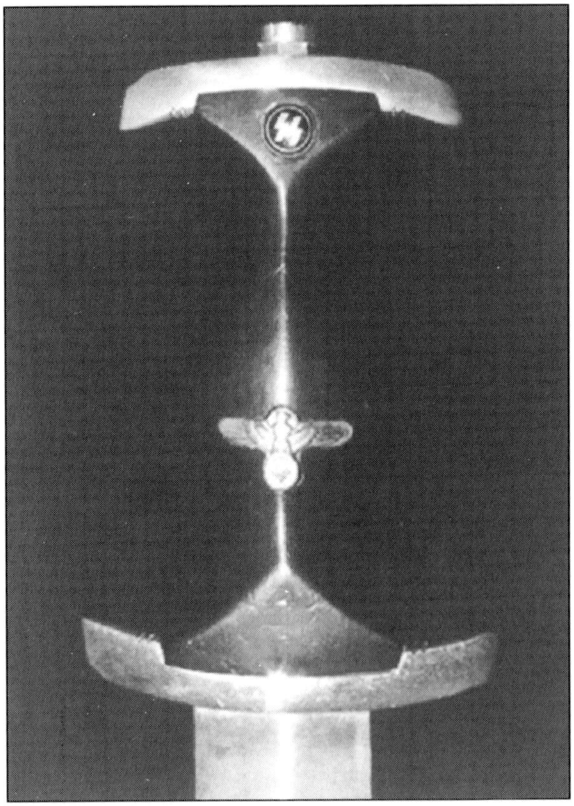

Three different views of a bogus Himmler dedication which has been applied to an otherwise genuine SS dagger. The proofmarks on the reverse blade look extremely impressive, but would only relate to a standard 1933 pattern SS dagger produced after 1934, and not a Himmler Honour dagger. This is due to the fact that all 200 examples of the genuine Himmler Honour dagger were manufactured by one maker, Carl Eickhorn, Solingen. Additionally the RZM and its proofmark were not in use at the time the Himmler dagger was awarded in 1934. Technically the inscription on this fabrication is quite good, however it has been applied too low down the blade as a result of the numerous SS and RZM proofmarks, and Maker's control number on the upper blade.

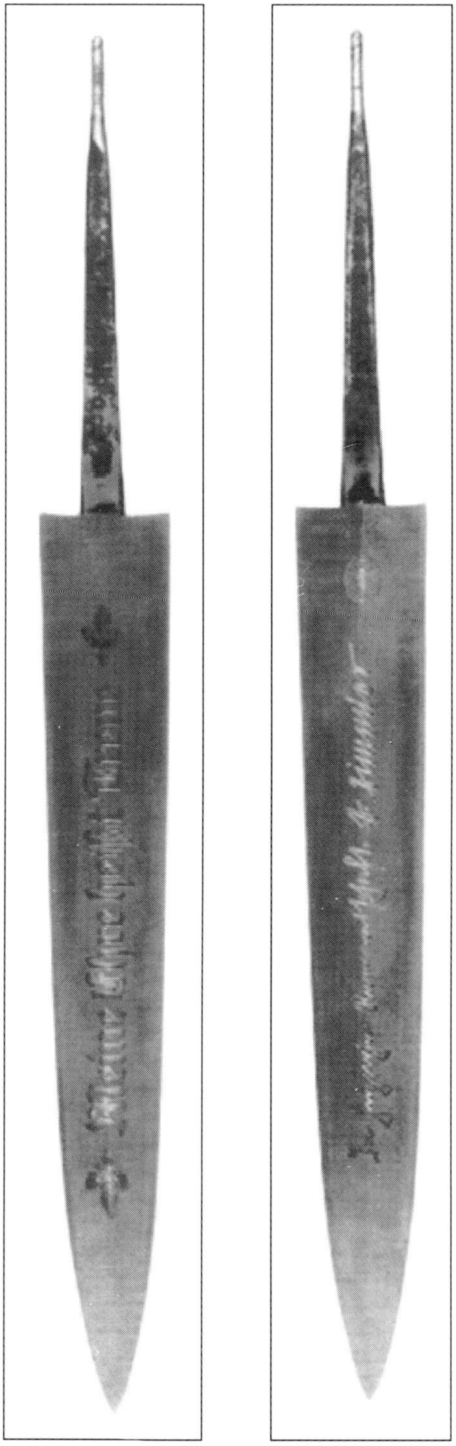

Current production SS Himmler Honour dagger blade made in Solingen with an artificial Damascus blade. The SS motto and Himmler dedication are well executed using original templates. The inscription lettering is highlighted in gold. It should be borne in mind that this type of blade was not a standard feature of the original 200 Himmler SS Honour daggers.

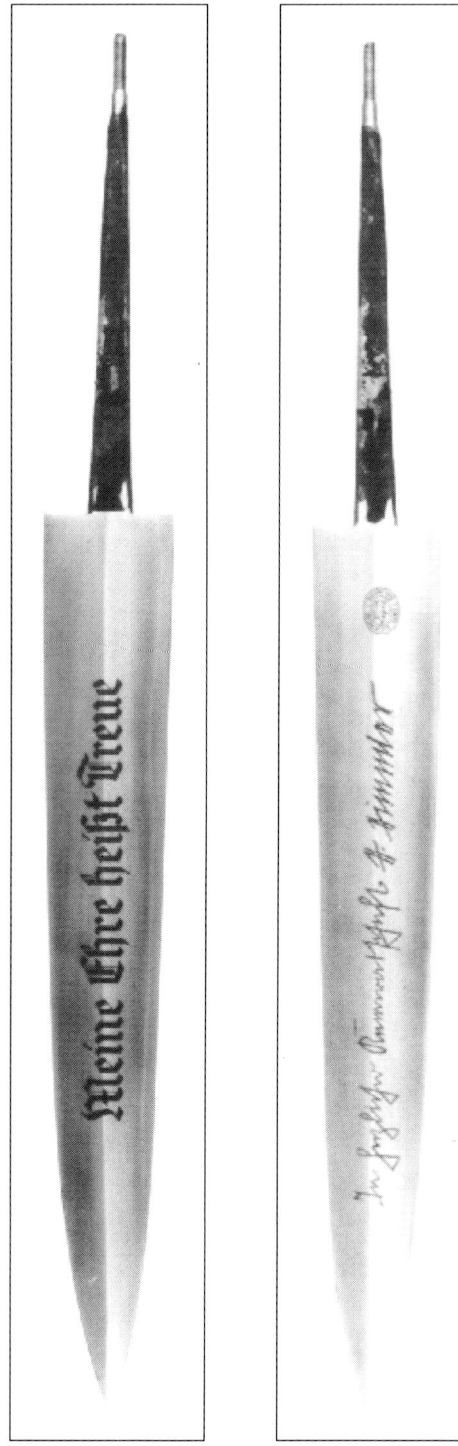

Reproduction blade for the SS Himmler Honour dagger. This extremely well made blade is currently being produced in Solingen using original inscription templates. These blades do not have the sharp central ridge characteristic of many reproductions. The main point to observe is the proofmark which is positioned too far from the ricasso thereby moving the Himmler inscription too close to the blade tip.

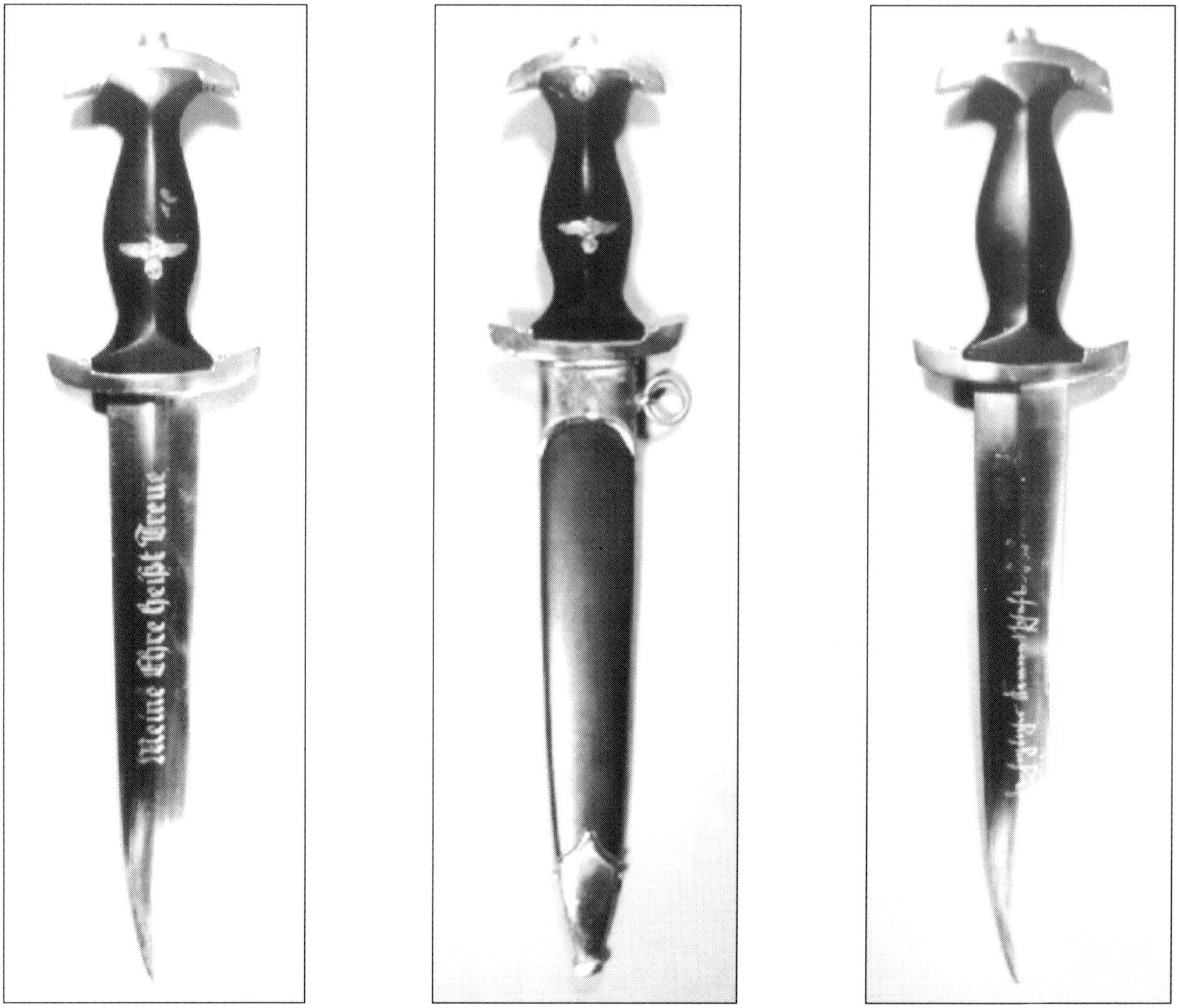

Three different views of a genuine 1933 pattern SS dagger which has had a bogus Himmler dedication engraved onto the reverse of the blade. Original dedications were never engraved but were acid etched from a waxed template. This crude attempt at deception has ruined a perfectly good dagger. Also the faker has tried to erase Himmler's name which was not appropriate - only SS blades with Rohm dedications were ordered to have the name erased.

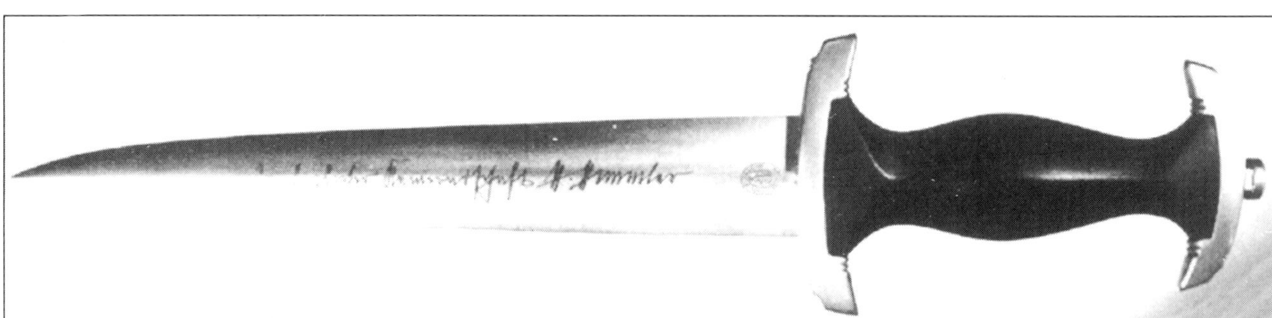

The reverse side of a genuine 1934 Himmler Honour dagger. Note the style of script on the Himmler dedication and the positioning of the Eickhorn oval proofmark. This example is the only correct and acceptable configuration on this dagger.

SS HONOUR DAGGER

The outstanding quality of this dagger both in its workmanship and material composition make it a difficult item to reproduce to a standard which would pass close scrutiny. In the main all of the dagger and scabbard fittings were of German silver with the exception of the less robust pieces such as the tang, nut, scabbard fitting retaining screws and the scabbard throat fitting which were silver plated. Also the scabbard throat was thicker than that found on regular SS daggers and is a positive feature to aid in reproduction recognition.

The scabbards were covered in black leather which was fitted to the scabbard in the same way as SA Honour daggers being tailored to fit around the scabbard fittings and not under as is the practice on many reproductions. The blades were genuine Damascus steel of the maidenhair pattern and has the SS motto on the obverse side raised in high relief with an oakleaf spray at each end of the motto. The whole of the motto and oakleaf decoration were gilded. The reverse blade ricasso had the Eickhorn proofmark gilded in high relief. The reverse tang of the blade bore the word "DAMAST" stamped into the tang.

The fittings of the SS Honour dagger were identical in design and material content to the SA Honour dagger originating from the same Maker, Carl Eickhorn, Solingen. Consequently the comments made regarding the SA Honour dagger apply equally to its SS counterpart. In addition to the complete reproduction SS Honour dagger there have also been various types of post-war Honour style crossguards and other fittings available which have been used to fabricate SS Honour daggers by the expedient of marrying together reproduction and genuine SS dagger parts.

The most common mistake which is made in fabricating SS Honour daggers occurs with the blade where the fakers generally tend to utilise plain SS blades (quite often genuine) or a modern blade with an artificial Damascus finish. The pattern normally found on the modern artificial Damascus blades is of the rosebud design rather than the maidenhair of originals. Although reproduction artificial Damascus SS blades with the maidenhair pattern are available. Both the SS and SA Honour daggers were made by Carl Eickhorn, but whereas the SA Honour dagger was available with a plain blade, the SS Honour dagger blade was invariably of genuine Damascus steel.

A distinction should be made between what were actual SS Honour daggers and those pieces which although genuine were presentation daggers for which there was a whole different criteria for bestowal. Generally speaking the SS Honour dagger was awarded and had its requisite visible ornamentation whereas presentation daggers were not actually in the same category and could be presented to an SS member on a variety of occasions such as retirement, Sport's Days, promotions etc. These SS presentation daggers did not have a standard form and could range from merely a blade dedication to a full blown Damascus blade. However the characteristic which virtually all of them had in common was that there was no external distinction evident on the dagger such as ornamented crossguards, etc.

These presentation daggers do not exactly fall into any specific category due to the diversity of their appearance, but generally speaking they were either standard 1933 or 1936 pattern SS daggers with embellished blades. Due to presentation daggers being purchased on an individual basis for bestowal they could be acquired from any authorised Maker of SS daggers whereas actual SS Honour daggers were only purchased by the SS Main Office from a single Maker, namely Carl Eickhorn. Therefore it is not uncommon to encounter a wide variety of Maker's proofmarks on this type of presentation dagger. As a consequence of the appearance of different Makers' marks on these presentation daggers a great deal of confusion exists in the mind of collectors when encountering most SS presentation daggers.

Quite often a collector will reject what he believes to be a phoney SS Honour dagger on the grounds that it bears a proofmark of a Maker other than that of Carl Eickhorn. Whilst the presumption that this makes the dagger a fake is correct if it is a true Honour dagger, it does not necessarily have to be true if the piece is in fact an SS presentation dagger. Therefore it is essential before coming to a firm conclusion about the authenticity of an SS dagger to first determine whether it is a true Honour dagger or is in fact a presentation dagger which could quite legitimately bear a Maker's mark other than that of Carl Eickhorn.

It was never the intent to give credibility to fantasy daggers by further documentation in this book, however one particular strain of fantasy SS presentation daggers needs to be dismissed once and for all. These daggers take several forms centring around the theme of an ivory handled SS presentation dagger for award to Leaders in the SS such as Julius Schreck, Gottlob Berger, Sepp Dietrich and others. The general form of these daggers is that of an embellished 1933 pattern SS dagger. In most instances they were meticulously assembled using original SS dagger parts but having the black ebony grip replaced by a white ivory grip. The scabbard either SS or SA were completely stripped of their painted finish and had their centre panels engraved with appropriate Nazi looking decoration such as SS runes, oakleaves and acorns etc. The scabbards were then silver plated to give them a professional finish. They feature superb quality Damascus blades usually genuine, not artificial, although some plain SS blades were also used and had personalised dedications etched on their blades. These particular fantasy daggers were manufactured for an English dealer as early as the 1960's and have been sold worldwide for astronomical sums. These daggers were only produced in very limited quantities and were fed to the collector market gradually in order to substantiate their authenticity and to command the highest prices possible.

RECOGNITION CHECKLIST

BLADE

- The RZM proofmark should not appear on the blade of any genuine SS Honour dagger.
- Reproduction Honour daggers have the blade motto etched rather than in high relief.
- On reproductions with simulated Damascus blades featuring a gold finished blade motto with an oakleaf at each end, the motto and bottom oakleaf are applied too close to the tip of the blade.
- The only form of decoration which should appear on the blade of an SS Honour dagger is a gold "Mein Ehre heisst Treue" motto decorated at each end with a gold oakleaf spray. Any additional inscriptions etc. are spurious.
- Poor quality artificial Damascus finish usually of the small rosebud pattern is a feature of modern reproduction SS Honour blades. Maidenhair was the pattern used on originals.
- A plain SS dagger blade (whether genuine or reproduction) bearing only the SS motto is indicative of post war fabrications.
- The use of a Maker's proofmark other than that of Carl Eickhorn should be viewed with suspicion.
- The Himmler dedication should not appear on the reverse of the blade of the 1936 SS Honour dagger: this was a feature restricted to the 200 SS Honour daggers awarded in 1934, and was never applicable to this later type of SS Honour dagger.
- "SS Honour daggers" with white ivory grips and various blade inscriptions to SS and other Nazi notables would be rejected as post war fantasies. These fantasy daggers invariably feature genuine parts and utilise real ivory for the grips and have the look and feel of a genuine article. They were however the creation of and English dealer who had them craftsman made in very limited quantities from the mid-1960's through to the 1980's.

SCABBARD

- Scabbard fittings which have been engraved should be viewed with suspicion. Original fittings were always die struck.
- Genuine SS Honour daggers were invariably covered in fine grain black leather. Black painted daggers should be viewed with suspicion.
- The leather scabbard covering should be fitted flush around the upper and lower fittings and not underneath as is the practice with some reproduction scabbards.
- The scabbard throat fitting on genuine Honour daggers is somewhat thicker than that found on

genuine standard SS dagger scabbards and also the throat fitting of modern reproductions.

- Scabbards with ornately engraved patterns in the centre panels are post-war embellishments: these include runic symbols, swastikas and other types of Nazi symbolism.
- The scabbard fittings of genuine SS Honour daggers were of German Silver. Modern reproduction fittings are usually just thinly plated alloys.

GRIP

- The use of a white ivory grip (whether genuine or artificial ivory) is a characteristic which will be encountered on post-war fantasy creations and was never an authorised option on the genuine SS Honour dagger.
- The use of black plastic to make the grips is a characteristic of modern Spanish reproductions. The grips for genuine SS Honour daggers were always of polished black ebony wood.
- The use of aluminium or plated copper grip insignia is a feature of modern reproductions. Genuine grip insignia for the Honour dagger were always silver.
- The initials of an individual inserted into the round recess where the SS rune normally fits is a feature of post-war fantasy daggers.
- Hand engraved crossguards are a feature of a modern style of embellishing plain ordinary SS and SA crossguards to give the appearance of Honour crossguards. Original crossguards were always cast in high relief.
- The use of a floral or other type of crossguard design which diverges from the correct oakleaf and acorn design of original SS Honour crossguards is characteristic of modern reproduction spare parts assembly crossguards.
- Any form of substitution or embellishment on the actual wooden grip should be viewed with suspicion as the actual ebony grip part of the SS Honour dagger was identical in all respects to that of the standard 1933 pattern SS dagger.
- These points should be viewed in conjunction with those of the grip sections for the 1933 pattern SS dagger, 1935 SA Honour dagger and 1938 SA High Leader's dagger.

PROOFMARKS

As previously related the only legitimate Maker's proofmark which should appear on any genuine SS Honour dagger is that of Carl Eickhorn. The Eickhorn proofmark should appear on a maidenhair patterned genuine Damascus blade raised in high relief and gilded.

SS PRESENTATION DAGGERS

The appearance of another Maker's proofmark on what may appear to be a genuine SS Honour dagger could indicate that the piece is an SS presentation dagger rather than an SS Honour dagger, and that it is not necessarily a reproduction. The RZM proofmark however should never appear on any SS presentation dagger either: as these two types of daggers were in their own different ways non-regulation private purchase items, and therefore were not subject to RZM regulations. SS presentation daggers were similar in appearance to the Honour dagger with the exception of the scabbard decoration which was more eloborate on the presentation dagger. The style and form of genuine SS presentation daggers did vary although not to the extent of some of the more outrageous reproduction and parts assembly daggers now on the market. The use of the Himmler Honour dagger dedication on the reverse blade of an SS presentation dagger is indicative of post-war reproductions especially those emanating from Spain. Also some of the good quality German reproduction SS blades carry a spurious Himmler or Rohm dedication. Although presentation daggers were made by several Solingen manufacturers the principal supplier of presentation daggers was the same as the SS Honour dagger, Carl Eickhorn.

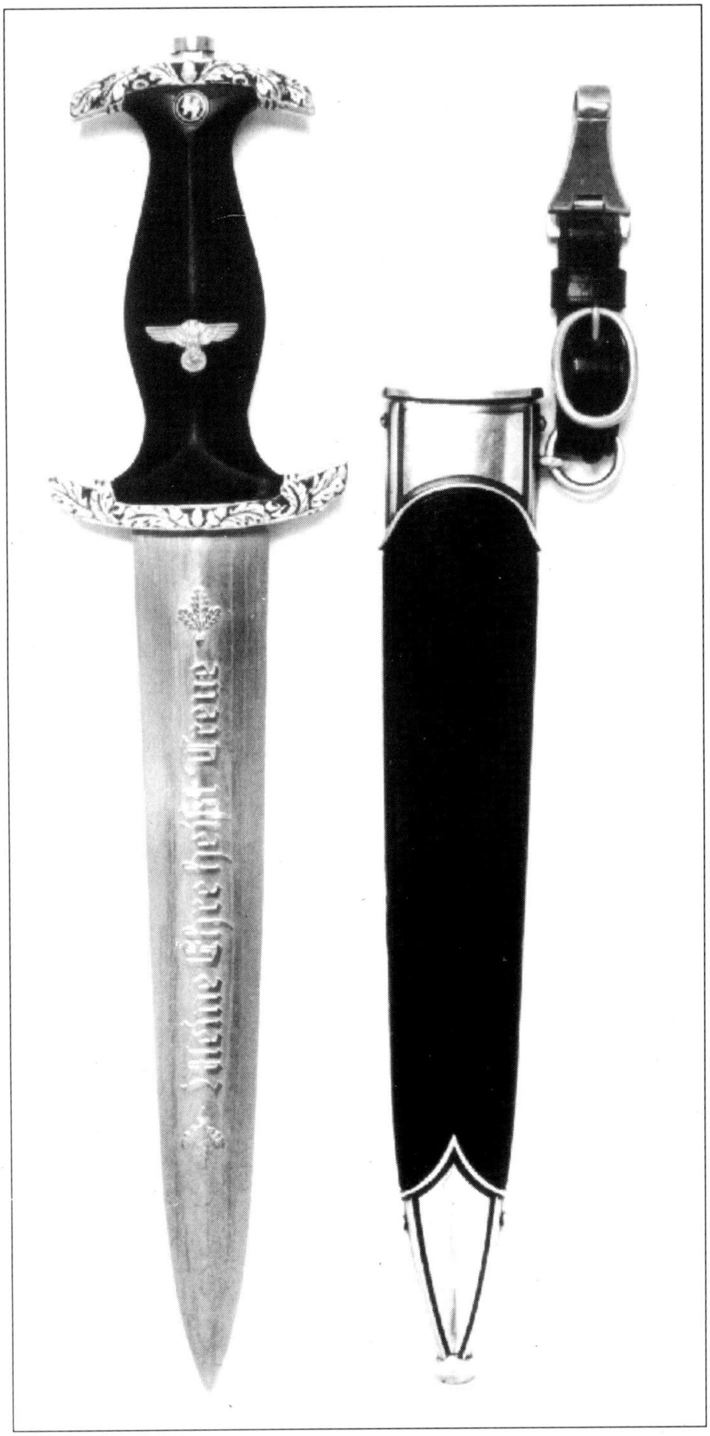

Obverse and reverse sides of the 1936 pattern SS Honour dagger. This is a genuine example with correct scabbard decoration, oakleaf crossguards and maidenhair genuine Damascus blade. This genuine dagger is a good comparison piece which will expose the shortcomings of most reproduction SS Honour daggers currently on the market.

1936 CHAINED SS DAGGER REPRODUCTIONS

The reproduction characteristics of the 1936 pattern SS dagger are the same as those for its 1933 predecessor except for the scabbard and attached hanging chains. Therefore only the characteristics for these parts of the dagger will be dealt with in this section and should be used in conjunction with the other reproduction characteristics for the 1933 pattern SS dagger. Additionally all of the characteristics of reproduction scabbards related in the previous section can also be applied to the 1936 scabbard. Genuine chained SS daggers frequently had RZM proofmarked blades although many SS members who qualified for award of the chained dagger often chose to retain the 1933 pattern dagger and married it to the new chained scabbard. Genuine blades will also be encountered which feature a combination of RZM and Maker's proofmark.

RECOGNITION CHECKLIST

SCABBARD

- ➢ A centre scabbard fitting which is noticeably different in either style or material composition could indicate a converted 1933 pattern scabbard.
- ➢ A badly fitting centre scabbard mount.
- ➢ Poorly defined detail on the centre mount swastika decoration having a flat appearance instead of a sharp distinct outline.
- ➢ Suspension rings to attach the chains can be evidence of a converted 1933 pattern scabbard or some post-war reproductions. Original chain attachments were always of the flat ramp type.
- ➢ The centre mount should be held into position by a single dome headed screw in the centre of the fitting on one side and another screw on the bottom edge of the fitting on the other side. Many reproductions have these screws missing with the fitting jammed into position or feature just one screw in the middle of one side of the fitting.
- ➢ Ensure that the top scabbard fitting is of two piece construction with correct brass scabbard liners, Many reproductions of Spanish extraction have the top fitting made in one piece with the scabbard liners incorrectly brazed into position.
- ➢ The centre band on many reproductions is wider at each end than originals by approximately 10% and sometimes more, and the securing screw is off centre. Originals always had the screw mounted in the centre.
- ➢ The centre scabbard mount of some reproductions has a crude moulding seam visible on both sides.

CHAINS

- ➢ Many reproduction chains have extremely poor detailing showing areas of pitting on the runes and skull and crossbones. This type of reproduction chain had the links cast rather than being die struck as originals were.
- ➢ Original chain links had a very fine background pebbling which is usually either missing or poorly defined on reproductions.
- ➢ Reproductions chain links are either undersize from shrinkage or oversize due to over compensation in copying the link.
- ➢ The reverse of reproduction chain links and catches often exhibit indentations or small bumps as a consequence of crude casting.
- ➢ The two bands which join the chain links on reproductions often have an oval shape whereas originals were flat and elongated and only rounded at the ends.
- ➢ The chain links of some post-war reproductions are extremely thick.
- ➢ Ensure that the links have been assembled in the correct order i.e. moving away from the scabbard:

top set should be SS rune then Death's Head; bottom set should be Death's Head then SS runes then Death's Head then SS runes. Some post-war assembled chains have been put together in the wrong combinations.

- Ensure that the chain has the correct number of links i.e. 2 upper and 4 lower. Some reproductions have the wrong number of links. One Spanish reproduction in particular features one upper link and three lower links.
- The material composition of the links is not an ironclad guarantee in identifying reproduction chains as the material composition of originals chains underwent several changes, and have been encountered as nickel or silver plated steel, iron, nickel and even alloy on some later examples. Although there is no evidence of original chains being manufactured from the very soft lead type alloy which has been used to manufacture some post-war reproduction chains.

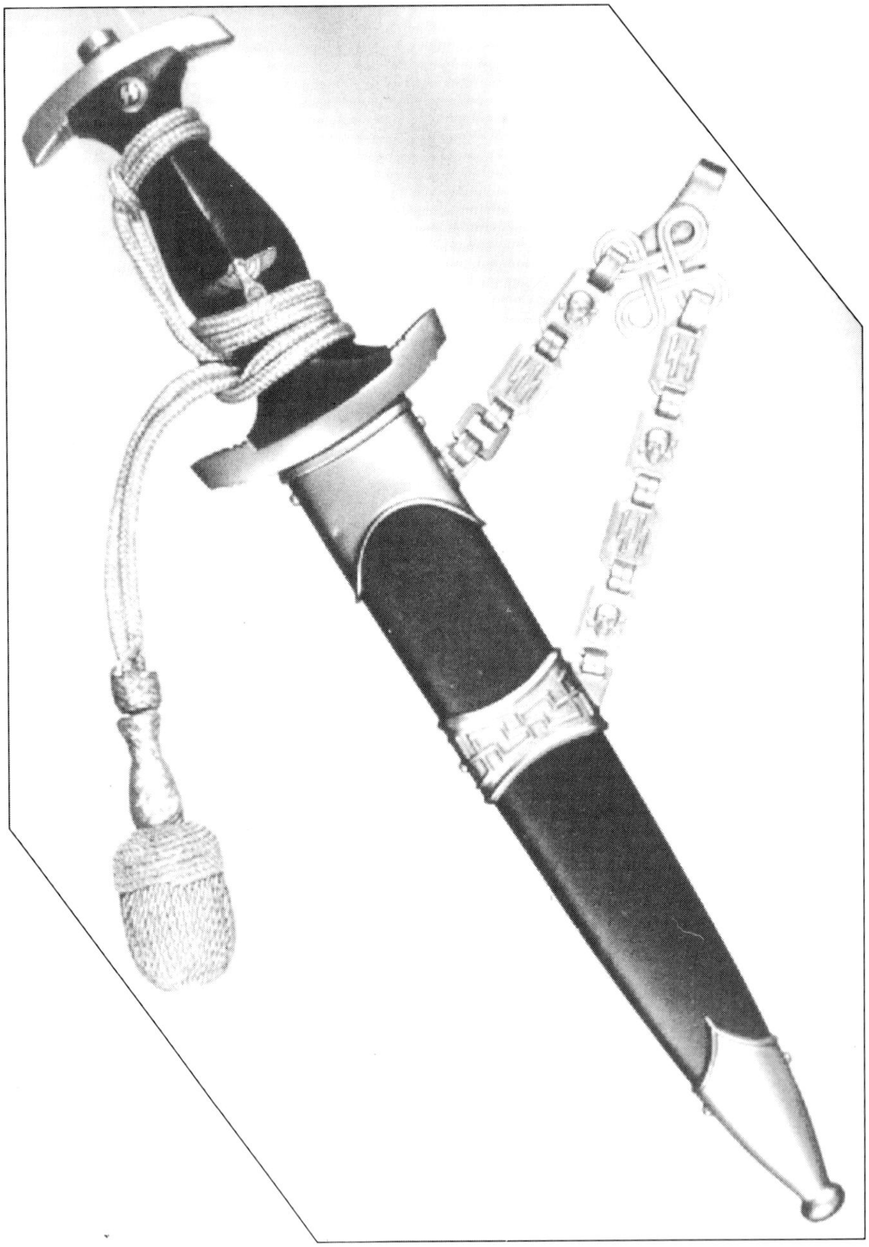

This is an excellent example of a genuine 1936 pattern chained SS dagger, complete with portepee knot. Note the configuration and clarity of the hanging chain links and centre scabbard mount.

Five different views of a current Spanish reproduction chained SS dagger. This particular example is very crudely made, and has more shortcomings than can be detailed here. However, briefly, there are no retaining screws on any of the scabbard fittings, the lower section of the chain has three instead of four links, and the top scabbard fitting has been cast in one piece. The black plastic grip has an oversized eagle grip inlay, which is too deeply recessed. The blade on this piece, although having a good polish, has a pathetic blade motto, which appears to have been cast at the same time as the blade. These photographs also show the abysmal attempt at an RZM proofmark, with an M7/14 control number. Due to the poor blade to scabbard fit of these daggers they also have a plastic blade washer, which was never a feature of originals.

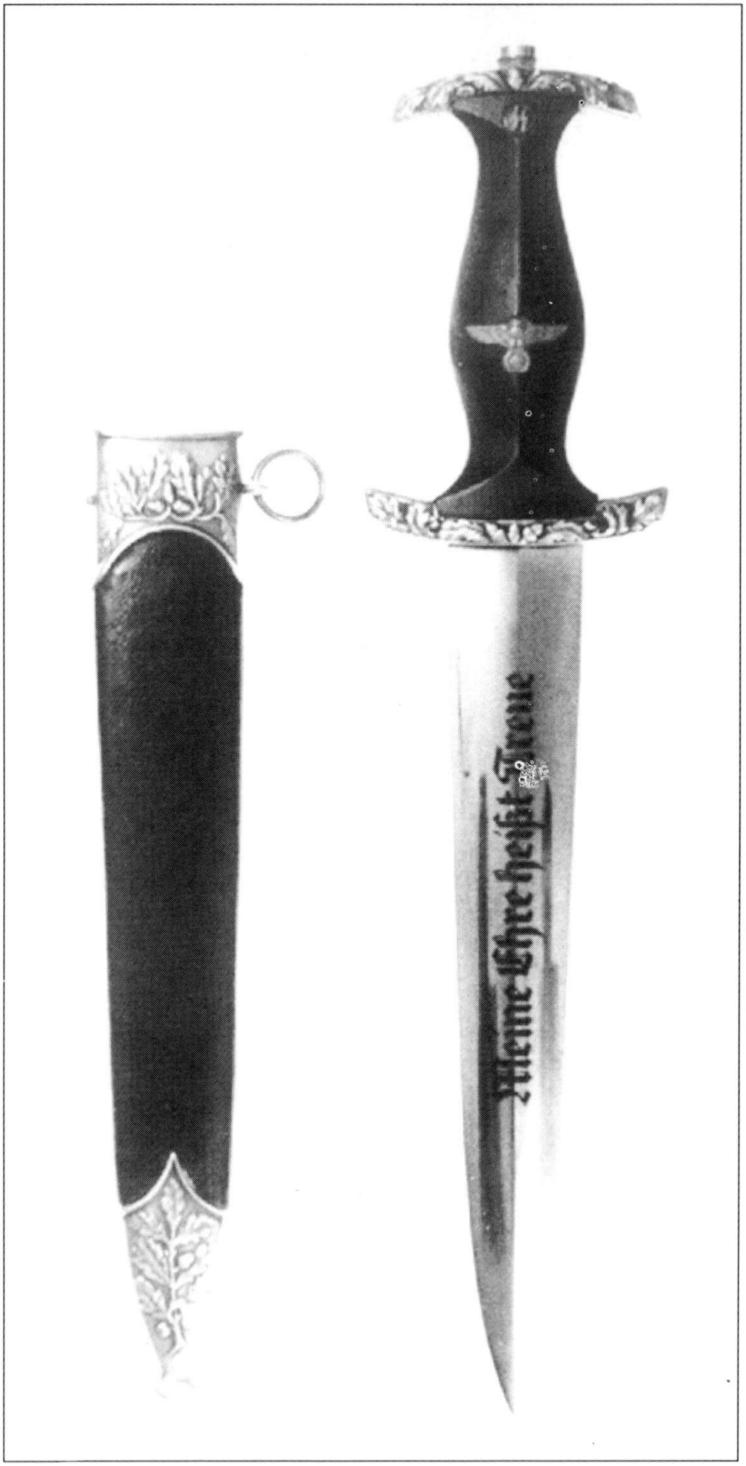

A superb example of a genuine SS Presentation dagger.

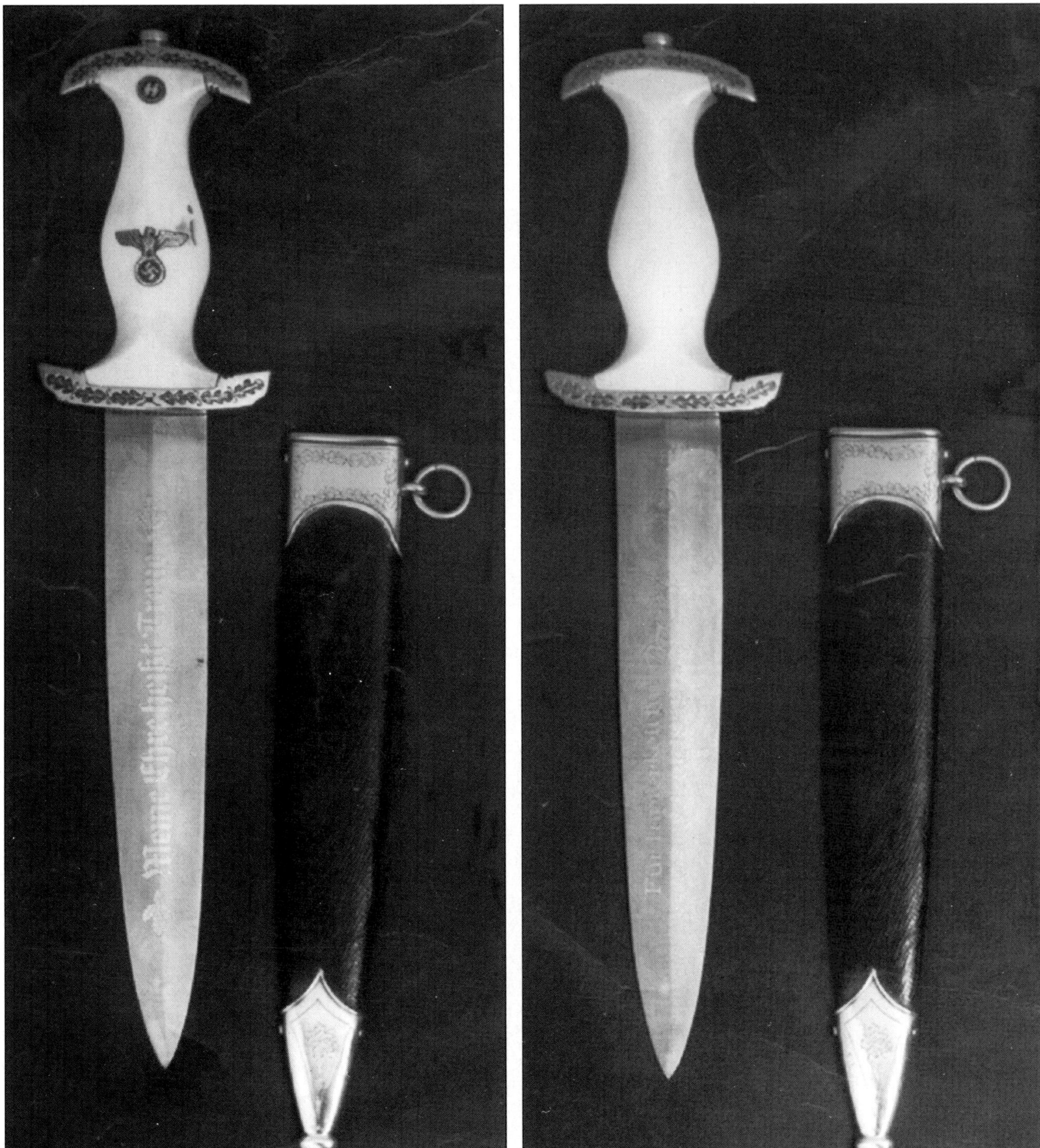

Obverse and reverse sides of a reproduction SS Presentation dagger made in the late 1960's. The scabbard has silver fittings with fine grain leather covering. The blade motto and oakleaf decoration are gold filled onto the Damast finish. The fitting on the grip and scabbard have been craftsman engraved with highlight toning. The grip is of genuine ivory with silver inlaid SS runes and eagle insignia. The reverse blade has a personalised dedication with the presentation date of 1942, however the obverse RZM and SS proofmarks carry a date of 1936. These superb quality reproduction daggers were made in relatively small quantities and will be encountered with presentation inscriptions to well known SS personalities.

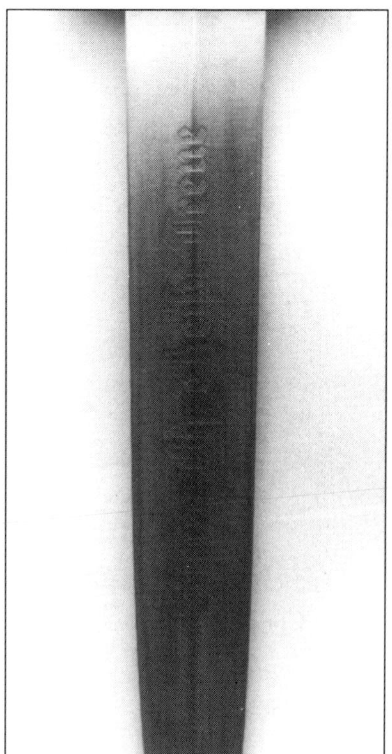

Five different views of a Spanish reproduction SS presentation dagger. All the fittings are crudely cast with black plastic grip. The blade has a matt grey finish with poorly executed motto and a spurious Himmler dedication.

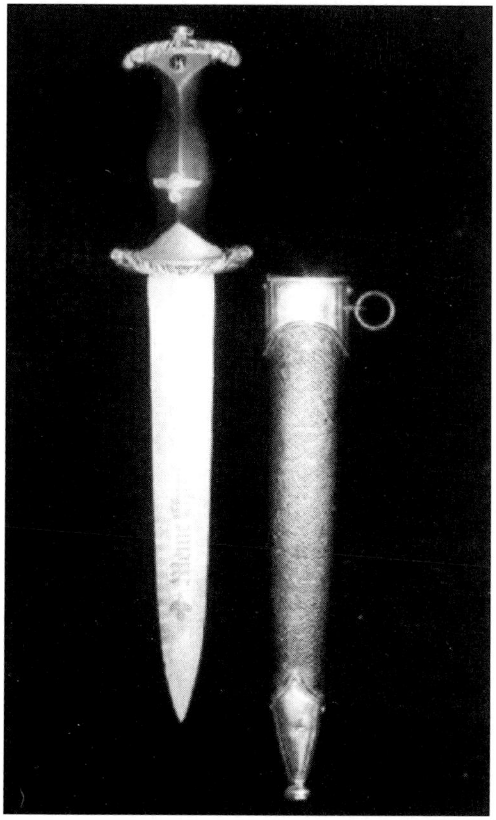

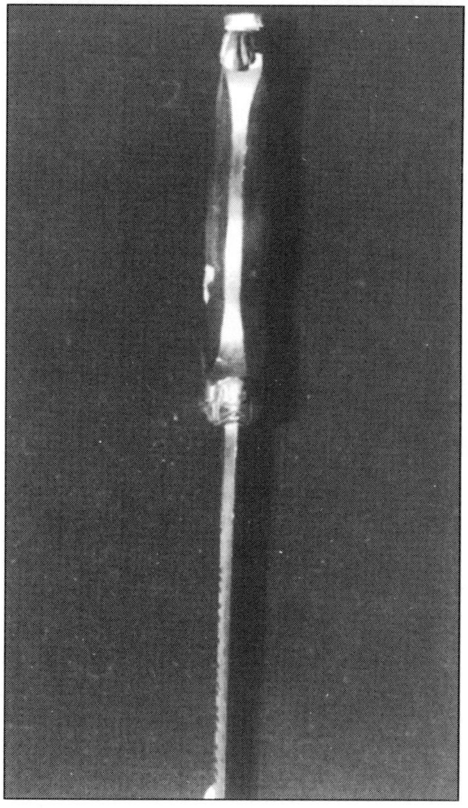

Three different views of a reproduction parts assembly SS Presentation dagger. Note on the side view the totally spurious use of a metal shell on the side of the grip. This style of grip was never a feature of any original SS dagger, neither was the use of two separate grip plates. Finally, the grip eagle has been positioned in a completely arbitrary manner, being too low down the grip, and also slanting at an awkward angle.

SA DAGGER REPRODUCTIONS

The SA dagger is undoubtedly the most evocative Third Reich era dagger. Even the individual who does not collect militaria or even have the most rudimentary knowledge of Nazi Germany can almost immediately recognise this dagger's form as being Nazi German. So deeply etched is this dagger in the public mind that it is immediately synonymous with Hitler's Third Reich.

The familiarity with which we collectors all treat this dagger needs to be tempered with some caution for the SA dagger was being reproduced almost before the guns of World War II had fallen silent. Due to the close association between the SA dagger and the Nazis, it was immediately in demand as a souvenir for Allied servicemen returning home after the war. This demand for Nazi souvenirs was further stimulated by large numbers of fresh Allied troops arriving in Germany as part of the Army of Occupation, many of whom were also seeking war relics especially Third Reich dress daggers. The expanding and extremely lucrative demand for Nazi daggers was soon satisfied by the old established Solingen dagger Makers who had quite substantial parts remaining in their inventories. These leftover parts were assembled and then sold off to servicemen. So great was the demand for SA daggers after the war that they were even exported from Germany to the USA and England. Unlike the earlier "parts assembly" daggers these "export pieces" were easily identifiable for they carried an obligatory export stamp bearing the word "Germany" etched into the blade ricasso. (This not only applied to the SA dagger but also the Hitler Youth knife and other items exported at that time). Examples of this type of dagger have also been observed with "Germany" die struck into the tang.

A further post-war phenomenon was the parts assembly SA dagger which featured a mixture of wartime and post-war fittings. This occurred due to stocks of particular original dagger parts being exhausted and new parts being manufactured to complete the dagger. The newly manufactured pieces were very often manufactured to a different standard and utilised inappropriate materials. This frequently caused these types of dagger to have badly fitting or mismatched parts. These daggers were produced using various dagger Maker's proofmarks depending on the origin of the blade, and also the RZM proofmark. A post-war parts assembly dagger was also marketed with a proofmark not used or documented during the period 1933-1945. This took the form of initials "B & A". The B & A daggers invariably have reddish brown plastic grips of post-war manufacture and were in the main marketed without scabbards; although examples have been encountered where scabbards have been added as a later embellishment.

In addition to the post-war parts assembly SA daggers there have also been a variety of complete reproduction SA daggers manufactured in Spain, Germany, England, the USA and elsewhere. Most of the complete reproductions have numerous very distinct characteristics which will enable the collector to identify them as reproductions. These points are listed at the end of this chapter.

Much more insidious even that blatant reproductions is the long standing practice of embellishing very ordinary but perfectly genuine SA daggers to boost their market value. The types of embellishment can take a number of forms which can include any or all of the following practices: "minting" a dagger which entails polishing the wooden grips to a high sheen; cleaning or even replating the fittings; buffing the blade and refinishing the scabbard. This newly "minted" dagger can then be further enhanced by the addition of genuine Maker's or RZM tags which are readily available and can be purchased quite inexpensively. This may seem like a lot of trouble to take on a humble SA dagger, but a mint example will fetch twice as much (or more) than a middle of the road dagger, and virtually every collector is looking for a "mint" example of whatever he is collecting and is quite prepared to pay the price for it.

The next stage in embellishment is the addition of bogus inscriptions applied to the blade of an ordinary, but otherwise genuine SA dagger. These blade inscriptions take a wide variety of forms and can vary greatly in quality. They are usually executed in three main ways: by photo-etching, engraving or acid etching. Sport's Day presentation inscriptions are the most common and can sometimes be quite wordy and even elaborate, or they can just bear an individual's name. When encountering inscribed SA blades it is prudent to not only scrutinise the quality of the inscription but also its wording for many post-war applied inscriptions feature some really silly mistakes in them. Sometimes it is just the incorrect use of say "Der", "Die", "Das"; all three words have the same literal meaning but are frequently used for the wrong gender or tense. Also look for spelling mistakes: a prime example of this occurred to the author recently when being offered an Imperial German dress sidearm with a blade inscription. It was observed that the French spelling of the word "Roi" meaning "King" had actually been misspelt by a recent forger as "Roy" - this is obviously a case of a person spelling the word "Roi" phonetically. (French was frequently used in Imperial Germany as the diplomatic language of the court: the wording on the Blue Max "Pour le Merite" is just one instance of the use of French language on German militaria.) Although this example is Imperial rather than Nazi German, the same principle applies to Third Reich daggers. For this purpose of detecting wrongly spelt words a German/English dictionary is an absolute essential for the serious collector.

Embellishment is not restricted to the blade of SA daggers, but has also been encountered on the scabbard and its fittings, also the grip and its associated crossguard fittings. Runic symbols on the body of the scabbard have been observed and also a variety of engraving applied to the fittings of the dagger taking the form of oakleaves, acorns, laurel wreaths, swastikas, initials, names etc. An important fact to bear in mind is that there were a host of regulations governing every aspect of the SA dagger. The regulation which covered the use of inscriptions, etching, engraving etc. in brief stated that the SA dagger can be used as a presentation piece and have inscriptions applied to them; however the inscription whatever form it took had to be applied in such a way that under no circumstances should any part of the inscription be outwardly visible when the dagger was sheathed and being worn in the regulation fashion. Quite obviously this regulation precludes the use of engraving on the scabbard and visible fittings, hence the collector should draw his own conclusions when encountering external embellishments on any standard SA dagger.

1933 PATTERN SA DAGGER REPRODUCTIONS

In most instances the reproductions which will be encountered of the standard 1933 pattern SA dagger carry an RZM proofmark. This is true of both early German reproduction blades and the later Spanish reproductions. At the time these reproduction daggers were produced in the 1960's the market value of an original SA dagger was so low as to preclude the use of good quality materials or lengthy and costly techniques to make a reproduction. Consequently the majority of these blades tend to be of an inferior quality which would not pass close examination. In addition to the RZM proofmark the other characteristics shared by most of these early blades is the poor quality of the blade etching which is far too shallow, and is in most cases incorrectly positioned on the blade. A recurring characteristic of reproduction Party form daggers is a sharp central ridge on the blade. However this characteristic alone should not be used in isolation to determine authenticity of an SA or any other dagger: for it should be borne in mind that original specifications for the SA and SS daggers required a well defined central ridge, and that many of the craftsmen who produced the early genuine SA blades considered a pronounced central ridge to be the mark of a superior quality blade. Therefore a distinction should be made between a sharp central ridge which manifests itself as a line down the centre of the blade and a good quality genuine blade with a pronounced yet rounded central ridge.

RECOGNITION CHECKLIST

BLADE

- Etching of the SA motto is too shallow on many reproduction blades.
- Most reproductions of the standard SA dagger bear RZM proofmarks.
- Incorrect positioning of blade motto usually applied too low down the blade.

- A sharp central ridge on the blade is a common characteristic of reproductions. However this point requires close observation for many good quality original blades will also be encountered with a pronounced central spine.
- The word "Germany" on the blade ricasso or tang was only used on post WWII production daggers intended for export.
- The "B & A" proofmark on an SA blade indicates post-war manufacture.
- The most commonly used RZM M7 Maker's control numbers on reproductions are: M7/11; M7/33; M7/36; M7/66; M7/85; and M7/104. The latter control number has appeared on post-war parts assembly daggers.
- The RZM proofmark applied to the obverse ricasso is a feature found on some reproductions. The positioning of a proofmark was not practiced during the Third Reich period. RZM proofmarks were always applied to the reverse ricasso of genuine SA daggers.
- Poorly executed etching of the blade motto or proofmark showing areas of spotting where the etching is breaking up.
- A flat tang is indicative of modern reproductions, especially those emanating from Spain.
- The absence of billet clamp marks is a feature of many reproduction blades.
- On looking down the flat surface of a reproduction blade there is almost always a waviness which is rarely seen on good quality original blades.
- Some Spanish blades are extremely thin and have a very cheap looking plate applied over them. This plating also extends over the blade motto. This was never a feature of originals.
- Central spine slightly off centre.
- Poor fitting of blade to lower crossguard is a feature of some parts assembly daggers.
- A felt or leather blade washer is usually used to mask a badly fitting blade. The only genuine Party form daggers which legitimately had a blade washer were the NPEA dagger and some of the SA Honour daggers where the washers were used as a buffer pad to protect quality gilt fittings.
- Current reproduction German blades are slightly narrower at the top by approximately two millimetres.

SCABBARD

- The absence of scabbard liners is indicative of some reasonably good quality Spanish reproductions currently in circulation.
- Some Spanish reproductions have an oversize suspension ring which is also approximately 50% thinner than originals.
- The lower scabbard fitting on some reproductions has a very rounded appearance especially around the ball tip which has a much more ovoid shape than on originals.
- Long thin scabbard liners brazed into position. Original liners were wide and ribbed with a tongue shape at the base and were riveted into position on the throat attachment.
- Most of the upper scabbard fittings on Spanish reproductions are of one piece construction. Original fittings were always two piece: consisting of an outer locket and inner throat sleeve to which the liners were riveted.
- Virtually all reproduction scabbards are devoid of the lead tip former which was positioned on the inside tip of the scabbard and acted as a counter balance and a soft blade stop on originals. It should however be mentioned that some later examples of genuine SA daggers will also be encountered without the lead inner former sleeve.
- Generally speaking the top and bottom scabbard fittings should match the dagger fittings in their material composition i.e. being either all nickel silver or all nickel plated. A mixture of different fittings on the scabbard and dagger is indicative of parts assembly daggers and/or replacement

scabbards.

- Reproduction scabbards invariably have a painted finish which usually tends to be too brown instead of having the slightly reddish hue of genuine brown painted SA scabbards. Also reproduction scabbards have as yet not been encountered with the early (anodised) type of finish.

GRIP

- Plastic grips are only found on reproductions.
- Early Spanish reproductions used a stained softwood to make the grips which had a very coarse grained appearance totally dissimilar to original wooden grips.
- Incorrectly positioned eagle inlay which is usually mounted too high in the centre of the grip of reproductions. Originals were always positioned in line with the thickest part of the grip.
- Some early Spanish reproduction grips had a flat SA rune which was not enamelled. Originals were always enamelled.
- Small gaps around the eagle and rune grip inlays are indicative of some reproductions and also modern replacement grips.
- Some Spanish reproductions feature an eagle inlay of completely incorrect form having an eagle with square wings and tapered wingtips.
- Some modern eagle inlays have an eagle with a cone shaped head and a large hooked beak.
- On some reproduction eagle inlays the swastika is oversized and too thick having a flat appearance. Also the detail on the edges of the swastika legs is very poor with the end section of the bottom leg missing on some examples observed.
- Some post-war grips produced in Germany have extremely sharp edges in the area of the central ridge and the upper and lower "V" shape of the grips.
- A distinct feature of many reproduction grips is that the upper and lower necks of the grip are of virtually the same diameter giving the grip a far too symmetrical appearance. Original grips always had a thinner upper neck with the bottom neck being considerably broader: designed to fit snugly into a clenched hand to compliment the contours of the natural grip of the hand which is broader at the top and narrower at the bottom.
- The tang locking nut on many reproductions are of incorrect size. The two main types observed are a thin flat button with a very narrow nut section. The second type has a very thick flat button also with a narrow nut section. Although there was some variation in locking nuts on original SA daggers, their form was always quite similar. A consistent feature of reproductions is the flat topped button whereas originals invariably had a slightly domed top.
- A further characteristic of tang locking nuts on reproductions is the depth of the screw socket on the nut which tends to be considerably shorter on most reproductions.
- Significant gaps between the upper and/or lower grip and the metal fittings is indicative of either poor quality reproductions or mismatched parts assembly daggers.
- The underside of the crossguard has a gauged out trench on some part assembly daggers to facilitate a superficially snug blade to crossguard fit.

HANGERS

Some reproductions especially the current German examples feature the short SA style hanging strap. However these are of very inferior quality even when compared to some late poor quality genuine hangers. The leather tends to be very thin and machine stitched with narrow thread. The buckle and belt clip are usually nickel plated iron rather than nickel silver which was the material composition of most original fittings. The belt catch has a very narrow end and is triangular shaped: the catch also tends to be considerably flatter than originals were.

As previously indicated the vast majority of reproduction SA daggers tend to exhibit the RZM proofmark with various M7 Maker's control numbers. However actual Maker's proofmarks have been encountered including those of Tiger, E P & S, F W Holler, and Eickhorn. In most instances these Maker's proofmarks were very badly etched, and in some cases of incorrect form. The RZM proofmark has been observed appearing on the obverse blade ricasso just above the SA motto. This was never an approved positioning for the RZM proofmark or any other Maker for that matter. Proofmarks on genuine SA daggers were always applied to the reverse ricasso of the blade. Consequently proofmarks of any type applied to the obverse of the blade of any SA dagger are spurious and should be regarded as reproductions. The most frequently encountered RZM M7 control numbers on reproduction SA blades are the following: RZM M7/11; M7/33; M7/36; M7/66; M7/85 and M7/104.

N.B. Double proofmarks will be encountered on some SA daggers, having a Maker and RZM proofmark. This configuration of proofmarks is perfectly legitimate and usually indicates that the dagger was a special purchase item produced after 1935. Although of later manufacture these double proofmarked SA daggers were usually of a better quality than their RZM contemporaries and would often feature early 1930's style nickel silver fittings.

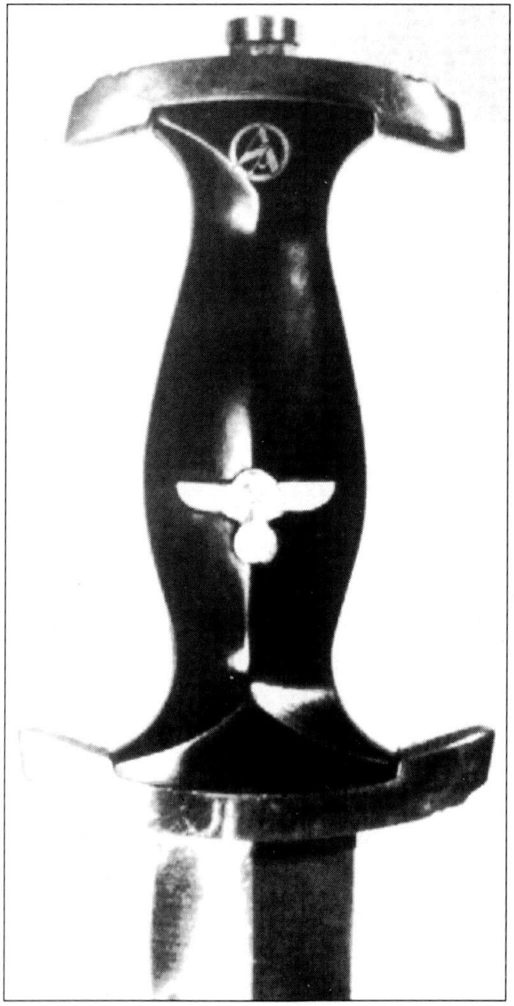

The post-war "B A" parts assembly SA dagger. Note the sharp central ridge of the blade and the loose fit of the grip insignia.

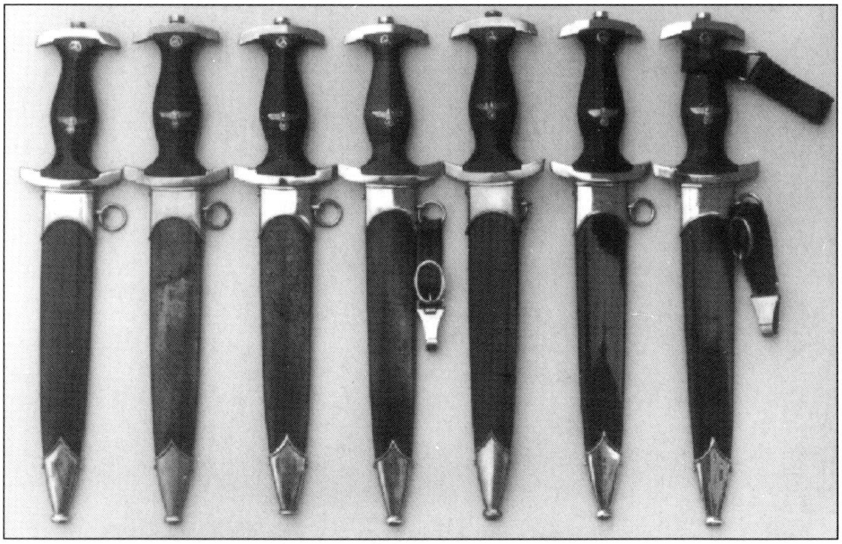

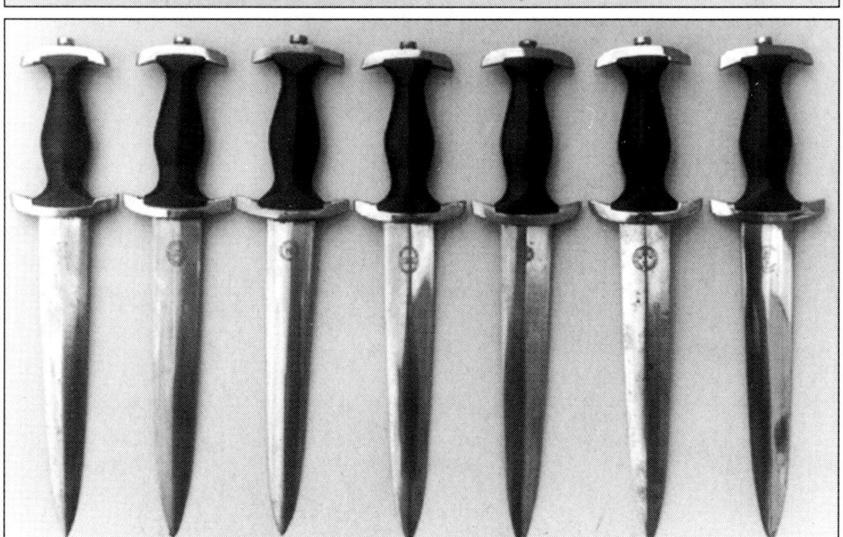

These three photographs picture different aspects of seven genuine SA daggers. The daggers were all produced between 1933 and 1936 by a variety of Solingen dagger Makers and graphically illustrate the diversity of genuine SA daggers. The daggers vary in overall length, scabbard length, grip size, composition and size of fittings etc. It is probably true to say that no two Makers produced a dagger with the exact same specifications prior to 1934. This lack of uniformity was somewhat regulated following the introduction of RZM controls in late 1934. Due to the disparity in the specifications of genuine SA daggers it is not possible to give an absolute dimension for genuine examples of this dagger.

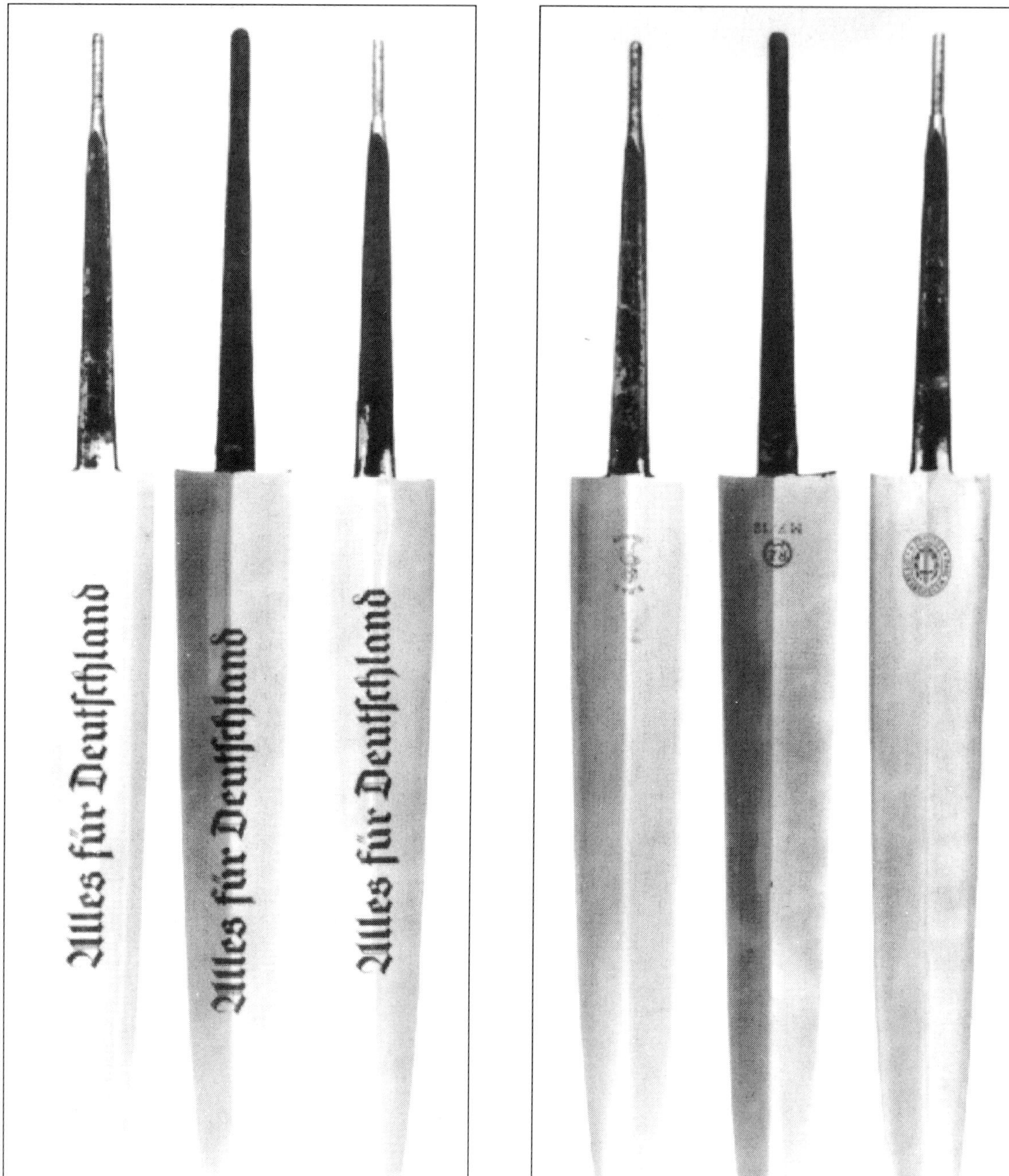

Three different reproduction SA dagger blades. These Solingen made blades are drop forged and finished to a very high standard. All three examples exhibit different styles of blade motto and a variety of Maker and RZM proofmarks.

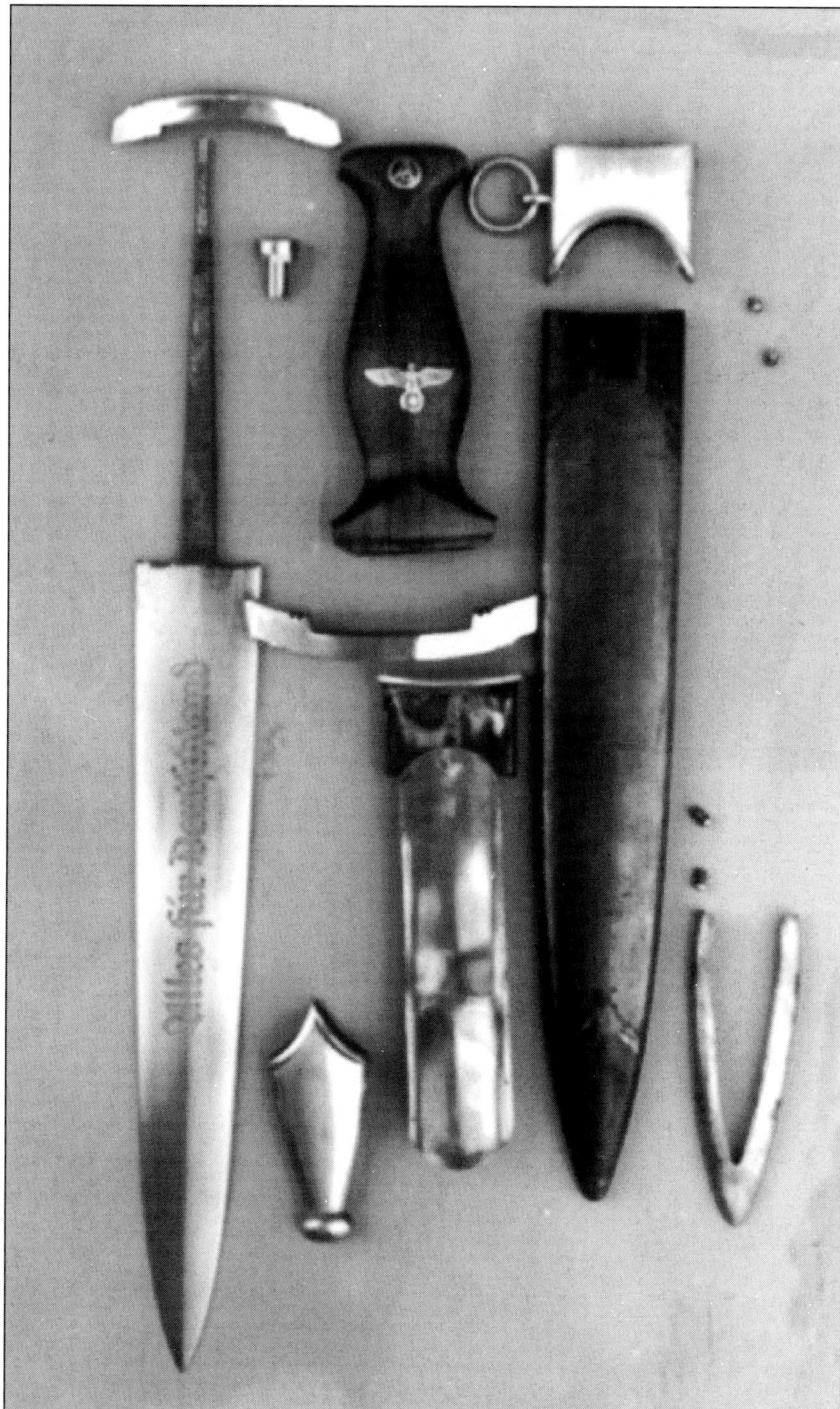

Disassembled view of a genuine SA dagger showing all the component parts which made up a genuine 1933 pattern SA dagger.

SA ROHM HONOUR DAGGER

In 1934 a special honour dagger was instituted for serving SA personnel who were SA members prior to December 31st, 1931. This dagger is identical in every respect to the standard 1933 pattern SA dagger with the exception of an inscription etched onto the reverse side of the blade. This inscription took the form of a dedication in the hand writing of Ernst Rohm, Chief of Staff of the SA, and read "IN HERZLICHER FREUNDSCHAFT ERNST ROHM" (IN HEARTFELT COMRADESHIP, ERNST ROHM).

135,860 Rohm daggers were awarded. This figure included 9,900 members of the SS who had been members of the SA within the qualifying period. Within months of this dagger appearing Ernst Rohm fell from grace with Adolf Hitler and was murdered along with hundreds of other high SA officials in "The Night of the Long Knives". Following the massacre of June 30th, 1934 all vestiges of Rohm's tenure as SA Chief were expunged including the dagger bearing his name.

SA members who had been awarded the Rohm dagger were ordered to replace the weapon with a standard 1933 model dagger. This order has led to many different variations of the 1934 "Rohm" dagger surviving. A very small number of daggers still exist bearing the full Rohm inscription. The daggers which have had the inscription erased come in a variety of forms. Some inscriptions were crudely ground off by individual SA members either erasing the whole inscription or just Ernst Rohm's name. Another option was to have the inscription totally or partially erased by a professional cutler. Due to the erasure of the inscription being left up to the individual SA member, three different types of Rohm daggers now survive: FULL INSCRIPTION, PARTIAL INSCRIPTION, FULLY ERASED. Each of these types of dagger has a different value.

The Rohm dagger was manufactured by several dagger Makers, however the most frequently encountered Maker on this particular SA dagger is E.P. and S. (ERNST PACK and SOHN): though the Makers proofmark has sometimes been obliterated along with the erased Rohm inscription.

Although this dagger is identical to the standard SA dagger most Rohm daggers appear to feature a very light brown wooden grip.

As previously noted there are three different prices for the different types of Rohm dagger ascending in value from the fully erased to the full inscription dagger which in today's market commands a premium price. This high price tag for what is after all just a standard 1933 pattern SA dagger has prompted the less scrupulous elements of the collecting/dealer fraternity to apply bogus Rohm inscriptions on to standard plain blade daggers.

SA ROHM HONOUR DAGGER REPRODUCTIONS

The Rohm Honour dagger has been reproduced in its entirety, and the characteristics of these reproductions are virtually the same as those for the standard SA dagger merely with the addition of the Ernst Rohm blade dedication. The aspect of the Rohm dagger which should be of paramount concern to the collector is not the blatant reproduction but the use of fake blade dedications on otherwise genuine SA daggers.

There are a number of ways to approach the subject of fake Rohm daggers: the most obvious being to identify the actual fake dedication. However the quality of many of the current etched blade dedications is so good as to be virtually impossible to detect. One particular batch of etched blades currently coming out of Germany have allegedly been acid etched from an original template. Therefore bearing in mind the sophistication of these current dedicated blades a number of other factors need to be added into the equation when trying to assess the authenticity of any Rohm Honour dagger.

There are two principle methods used to fabricate a fake Rohm dagger: the first is to substitute a currently produced Solingen etched blade for the blade of an ordinary but otherwise genuine SA dagger. The second method of fabrication is to have the blade of an ordinary genuine SA dagger acid etched with the Rohm dedication. Where a modern good quality Rohm dedicated blade has been used it is necessary to closely observe every other part of the dagger and not just be blinded by the Rohm inscription. It should be determined that the fittings of the dagger are of a contemporary period with the original Rohm Honour dagger i.e. early 1934. In this period virtually all SA daggers had nickel silver fittings and the anodised finished scabbards. If the Rohm blade is married to fittings which are obviously of a later vintage, being the plated type found on RZM period SA daggers, then it is reasonably safe to assume that the blade does not belong with the rest of the dagger fittings and is a modern substitution. A further means of identifying a substituted Rohm blade is to closely observe the way the blade fits into the lower crossguard, and just as important how well the blade fits into the scabbard: as most collectors will know scabbards and blades from different Makers of SA daggers rarely fit together properly when mixed. This can manifest itself in several ways: by the dagger having too tight a fit in the scabbard, being too loose in the scabbard, or being unable to push the blade home fully into the scabbard allowing a small gap between the scabbard throat and crossguard. There is little doubt that as more of these good quality fake Rohm blades find their way onto the market that this type of fabrication will become more widespread. However up until recently the most prevalent type of fake Rohm Honour dagger is the second type mentioned with a modern acid etched dedication being applied to a genuine Third Reich era SA dagger.

Fake acid etched Rohm dedications applied to the genuine SA dagger blades have been around for many years, and the quality of the fabrication has improved markedly over the years to a point where they are now extremely difficult to detect. It is estimated that something in the region of four out of five Rohm daggers in circulation and in collections are genuine daggers with fake dedications. Due to the quality of these fake dedications it is necessary for the collector to be aware of a number of basic facts about the Rohm Honour dagger which do not necessarily pertain to the actual dedications. The number of dagger Makers who actually produced the Rohm Honour dagger was quite limited, and the names of these known Makers will be provided at the end of this section. Eliminating an inappropriate Maker is only one of many means which can aid in detecting a fake Rohm dagger. Probably the most blatant mistake made by the faker is to use a genuine SA dagger bearing an RZM proofmark to which a modern spurious Rohm dedication is added. This was totally inappropriate as RZM regulations governing issue of any SS dagger did not come into force until quite some time after Ernst Rohm was murdered! This RZM connection is an example frequently quoted as a means of identifying fake Rohm daggers; however this obvious mistake is not one which will be regularly encountered and is an oversight long ago rectified by the fakers.

There are more subtle means of identifying fake Rohm daggers. One relates to which type or period of Maker's proofmark appears on the dagger blade. This is especially true of the Carl Eickhorn proofmark which on genuine Rohm daggers is of the early squirrel within an oval proofmark: whereas some genuine SA daggers made by Eickhorn with the later proofmark have been observed bearing fake Rohm blade inscriptions. These examples are given to expand the possibilities for detecting fake Rohm daggers, but probably the most telling comment in view of the seemingly large number of Rohm daggers currently on the market is that they could not possibly all be genuine examples: for there were undoubtedly very few staunch followers of Ernst Rohm who would have been prepared to retain the full inscription on their SA dagger after it was ordered to be erased following Rohm's murder and who would risk the severe penalties for disregarding the erasure order.

Experience shows that Ernst Pack was the most prolific producer of Rohm Honour daggers, and of the handful of known Makers of this dagger Pack is the only manufacturer who would appear to have made any outward distinction on the Rohm dagger in order to distinguish it from a regular SA dagger. The prominent feature of a Rohm dagger made by Pack is the grip; on virtually every genuine Rohm dagger observed the wooden grip is a different shade of brown to that found on regular SA daggers: being much lighter brown and not having the same reddish hue. This anomaly enables one to usually be able to identify a Pack manufactured Rohm dagger even when in its scabbard. There has always been a ready acceptance by collectors of Rohm Honour daggers bearing the Ernst Pack "E P & S" proofmark. However some caution should be exercised even with the Pack dagger, for fakers who are aware of this acceptability frequently use ordinary but genuine Pack SA daggers with the ("E P & S") proofmark as a home to place a spurious Rohm blade dedication knowing it will arouse less suspicion than other Makers. The more knowledgeable fakers will even go so far as to replace the ordinary grip with one from an erased (and consequently less valuable) Rohm dagger made by Pack thus completing a very believable combination.

A common explanation often given in support of a Rohm dedicated blade which perhaps does not look 100% correct is that it is "a Maker's variation". Although this statement does have some basis in fact it probably only accounts for an insignificant number of so called "variations". The only way in which a variation would be acceptable is perhaps in the depth or positioning of the etched dedication: for although the Rohm Honour dagger was produced by several different Makers the actual character and style of the dedication was identical in every detail irrespective of the Maker. This is due to the fact that the blade dedication is an exact facsimile of the handwriting and signature of Ernst Rohm, and a copy of this dedication was provided in template form to each of the approved manufacturers. Bearing this in mind there is absolutely no scope whatsoever for even minor deviations from the original Rohm dedication: such as different strokes on the letters or a rounded form of script instead of the correct angular handwriting style of Ernst Rohm. The rounded form and misplaced strokes are characteristic of many of the post-war dedications which have been spuriously added to otherwise genuine SA daggers.

The Rohm Honour dagger has been the subject of reproduction and faking for many years. They range in quality from the blatant Spanish reproductions to superb quality Solingen made Rohm inscribed blades which are currently available. Many Rohm daggers are genuine standard SA daggers which have had a bogus Rohm inscription applied usually by acid etching although examples have been observed where the inscription has been hand engraved, a process which was never used on original Rohm daggers. The quality of etching on many acid etched Rohm daggers is quite good and of a quality that would pass most inspections. However the inscriptions are often applied to inappropriate daggers of late production with blades bearing RZM proofmarks. This type of blade is totally inappropriate for RZM regulations were not yet in force when the Rohm dagger was first awarded. Poorly applied etching of the inscription and also its incorrect positioning on the blade is another indicator: others are listed at the end of this chapter.

SA Honour and High Leader's daggers appear on the market in a number of forms. The easiest by far to detect are the Spanish reproductions which are extremely bright and gaudy and would not pass even the most rudimentary inspection as an original. Spanish examples of this dagger have also been encountered with the Rohm inscription on the reverse of the blade which was totally inappropriate for this type of dagger. Good quality reproductions of the High Leader's dagger are currently in circulation, many with Solingen made blades. The quality of the crossguard fittings varies and can be brass castings which have been silver plated or alternatively ordinary but genuine SA crossguards which have been used with engraving applied to stimulate the appearance of the High Leader's dagger crossguard. Similarly scabbard fittings are embellished with decoration either cast or engraved. In some instances the centre panel of the scabbard is left with a brown painted finish, or alternatively simulated leather is used to give the superficial appearance of originals.

The chains used to suspend the 1938 High Leader's dagger have also been reproduced in various qualities. There are also examples which are just pure invention.

As can be judged at the end of this chapter the number of different characteristics to be observed on the various types of reproduction SA dagger is quite bewildering. Consequently each type of dagger has been dealt with separately: although some characteristics are the same on several dagger types which does cause some repetition, but which was deemed necessary for clarification of the points.

In addition to the full Rohm inscription there are two other categories of genuine Rohm Honour dagger: the partial inscription which has the Ernst Rohm signature removed, and the fully erased inscription. Both of these types of dedication have a higher market value than just a plain ordinary SA dagger: this is especially true of the partially erased Rohm dagger. The increased values of these types of

Rohm dagger are obviously nowhere near that of a fully inscribed blade. However there are a couple of minor underhanded practices which are carried out to squeeze that extra little bit higher price out of an ordinary but genuine SA dagger. Genuine SA daggers have been observed with spurious Rohm dedications applied to their reverse side and then having the "Ernst Rohm" portion of the inscription ground or polished off to simulate the original erasing technique. This practice has the effect of increasing the value without arousing the same kind of suspicion and close inspection that a full Rohm inscription would attract. The other type of practice used to simulate the appearance of a former Rohm dedicated dagger is to lightly grind or polish the reverse of the plain genuine blade to give the suggestion that this is a fully erased former Rohm dagger.

In seeking to detect reproduction Rohm Honour daggers most of the points which pertain to the standard SA dagger should be applied to the Rohm dagger also. Consequently these points have not been repeated in this section. The main emphasis for the points to observe on the Rohm dagger are principally directed towards identifying dedications spuriously applied to ordinary unetched but otherwise genuine SA daggers.

RECOGNITION CHECKLIST

BLADE

- ➢ The use of an RZM proofmark is not appropriate on any genuine Rohm Honour dagger.
- ➢ The letters within the blade dedication being too thickly formed is a characteristic of some reproductions.
- ➢ The use of engraving to execute the dedication is a style only used on spurious inscriptions. Genuinely inscribed blades were always acid etched.
- ➢ The dedication should always be clearly and sharply applied and should not show any areas where there are any breaks in the letters.
- ➢ Some good quality currently produced blades from Germany not only have a spurious dedication but also an "E P & S" proofmark which is a forgery. It is oversized with spidery letters of inconsistent form and a very poorly defined figure within the proofmark.
- ➢ Dedications applied to the blade either uneven or at an angle: originals were always applied up the centre of the blade.
- ➢ Dedications applied too low down the blade. This usually occurs because the original proofmark has been applied lower down the blade. The proofmark on virtually all original Rohm daggers was applied very high on the ricasso close to the crossguard in order to accommodate the blade inscription.
- ➢ Some reproduction Rohm daggers produced in Spain have the characteristic sharp central spine which appears to cut the dedication in half.

SCABBARD

- ➢ The scabbards used on original Rohm Honour daggers had the solid nickel fittings rather than the later plated type.
- ➢ See also recognition checklist on 1933 pattern SA reproductions.
- ➢ Genuine Rohm scabbards invariably feature an anodised finish.

GRIP

- ➢ Grips on the Rohm Honour dagger were always of wood never plastic.
- ➢ The grips of the majority of genuine E P & S Rohm daggers tend to be a lighter shade of brown than normal.
- ➢ See also recognition checklist on 1933 pattern SA reproductions.

SA Rohm Honour daggers always carried a Maker's proofmark. No genuine examples have been encountered with a complete inscription minus a Maker's proofmark. However Rohm daggers with partial or fully erased inscriptions will be encountered without a Maker's proofmark. This is due to the proofmark being erased along with the Rohm inscription. There are in total 8 known documented Makers of genuine Rohm Honour daggers which are as follows: Ernst Pack & Sohne (E P & S); Carl Eickhorn; Richard Herder; Gottlieb Hammesfahr; J A Henckels; C G Haenal; Anton Wingen; and Eduard Wusthof.

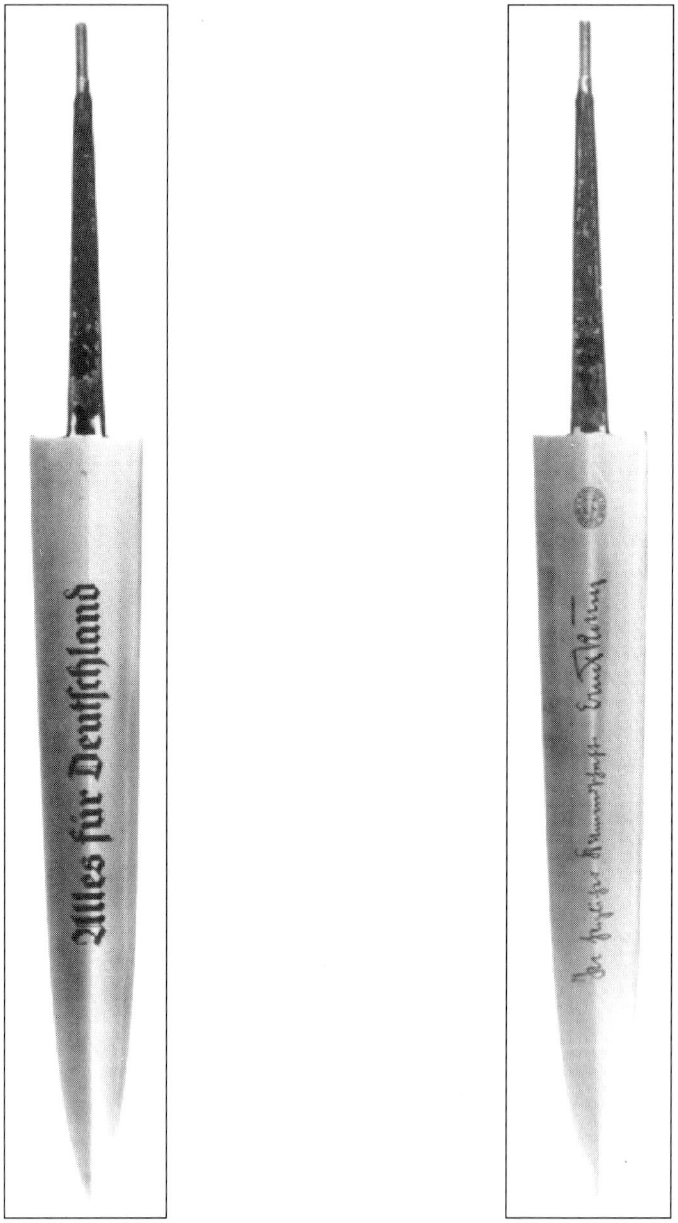

A reproduction Rohm Honour dagger blade currently being manufactured in Solingen using original templates for the SA motto and Rohm inscription. These reproduction blades bear the oval proofmark of Carl Eickhorn, although this proofmark will be encountered on genuine Rohm daggers it is positioned further away from the crossguard than original examples.

Two genuine SA Rohm dagger blades. Both blades are by E.P. & S who was the principal Maker of this dagger. The top example has a partial inscription with Ernst Rohm's name only erased. On the bottom is a fully erased Rohm inscription.

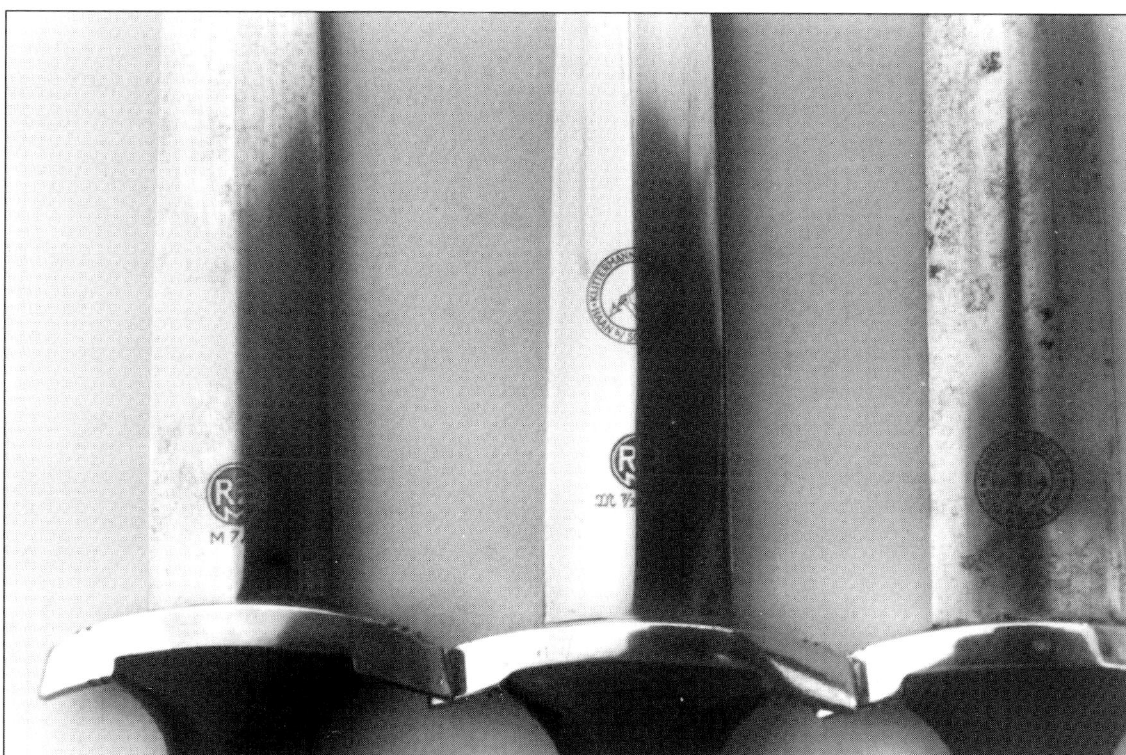

Three genuine SA daggers showing the proofmarks on the reverse blade. On the left is an RZM proofmark applied to genuine SA blades produced after 1935. The blade on the right was produced prior to 1935 and bears the Maker's proofmark. The dagger in the centre displays both the RZM and Maker's proofmark, indicating it was a private purchase item produced after 1935.

1935 SA HONOUR DAGGER REPRODUCTIONS

Reproductions of the 1935 pattern SA Honour dagger have been on the market for over thirty years. The examples manufactured in Spain which are still currently available are extremely attractive and decorative display pieces, but upon close inspection lack the fine detail and superb workmanship of originals. There is a good quality Honour dagger which has been manufactured in Germany since the late 1960's which is of a high enough quality to require very close scrutiny. Characteristics of this and the Spanish reproductions will be listed in this section.

Original SA Honour daggers although being basically the same did have some slight variations in style, and were available with both plain and Damascus blades. However one of the Spanish reproductions Honour daggers which has been on the market for some time features a variation which was never used on any original 1935 Honour dagger. This takes the form of a spurious Rohm inscription which is applied to the reverse blade, and as the original examples of this dagger post dated Ernst Rohm's tenure of office by between one and four years there is no conceivable justification for this type of inscription being applied to any genuine post-1935 Honour dagger.

A common feature of many reproduction Honour daggers of Spanish origin is the use of an RZM proofmark on the blade. Although RZM regulations were in force at the time original Honour daggers were produced and RZM regulations did apply to the SA Honour dagger, the RZM proofmark was not applied to the blade of the 1935 pattern Honour dagger. This anomaly was due to the fact that the Honour dagger was a special purchase item which was awarded rather than issued. This technically put it outside of RZM regulations thus allowing the manufacturer of the dagger to apply his own proofmark whether it was acid etched on a plain blade or in gold relief on a Damascus blade.

Due to there being no special hangers or other accoutrements on genuine SA Honour daggers there has always been plenty of scope for embellishing the crossguards and scabbard fittings of ordinary but otherwise genuine SA daggers in order to give them a superficial appearance of being an Honour dagger. In most cases these daggers with embellished fittings tend to have a plain blade just bearing the acid etched "Alles fur Deutschland" motto and do not usually have Damascus blades. These embellished daggers also invariably feature a standard SA brown painted steel scabbard rather than being leather covered.

In addition to reproduction and embellished Honour daggers there have also been Honour dagger crossguards reproduced which were intended to substitute the fittings of a genuine standard SA dagger to give it the appearance of being a 1935 pattern Honour dagger. These fittings have been encountered in several styles: some of which never actually appeared on any genuine Honour dagger - the most striking being a floral design. The quality and material composition of these replacement fittings are quite diverse ranging from the above mentioned floral type which were superbly cast and silver-plated. Other examples of an inferior quality have been encountered made from plated zinc and even the soft lead alloy used to make the poorer quality Nazi badges.

Scabbards of SA Honour daggers always require close inspection. Original examples could be either brown painted steel with a thin brown leather covering. Reproduction scabbards have been produced in both these styles and will be encountered both with and without decorated scabbard fittings. There have also been examples of ordinary but genuine SA scabbards being covered in genuine or simulated leather. However these usually display two telltale characteristics: either bunching of the leather around the upper and lower fittings where the material has not been fitted flush under the lockets, or a slightly raised open end to each fitting where the edges of the lockets have been slightly flared to enable the material to be accommodated under the fittings. Neither of these examples was ever characteristic of original SA Honour daggers.

RECOGNITION CHECKLIST

The reproduction characteristics to observe on the 1935 SA Honour dagger are virtually the same as those for the standard 1933 SA dagger with the following additions:

BLADE

- The RZM proofmark should not appear on any genuine Honour dagger.
- A Rohm inscription on the reverse blade is only found on reproduction Honour daggers.
- Reproduction Honour daggers have the blade motto etched too shallow.
- On reproductions with simulated Damascus blades featuring a gold blade motto with an oakleaf at each end, the motto and bottom oakleaf are applied too close to the tip of the blade.
- On reproductions with plain blades the motto is often applied too high up the blade, close to the lower crossguard.
- The only form of decoration which should appear on the blade of an Honour dagger is a gold "Alles fur Deutschland" motto decorated at each end with a gold oakleaf, and this should only be on a Damascus style blade. Any other form of blade ornamentation such as a bust of Adolf Hitler or Hermann Goering's Aunt Helga should be rejected as a totally counterfeit post-war fantasy!

SCABBARD

- Scabbard fittings which have been engraved should be viewed with suspicion. Original fittings were always die struck.
- Decorated scabbard fittings on the Honour dagger were made as an integral part of the scabbard with the decoration being die embossed. The only separate piece on a genuine scabbard should be the throat liner insert.
- Reproductions with decorated fittings have the top and bottom locket placed on the scabbard as separate pieces and held into position with two screws each. Originals have no screws on the bottom fitting and two on the top fitting to hold the throat insert in place.
- Genuine scabbards with separate plain fittings should have a painted scabbard.
- Genuine scabbards with decorated fittings should have a leather covering. This leather should be fitted around the upper and lower fittings and not underneath.
- Scabbards with ornately engraved patterns in the centre panels are a post-war embellishment. Other types of spurious embellishments include the addition of runic symbols, swastikas, and other types of Nordic or Nazi symbolism. Strict SA regulations governed the type of inscriptions or decorations which could be applied to a dagger, and a regulation did specifically forbid the use of any unauthorised outward decoration on the dagger.

GRIP

- The decoration on the crossguards of Honour daggers was always cast in high relief. Genuine crossguards were never engraved to achieve the oakleaf decoration effect. This engraved style is indicative of post-war embellishments.
- Post-war engraved crossguards always appear to be too small: often giving a slight overhang on the edges of the grip.
- Casting seams on the crossguard either across the front or on the top of each arm are a feature of reproductions.
- The grooves on the crossguard are very shallow and poorly defined on many reproductions, and on some examples the underside grooves on the lower crossguard are totally absent.
- A floral pattern with a cast or engraved design is a feature of some reproductions. The floral design never featured on original SA Honour daggers.

- Very poor detail on the oakleaves and acorns which on originals were always exceptionally well defined.
- Very narrow crossguards with a thin single row of oakleaves is a characteristic of replacement cast grips. These grips are approximately 1/3 narrower than originals.
- Fittings with a garish looking gold finish are a feature of a Spanish reproduction dagger which has been on the market since the 1970's.

A genuine SA Honour dagger taken from the 1937 Eickhorn Kundendienst. Note the style of the crossguard decoration, and the plain edging lines around the top and bottom scabbard fittings. The scabbard has the Eickhorn authenticity seal attached.

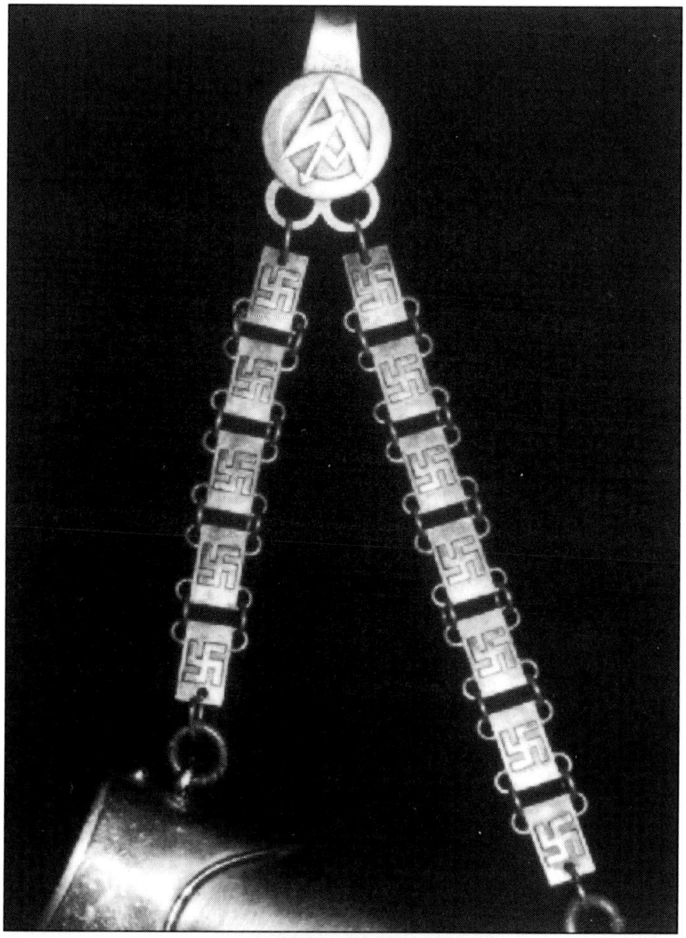

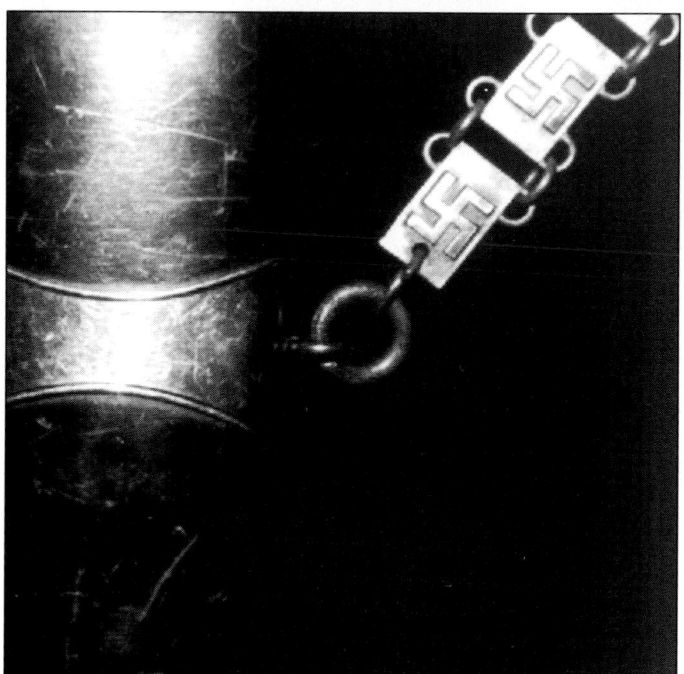

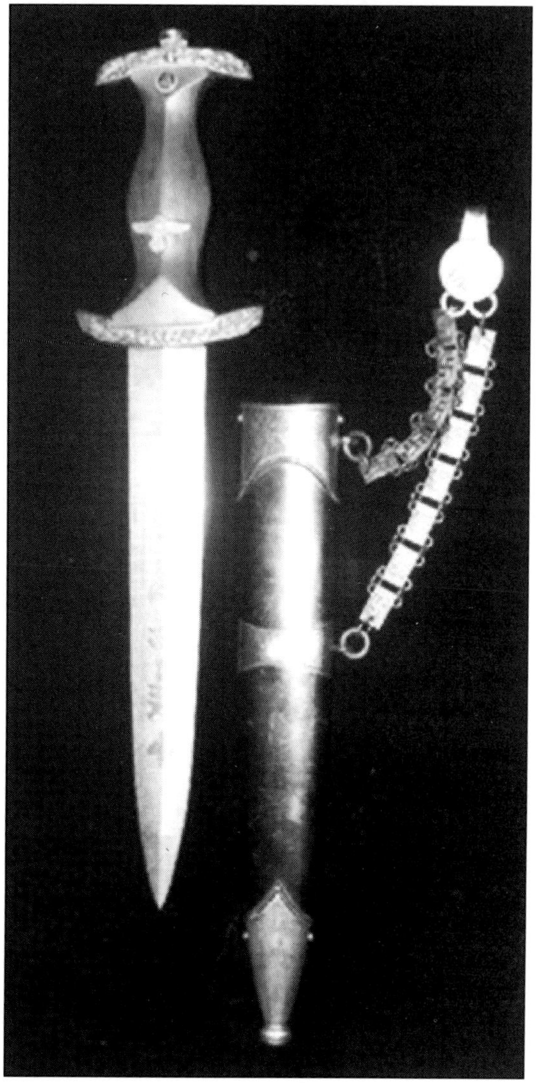

Three different views of a reproduction SS High Leader's dagger, believed to have been produced in Germany. Although the actual form of the scabbard is quite good, the quality of the hanging chains is poor, having thin wire loops to interlock the links, instead of H-shaped bars. The dagger with artificial Damascus blade is quite attractive however it is let down by the badly positioned grip eagle inlay and the engraved crossguards.

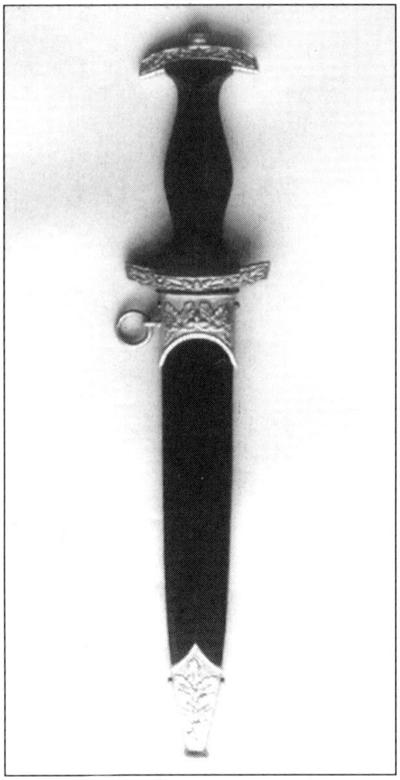

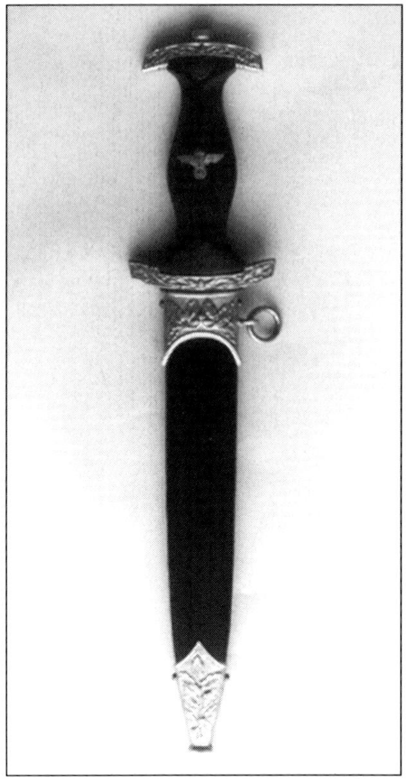

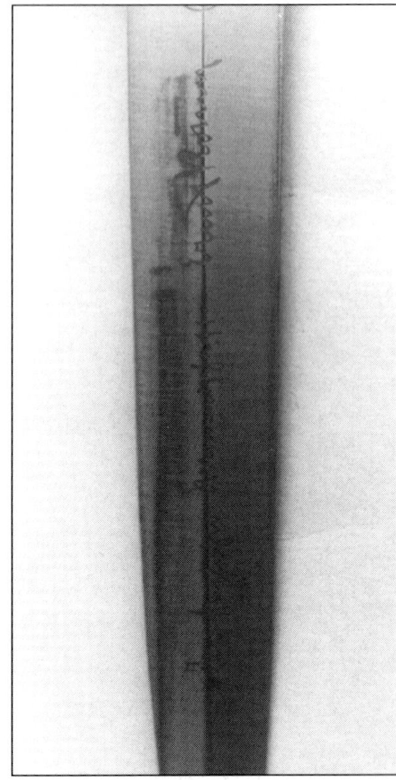

Six different views of a Spanish reproduction SA Honour dagger. Note the usual Spanish quality blade with a matt grey finish, and the poorly executed blade motto and proofmark. Also the Rohm inscription was not appropriate for this dagger.

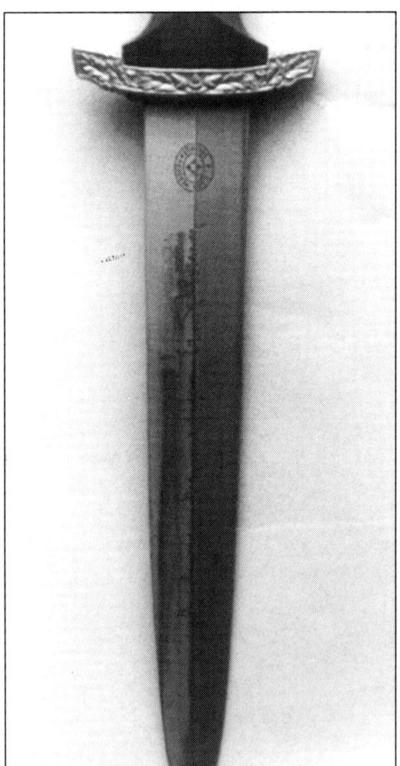

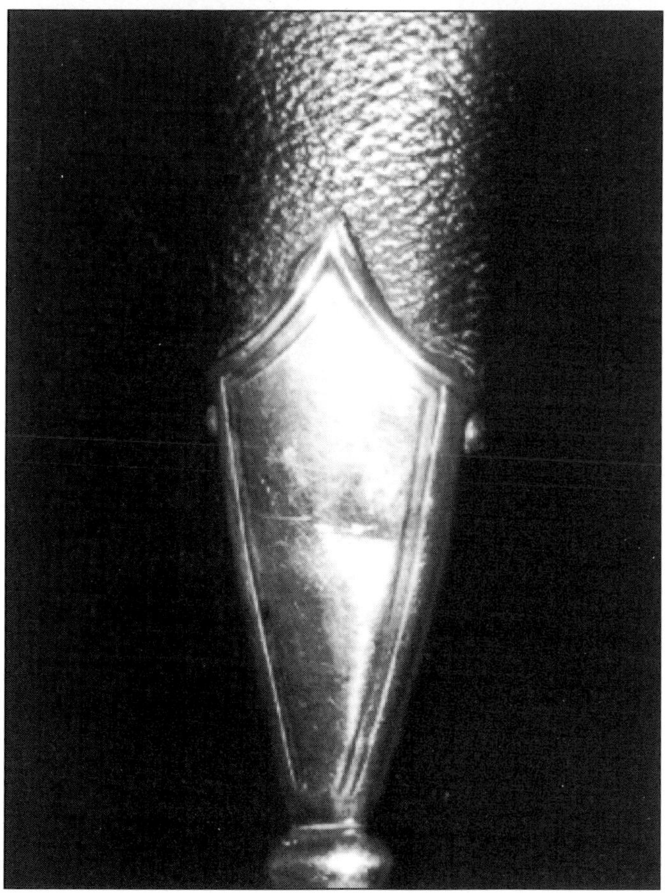

These photographs give a comparison between a genuine SA dagger scabbard and an embellished scabbard masquerading as an SA Honour dagger scabbard. The leather covered "Honour" scabbard is an ordinary SA scabbard which has been decorated and covered in leather. Note the bunching around the rim of the scabbard fittings.

Obverse and reverse sides of two different types or reproduction artificial Damascus blade. The example on the left is an SA Damascus blade with the SA motto on the obverse in gold highlights. The reverse bears the Ernst Rohm dedication - this style of blade was not normally a feature of genuine Rohm Honour daggers. The example on the right is a reproduction SA Honour blade, similar to the left example but without the Rohm dedication. These blades are currently produced in Solingen to a very high standard.

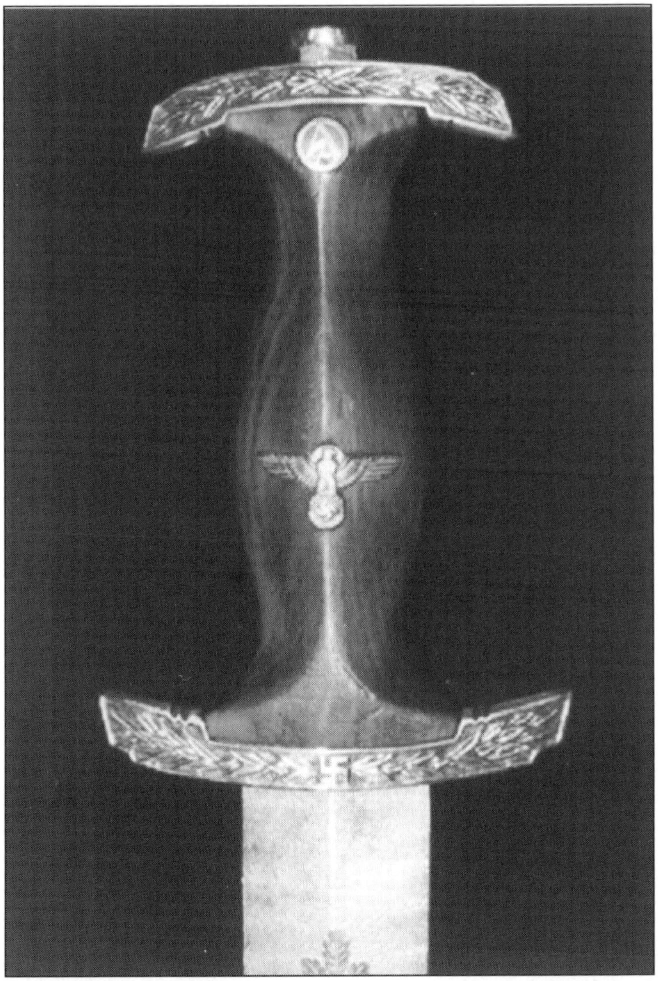

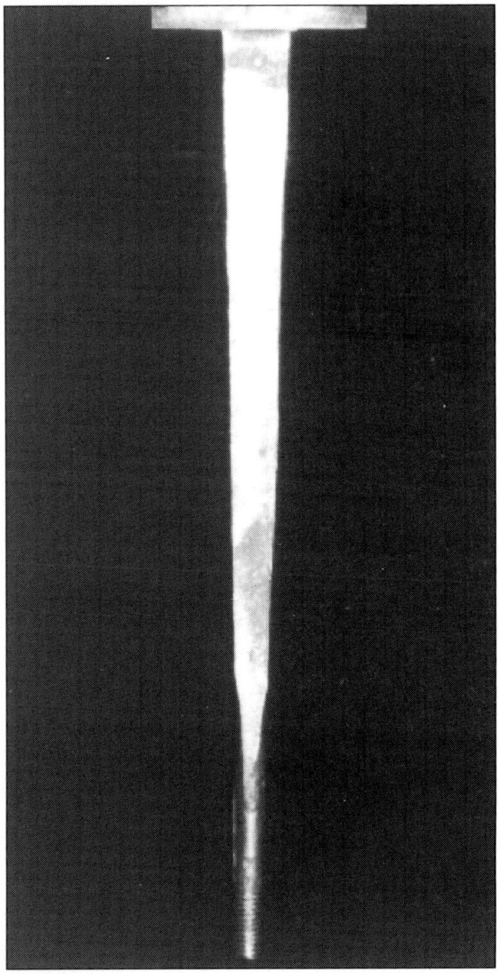

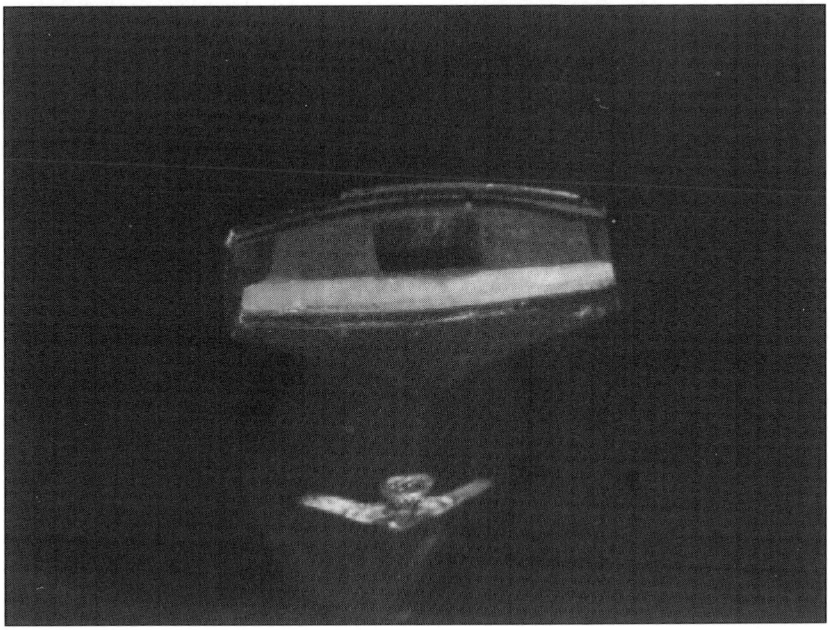

Three close-up views of a reproduction SA presentation dagger. Note that the blade on this piece is narrower than normal, as is the grip. The grip eagle inlay is incorrectly mounted and is also undersize, having very narrow wings. Note the engraved crossguard decoration which features a swastika in the centre of the lower crossguard, this was never a feature on original crossguards. The close-up picture shows where the inside of the grip has been filed to accommodate the bogus crossguard.

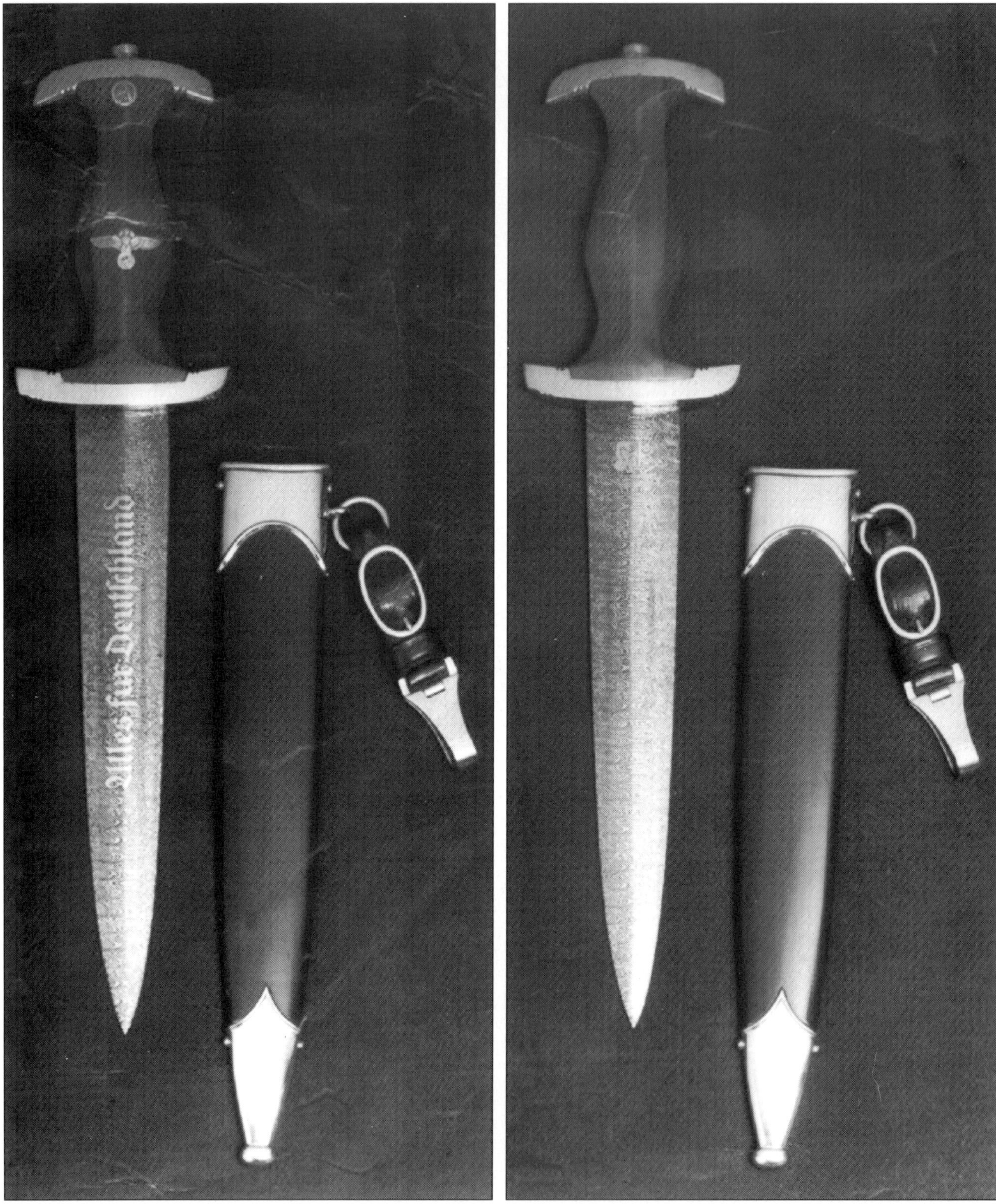

This SA presentation dagger is a superb example of a parts assembly fabrication using genuine SA dagger parts married to a modern reproduction artificial Damascus blade.

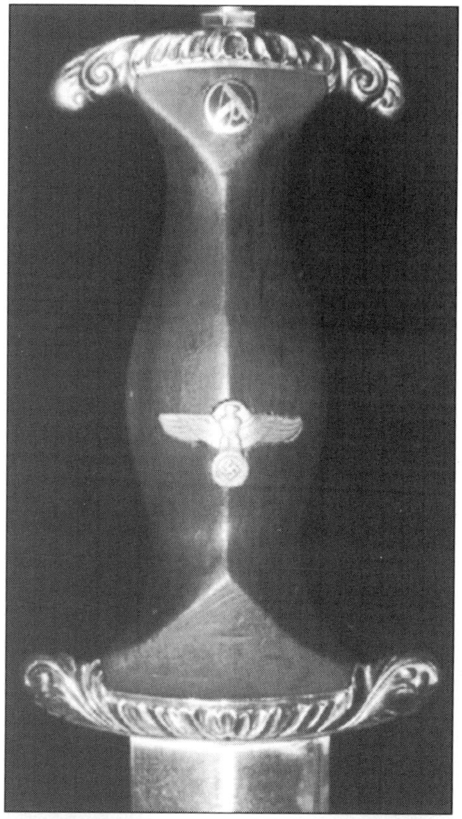

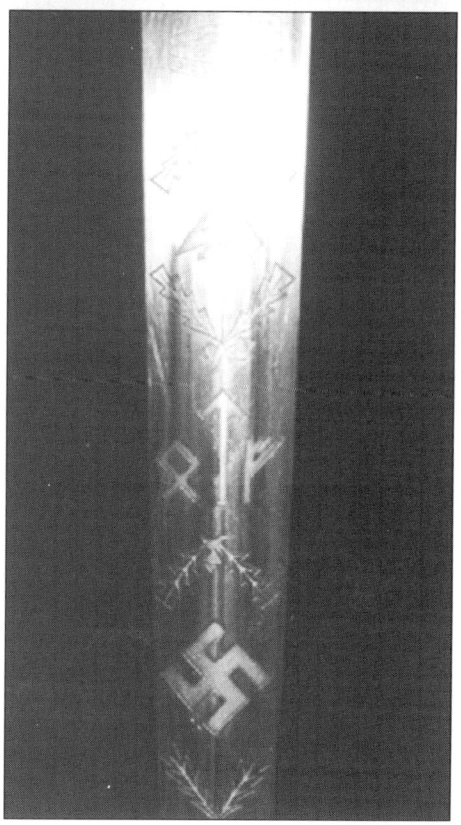

Three different views of a genuine SA dagger, which has been embellished in the post-war era, to give it the appearance of a presentation dagger. Note the floral decoration on the crossguards, which has been engraved rather than cast as originals were. Also, the blade has been extensively decorated with numerous Nazi and runic symbols, all of which are completely bogus.

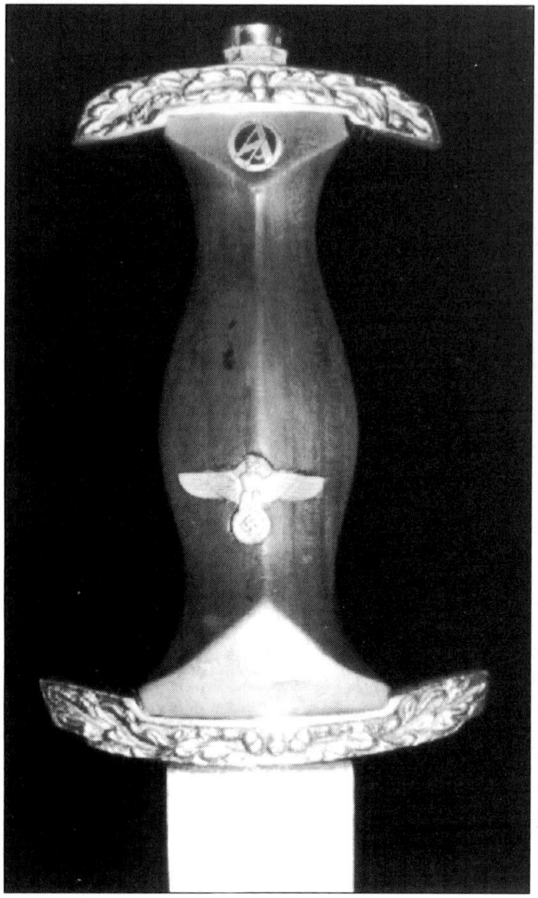

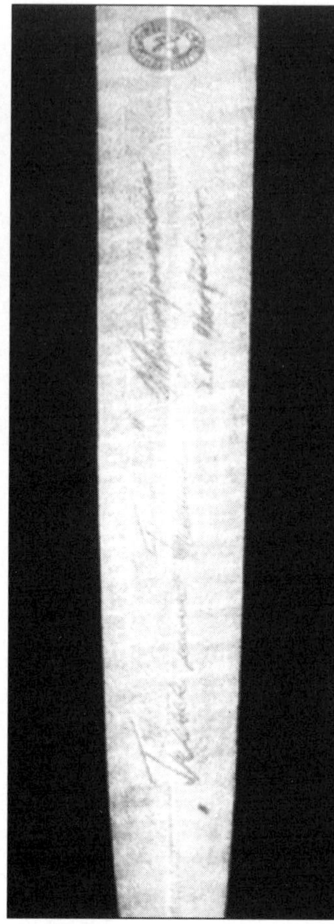

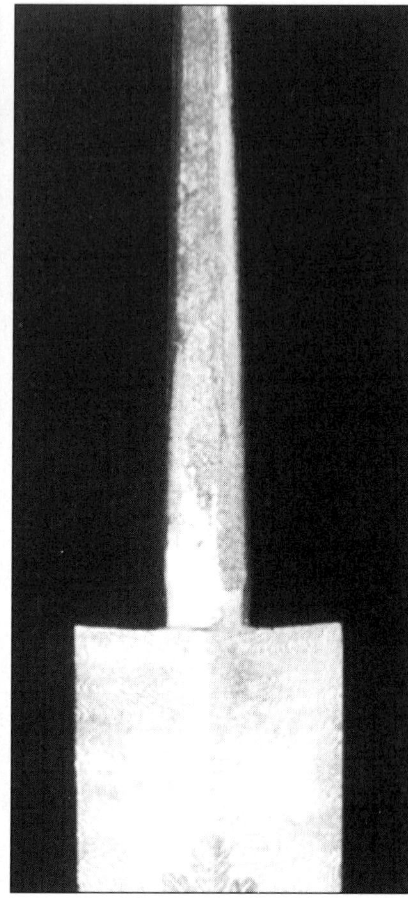

Four different views of a reproduction SA presentation dagger, with artificial Damascus blade and spurious blade dedication. The tang of this blade has been very crudely filed in a manner one would not expect to see on a blade of this alleged quality. The crossguards, which have been engraved, have been quite crudely executed, and the grip inlays have been inserted crookedly. Finally, the bogus P. D. Luneschloss proofmark has been applied to the ricasso unevenly, too far to the right.

1938 SA HIGH LEADER'S DAGGER

Reproductions of the 1938 SA High Leader's dagger are usually just up-market versions of the 1935 SA Honour dagger. In most cases only part of the reproduction which differs is the scabbard. Consequently in relationship to reproductions all of the characteristics previously stated for the 1935 Honour dagger should be applied to identify reproductions of the 1938 High Leader's dagger taking into account the additional points on the scabbard.

As well as straightforward reproductions of this dagger there are also the usual "embellishments" as previously stated for the 1935 SA Honour dagger. However there are several additional fabrications which apply exclusively to the 1938 High Leader's dagger, and as with outright reproductions these fabrications predominantly manifest themselves on the scabbard.

A further feature which relates to fabrications of the 1938 High Leader's dagger is the use of a variety of chained suspension scabbards which are in themselves genuine items but are totally inappropriate when married to the SA High Leader's dagger. The types of scabbards used in various fabrications are quite diverse and include: the 1936 NSKK chained scabbard, the 1936 SS chained scabbard, 1936 NPEA Leader's chained scabbards, converted 1933 SA and SS scabbards and innumerable types of chains - real, reproduction and fantasy in a wide variety of combinations.

A consistent feature of genuine 1938 SA High Leader's daggers was the brown leather covered scabbard, a characteristic which some reproducers have overlooked. It is therefore wise to treat any High Leader's dagger with a brown painted scabbard with a degree of scepticism. A further characteristic found on the majority of genuine SA High Leader's daggers is that all three scabbard fittings are relatively plain with the exception of a grooved outline following the contours of the inside edge. However many post-war reproductions tend to go a bit over the top when it comes to decoration of the scabbard fittings. This is especially true of the Spanish reproductions.

A single point which is of a great help to the collector is that the proofmark on any SA High Leader's dagger should always be that of Carl Eickhorn and should appear high on the reverse ricasso in gold relief on a Damascus steel blade. The appearance of any other Maker's or RZM proofmark should render the piece suspect.

RECOGNITION CHECKLIST

With the exception of the scabbard all points to observe relating to reproductions of the 1938 SA High Leader's dagger are the same as those for the 1935 SA Honour dagger.

SCABBARD

- ➢ Ensure that the suspension chain contains the correct number of links i.e. five upper and seven lower.
- ➢ Genuine suspension chains were silver with gold swastikas in high relief.
- ➢ Swastikas should be square on an oblong link and finely detailed. Many reproduction chains have badly formed swastikas with a very shallow relief. Some reproductions feature square swastikas positioned at a 45 degree angle giving a circular effect (not to be confused with a sunwheel swastika which would also be incorrect).
- ➢ Ensure that the interlocking rings which join the links are of correct form and composition. Originals were always well formed and silver plated whereas reproductions often have an oval shape and are extremely thin.
- ➢ The holes for locating the loops are a separate "U" shaped appendage on the corner of each link whereas reproductions have holes drilled in each corner from a flat panel which is part of the link. Therefore the link requires close examination. Original links are an oblong with loops at each corner, and reproduction links are made in an "H" shape then drilled on the end of each arm.

- ➢ The links of the suspension chain should not have as a decoration round SA symbols, swastikas within a circle, arrows, Death's heads, SS runes or any other form of spurious decoration.
- ➢ The belt clip fastener should have a large SA lightening bolt insignia on originals. Any other type of insignia on the fastener such as the NSKK oakleaves within a shield or the SS Celtic swirl style fastener is a post-war fabrication.
- ➢ A centre scabbard ramp fitting with the cubic interlocking swastika decoration running around it is a converted 1936 chained SS scabbard.
- ➢ A centre ramp scabbard fitting not of the same basic design as the top and bottom scabbard fitting is indicative of a converted 1933 SA or SS scabbard which has had a modern centre ramp added.
- ➢ The suspension chain attachment on the centre ramp of reproduction High Leader's daggers is usually just a ring with a swivel which is of the same style as the upper fitting ring: whereas original centre ramp attachments are usually a flat appendage protruding from the side of the fitting.
- ➢ Many reproduction suspension chains feature two large scabbard attachment loops (one at the end of each chain) similar in size and form to the hanger loop on the 1933 SA scabbard. This is a style never documented on the chains of original High Leader's daggers.

PROOFMARKS

Carl Eickhorn of Solingen was the only authorised manufacturer of the SA High Leader's dagger, and only his proofmark should appear on the reverse ricasso of the blade. The appearance of any other Maker's or RZM proofmark should be viewed as suspicious.

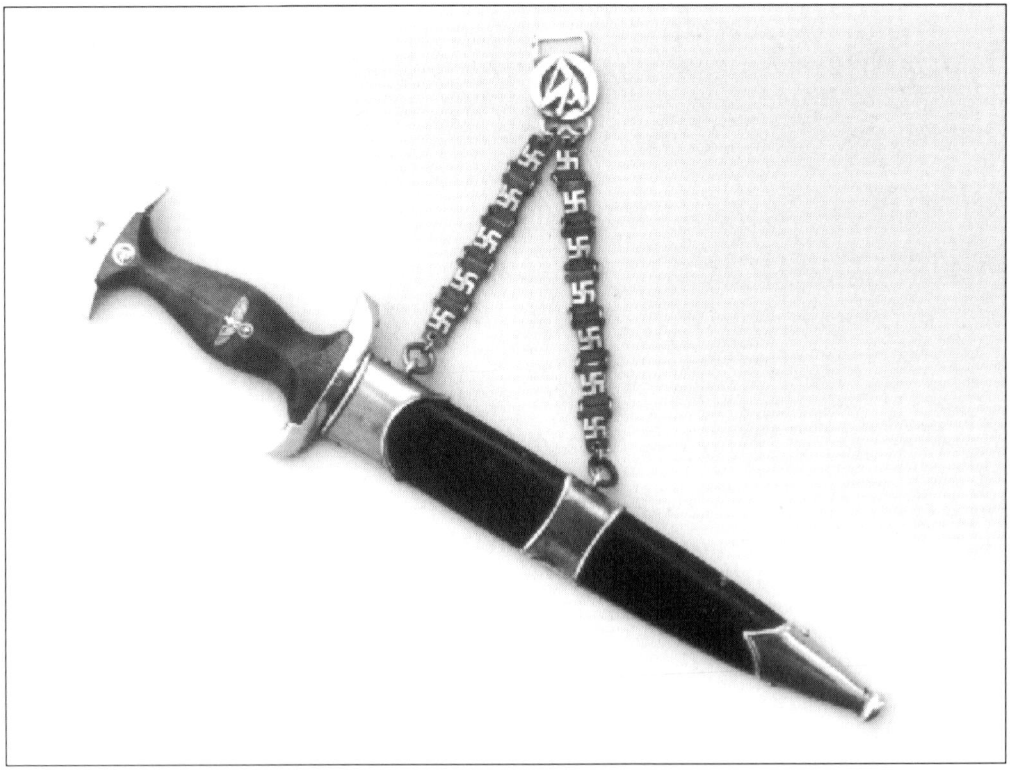

Obverse view of a genuine SA dagger which has been married to a 1936 pattern NSKK scabbard, suspended from reproduction SA High Leader's Honour dagger hanging chains.

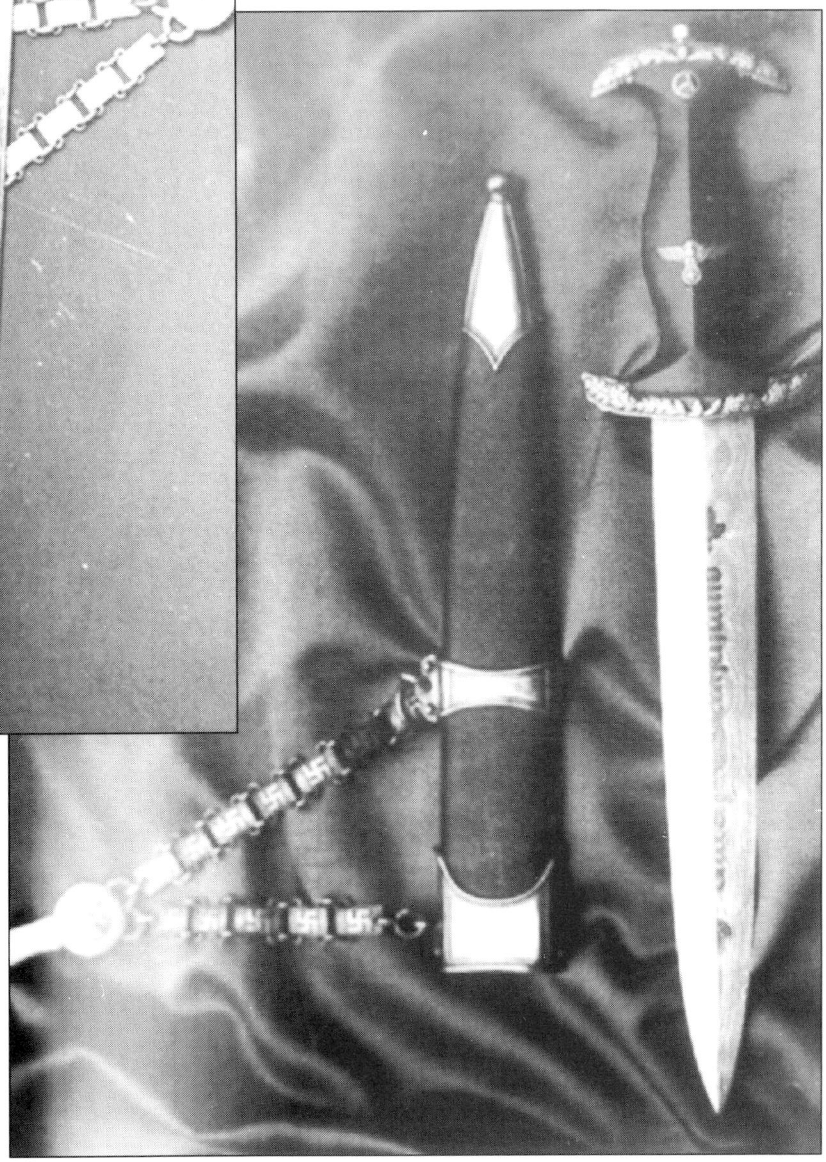

Two different examples of genuine 1938 SA High Leader's Honour daggers. Note the minor variation in the chain attachment on the centre scabbbard ramp.

SA FELDHERRNHALLE DAGGER

The rarity and extremely high value of the Feldherrnhalle dagger puts it outside the scope of all but a few wealthy or very lucky collectors. Although it is highly unlikely that the collector will ever encounter a genuine example of this dagger, nonetheless details of Feldherrnhalle reproductions will be detailed here.

Whilst researching reproductions of this dagger one fact became very evident from all sources - that almost all reproductions encountered by collectors and dealers over the years have been of an excellent quality and in almost every case were being passed off as "originals" by the vendors and never as actual reproduction pieces.

There would appear to be at least two and possibly more manufacturers of reproduction Feldherrnhalle daggers: this fact is born out by the contrasting characteristics which have been observed on different reproductions of this dagger. There has also been some very smart marketing by the reproducers whereby they have limited the distribution of this reproduction dagger in order not to flood the market and thus diminish the dagger's plausibility when it does appear as a "genuine" Feldherrnhalle dagger.

Carl Eickhorn was the sole manufacturer of the original Feldherrnhalle dagger and the good quality reproductions invariably reflect this by carrying the correct Carl Eickhorn proofmark.

The gold finish of reproductions of this dagger tends to be very bright with a new appearance rather than the subdued gilt finish of originals. It has also been determined in discussing this dagger with a number of collectors and dealers that the general consensus is that most examples encountered are approximately 10% undersize when compared to originals. Further in almost all cases the reproductions have been offered without hanging straps.

Detecting reproductions of this extremely rare dagger has been further compounded by the appearance in recent years of spurious examples with a variety of embellishments such as white ivory grips, the SA motto in a fancy etched panel and reverse blade dedications bearing a Viktor Lutze facsimile signature. Both the dedication and signature are acid etched and are completely bogus.

With a five figure price tag the Feldherrnhalle dagger is well worth reproducing to a very high standard, including genuine ivory grips. Consequently the collector should not take superficial quality of manufacture as the sole criteria for assessing the authenticity of any example of this dagger.

RECOGNITION CHECKLIST

BLADE

- ➢ Carl Eickhorn was the only authorised manufacturer of this dagger: any other Maker's proofmark or RZM proofmark is incorrect.
- ➢ Spurious dedications applied to the reverse of the blade, often having a facsimile Viktor Lutze signature.
- ➢ The "Alles fur Deutschland" motto incorrectly positioned on the blade being applied centrally on the obverse blade instead of being applied closer to the crossguard approximately 2/3 of the way up from the blade tip.
- ➢ The blade motto being incorrectly applied reading from crossguard to tip instead of vice versa.
- ➢ The use of photo-etching to execute the blade motto: originals were always acid etched.
- ➢ The blade motto appearing within a decorated photo etched panel with a blued background. This is a spurious embellishment: original blade mottos were always plain and completely unadorned.

SCABBARD

- ➢ The use of wooden scabbard liners instead of the correct metal type.
- ➢ Scabbard throat fitting oversize causing a slight bulge.

- Incorrect positioning of the scabbard throat retaining screws being mounted too close to the edge of the throat instead of being approximately 1/4 inch from the edge as is the case with the screw positioning on original scabbards.
- The pebbled central panel of the reproduction scabbards has a discernible swirl pattern similar to but not as pronounced as that found on the reproduction Army scabbard. Original scabbards have irregular pebbling.
- The two scabbard bands should be held in place by a single recessed screw on the edge of each band. Some reproductions observed are totally devoid of any scabbard band retaining screws.

GRIP

- Bulbous shaped grips lacking the hour glass shape of originals.
- The use of dyed softwood to make the grips instead of fruitwood, usually pear or cherrywood, similar to that used on the standard SA dagger is a feature of many reproduction Feldhernhalle grips.
- Reproductions have the upper grip recessed too high into the pommel.
- The crossguard definition is not as good on reproductions and lacks the fine background pebbling on the SA insignia.
- The eagle pommel on reproductions lacks the fine detail of originals especially in the wing and breast fletching.
- The lower wing feather of the original has seven distinct finely detailed feathers on each wing whereas reproductions only have six distinct feathers; the seventh next to the eagle's leg is very indistinct.
- The tang locking nut on originals has two grooves forming a cross. Locking nuts on reproductions are either a single groove or two holes.
- The wreathed swastika has very sharp edges on reproductions: originals have a much smoother and more rounded appearance.
- The background pebbling of the swastika is very poor on reproductions often being nonexistent.

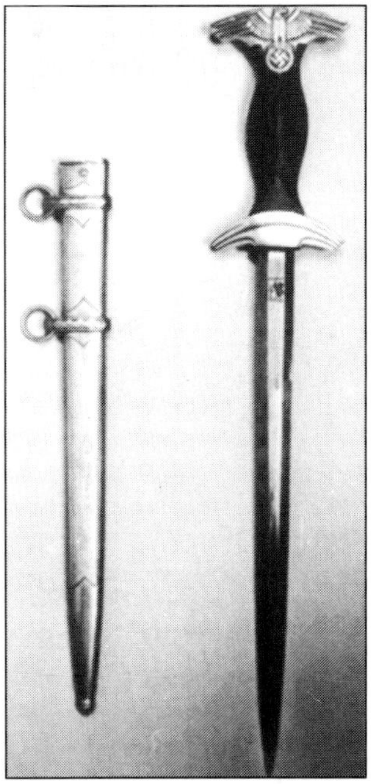

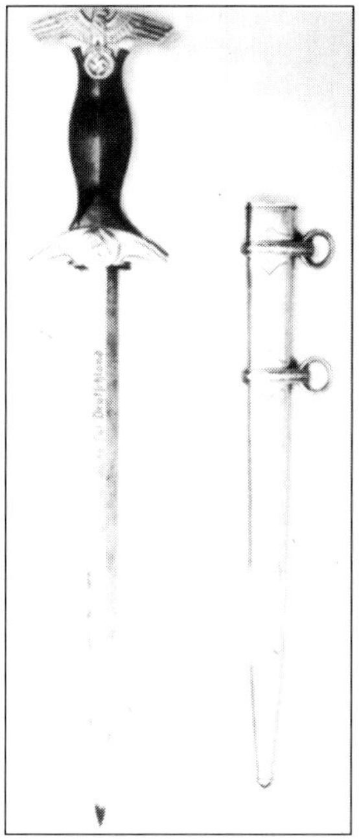

Obverse and reverse sides of a genuine SA Feldherrnhalle dagger and scabbard. Note the sharp detail of the fittings and the well executed obverse blade motto and reverse blade Maker's proofmark of Carl Eickhorn.

HITLER YOUTH REPRODUCTIONS

YOUTH KNIFE: FARTENMESSER

A knife was introduced in 1933 for use by Hitler Youth members of *all* ranks. This took the form of a sheath knife of a type which was quite common at the time and is indeed still produced today. It was intended to be a functional knife rather than an ornamental dress item. The knife was single edged with the blade bearing the Hitler Youth motto "Blut und Ehre" (Blood and Honour) etched into the obverse side of the blade. The etching was executed in a normal script style. The handle of the knife was of checkered black plastic with the Hitler Youth diamond inset into the obverse side. The diamond was of the normal red and white enamel with the black enamelled swastika in the centre. The scabbard which accomodated the knife was of metal painted black with a black or brown leather hanging attachment riveted to it.

Early examples of the Hitler Youth Fartenmesser will be encountered bearing various Maker's proofmarks; their position can be either on the ricasso or etched laterally on the reverse side of the blade. In keeping with other Party organisations such as the SA and SS, production of the HJ knife came under the control of the RZM in late 1934. Consequently later examples of the knife bear the RZM proofmark and Maker's control number and also combinations of both RZM and Maker's proofmarks.

In 1938 the use of the motto "Blut und Ehre" was discontinued on the Hitler Youth knife. All knives produced after that date under RZM control bear no motto whatsoever, although private purchase examples with the motto could be acquired.

It is worth mentioning at this point that there is a never ending stream of Hitler Youth knife variations (in addition to the modern reproductions) with the HJ diamond appearing on the scabbard or having no diamond at all. Additionally they will be encountered with staghorn grips, wooden grips and even in bayonet form. Etching applied to the hilt and also the blade of HJ knives was never a standard feature, nor for that matter was it ever authorised. Over the years individuals have attempted to give bogus credence to Hitler Youth knives which fell into the variation category calling them "Presentation knives", "Honour knives", and a variety of other terms. Also it has been suggested that members of the DJ had their own authorised knife, when in fact they were just unofficial versions of the Hitler Youth knife. As with all Third Reich edged weapons many variations existed, but it should be borne in mind that *officially* there was only one pattern of Hitler Youth knife, and also the Hitler Youth was the only Nazi youth organisation which was authorised to wear this type of knife.

RECOGNITION CHECKLIST

BLADE

- ➢ A straight blade is indicative of modern Scout knives. The Hitler Youth knife had a slight lozenge shape to it.
- ➢ The use of the "Blut und Ehre" motto on the blades produced after 1938. RZM proofmarks for the period normally carried a date with them.
- ➢ A proofmark etched into the obverse ricasso in company with a "Blut und Ehre" inscribed blade is a combination found on reproductions. The correct positioning for proofmarks is on the reverse blade.
- ➢ The use of the word "Solingen" in large letters on the ricasso is a style used on post-war produced Scout knives.
- ➢ The word "Germany" on the blade ricasso is a feature of post-war produced knives which were made for export.
- ➢ A photoengraved "Blut und Ehre" motto is a feature only found on the blades of modern reproductions. Third Reich period blades always had the motto acid etched.

- ➢ The positioning of the "Blut und Ehre" inscription should be examined closely as reproduction etched blades frequently have the etching applied too close to the tip, too high on the blade or slightly sloping.
- ➢ The etched motto on some reproductions is missing the exclamation mark at the end of the word "Ehre"
- ➢ Some recent reproduction blades have a high chromium content which tends to give them very bright appearance.
- ➢ The "Blut und Ehre" motto applied to the reverse blade: this was never a feature on genuine Third Reich Hitler Youth knives.

These points are as follows:

- ➢ A Maker's proofmark appearing on a plain bladed HJ knife without RZM proofmark or Maker's control number should be viewed with suspicion.
- ➢ A proofmark (usually RZM) applied horizontally across the obverse ricasso is a common feature of reproductions.
- ➢ The appearance of any proofmark appearing on the same side of the blade with the Blut und Ehre motto.
- ➢ In most cases reproductions have the proofmark applied to the ricasso whereas most originals had their proofmark (either RZM, Maker or both) applied to the middle of the reverse blade.
- ➢ The RZM proofmark on original HJ knife blades was smaller than that used on daggers, and it usually took the form of a single line circle terminating in the "M" of "RZM". Many reproductions feature a larger RZM proofmark similar to that applied to reproduction SS daggers. The style of the proofmark is also slightly different to that found on most genuine HJ blades in that it has two lines forming the circle around th RZM logo.
- ➢ The most frequently encountered RZM proofmarks on reproductions are RZM M7/2; M7/11; M7/13; M7/33; M7/36 and M7/66.

SCABBARD

- ➢ Scabbard constructed from alloy materials are a feature of modern reproductions. Genuine HJ scabbards were always made from sheet steel. Testing with a magnet will identify an alloy scabbard immediately as these are nonferrous and will not hold a magnet.
- ➢ A slightly flared lip on the mouth of the scabbard is a feature of modern reproduction scabbards. Originals were always straight.
- ➢ The absence of a small rivet on the neck of the scabbard is indicative of reproductions.
- ➢ A slightly raised edge around the mouth of the scabbard is a feature of some reproductions.
- ➢ The use of plastic to make the belt suspension strap is only found on reproductions. Genuine straps were always of leather.
- ➢ When leather is used for the belt suspension strap it is often considerably thinner than that found on originals, and will sometimes feature a vertical line running down each side of the strap.
- ➢ The use of plastic studs as a fastener for the grip buckle is a feature of modern reproductions. Original studs were always made of metal.
- ➢ Hollow head rivets on the suspension strap are a feature of some reproductions whereas most rivets were slightly domed having the flat part of the rivet on the reverse side.

GRIP

- ➢ The Hitler Youth diamond insignia should be examined closely to ensure it has the correct appearance for although there were some slight variations in style, most diamonds irrespective of Maker conformed quite closely to a standard design; whereas reproduction diamonds tend to come in a variety of styles some of which are mentioned here: a diamond without any border around its edges; a diamond with a very narrow border around its edges; a diamond with a thick raised border around its edges; a diamond with the left and right sections being too large (this appearance is usually caused because the swastika in the centre is too small); a swastika with thin spidery arms which are not exactly square; overall most reproduction diamond inlays tend to be marginally larger than originals.

- Ensure that the diamond insignia is relatively flush in the grip and is not recessed or too protruding which is sometimes the case where too much adhesive has been applied.
- Do not place too much trust in the test of shaking the knife to see if the grip inlay is loose as loose inlays are no more a guarantee of originality than static ones are of being reproductions. This test should only be used as a guideline in conjunction with other points observed.
- The absence of rivets holding the grips in place is a feature of some poor quality reproductions which had the grip plates glued into position.
- Of special note is an embellishment which was added to the neck and pommel of good quality genuine Hitler Youth knives. This took the form of photo-etching decoration usually around a form of Hitler Youth insignia. The decoration being executed on the whole of the upper metal parts of the grip, both obverse and reverse. This form of embellishment was completely spurious and was never an authorised option of any Hitler Youth Fahrtenmesser. This process carried out on genuine HJ knives was in an effort to boost the market price of an otherwise ordinary knife at a time when the basic HJ knife was only worth a few Pounds/Dollars and was aimed at the collector looking for something a little bit different. These embellished HJ knives were personalised by a dealer in the North of England during the late 1960's and 70's: he was the same dealer who was responsible for introducing the "K98 Waffen SS presentation bayonet" which was similarly decorated on the grip with photo-etching which was also applied in decorative panels to the blades of ordinary but genuine K98 bayonets.

PROOFMARKS

With the Hitler Youth Fartenmesser being introduced at the very beginning of the Third Reich in 1933 a number of different Maker's proofmarks will be encountered on genuine HJ knives. The proofmark on Hitler Youth knives was usually positioned quite differently from all other daggers being placed on the blade of the knife instead of on the ricasso as was the case with daggers. The proofmark was invariably applied to the reverse of the blade with the motto "Blut und Ehre" appearing on the obverse side of the blade. When the RZM came into being in 1934 the Hitler Youth knife was then regulated by this organisation. Consequently the RZM proofmark and Maker's M7 control number began appearing on blades produced from 1935 onwards. The RZM proofmark did not always appear on the blade exclusively for in many instances in addition to the RZM proofmark and the Maker's M7 control number the Maker would also apply his own logo. In addition to the RZM proofmark and M7 control number most HJ knives produced after 1935 also have the date applied under the M7 code. This dating affords some assistance in identifying the reproduction knives with the "Blut und Ehre" motto: for due to this motto being discontinued in 1938 any RZM proofmarks with dates later than that in conjunction with the "Blut und Ehre" motto should be viewed with suspicion. In the past there has been a simplistic rule of thumb used to identify reproduction HJ knives which goes something like "knives with the Blut und Ehre motto should only have a Maker's proofmark on the blade and that any Blut und Ehre blades bearing the RZM proofmark are reproductions". This is obviously not the case as Hitler Youth knifes continued to be produced with the Blut und Ehre motto for at least three years after the RZM came into being. Probably a more telling observation would be a plain bladed HJ knife with a Maker's proofmark and no RZM proofmark.

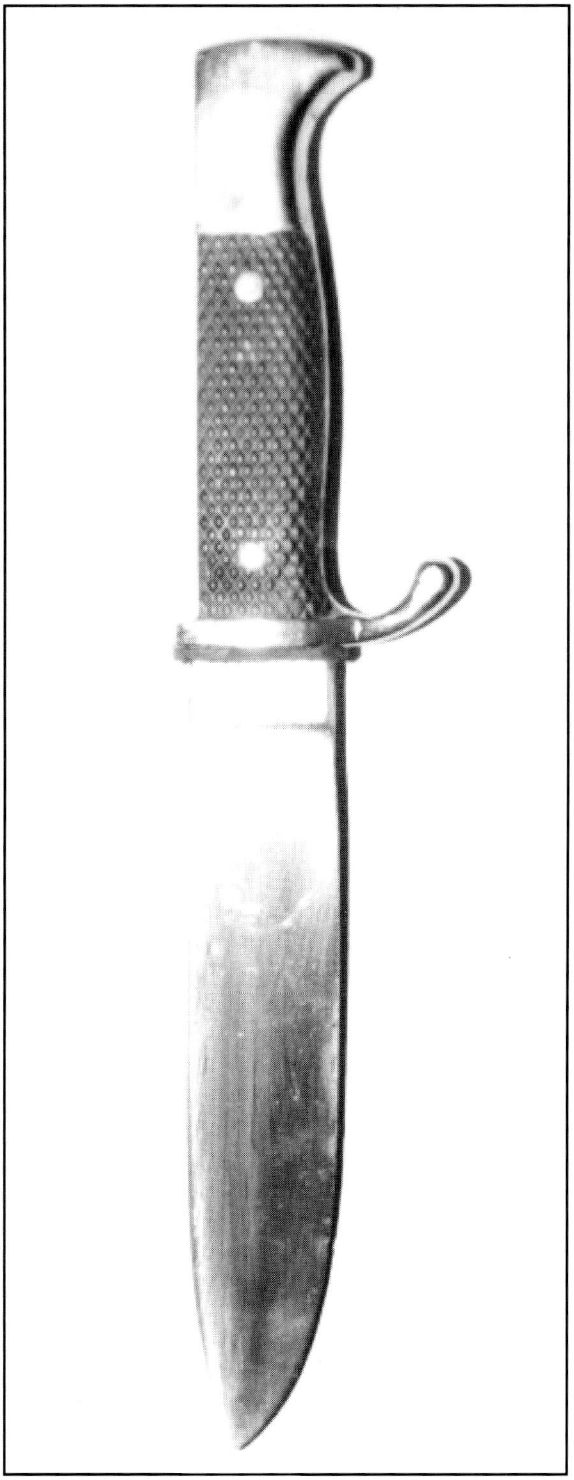

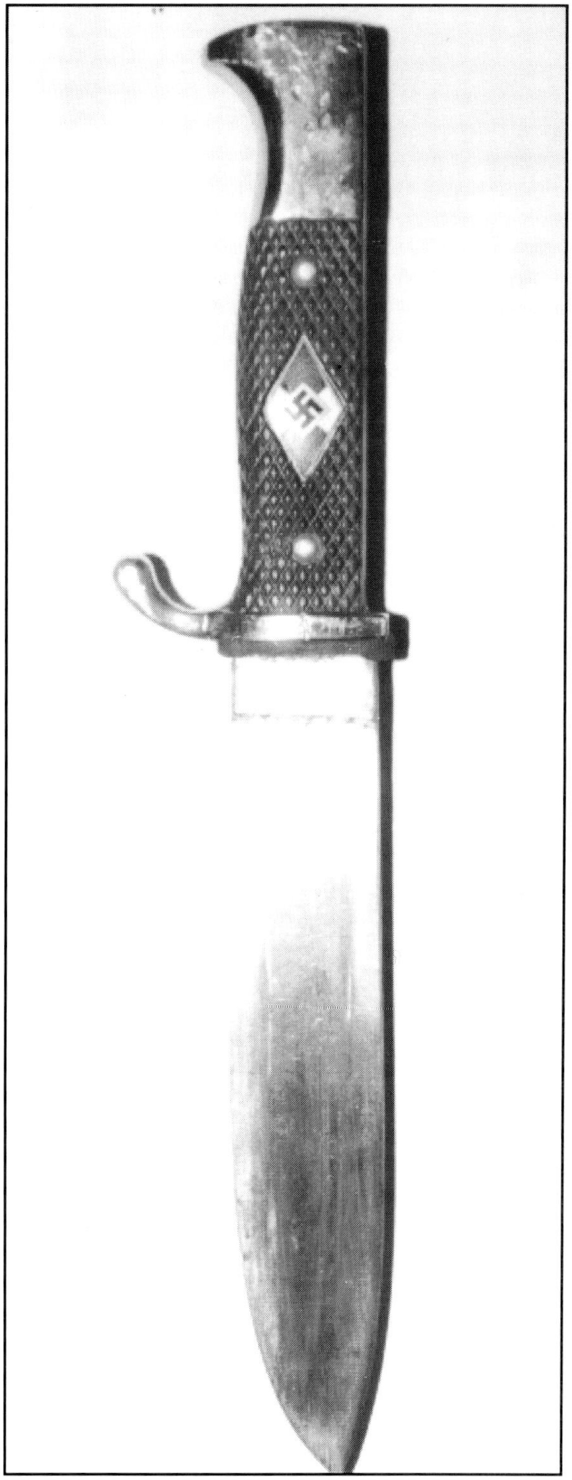

Obverse and reverse of a reproduction Hitler Youth knife. The HJ diamond insignia is deeply recessed with an elongated shape. An attempt has been made to "distress" the pommel in an effort to age the piece.

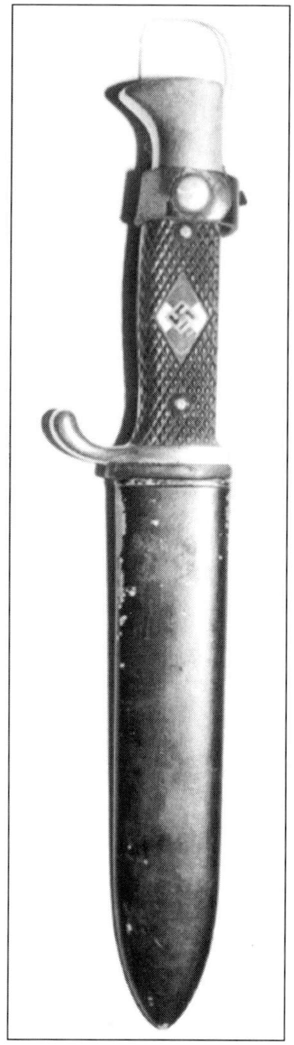

The three Hitler Youth knives above are examples of modern Boy Scout knives which have had bogus HJ insignia inserted into the grip. Note the poor fit of the insignia and the attempt to fill in the gaps around the diamond. The proofmark on the left is a post-war type with "Solingen Germany" below the trade name of the Maker.

Three different reproduction Hitler Youth knives. Although the overall style is the same, each knife has its own particular characteristics. Note the slight differences in overall length and the varying thickness' of the blade ricasso. Also the HJ diamond insignia is slightly different on each example.

Four different views of a reproduction Hitler Youth knife with a sawback blade. This knife is relatively new to the market and is very well made. The scabbard throat does not have the usual lip, however the blade does not fit well into the scabbard hence the thick rubber blade washer. The scabbard is well finished in black enamel paint and a black leather belt loop with retaining stud fastener. The hilt and crossguard are both nickel plated. The blade has a dull grey appearance.

Obverse and reverse of three different reproduction Hitler Youth knives. The example on the left has stainless steel hilt and crossguard with a regular steel blade. The middle knife features stainless steel fittings and blade. On the right is a nickel plated knife with aluminium scabbard. All three of these reproductions exhibt post-war proofmarks.

Five different examples of post-war Hitler Youth knife proofmarks. The middle left blade ricasso shows evidence of grinding to remove a tell-tale post-war proofmark.

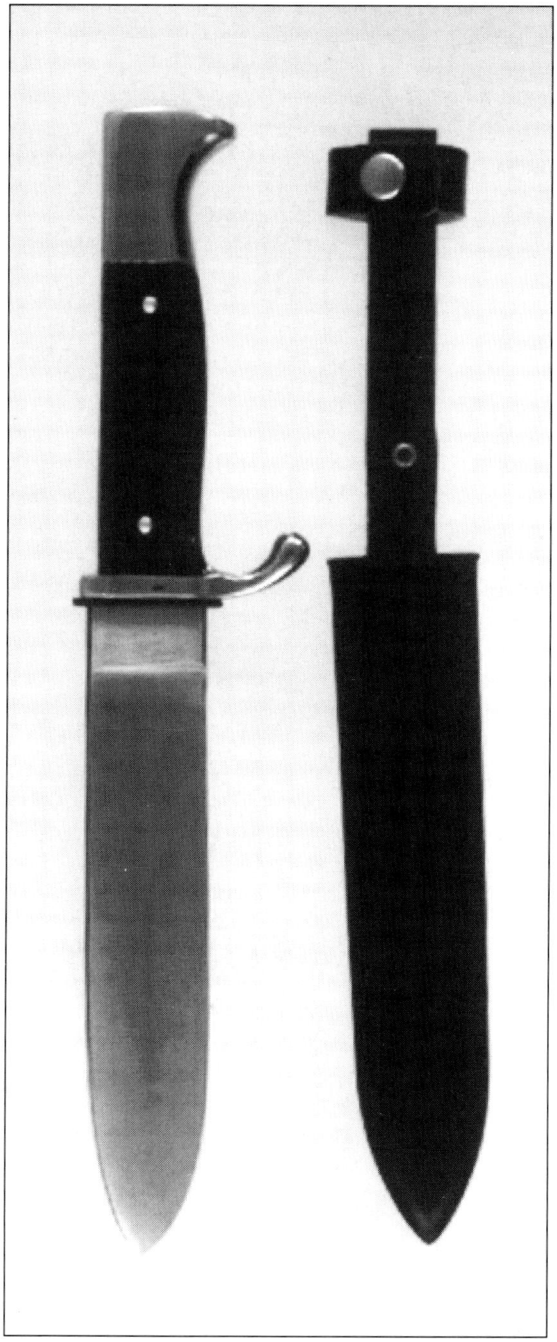

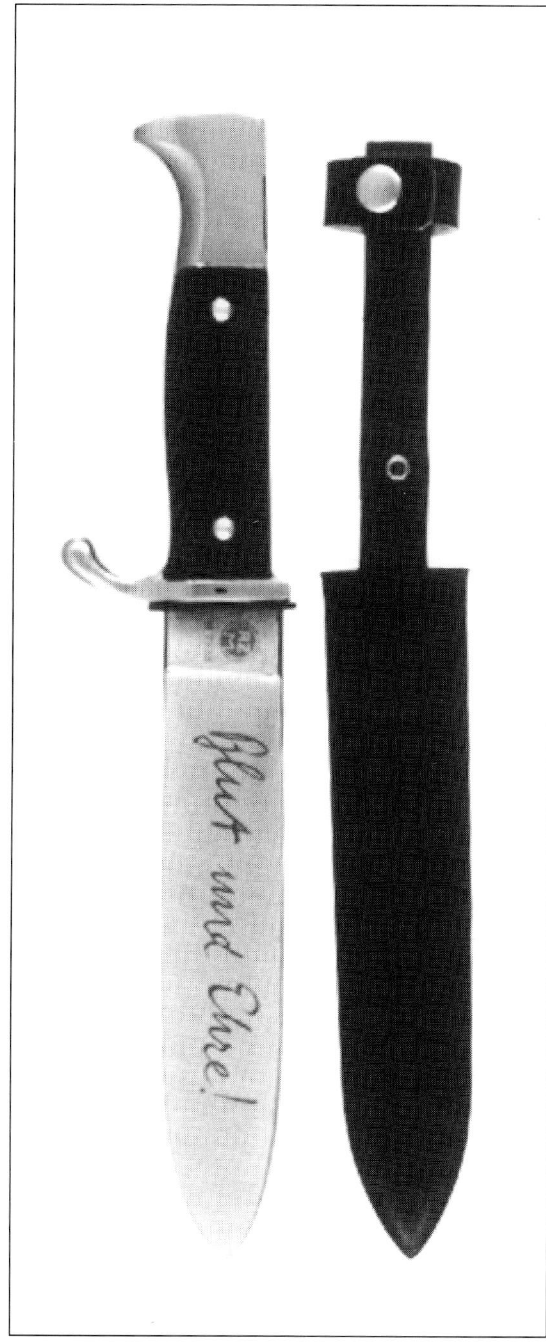

Obverse and reverse views of a reproduction Hitler Youth knife and scabbard. These particular pieces are currently produced in Germany and are manufactured without the HJ diamond grip inlay, this is added at a later date. Note the straight blade and oversize ricasso, also the thin buffer pad. The scabbard exhibits the characteristic flared throat of many current reproductions.

HITLER YOUTH LEADER'S DAGGER

In 1937 a dagger was introduced for wear by Hitler Youth leaders with the rank of Gefolschaftfuhrer and above. Prior to the introduction of this dagger no distinction was made between leaders and ordinary youth members in the edged weapon area. The dagger which is more reminiscent of a letter opener than other Third Reich daggers had a stilletto blade which was very similar to the Army dagger blade being double edged with a double bevel and a flat central section on which appeared the Hitler Youth motto "Blut und Ehre" (Blood and Honour). Unlike the Youth knife, the inscription on the Leader's dagger was acid etched in block print.

The wooden grip of the dagger was wrapped in a silver wire. The pommel, ferrule and crossguard were of either aluminium or silver plated. The metal scabbard was wrapped in a very dark blue leather (which with age often appears black). The scabbard fittings were also of aluminium or silver plate. The upper scabbard fitting bears the Hitler Youth eagle in relief. The Hitler Youth diamond symbol appears engraved on the pommel. A set of plain black leather hangers with silver oval buckles and clasps were a standard fitting with this dagger.

The Hitler Youth Leader's dagger was a presentation piece and as such was accompanied by an embossed leatherette presentation case and an award document (Urkunde) both of which are extremely rare and collectable in their own right. It is very unusual to find the Hitler Youth Leader's dagger in its original case although reproductions of the case are also made these days.

In terms of rarity the HJ leader's dagger would appear somewhere in the middle of the scale and is consequently a much copied and reproduced edged weapon.

BLADE

- A lightly etched Blut und Ehre motto.
- Incorrect positioning of the blade motto being located too close to the tip instead of being in the upper half of the blade as on originals.
- The use of an oversize RZM proofmark which extends over all three surfaces of the blade ricasso.
- The RZM proofmark used on most reproductions is quite bold but does show some patchy areas instead of being an overall firm impression.
- The recesses of the letters of the blade motto were filled in with a dark material on originals to highlight the motto. Most reproductions do not feature this and where they do it has usually been painted on and is flaky in areas.
- Some of the early reproductions of German origin utilised Army dagger blades which are longer than the blades on original Hitler Youth daggers by approximately an inch.
- Blades bearing the inscription "Fur Verdienste Um Die Deutsche Jugend" (For Meritorious Service in the German Youth) which appears on the reverse side of the blade are post war fakes. This inscription was never documented on the blade of any original Hitler Youth Leader's dagger.
- Blades with a matt grey or satin finish are of post war manufacture.

SCABBARD

- An all metal scabbard with a pebbled finish is a feature of one particular type of reproduction.
- A thick bulky synthetic leather binding causing bulging especially around the scabbard fittings.
- Poor definition on the insignia of the upper scabbard fitting.
- A crooked swastika on the upper scabbard fitting insignia.
- A scabbard insignia of incorrect form with the eagle facing directly outwards. The correct pose for the eagle was in quarter profile with the eagle in a descending pose rather than a static one.
- A large round headed screw located almost in the centre of the reverse of the upper fitting for securing the scabbard liners. Original examples of this screw were smaller and mounted closer to the

scabbard throat.

- The rim of the scabbard throat which holds the liners is quite thin on reproductions and slightly rounded instead of the relatively thick, square rim found on originals.
- The upper scabbard insignia should be situated centrally on genuine fittings. Some reproduction insignia are mounted too close to the throat.
- The upper scabbard fitting on some reproductions is too large and makes the insignia look undersized.
- The reverse upper fitting of some reproductions are completely devoid of any retaining screw.

GRIP

- Reproduction crossguards are noticeably thinner than originals.
- Some reproduction crossguards are virtually straight instead of having the slightly upturned shape of originals.
- Grips with binding over a plastic shell are a feature of reproductions. Genuine grips always had a wooden shell.
- Grips bound with an aluminium type wire are incorrect: the wiring of originals was silver.
- An incorrectly shaped grip having a bulge at the top and having a noticeable sharp taper into the ferrule: this type of grip looks very much like a Doner Kebab. The shape of original grips featured a gentle taper from the pommel to the ferrule.
- The Hitler Youth diamond insignia at the top of the pommel is very poorly executed with a spidery slightly misshapened swastika. The overall detail is poor.
- Brass or zinc used to cast the pommel on reproductions which gives poor definition to the fittings. Originals were made from steel then nickel or silver plated.

PROOFMARKS

The only proofmarks which should appear on genuine Hitler Youth Leader's daggers are those of the RZM along with the Maker's M7 control number. Some early reproductions which used genuine Army blades bear Maker's proofmark on their reverse side: this was never a feature of original HJ daggers. Also the etching of the blade motto "Blut und Ehre" is very poorly executed on these blades showing areas of spotting where the etching is breaking up. Due to the additional lengths of these blades the motto looks out of place as it has been executed in the middle of the Army blade. As previously mentioned in most instances where the RZM proofmark has been used on reproductions its size is too large and the form is incorrect. In summaration only the small RZM proofmark should appear on the reverse ricasso, and should occupy only the flay centre panel of the blade. The two Maker's RZM M7 codes associated with original Hitler Youth Leader's daggers are RZM M7/36 E F Horster and RZM M7/66 Carl Eickhorn.

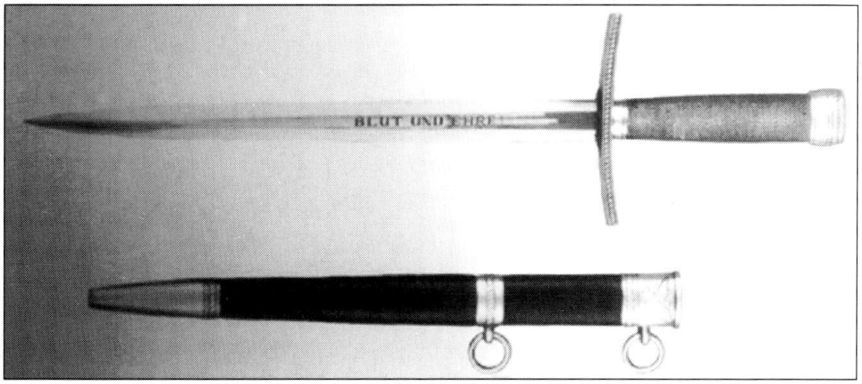

Obverse view of a genuine Hitler Youth Leader's dagger with leather bound scabbard.

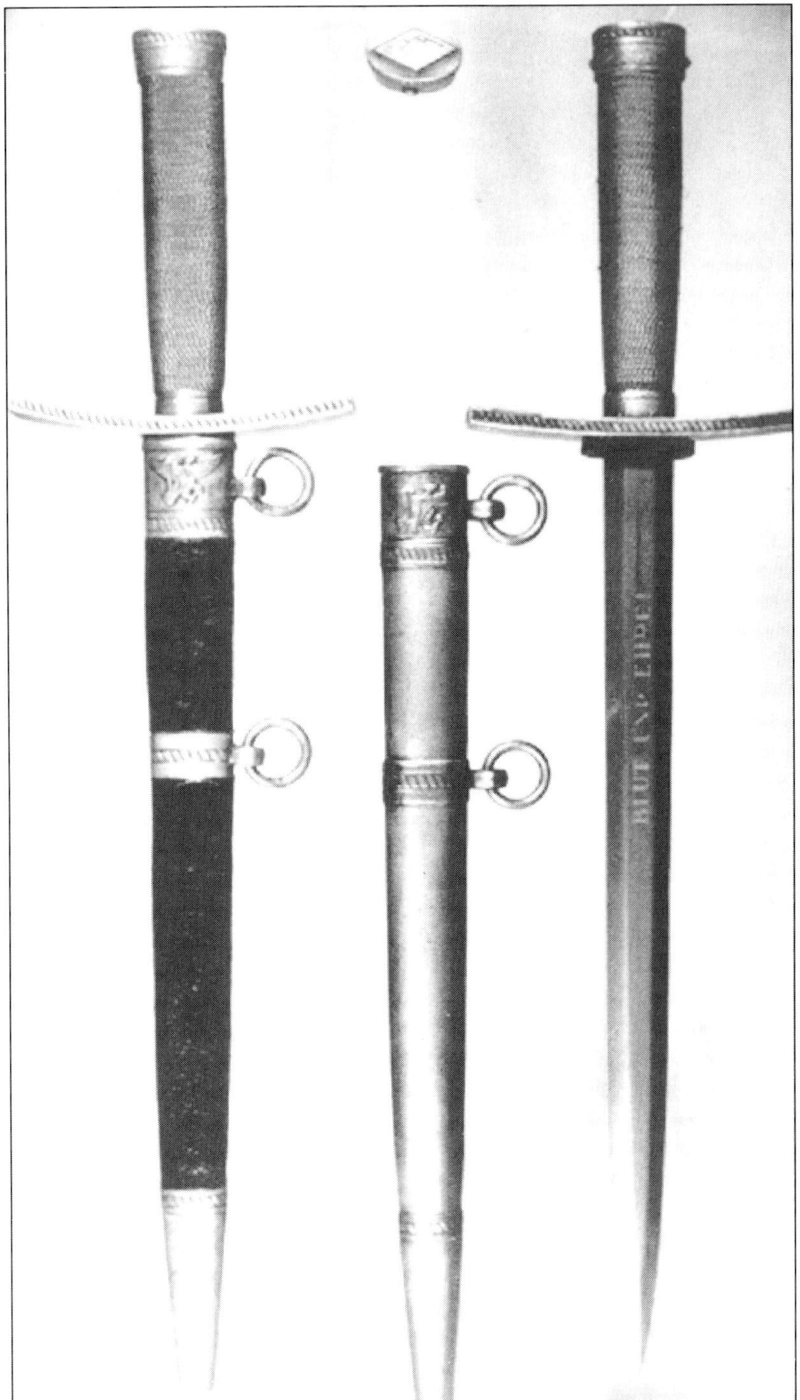

Obverse view of two different types of genuine Hitler Youth Leader's dagger. Example on the left with leather bound scabbard and on the right with a plain silver finished scabbard.

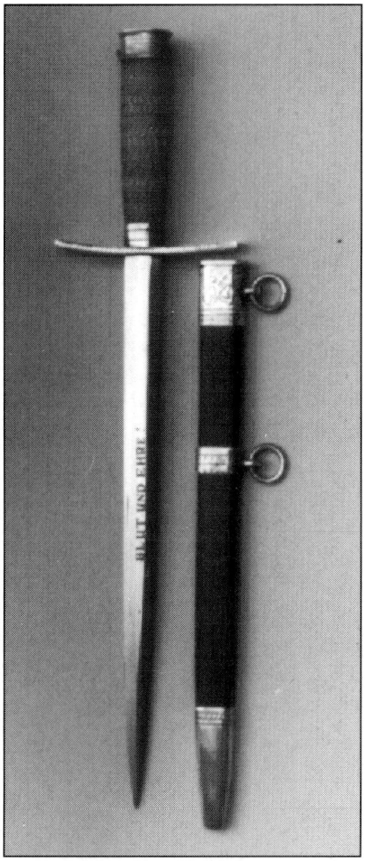

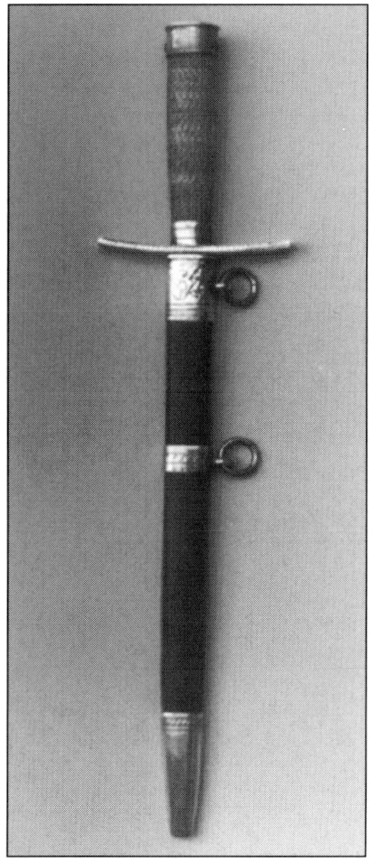

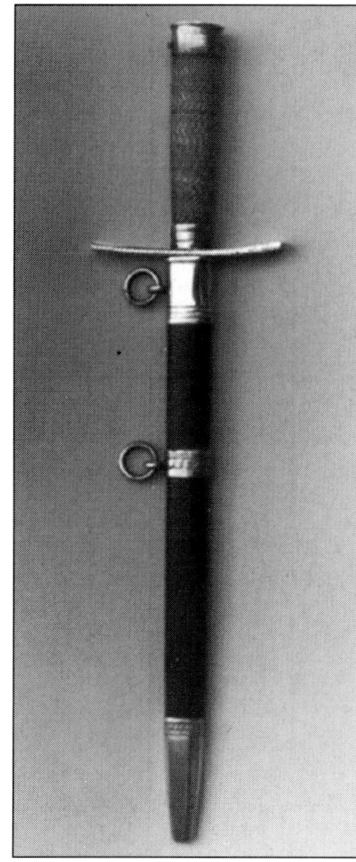

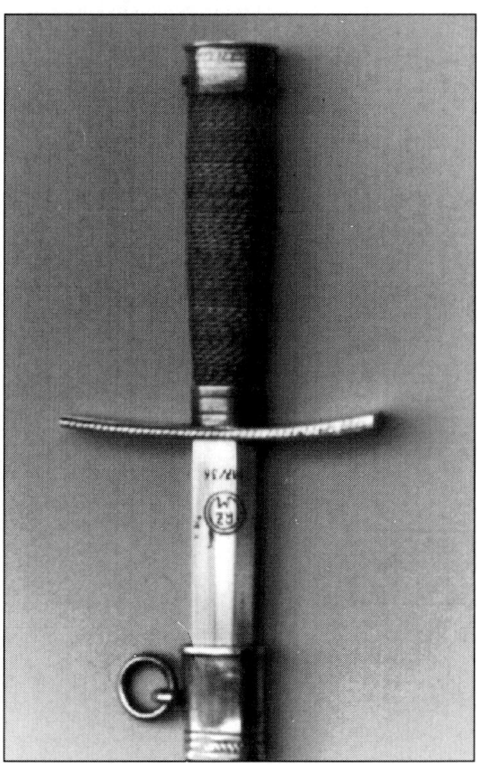

Four different views of a Spanish reproduction Hitler Youth Leader's dagger. Note the badly shaped scabbard and oversized scabbard fittings. The grip of this reproduction is very poorly bound with a coarse wire and does not have the correct tapering shape of originals. Also of note is the poorly etched and oversized RZM proofmark. The scabbard fittings are made from a thin tinny material and have very poor definition.

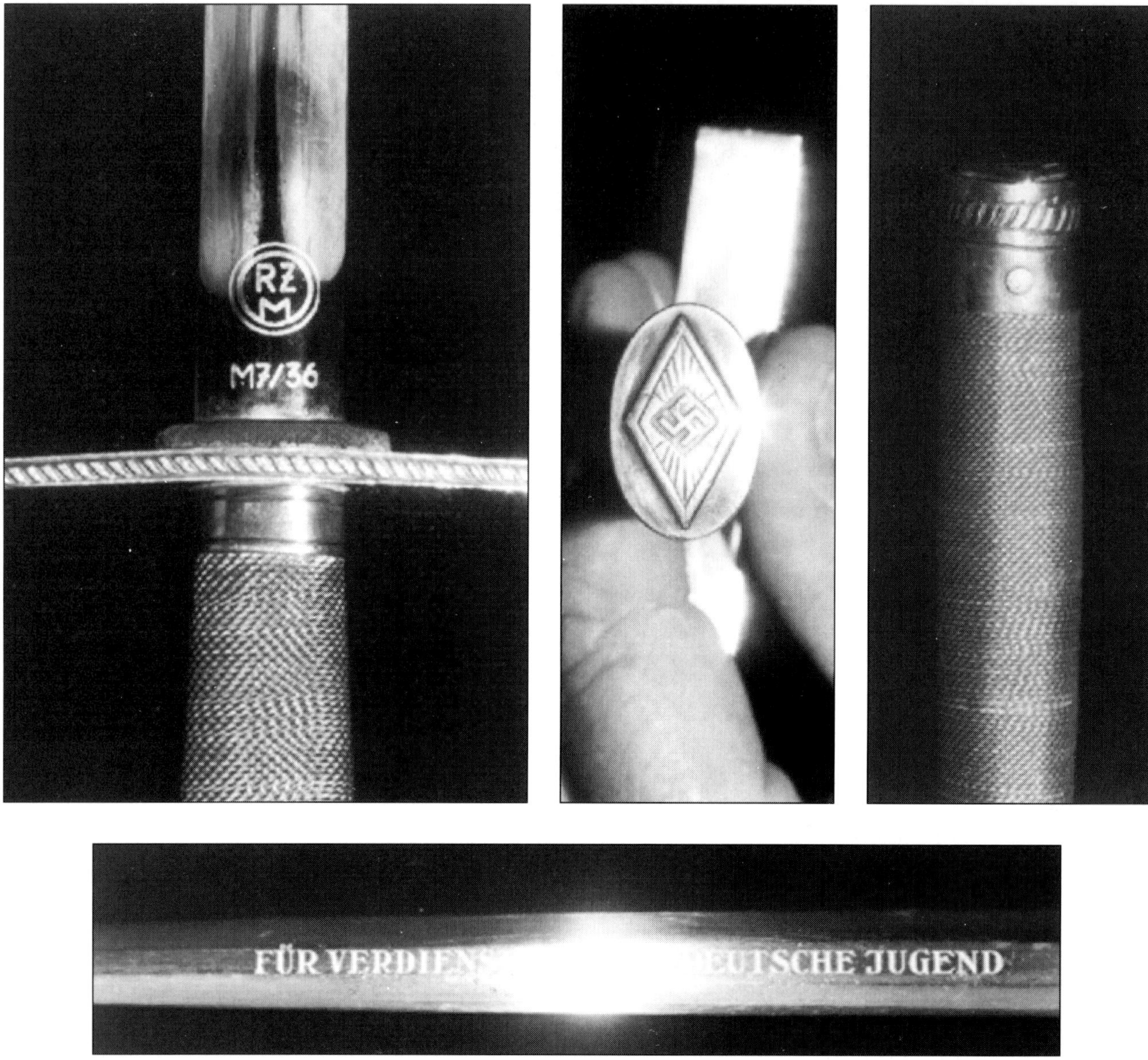

Four different views of a reproduction Hitler Youth Leader's dagger which features a spurious reverse blade inscription relating to alleged faithful service in the Youth Organisation. Note that the pommel is held in position with a flat-headed nail and also the poor definition on the end of the pommel. The RZM proofmark is oversized as is the M7/36 control number.

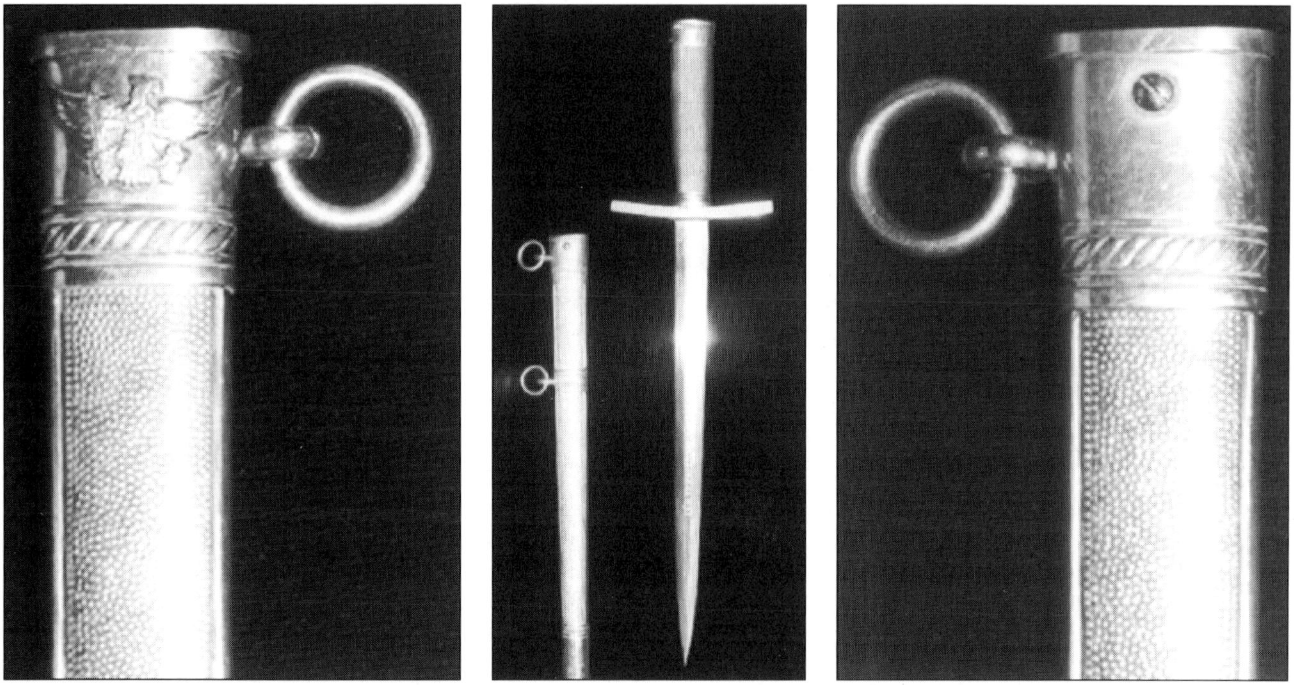

Three different aspects of a reproduction Hitler Youth Leader's dagger, with silver scabbard and pebbled finish. Note the top scabbard fitting is an integral part of the scabbard and has a HJ eagle insignia which is facing outwards instead of being in an angled ascending flight. The crossguard is extremely thick and bulky and lacks the clear upswept shape of originals. Note the large round headed screw used to secure the scabbard liners.

Three different views of a reproduction Hitler Youth Leader's dagger with leather covered scabbard. Note the bulges in the leather seams of the wrapping and also the poor detail of the HJ insignia on the top locket. This dagger has a crossguard which is almost straight instead of having a slightly upswept shape. Also note that the top scabbard fitting has been jammed into position rather than being located with a screw.

NSKK DAGGER REPRODUCTIONS

Initially the members of the NSKK wore the standard 1933 pattern SA dagger without any organisational distinction. In 1936 the NSKK through their leader Huhnlein were authorised to wear a black painted scabbard instead of the brown SA type but still retained the actual SA dagger with the SA grip inlays. After 1936 daggers were manufactured with the black scabbard and were marketed by the Makers as NSKK daggers. At the time the new scabbard colour was adopted the existing SA scabbard was authorised to be repainted, and examples will be encountered today which show signs of the overpainting: due to many of the early brown anodised versions merely being overpainted black. Other options available were to have the scabbard professionally stripped and repainted or merely to purchase a new black NSKK type scabbard from the Maker. It is only conjecture but this last replacement option may account for the fact that many early NSKK daggers encountered have such poorly fitting scabbards.

A seldom documented anomaly is the NSKK Rohm Honour dagger which has been overlooked in the past or has merely been bundled together with the SA Rohm daggers. At the time these daggers were awarded to the SA in 1934, members of the NSKK who had formerly been members of the SA motor section prior to the integration of the two organisations were also authorised to be awarded the Rohm Honour dagger. Also between the award of the dagger in 1934 and the 1936 change of scabbard colour many SA men who had been awarded the Honour dagger in 1934 had in the intervening two years transferred to the NSKK. Due to the daggers of both organisations being identical between 1934 and 1936 no real difference was visibly evident: however after the NSKK adopted the black painted scabbard in 1936 existing NSKK members who retained a Rohm dagger with either a scrubbed, partial or whole inscription on the blade would have transferred the dagger into the newly adapted black painted scabbard. Thus two years after the death of Ernst Rohm many NSKK members ended up with an "NSKK" Rohm Honour dagger by default.

In every other respect the 1933 pattern NSKK dagger had identical characteristics to that of the 1933 pattern SA dagger.

1936 PATTERN

The chained NSKK dagger introduced in 1936 was in direct response to the chained SS dagger introduced just a short while previously. Not to be outdone by the SS Adolf Huhnlein sought to have a chained dress dagger for the NSKK as well. The dagger was the same basic 1933 pattern NSKK dagger with the addition of suspension chains. The scabbard was modified with the addition of a central ramp to accommodate the lower suspension chain which consisted of 5 discs joined by inter locking rings whilst the upper chain consisted of 4 discs joined together in the same manner. The two chains were joined on a catch with a belt loop clip: this was decorated with an oakleaf design. The discs on the suspension chains were alternately decorated with sunwheel swastikas and eagles.

The centre ramp scabbard mount on this pattern of NSKK dagger will be encountered with a retaining screw on the opposite side to the chain attachment and also without. Additionally examples will be encountered with three discs in the upper chain instead of the customary four: although this is more usual on the Marine NSKK dagger. The reverse of the suspension chains were marked with the following lettering "MUSTERSCHUTZ NSKK KORPSFUHRUNG" on the last link next to the suspension catch of the upper chain, and the RZM proofmark and an M5 Maker's control number should appear on the opposing link on the lower chain.

All daggers of the NSKK came under RZM inspection controls: consequently the 1936 NSKK dagger carried the RZM proofmark and Maker's control number rather than the Maker's own logo proofmark. This was true for all NSKK daggers produced during this period. However it should be remembered that some long standing NSKK members might have preferred to retain their existing 1933 pattern dagger and merely purchase the new 1936 pattern scabbard with suspension chains, therefore it should not be regarded as suspicious to find an early dagger with a Maker's proofmark in the latter 1936 scabbard bearing RZM proofmarks.

The 1936 chained NSKK dagger will be encountered with two different types of fittings: early examples produced had nickel silver fittings on both dagger and scabbard however latter examples featured nickel plating over base metal. These latter examples have a tendency for the plating to lift and/or bubble in much the same way as the later RZM marked SA daggers do.

The reproduction checklist for the 1933/1936 pattern NSKK daggers is the same as that for the 1933 pattern SA dagger.

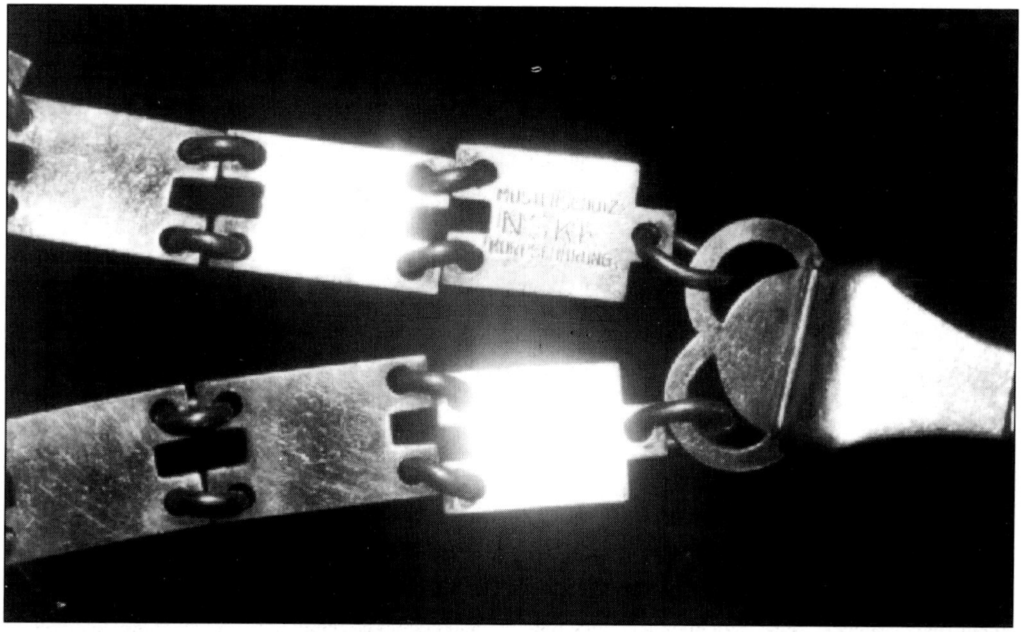

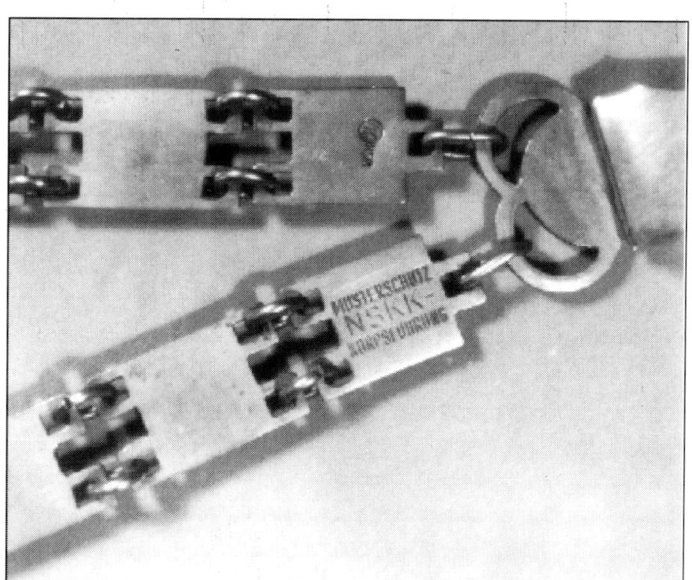

Comparison photographs of NSKK 1936 pattern hanging chains. The top set are reproductions; note the thick interlocking rings when compared to the genuine set of chains in the bottom photograph.

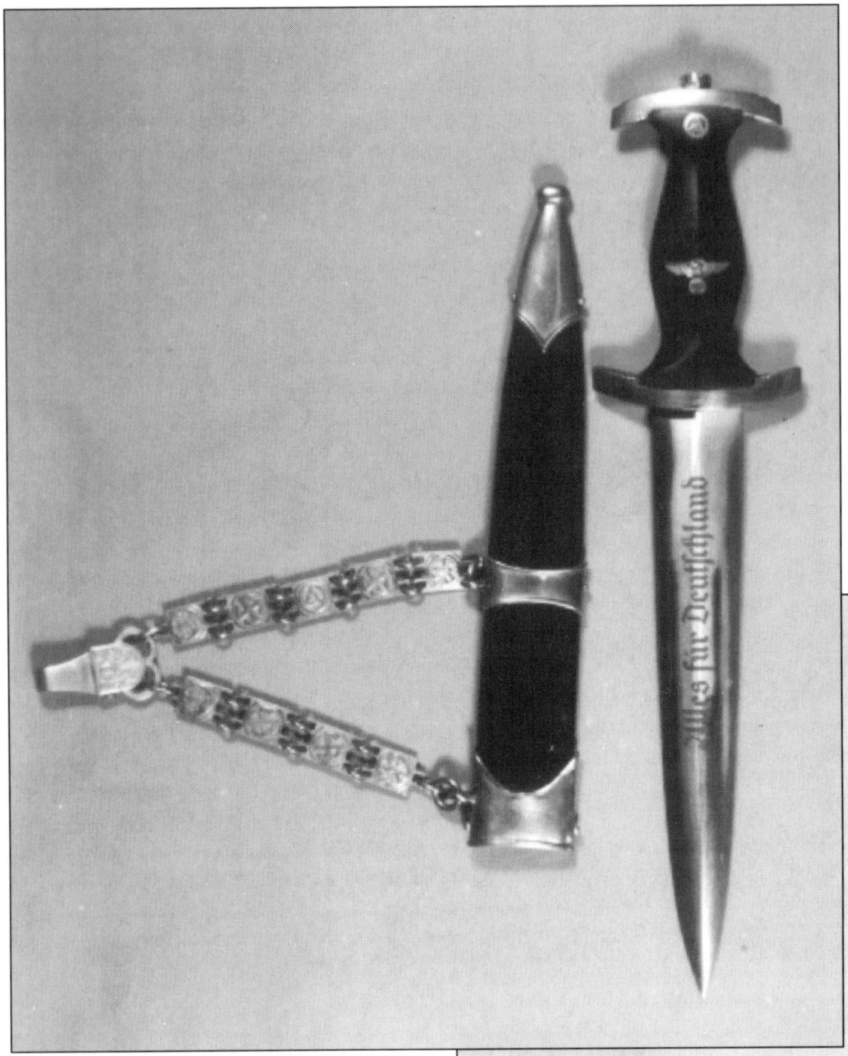

Obverse side of a genuine 1936 pattern chained NSKK dagger. The blade retains its original polish which highlights the quality of the blade motto etching. The hanging chains have the correct configuration of four upper and five lower links. Note the crisp detail of the links design.

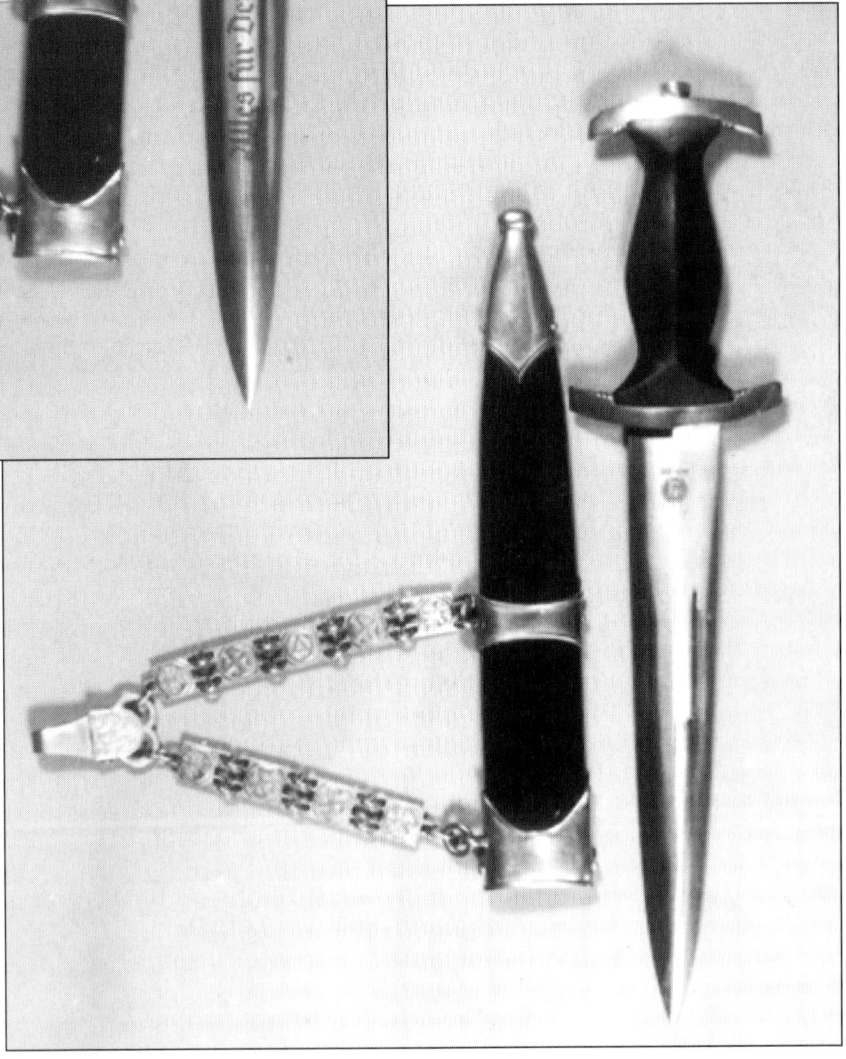

Reverse view of a genuine 1936 pattern NSKK dagger. Note the excellent crossguard to grip fit and the clarity and position of the RZM proofmark and Maker's control number.

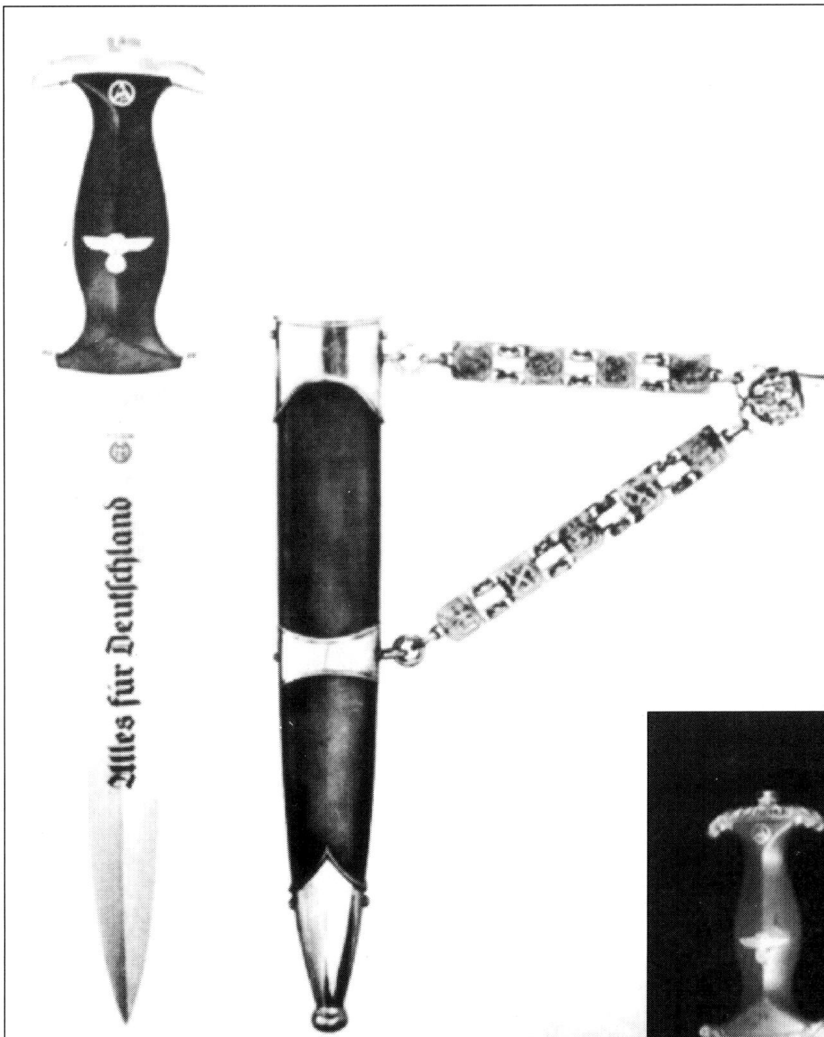

(Left) A reproduction 1936 pattern NSKK dagger. The detail of both dagger and scabbard is quite good, however this piece is let down by its blade which has a sharp central ridge. Also the RZM proofmark has been incorrectly applied on the obverse ricasso instead of the reverse. The blade motto and proofmark should not appear on the same side of the blade. Note the incorrect type of interlocking rings and their over wide spacing. Also the centre scabbard ramp has been mounted too low.

(Right) A parts assembly 1936 pattern NSKK presentation dagger. This piece is well put together utilising a genuine SA dagger which has had its crossguards engraved with a floral decoration. The scabbard is a genuine 1936 pattern NSKK type, however the hanging chains are reproductions. Note the thin wire interlockers on the hanging chains.

Civil Service Daggers

In all there were seven German civil service organisations authorised to wear a dress sidearm during the Third Reich era . These were: the Feuerwehr/Fire Service; Postschutz/Postal Protection Service; Wasserschutzpolizei/Water Protection Police; Deutsches Reichsbahn/National Railways; Deutsches Rotes Kreuz/German Red Cross; Diplomaten und Staatsbeamte/Diplomatic and Government Officials; and Zolldienst/Customs Officials.

The Feuerwehr was one of the few organisations in existence during the Nazi period that did not include the swastika symbol on its dress sidearm. The absence of any specific Nazi symbol often makes Feuerwehr daggers difficult to date and actually ascribe to the years 1933-1945. The same style of Fireman's dagger was in use during the Imperial, Weimar Republic and Nazi period with very little change or modification. Also the same weapons are still being produced in Solingen today, to the same standards and indeed by the same Makers as those being made prior to 1945. Therefore it is extremely difficult to draw a line between what is a genuine Third Reich Feuerwehr sidearm and what is either pre-1933 or post-1945.

Daggers of the Postschutz are quite rare and much sought after by collectors. They have been reproduced with varying degrees of success, however most of the convincing reproductions tend to be parts assemblies using some genuine elements. Frequently the hanging chains on the scabbard of these fabrications are taken from 1st pattern Luftwaffe daggers, and require close examination.

The Water Protection Police dagger has been reproduced quite successfully. However due to its close similarity to the Kriegsmarine dirk, this Police dagger is most frequently encountered as a parts assembly fabrication: usually taking the form of a genuine Kriegsmarine scabbard, blade and crossguard applied to a reproduction leather bound Police grip and flaming ball pommel. A further simple expedient used to increase the value of genuine Water Protection daggers is the addition of a good quality reproduction Police eagle insignia affixed to the grip of a genuine dagger. This practice has come about because only a small number of early original Wasserschutzpolizei daggers were issued with the grip insignia. Most later examples were devoid of this insignia, and the presence of the Police insignia can therefore increase the value of a genuine dagger by as much as 20%.

Reichsbahn daggers are valued in the middle to upper price range, and as such have been widely reproduced: in some instances to quite a high standard. The Reichsbahn Wasserschutzpolizei is a rare dagger which unfortunately has many characteristics in common with the humble Army dagger: namely the blade, scabbard and crossguard, all of which are virtually identical. These similarities make this dagger susceptible to parts assembly fabrications using the aforementioned Army dagger parts allied to a reproduction grip, ferrule and pommel. The main points to observe are the scabbard suspension loops which are of a different design on the Reichsbahn Wasserschutzpolizei, although the overall shape and pebbling are the same as those on the Army dagger scabbard.

The two types of DRK sidearm have both been reproduced, although the DRK Subordinate's is the more commonly encountered. The complicated grip securing system on the DRK Leader's dagger has never been successfully reproduced, and this area is always a good indicator when examining a DRK dagger.

The Diplomat's dagger is one of the most attractive Third Reich daggers and one of the more expensive types. As such it has been extensively reproduced, both as complete daggers and in parts assemblies. The Diplomat's dagger has some similarities to the common Army dagger, namely the blade and scabbard which make it an ideal subject for parts fabrication using genuine Army dagger parts. Most reproductions tend to use white plastic for the grips rather than the mother-of-pearl of originals. The most common type of reproduction has the silver finish, however examples are available with a gold wash.

The Third Reich Customs service was separated into two branches: Land Customs and Water Customs. The original daggers for both organisations were identical in style and only differed in the colour of the leather binding of the scabbard and grip (green for Land Customs, blue for Water Customs), and the material composition of their fittings: Land Customs being silver and Water Customs being gold. Original Land Customs daggers were not of a particularly high quality, consequently many originals are often mistaken for reproductions and vice versa. The Water Customs dagger is worth more than three times as much as its Land Customs counterpart, consequently many genuine Land Customs daggers have been gold dipped and had their leather dyed blue in order to pass them off as genuine Water Customs daggers.

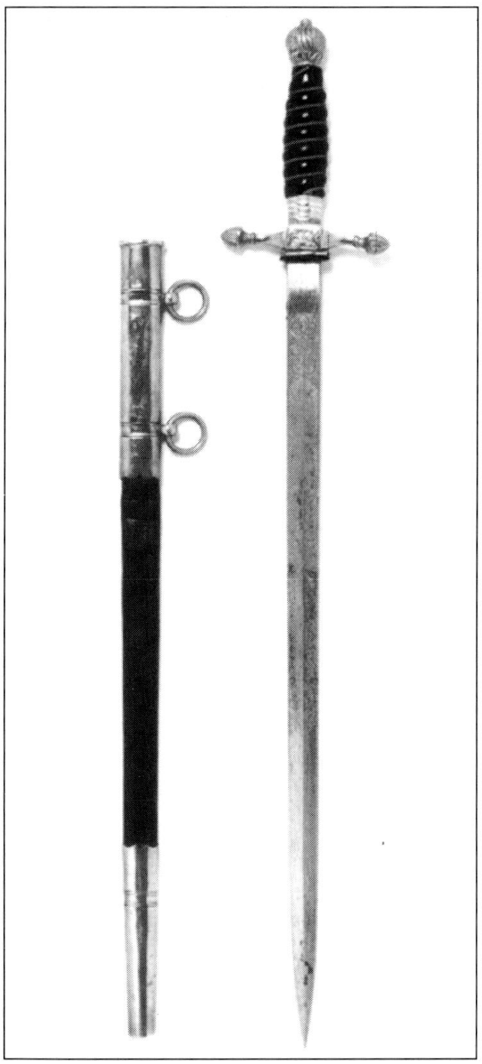

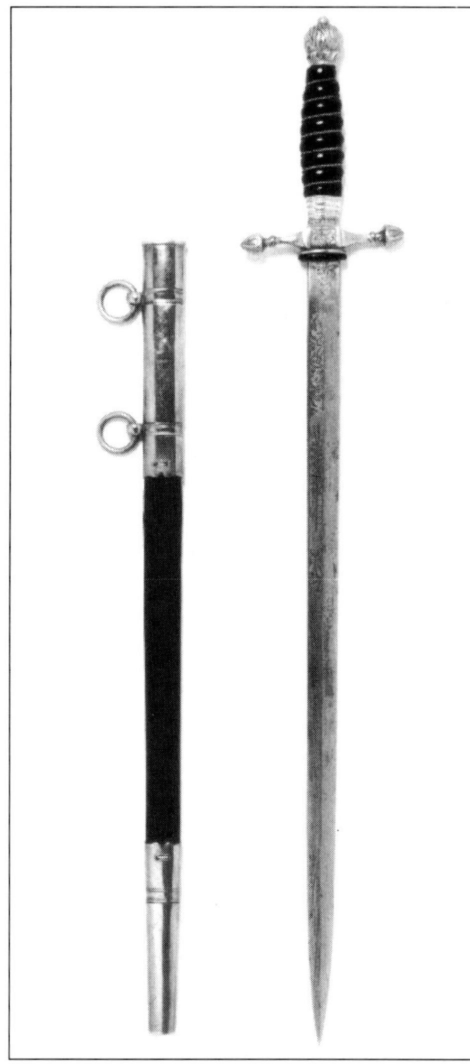

Obverse and reverse sides of a genuine Feuerwehr dagger by W K C. This dagger dates from the Nazi era and displays a style which was consistent both prior to and after World War II. This dagger with a floral design etched blade is slightly longer than most examples, but shows all the characteristics and design found on this pattern of dagger from most periods.

POSTSCHUTZ REPRODUCTIONS

RECOGNITION CHECKLIST

BLADE

- A blade bearing a proofmark other than Paul Weyersburg, Solingen should be viewed with suspicion, although genuine examples have ben encountered devoid of any proofmark.
- The use of the RZM proofmark would indicate a reproduction, as RZM regulations did not apply to the Postschutz.
- The length of the blade should be measured against the scabbard, as a short blade could indicate that it originated from an RLB Subordinate's dagger.
- The absence of a billet clamp seam is a feature of Spanish reproductions.
- A crudely formed tang is invariably found on reproduction blades.
- The central ridge on reproductions is rounded whereas original blades had a clearly defined ridge running the full length of the blade.

SCABBARD

- A scabbard bound with leather, either black or dark blue, would indicate the use of a 2nd pattern RLB scabbard. The Postschutz scabbard should be plain steel painted black.
- The absence of a central scabbard band would indicate the use of a 1st pattern RLB scabbard. The RLB type only has one upper suspension ring.
- A scabbard with only one fitting at the bottom and the triangular gate suspender at the top would indicate the use of a 1st or 2nd pattern RLB Subordinates's scabbard. The only similarity between this type of scabbard and the Postschutz is that they are both sheet steel painted black. This type of scabbard was observed on one fabricated Postschutz dagger where an RLB Subordinate's blade had been used in the fabrication.
- Current Spanish reproductions utilise brass to construct the scabbard fittings which is then very lightly nickel plated. Original fittings were always of heavy nickel silver.

GRIP

- A grip made from softwood rather than the ebony or hardwood of originals is a feature of reproduction grips. A broad grain is always discernible in softwoods such as pine rather than the close fine grain of hardwoods.
- Grips should be observed for their density of colour as originally produced grips, either ebony or stained hardwood, tend to maintain their colour even after 50 years. Currently produced grips have a thin inferior quality stain applied to them, of the modern, fast drying type which does not penetrate to wood to the same extent as the traditional types. Consequently modern grips often demonstrate a shallow colour density, and often the stain can be smudged or uneven as they are susceptible to moisture since most modern stains are water soluble.
- The grip inlay having gaps around its edge is indicative of modern reproduction grips. Genuine grips have the inlay inset virtually perfectly.
- The grip inlay situated precisely in the centre of the grip is a feature of some reproductions. The original grip inlays were always positioned slightly above centre.
- Post-war produced wooden grips are often incorrectly turned and can exhibit extreme characteristics which were not a feature of originals: i.e. the top and bottom necks of the grip are too narrow; the centre section has a pronounced bulge; or each end having been turned, too much or too little, does not fit into the pommel or crossguard correctly causing an overlap on either the pommel and

crossguard fittings or each end of the grip.

- Crossguards which bear no issue serial number or D R P identification code on their underside should be viewed with suspicion.
- Where the serial number and D R P code are present make sure the stamping is first on the correct arm i.e. serial number on the left arm and D R P on the right, and that second the stamping is executed in the correct form i.e. the numbers and letters should be 0.5mm thick whereas the stampings on reproduction crossguards are twice as thick as that and in some cases even more. Also the numbers and letters are noticeably uneven on reproduction crossguards, and are not as evenly struck being too deep in some parts and too shallow or even nonexistent in others.
- The crossguards of some reproductions are slightly undersize and exhibit this in the depth in the crossguard which is approximately 1/3 narrower than originals. The slightly smaller size at the base of the crossguard causes an odd looking uneven fit into the scabbard throat which tends to look marginally off centre.
- The inset swastika of the crossguard has too wide a shape, and is noticeably thicker than originals having a bulky appearance. This swastika is also usually black painted on reproduction crossguards instead of the inlaid black enamel of originals.
- The internal recesses of the crossguard and pommel of reproductions are quite crudely finished and invariably exhibit a rough finish.
- The grip inlays of originals were usually nickel or silver plated. Examples of reproductions inlays have been observed in aluminium and copper, the latter being thinly plated.

PROOFMARKS

The proofmark of Paul Weyersburg is the only Maker's proofmark which should be present on the blade of a genuine Postschutz Leader's dagger. The use of the RZM proofmark or control number was not appropriate for the Postschutz, for even though the Postal Protection Force did become a nominal part of the SS in 1942, the organisation was not subject to RZM control or regulations in regard to the Postschutz dagger.

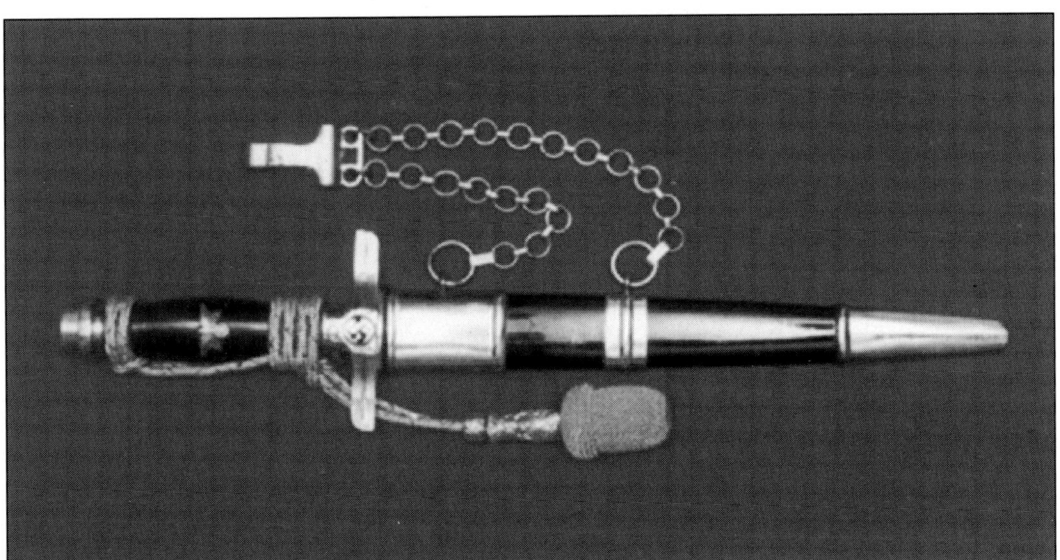

A genuine Postschutz Leader's dagger with correct hanging chains and portepee knot.

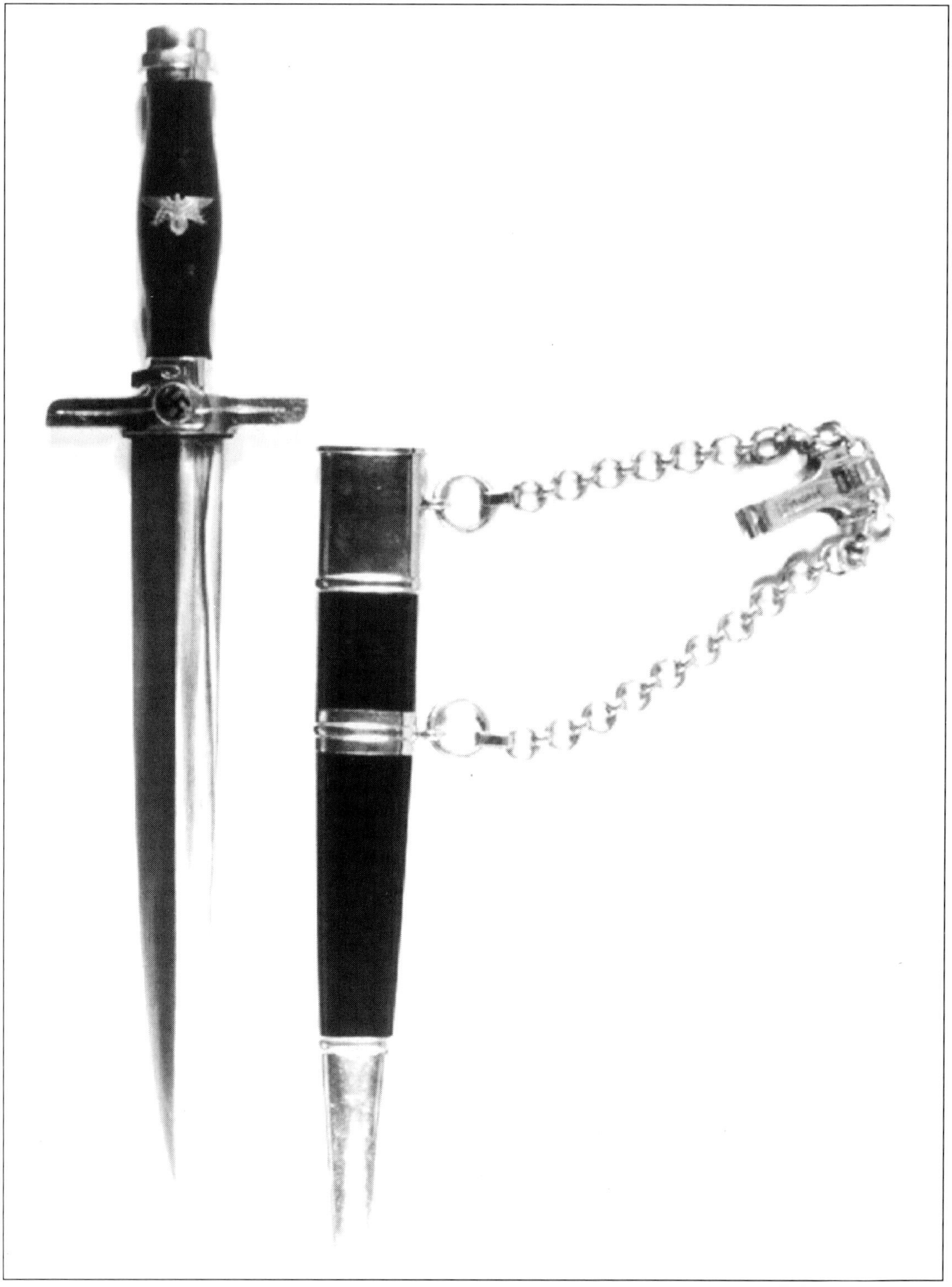

Obverse view of a genuine Postschutz Leader's dagger. Note the crisp detail of the dagger and scabbard fittings especially when compared to most current reproductions. This photograph also shows the reverse detail of the hanging chains and belt clip.

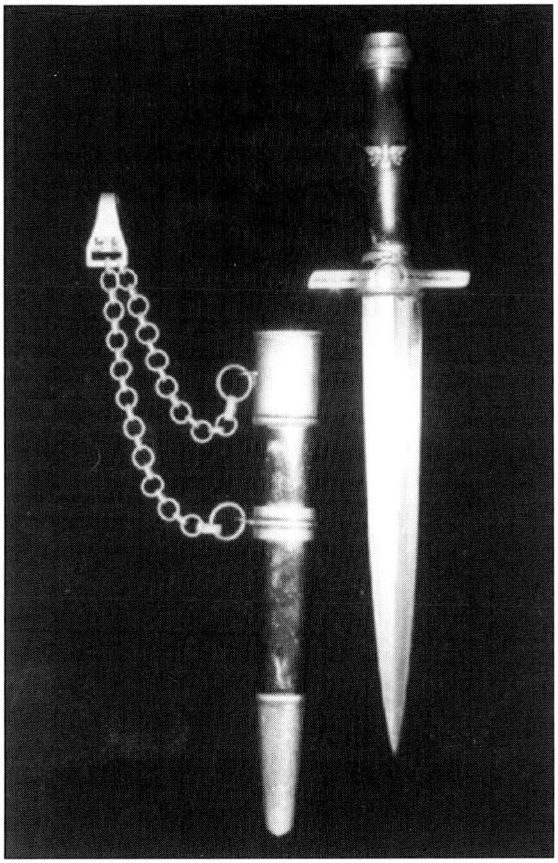

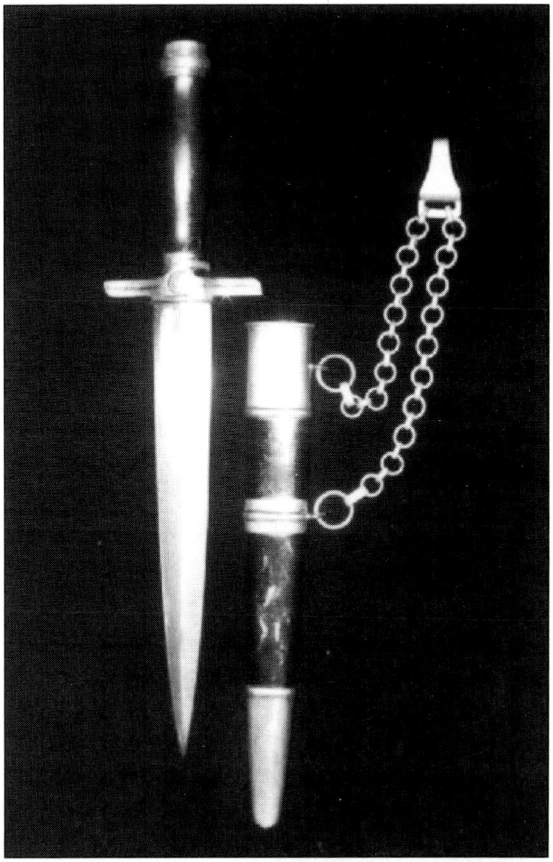

Obverse and reverse views of a reproduction Postschutz Leader's dagger. Superficially this German reproduction has quite a good overall appearance but suffers from the usual use of inferior materials which are plated brass castings and now have a gold appearance where most of the poor quality silver plating has rubbed off. As can be noted from these photographs the blade has an incorrect shape being too wide at the ricasso and tapering too sharply to the point. The central ridge is also not as sharp and clearly defined as that found on originals. The chains have links which are somewhat thinner than originals and also fit into a rectangular slot in the beltclip instead of into two separate holes.

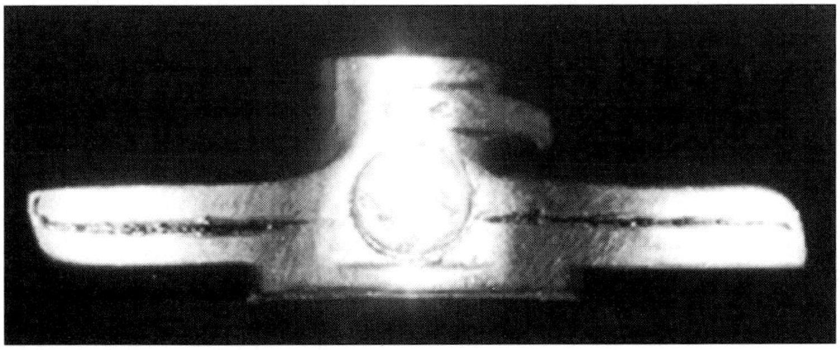

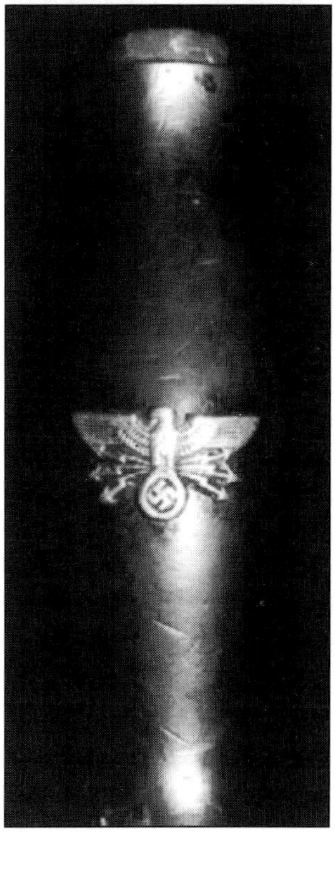

Close-up detail of the grip and crossguard of the same reproduction Postschutz Leader's dagger. Note the exceptionally poor detail on the crossguard where the eagle's eye is barely visible, and also the poor shape and definition of the whole crossguard, but particularly the swastika inlay which is actually incorrectly mounted being situated sitting on the bottom rim of the crossguard. The wooden shell grip is made from softwood rather than hard, but of particular note is the grip inlay insignia which lacks any detail on the eagle and has been mounted onto the grip with epoxy adhesive.

RAILWAY REPRODUCTIONS

Due to the considerably high prices which genuine Bahnschutz daggers now realise on the collector market there have been a number of reproductions in circulation for many years. The Bahnschutz dagger is one which the Spanish reproducers have not yet exploited to the same extent as the Nazi military and Party form daggers.

Most of the reproductions which have been encountered by the author over the past 20 years would appear to have been of German Manufacture and have leaned heavily on castings to produce most of the component parts of the daggers. Many of the examples examined have been constructed from materials completely unlike those found on original Bahnschutz daggers: usually being of brass castings rather than aluminium as originals were. These brass castings have probably been copied from original fittings which accounts for their size being slightly smaller than originals, due to shrinkage in the moulding process. The use of brass in constructing reproduction fittings for the Bahnschutz daggers tends to give the reproductions a very heavy feel as opposed to the originals which were a relatively lightweight dagger.

The blades found on most Bahnschutz reproductions tend to be post-war reproductions of the Army style blade or even actual blades from a genuine Army dagger. This takes us into the second category of reproductions of the Bahnschutz dagger which is the parts assembly fabrications which are parts from genuine Army daggers (such as the blade and scabbard) which have been modified in order to copy the shape and style of a Bahnschutz dagger. The technique of using genuine spare parts to compose a fabrication is especially prevalent on the Railway Water Protection Police dagger which has many similar characteristics to that of the Army dagger: namely the blade, crossguard and scabbard which only requires a modification to the scabbard bands. In fact the genuine Railway Water Protection Police dagger is little more than a modified and over embellished Army dagger; consequently when encountering examples of this dagger it is always prudent to look for evidence of modification rather than just a blatant reproduction.

The subject of the "1935 pattern Bahnschutz dagger" has already been dealt with in the main text of this chapter, however in view of the comments made there this piece also needs to be examined from the reproduction pint of view. Whatever one's opinion may be about this particular pattern of dagger they are on the collectors market as a genuine Third Reich period produced dagger, and have as a consequence been the subject of reproduction and fabrication. This latter form is the most commonly encountered due to the close similarity between this dagger and the standard 1935 pattern Army dagger. In fact the only thing which separates the two is the colour of the grip being black or deep purple. Several types of reproduction grips in the Army style, but being black in colour, have been produced since World War II as replacements with which to modify genuine Army dagger into "Bahnschutz daggers". This simple expedient can virtually double the price of an otherwise common but genuine Army dagger without the necessity for major surgery.

The Spanish have produced a version of this dagger which is merely the standard Spanish reproduction of the Army dagger with a black plastic grip. The reproduction characteristics for this particular piece are the same as those for the Spanish reproduction Army dagger: the only additional points being a black plastic grip instead of celluloid one and being solid rather than having an inner wooden sleeve. The ridges on the grip spiral twist of these reproductions are very sharp and pronounced and also tend to be slightly oversize.

A German manufacturer is known to have produced black celluloid grips for the "1935 Bahnschutz dagger" as early as the 1960's which accounts for many of the examples of this dagger which appeared on the market at the same time and subsequently. These grips are marginally narrower than a regular Army grip and are noticeably longer by almost half an inch giving the grip two extra twists on the spiral.

A personal view of this particular dagger is that it is nothing more than a glorified Army dagger even when all the parts are original, and when containing reproduction parts in a fabrication it is probably worth something slightly less that a letter opener!

1938 BAHNSCHUTZ LEADER'S DAGGER

In 1938 a distinctive dress dagger was authorised to be worn by Bahnschutz Leaders with the rank of Oberzugfuhrer or above. This dagger featured an Army style double edged stiletto blade which bore no organisational motto only the Maker's proofmark on the reverse ricasso. The dagger fittings, pommel, crossguard and ferrule were silver plated, steel or nickel silver, however later examples tended to have cast aluminium fittings. The celluloid grip was a very deep purple with later examples quite often being black. The twist in the grip ran from top right to bottom left.

The metal scabbard was plated or finished in the same fittings as the corresponding dagger i.e. silver plate or aluminium. The crossguard bore the Reichsbahn symbol of a winged locomotive wheel and the domed top of the pommel had a raised stylised swastika decoration. The dagger had a set of fabric hanging straps with a purple velvet background and two black facing stripes. The oval buckles and other hanger fittings had an oakleaf decoration and were finished in silver. As originator of the piece Eickhorn is the most commonly encountered proofmark on the Bahnschutz Leader's dagger. A silver cord portepee with inter woven purple thread was authorised to be worn with the Bahnschutz Leader's dagger. Its overall length was 42cms or 16 1/2 inches.

RECOGNITION CHECKLIST

BLADE

➢ The use of an RZM proofmark on a Bahnschutz blade is totally inappropriate for this organisation.
➢ A dull matt grey finished blade is a characteristic of early Spanish reproduction blades for this dagger.
➢ A flat tang.
➢ The absence of billet clamp marks or seams.
➢ In most respects the points to observe for the Army and 2nd pattern Luftwaffe dagger blades can also be applied to Bahnschutz dagger blades.

SCABBARD

➢ Generally speaking most genuine Bahnschutz scabbards were made from aluminium. However genuine examples produced in a lightweight sheet steel have been encountered: these probably were produced in the early War years when aluminium was in short supply.
➢ Heavy steel or zinc alloy scabbards are post-war reproductions: the examples with a grey finish are of Spanish origin, although some of these scabbards may also have been chromed.
➢ Observe the scabbard tip carefully for evidence of the end decoration being brazed on separately.
➢ In most instances reproduction scabbards are considerably heavier than originals. A magnet test will detect a reproduction scabbard made from steel: aluminium originals being nonferrous will not attract a magnet.
➢ In common with many other reproductions, reproduction Bahnschutz scabbards often feature long thin wooden liners which were never a feature of original scabbards. Other types of reproduction scabbard liners are made of plastic.

GRIP

➢ The use of brass castings in constructing the grip fittings is a characteristic of modern reproductions. Originals were always die struck aluminium.
➢ Reproduction brass cast grip fittings have a thin silver or chrome plating applied over them giving them a very bright appearance rather than the subdued shine of polished aluminium.
➢ The inside grip fittings especially the crossguard should be closely observed for casting flaws and pitting which is an inevitable result of mould casting soft alloys such as brass.
➢ Reproduction crossguard, pommel and ferrules are usually noticeably smaller than originals by up to 10%: this is due to the reproduction casting mould being modelled from an original and also shrinkage during the mould casting process.

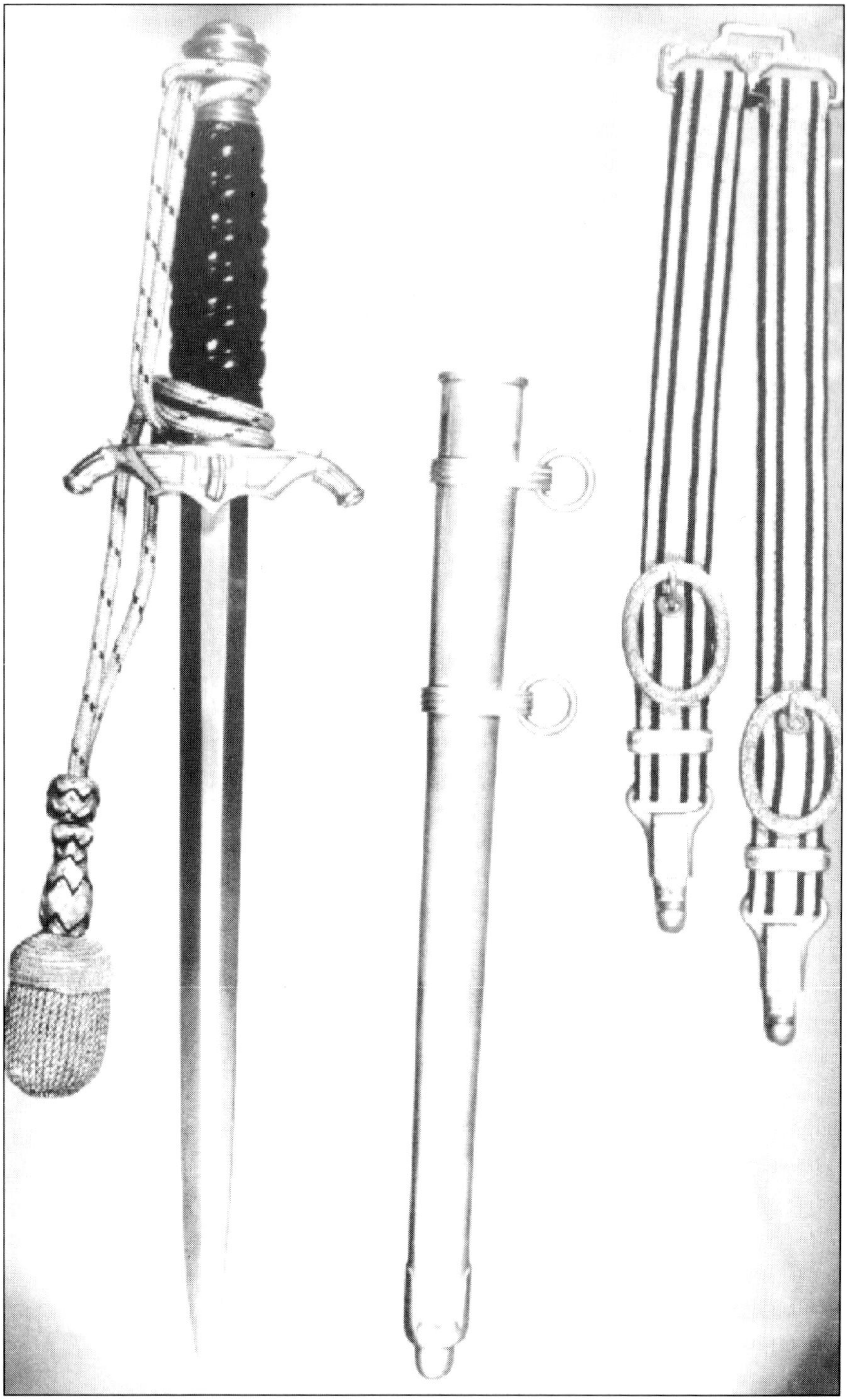

Obverse view of a genuine 1938 pattern Bahnschutz Leader's dagger, which has the correct portepee wrap for this type of dagger. The hanging straps illustrated are the regulation type for this dagger. Note the quality of the fittings on the dagger and scabbard.

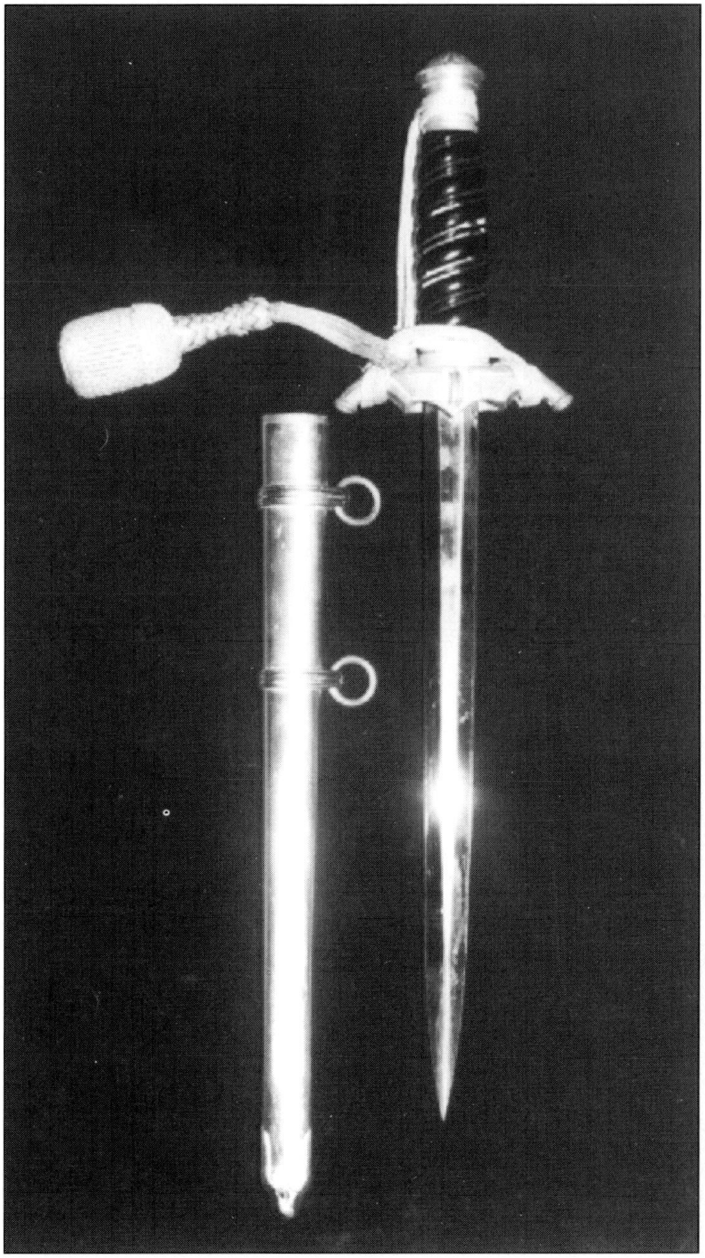

Obverse view of a modern reproduction Bahnschutz Leader's dagger. This piece really looks the business but upon close inspection the detail is nowhere near as fine as that found on originals and also the alloy fittings lack the class of an original. The blade of this reproduction has an extremely high polish giving it an almost plastic appearance. The grooves on the grip are much too sharp and the pommel neck is actually too big. The scabbard has a fine pebbled finish and exhibits a long lateral casting flaw towards the tip. The piece has had a genuine silver portepee added to disguise the reproduction shortcomings.

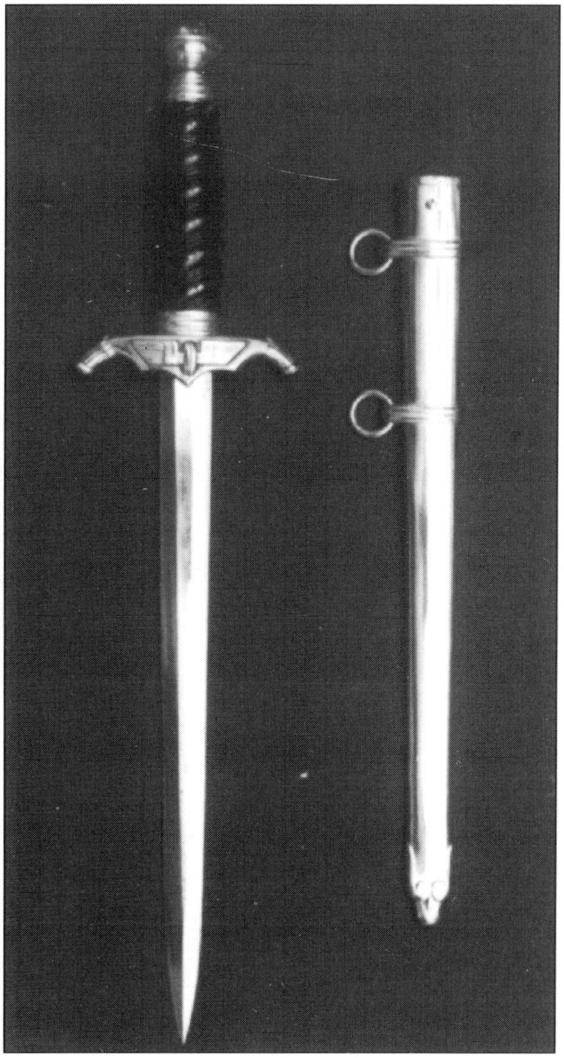

Obverse out of scabbard view of a genuine 1938 pattern Bahnschutz Leader's dagger.

RAILWAY WATER PROTECTION DAGGERS

Introduced slightly later in 1938 than the preceding Bahnschutz Leader's dagger, the Railway Water Protection Police dagger was only issued to a very limited number of police officers in this small organisation, and consequently it is one of the rarest of the production Third Reich daggers. The double edged stiletto blade was of Army style and bore no organisational motto whatsoever: the only blade marking being a Maker's proofmark applied to the reverse ricasso. The steel scabbard was identical in form to the Army scabbard with the pebbled finish. However the two scabbard bands were of a different design being composed of four narrow ribs running horizontally around each band. The crossguard was of the Army design bearing an eagle with outstretched wings clutching a wreathed swastika. The ferrule was just lightly ribbed, and bore no oakleaf decoration. The black celluloid grips had a spiral twist running top right to bottom left. The domed pommel bore the same stylised swastika as the Bahnschutz Leader's dagger. A set of double strap black leather hangers were worn with this dagger which featured oval buckles decorated with oakleaves as were the rest of the fittings. The most frequently documented Maker of the Reichsbahn Wasserschutz Polizei is that of Carl Eickhorn, Solingen.

RECOGNITION CHECKLIST

SCABBARD

- Examine scabbards closely for evidence of Bahnschutz bands being substituted for the Army oakleaf style.
- The swirling pattern characteristic of Spanish reproduction Army scabbards should be looked for due to the similarities between the two types of scabbards.
- Scabbards bearing the oakleaf decorated bands are Army dagger scabbards and not any kind of "variation" of a Railway Water Protection scabbard.

GRIP

- Oversized thick grips with sharp edges on the spiral twists are evidence of a reproduction grip.
- A ferrule with an oakleaf decorated design is just a standard Army dagger part.
- Genuine Bahnschutz ferrules have a lateral ribbed design.
- Most reproduction grips are made from bright plastic usually nylon and do not have the same deep tone as original grips which tended to be a deep purple rather than black.
- Reproduction pommels are usually brass castings and lack the fine definition of originals.
- Reproduction pommels also have a tendency to be undersized due to shrinkage from mould casting.
- The neck of the pommel on many reproductions is very narrow and lacks the finely detailed steps on the lower shoulder.

PROOFMARKS

Various Maker's proofmarks will be encountered on reproduction Railway Water Protection Police daggers especially if the reproduction has been fabricated using a genuine Army dagger blade. However when blatant reproduction blades have been used then the usual handful of Spanish applied proofmarks will be encountered; these include: F W Holler, Berlin; F W Holler, Solingen; Alcoso; and the ubiquitous RZM proofmark which was totally inappropriate for any Bahnschutz dagger. Good quality German reproduction Army dagger blades will be found in reproduction Railway Water Protection daggers; the most common proofmarks on these blades being: Carl Eickhorn (with small oval and the large squirrel proofmarks); Paul Weyersburg; Alcoso; and Ernst Pack & Sohne.

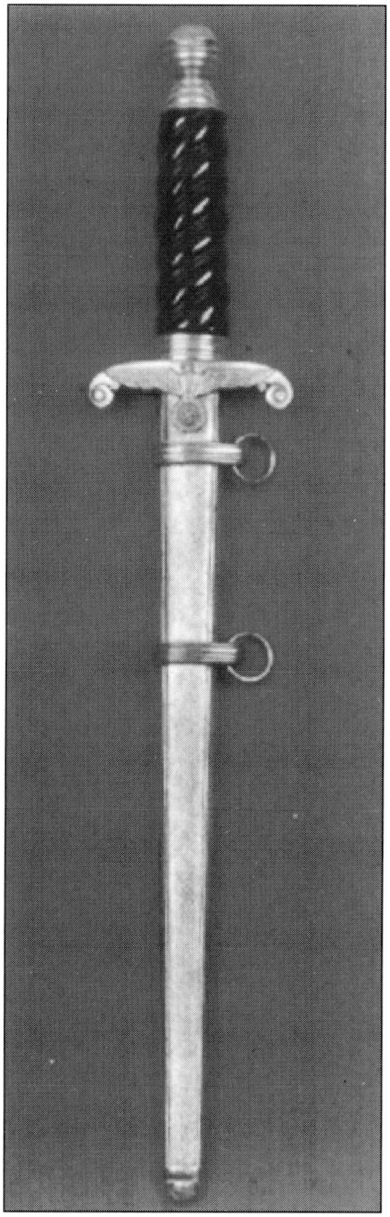

Two obverse views of the same genuine Railway Water Protection Police dagger. One view shows the overall appearance of the dagger whilst the other shows close-up detail of the crossguard and grip assembly.

WASSERSCHUTZPOLIZEI REPRODUCTIONS

Reproductions associated with the Water Protection dagger fall into two main categories: complete reproductions and converted genuine Navy daggers which have had the relevant parts substituted. Many of the characteristics of reproductions of this dagger are the same as those for the reproduction Navy dagger which in brief mainly deal with the quality of detail and the material composition of scabbard and fittings.

The question of substitution parts being added to genuine Navy daggers is a much more difficult issue to address: for in total there are only two parts which require replacing to fabricate a Water Protection Police dagger from an otherwise perfectly genuine Navy dagger. These are the pommel and grip. The pommels normally used to fabricate these daggers are: genuine examples of the early 1st pattern Navy pommel which had the flaming ball design, or post-war manufactured pommels. Two points will be helpful in identifying these different pommels. First genuine pommels for Water Protection daggers are slightly larger than those for the 1st pattern Navy dagger, especially around the neck of the pommel which needed to be slightly larger to fit around the thicker leather bound grip of the Water Protection dagger. Second most of the post-war produced pommels especially the earlier types were made from incorrect material being aluminium or Zinc castings lightly gold plated whereas originals were solid brass and fire gilded. Also many of the post-war pommels have the socket thread tapped slightly off centre, which makes them “wonky” when they are screwed into place and also gives them an uneven fit when they are located into the top of the grip.

The grips of genuine Water Protection daggers were always a wooden shell wrapped with blue leather and bound with twisted gold wire. However post-war productions or fabrications of the grips for this dagger rarely meet this specification. Most of the reproduction grips tend to be a plain plastic shell with artificial leather binding, and depending on the manufacturer are sometimes even the wrong shape. This usually occurs when the grips from reproduction Water Customs daggers are used to make up the reproduction. Fabrications of the grip invariably use a genuine celluloid Navy grip as a base over which to wrap imitation blue leather. However in most instances these fabrications suffer from two major faults: they are either very poorly finished where the leather is joined, or the grip has a very bulging appearance much larger than originals.

Although not a feature of most genuine Water Protection daggers some early examples had a gold police insignia applied to the middle of the obverse grip. The presence or absence of this insignia does not indicate a reproduction or fabrication. However where an insignia is present the style and method of attaching the insignia will help to determine whether the insignia is actually contemporary with the dagger or is a modern, post-war addition. This determination is absolutely essential for the presence of a police insignia on any genuine Water Protection dagger can greatly increase the value of the piece out of all proportion to the intrinsic value of the insignia. In observing genuine Wasserschutzpolizei daggers it is apparent that the provision for the insignia was made at the time of the dagger's manufacture: as two small holes were drilled through the grip and shell through which the two prongs of the insignia were inserted and then bent back inside the shell. This technique is very similar to that found on the grip inlay of Hitler Youth knives. In most instances where spurious Police insignia have been added to genuine Water Protection dagger they have been glued into position with an epoxy resin adhesive. Removing the pommel and looking inside the grip cavity will in most cases reveal whether the insignia has been applied in the correct fashion and is contemporary with the dagger.

RECOGNITION CHECKLIST

BLADE

- Blade etching too lightly applied.
- Poor definition on the Maker's proofmark.
- No provision made on the tang for the spring steel strip which holds the blade locking button.
- Crudely shaped tang.

- Square tang (the tang on genuine Navy blades were machine or hand filed when fitting the spring steel strip).
- It should be borne in mind in view of the aforementioned point that the absence of a billet clamp seam on the tang of a Naval blade does not necessarily indicate that the blade is a reproduction: as the billet clamp marks were frequently erased during the spring fitting process.
- Presence of a felt blade washer instead of the correct leather type.

SCABBARD

- Reproduction scabbards are invariably the lightening bolt type.
- The current Spanish reproduction scabbards have a cheap looking gold plating instead of a gilt finish.
- Reproduction scabbard bands are manufactured as a part of half the scabbard: the two halves then being joined together. Original bands were made as a single piece ring and then sweated onto the completed scabbard.
- The rings for the hanger loops are very poorly defined and too thick.
- The scabbard's throat screws are flat headed and screwed in flush with the side of the scabbard instead of being domed and protruding.
- The total absence of any scabbard throat screws.
- Absence of a scabbard liner.
- The use of thin wooden, plastic or tin slides usually just brazed, stapled or glued into position.

GRIP

- Poor detail on the pommel or crossguard castings.
- Incorrect twist on the grip spiral i.e. running top left to bottom right instead of vice versa.
- Grips with a plastic shell rather than a wooden one.
- The grip binding wire too thin. This can be either a slender double twisted strand or sometimes even just a single strand.
- The blade locking button is mounted too high on the crossguard of many reproductions.
- Undersized pommel giving a poor pommel to grip fit.
- The pommel screw thread off centre.
- Pommels made from alloys which are considerably lighter than the original brass fittings.
- A light weight crossguard made from white metal or alloy with very bright modern gold plating applied over the metal. Original fittings were cast from solid brass than gilded: period gilding has a much more subdued colour than modern plating.
- Badly joined leather covering with evidence of overlapping.
- A grip with a very bulbous appearance.
- Badly fitting grip leather.
- The use of modern alloy Police eagle such as those used on Police bayonets applied to the dagger grip usually be gluing.

PROOFMARKS

Three principal Makers have been identified as manufacturers of genuine Water Protection Police daggers: these are Carl Eickhorn, Paul Weyersburg and Alcoso. The most frequently encountered Maker's proofmarks on reproductions are: F W Holler, E F Horster, Krebs and Clemen & Jung. The last proofmark usually takes the post-war form of a shield within an oval whereas the genuine pre-war proofmark was just a shield with a "Z" in the middle. The question of Water Protection daggers fabricated from genuine parts poses further problems with proofmarks for where genuine blades are used they can bear any of the 17 authorised Makers of Navy daggers for the Nazi period. The use of genuine Navy blades used to fabricate Water Customs daggers makes it essential that the two points which distinguish the Water Protection Police dagger are closely examined i.e. the grip and pommel.

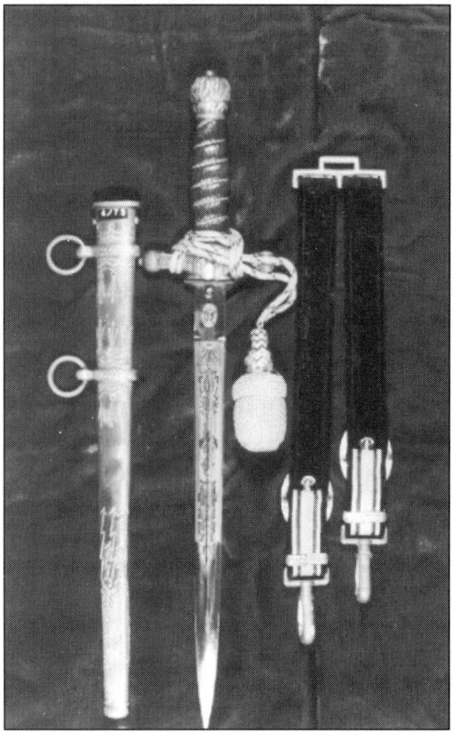

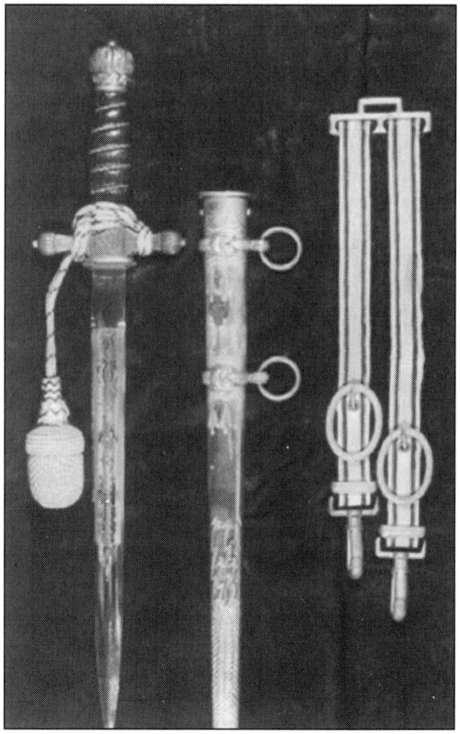

The two photographs above show the obverse and reverse sides of a genuine Water Protection Police dagger with the correct type of portepee knot and gold fabric hanging straps. This dagger is the later type *without* the Police grip insignia.

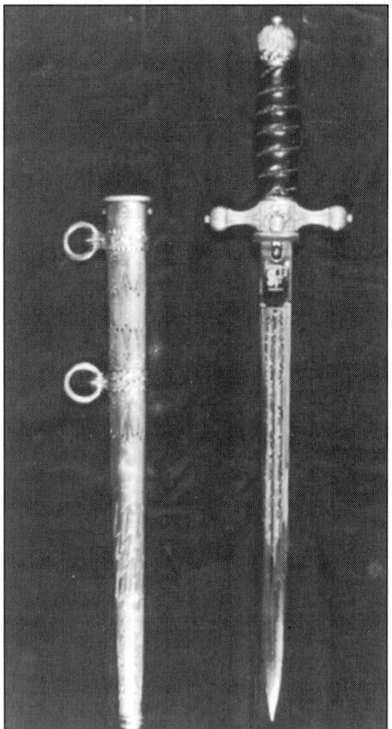

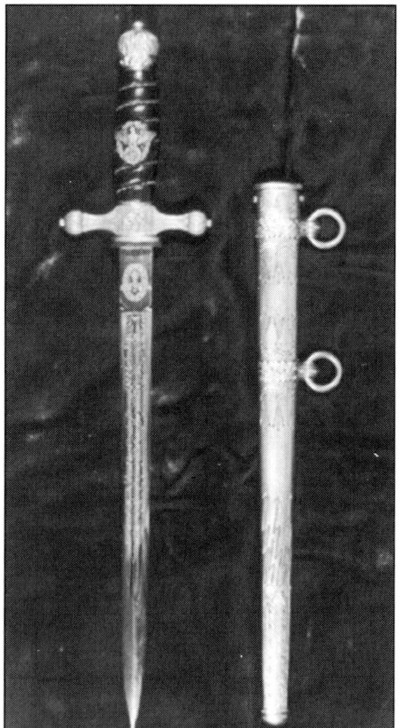

Obverse and reverse sides of a genuine Water Protection Police dagger. This is the early type of Police dagger which features the gold Police eagle grip insignia. Note the Police insignia proofmark on the obverse ricasso and the Eickhorn proofmark on the reverse ricasso. Carl Eickhorn was one of the principal Makers of this dagger.

LAND CUSTOMS REPRODUCTIONS

Reproductions of the Land Customs dagger are always difficult to quantify for many of the characteristics which are normally used to identify modern reproductions can in the case of Land Customs daggers also be related to some genuine examples of this dagger.

As well as straightforward reproductions there are also post-war parts assemblies of the Land Customs dagger to contend with which often feature mixed parts with daggers composed of plated and aluminium fittings, and in some cases the spurious use of Army dagger parts such as pommels and crossguards.

There are also post-war fabrications mainly based on genuine Army daggers with grips and scabbards being bound in green leather over the regular Army parts with new fittings being added to the standard Army scabbard.

It is virtually impossible to distinguish between genuine Land Customs dagger blades and pommels and these same parts from a genuine Army dagger. Therefore the main areas to be observed are the scabbard, grip and crossguard of any Land Customs dagger.

On the Spanish reproductions of the Land Customs dagger there are two main types of proofmark which should give the collector an immediate indication of the presence of a reproduction. The first is the use of the RZM proofmark on the blade which was never used on any genuine pre-1945 produced Land Customs dagger. The second type of proofmark to beware of is that of F W Holler for although Holler was a Third Reich period Solingen dagger Maker this firm is not normally encountered as a manufacturer of Land Customs daggers during the Third Reich era. Also "F W Holler" is the most common of the Maker's proofmarks encountered on Spanish reproduction blades, and due to the similarity of form the same blades are used on reproduction Army, Diplomatic and Land Customs daggers. The earlier reproduction blades bear the "F W Holler, Solingen" proofmark, and later reproduction blades bear the "F W Holler, Berlin" proofmark which in itself is a spurious proofmark - having the "Berlin" substituted for "Solingen".

"Carl Eickhorn" is the most commonly encountered proofmark on genuine Land Customs daggers. However the presence of an Eickhorn proofmark on a blade of any Land Customs dagger should not be taken as proof positive that the whole dagger is absolutely genuine. This fact is mentioned for reproduction examples of the Land Customs dagger have been encountered with genuine Army dagger blades bearing the Eickhorn proofmark substituted for a blatant Spanish reproduction blade. Similarly perfectly genuine Army dagger portepees are frequently added to reproduction Land Customs daggers as a smoke screen embellishment in order to pass the whole piece off as genuine.

RECOGNITION CHECKLIST

BLADE

All the points to observe on the blades of reproduction Land Customs daggers are the same as those for the reproduction Army and Diplomatic dagger blades. These points are quite extensive and have already been dealt with in the sections on "Army" and "Diplomatic" daggers. Consequently only a brief listing is given here:

➢ The spurious use of the RZM proofmark.
➢ The use of the "F W Holler" proofmark, either "Solingen" or "Berlin".
➢ Proofmark too lightly etched.
➢ Absence of billet clamp seams.
➢ Flat tang.
➢ Tang with new appearance having no firescale from tempering.
➢ Blade with rounded bevels, instead of having sharply defined edges on the blade flat.

SCABBARD

- ➢ A straight scabbard instead of being slightly tapered towards the tip.
- ➢ The straight line decoration on the three scabbard fittings is too thick and deeply etched and is usually situated too far away from the edge of the fittings.
- ➢ The scabbard rings are too large and have an incorrect rounded form, often with the hole for the hanger loop drilled slightly off centre.
- ➢ The absence of the straight line etching on the scabbard fittings.
- ➢ The leather section of the scabbard and the fittings being level. The fittings on original scabbards were always slightly raised above the level of the leather on the scabbard.
- ➢ An incorrectly shaped mouth to the scabbard being square or roughly formed instead of having the elliptical shape which corresponds to the shape of the blade.
- ➢ The absence of screws holding the scabbard fittings in place.
- ➢ When screws are used they frequently protrude slightly from the fittings, instead of being countersunk and flush as on originals.
- ➢ The scabbard having an irregular shape with bulges on the leather sections.
- ➢ The use of narrow brass, plastic or wooden scabbard liners.
- ➢ The total absence of any scabbard liners.
- ➢ The use of synthetic imitation leather to cover the scabbard.
- ➢ An unsightly overlapping of the leather binding or raised seams from stitching.

GRIP

- ➢ A pronounced bulge in the centre of the grip.
- ➢ Uneven appearance.
- ➢ Thin, straight grip lacking the slightly tapered shape of originals.
- ➢ A grip bound over a plastic shell instead of original wooden shell.
- ➢ The use of single strand wire to bind the grip.
- ➢ Pointed top on the pommel instead of being slightly domed.
- ➢ The use of brass to make the grip fittings. This alloy was never used on originals and gives the daggers a very top heavy feel.
- ➢ The presence of excessive moulding seams on the sides of the pommel and ferrule.
- ➢ A crossguard eagle with crooked wings instead of being slightly dipped.
- ➢ An eagle with straight wings would indicate the improper use of an Army crossguard.
- ➢ Grip grooves running in the wrong direction i.e. top left to bottom right instead of vice versa.

PROOFMARKS

As previously stated the "Carl Eickhorn" proofmarks most frequently encountered on genuine Land Customs daggers. However a wide variety of other Makers' proofmarks on genuine Army blades can and have been used married to reproduction parts. "F W Holler" is the most frequently encountered proofmark on reproduction Land Customs dagger blades. Also observed have been the "Alcoso" proofmark with the pre-1937 logo which would not have been applied to genuine examples of this dagger as the dagger was only introduced in August, 1937. Additionally the use of the RZM proofmark was not appropriate for any Land Customs dagger.

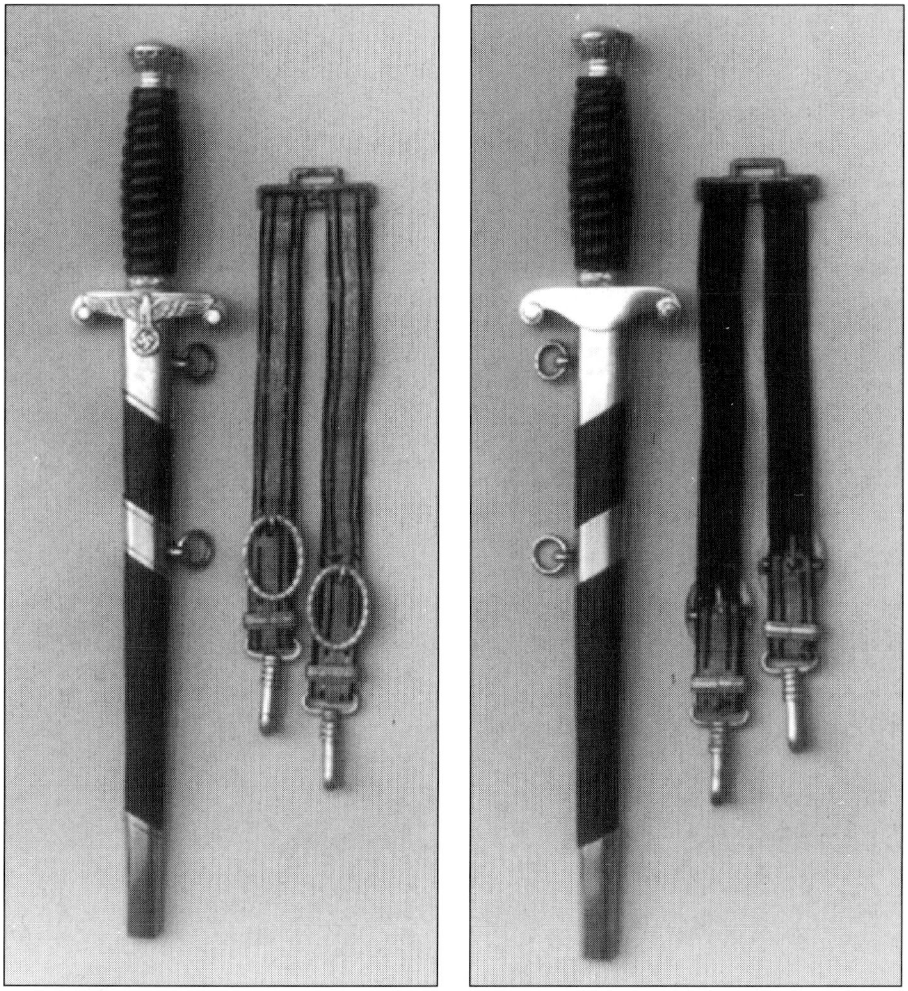

(Left) Obverse and reverse sides of a genuine Land Customs dagger by Carl Eickhorn, also illustrated are the correct fabric hanging straps for the Land Customs dagger.

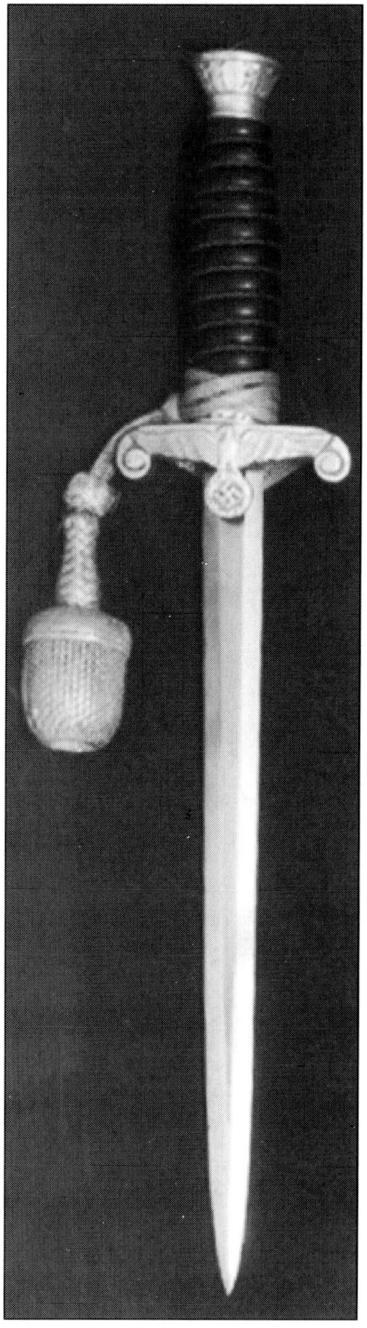

(Right) Obverse view of a reproduction parts assembly Land Customs dagger. The only genuine parts of this dagger are the portepee knot and blade, all other parts were fabricated in Germany in the 1960's for an English dealer. These daggers were produced in relatively small quantities but were exceptionally well made, and in some respects are better quality than many of the original Land Customs daggers!

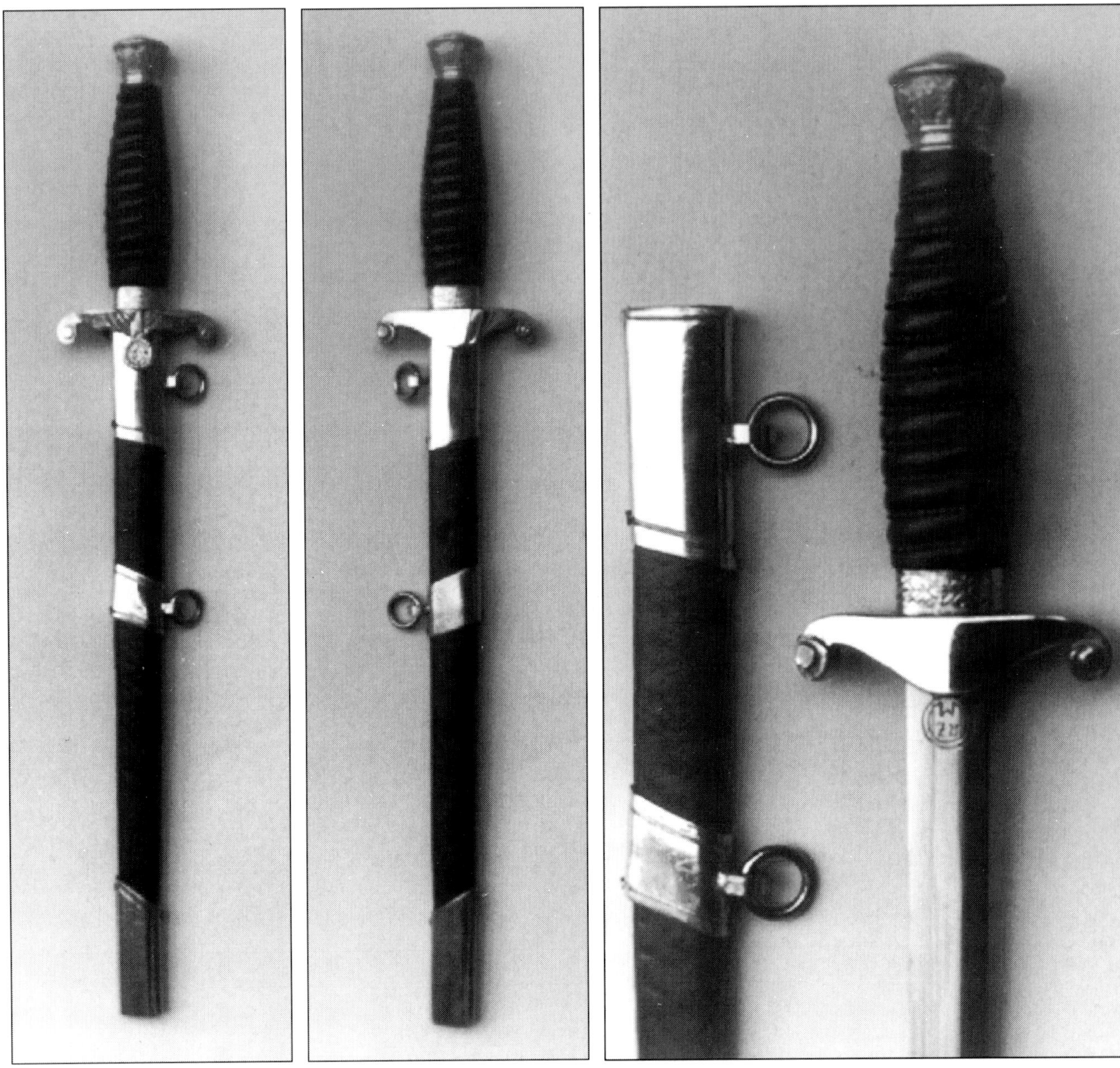

Obverse, reverse and close-up views of a Spanish reproduction Land Customs dagger. This dagger is of particularly poor quality when examined closely. The grip and scabbard are both bound with a cheap imitation leather covering. Note the bulbous grip and the spurious RZM proofmark on the reverse blade ricasso. The RZM proofmark should *not* appear on any Land or Water Customs dagger.

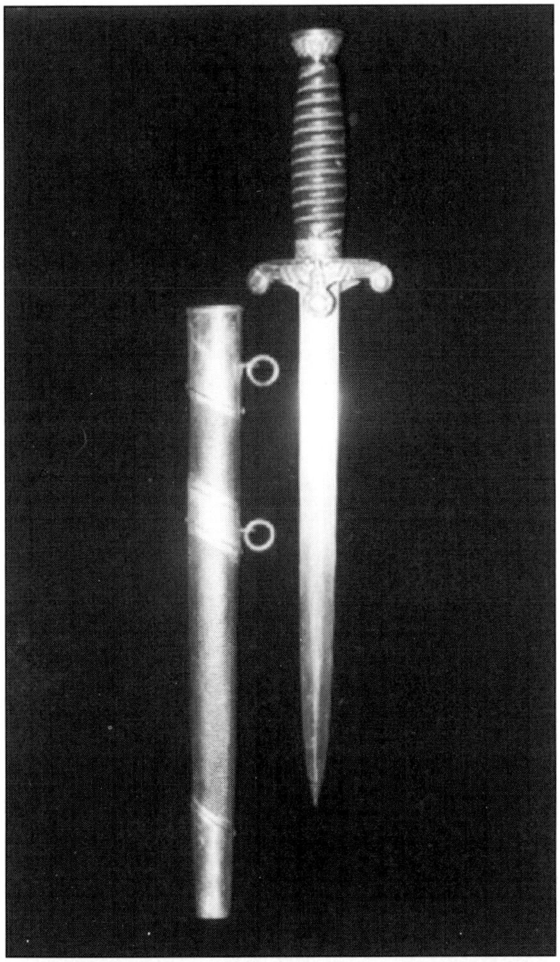

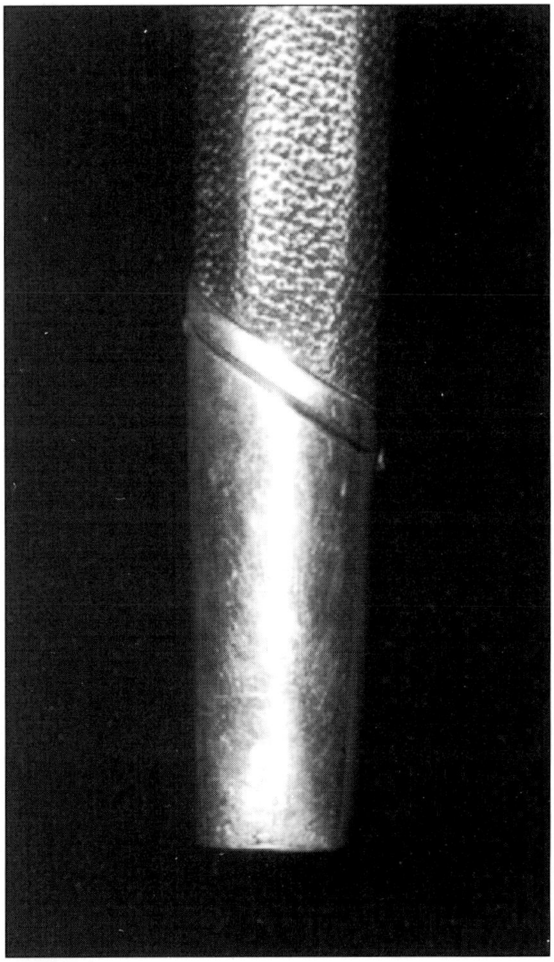

Three different views of a reproduction Land Customs dagger believed to have been made in Germany. Note the piece is well made and has quite good detail on the fittings although the ridges on the scabbard fittings are not as well defined as originals and the head of the eagle is slightly blurred.

WATER CUSTOMS REPRODUCTIONS

Water Customs reproductions are in some respects easier to detect than Land Customs: this is due to the good quality of the fittings of original Water Customs daggers which most post-war reproductions are unable to match.

Spanish reproductions of the Water Customs dagger are made from the same dies and materials as the reproduction Land Customs dagger, and consequently exhibit the same flaws in their construction. However these flaws are usually more evident in the Water Customs dagger where one is looking for a better quality in the fittings. Where the Spanish reproductions are gold plated the plating has the usual cheap looking bright finish unlike the subdued gilding of originals.

Some reproductions utilise brass to cast the fittings of the Water Customs dagger and merely polish the allot to give a gold finish. However these reproductions are usually quite easy to identify by their excessive weight and the inferior quality of the detail on the fittings especially the cross guard eagle.

In recent years several new products have come on the market which can gold plate most bas metals and alloys merely by immersion in a dip of gold solution. This solution can be used change the colour and nature of most items including the fittings of the Water Customs dagger. With the use of this solution the fittings of a genuine Land Customs dagger can be transformed into a Water Customs in a matter of minutes. The gold solutions come in two forms: a liquid dip in which small parts can be plated by immersion; and a paste which can be rubbed on to any metal or alloy giving an almost instant gold plating. These products are extremely expensive for they contain real gold, however they would still be cost effective when applied to the fittings of a good quality genuine Land Customs dagger in order to transform it into a Water Customs dagger. All that is then required to complete the transformation is to use a blue dye to change the colour of the grip and scabbard leather.

The same quick plating process can and has been used to convert genuine Army and Navy hanging straps into a set of Water Customs hangers. This process involved the fittings from the Army straps being removed and plated in gold solution and the fabric from the Navy hangers being cut to the correct size to replicate the fabric of Water Customs hangers. The newly plated Army fittings and the remodelled Navy fabric were then joined together to form an extremely believable set of Water Customs hangers. Due to the rarity of genuine Water Customs hangers there are very few collectors who have actually seen a genuine set of these hangers. Consequently this type of sophisticated fabrication of hangers is extremely difficult to refute or question when they do appear on the market. In over 20 years of collecting this author had only encountered one genuine set of Water Customs hanging straps, however in the past 18 months I have seen no less than 4 sets - 3 of which were undoubtedly modern fabrications! The quality of the fittings could not be easily faulted, the same was true of the material, but the single suspicious characteristic all three sets had in common was that they were extremely short. Their diminutive size was no doubt due to their tailoring from Navy hanging straps which are not of equal lengths.

RECOGNITION CHECKLIST

BLADE

All the points to observe on the blades of reproduction Water Customs daggers are the same as those for the reproduction Army and Diplomatic dagger blades. These points are quite extensive and have already been dealt with in the sections on "Army" and "Diplomatic" daggers. Consequently only a brief listing is given here:

- ➢ The spurious use of the RZM proofmark.
- ➢ The use of the "F W Holler" proofmark, either "Solingen" or "Berlin".
- ➢ Proofmark too lightly etched.
- ➢ Absence of billet clamp seams.
- ➢ Flat tang.
- ➢ Tang with new appearance having no firescale from tempering.
- ➢ Blade with rounded bevels, instead of having sharply defined edges on the blade flat.

SCABBARD

- A straight scabbard instead of being slightly tapered towards the tip.
- The straight line decoration on the three scabbard fittings is too thick and deeply etched on reproductions and is usually situated too far away from the edge of the fittings.
- The scabbard rings are too large and have an incorrect rounded form, often with the hole for the hanger loop drilled slightly off centre.
- The absence of the straight line etching on the scabbard fittings.
- The leather section of the scabbard and the fittings being level. The fittings on original scabbards were always slightly raised above the level of the leather of the scabbard.
- An incorrectly shaped mouth to the scabbard being square or roughly formed instead of having the elliptical shape which corresponds to the shape of the blade.
- The absence of screws holding the scabbard fittings in place.
- When screws are used they frequently protrude slightly from the fittings, instead of being countersunk and flush as on originals.
- The scabbard having an irregular shape with bulges on the leather sections.
- The use of narrow brass, plastic or wooden scabbard liners.
- The total absence of any scabbard liners.
- The use of synthetic imitation leather to cover the scabbard.
- Any unsightly overlapping of the leather binding or raised seams from stitching.
- A very bright gold plating on the scabbard fitting is characteristic of Spanish reproductions.
- Look for evidence of the leather being replaced which usually manifests itself as bunching of the leather around the scabbard fittings.
- Check the grain of the scabbard leather to ensure it has not undergone a colour change from green to blue. The dye will not always penetrate the recesses of the grain of the leather, and green can often be detected when viewed under a glass. Give special attention to areas around the scabbard fittings.

GRIP

- A pronounced bulge in the centre of the grip.
- Grip grooves running in the wrong direction i.e. top left to bottom right instead of vice versa.
- Uneven appearance.
- Thin, straight grip lacking the slightly tapered shape of originals.
- A grip bound over a plastic shell instead of original wooden shell.
- The use of single strand wire to bind the grip.
- Pointed top on the pommel instead of being slightly domed.
- The use of brass to make the grip fittings. This alloy was never used on originals and gives the dagger a very top heavy feel.
- The presence of excessive moulding seams on the sides of the pommel and ferrule.
- A crossguard eagle with crooked wings instead of being slightly dipped.
- An eagle with straight wings would indicate the improper use of an Army crossguard.
- Poor detail on the oakleaf decoration of the pommel and ferrule.
- Poor definition on the crossguard eagle.
- Look for evidence of a colour change on the grip leather from green to blue which will be especially evident around and under the grip wire binding.
- Very bright gold plating on the crossguard, pommel and ferrule is a characteristic consistent with Spanish reproductions.

PROOFMARKS

Carl Eickhorn is the Maker normally associated with the Water Customs dagger, however Paul Weyersburg is also known to have produced this piece. The most commonly encountered proofmarks on reproductions are the RZM proofmark, Alcoso pre-1937 type proofmark, F W Holler, Solingen; and F W Holler, Berlin.

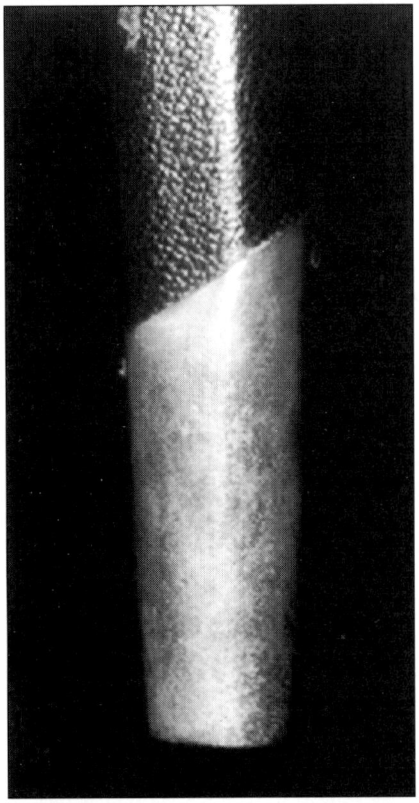

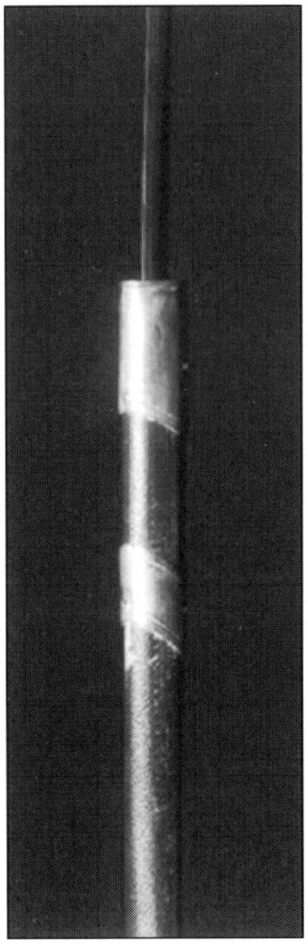

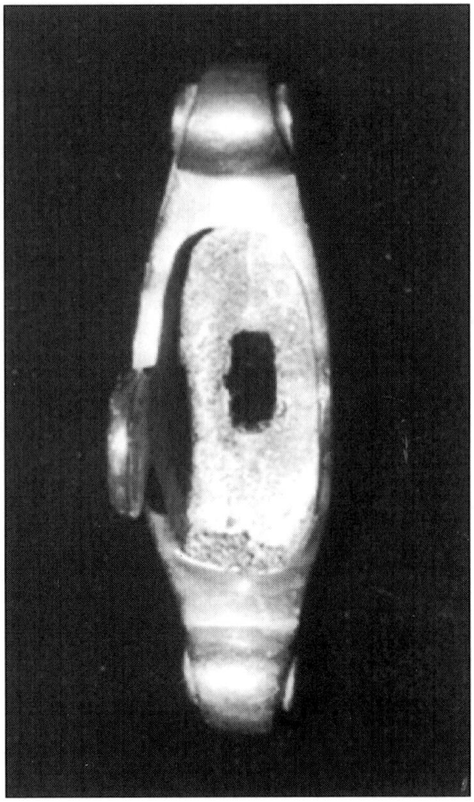

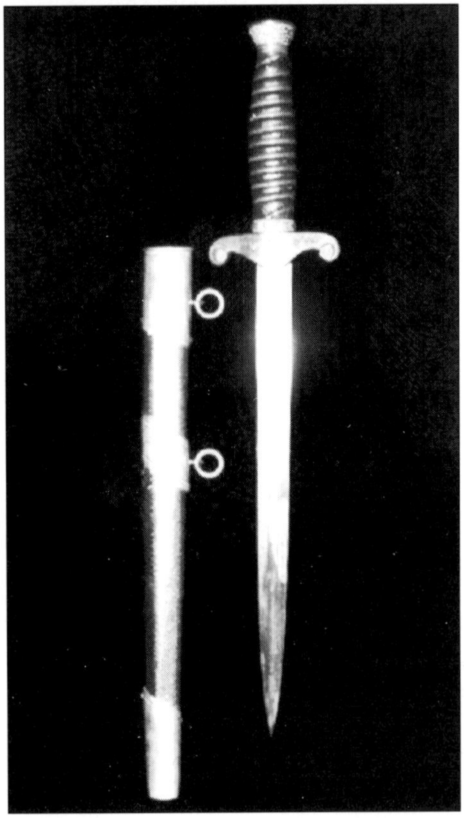

Four different aspects of a reproduction Water Customs dagger. Note the crude casting marks inside the crossguard, although the external detail is reasonably good. The scabbard and grip are well bound with a good quality imitation blue leather. Note that the bottom scabbard fitting is devoid of a diagonal groove on its upper portion.

DRK REPRODUCTIONS

The German Red Cross Officer's dress dagger and Subordinate's hewer have not been subject to any sustained attempts to reproduce them. Examples of reproductions of both the Leader's dagger and Subordinate's hewer have been documented over the year, however in almost all cases the quality has been quite poor in almost every aspect of their construction. This inferiority in quality appearing in any other type of Nazi dagger would in most instances be a positive attribute in successfully identifying a reproduction piece, but in view of the poor quality of many original Red Cross hewers the line between genuine and reproduction hewers is not always precisely definable. With the passage of over 50 years many original Red Cross hewers tend to exhibit varying degrees of loss of plating often revealing extremely poor quality pot metal fittings beneath. On many occasions I have observed an experienced collector rejecting Red Cross hewers as reproductions when in fact the piece in question was not so much a good reproduction as a poor quality original.

When encountering suspected reproduction examples of the Red Cross hewer the collector should mainly be aware of the errors in the overall dimensions of some reproduction hewers, often amounting to the item being up to 20% longer than originals with the blade ricasso being up to twice as long as original examples. Also on this type of reproduction hewer the saw-tooth back runs virtually the full length of the blade extending almost to the crossguard: whereas the saw-tooth on original blades normally terminated where the ricasso begins almost 3/4 of an inch from the crossguard. A further characteristic of some reproductions is that the blade is visibly narrower and somewhat thinner than is normal on genuine examples. Reproductions have also been encountered where the blade has been fitted into the grip incorrectly with the saw-tooth back edge of the blade being on the left side (when seen from the obverse view), whereas the correct positioning is for the saw-tooth to be on the right hand side of the hewer. The dimensions of the crossguard and pommel are relatively accurate on this type of reproduction hewer, however the narrower blade causes it to be off centre giving the hewer a very awkward uneven appearance.

Different types of grip plates have been observed on reproductions of the DRK hewer: namely plain black smooth plastic grip plates secured to the hewer handle by a single screw located in the centre and passing through both obverse and reverse grip plates. These grip plates are incorrect on two counts: first the genuine plates were always checkered plastic on the obverse side and plain plastic on the reverse; second, original grip plates should be secured with two screws, one at the top and one at the bottom of the plates. A further type of reproduction grip plate which will be encountered is made of wood stained black glued into position on the handle of the hewer. These grip plates are checkered, however the checkering has an irregular pattern which is approximately three times larger in its pattern than originals which featured a very fine form of checkering and displayed an overall even form of checkered pattern. Also original grip plates were *never* glued into position on any genuine Red Cross hewer documented to date.

The crossguard and pommel of reproduction DRK hewers have been observed constructed from brass or aluminium - neither of which alloy was ever used to construct genuine Red Cross fittings.

Reproduction DRK hewers are almost never found with a correct frog attached to them: indeed many do not even have a scabbard, let alone a frog. Reproduction scabbards tend to have a slightly better appearance than the actual reproduction hewer and are made from sheet steel or aluminium with plated brass upper and lower fittings. The scabbards are finished with a high gloss spray paint applied. Most scabbards would appear not to have any form of liner, consequently the hewer is very loose in the scabbard and has a tendency to rattle once inserted.

The Red Cross Leader's dress dagger has never been an extensively reproduced piece no doubt due to the fact that although the DRK Leader's dagger is a relatively scarce item it is not one of the more desirable Third Reich daggers. The examples of reproduction Red Cross Leader's daggers which have been observed have all been very good visually and would pass a cursory examination, although closer and more detailed inspection will reveal a number of characteristics which were not featured on original Third Reich period DRK Leader's daggers.

The most immediate observation to be made when examining DRK Leader's daggers is the shape of the grip which on some reproductions has a distinct bulge in the middle of the grip: whereas original grips were relatively straight along their whole length merely having a slight taper at each end where the grip meets the pommel and crossguard respectively.

The scabbard on Spanish reproductions of the DRK Leader's dagger are marginally wider than originals, and the taper is too sharp and has an uneven irregular appearance in the lower third of the scabbard towards the tip, although the actual point of the reproduction scabbard is approximately 25% wider than that found on original scabbards. As is the case with other Spanish reproductions the scabbard pebbling forms a distinct large swirling pattern; no discernible pattern should appear on Red Cross Leader's scabbards.

Original Red Cross Leader's daggers in most cases do not bear any Maker's proofmark which is externally visible on the blade: although they were frequently Maker marked on the tang section of the blade, but this is only visible be disassembling the grips of the dagger. Spanish reproducers have always proved to be very fond of putting spurious proofmarks on their reproduction blades even where it was not appropriate or necessary. Consequently reproductions of the DRK Leader's dagger which were produced in Spain invariably carry a proofmark externally visible on the blade: this usually takes the form of the spurious use of the RZM proofmark on the ricasso. The RZM proofmark was never used on original DRK daggers either externally or internally, therefore any Red Cross dagger encountered with a blade bearing the RZM proofmark should be rejected as a blatant reproduction.

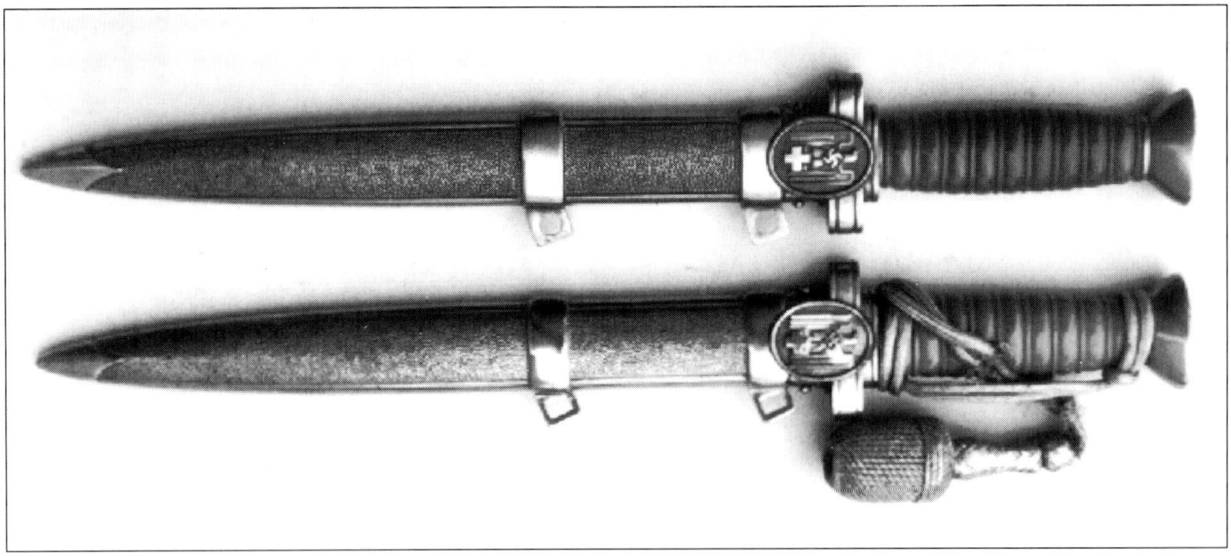

Comparison photograph of the obverse side of two genuine German Red Cross Leader's daggers. Whilst both daggers are identical in form they exhibit one minor variation, namely the scabbard hanger attachment loops. This is the only distinguishing feature between the regular Red Cross Leader's and Leaders of the Social Welfare department of the German Red Cross - round holes for Social Welfare, square holes for general Red Cross. The buckles on the hanging straps are the reverse of the dagger, i.e. square buckles for Social Welfare, oval buckles for regular Red Cross Leaders.

DRK LEADER'S DAGGER REPRODUCTIONS

RECOGNITION CHECKLIST

BLADE

- The tang on most reproduction DRK Leader's daggers tend to be the flat type.
- The raised central spine of the blade of reproductions is very pronounced and sharp.
- The ricasso of reproductions is extremely long, extending approximately one inch from the bottom of the crossguard cartouche. Originals normally have half that amount of ricasso showing below the cartouche.
- The spurious use of the RZM proofmark.
- Generally speaking the quality of reproduction Red Cross dagger blades is quite good and requires close inspection.

SCABBARD

- A scabbard slightly wider than originals is a feature of reproductions.
- The taper is too sharp and has an irregular appearance towards the tip.
- The plain inverted "V" section of the scabbard tip is wider than that found on originals and has a sharp rather than rounded end to it.
- The pebbling on the scabbard exhibits a swirling pattern similar to that found on reproduction Army scabbards, however the pattern is somewhat larger.
- The groove which extends around the perimeter of the scabbard on obverse and reverse sides is gouged out too deeply and is irregular in its width and depth - unlike the fine symmetrical design found on originals.
- The scabbard ramp cutout holes where the hanger catch is attached is too large on reproductions and invariably takes the square Red Cross shape. The round Social Welfare cutout holes have not been documented so far to date on reproductions (but this is not to say they may not have been manufactured).

GRIP

- The most obvious aspect on reproduction grips is the bulbous appearance in the centre of the grip: originals were virtually straight, only tapering slightly where it joins at the pommel and crossguard.
- Reproduction grips have been encountered in white and yellow made from plastic usually nylon. The white tends to be very bright showing no ageing, and the yellow does not have the richness of colour found on originals.
- The detail on the crossguard is not as sharp or clearly defined as that found on originals with the two lateral lines being quite indistinct.
- The oval Red Cross insignia on the crossguard lacks the sharp detail of originals, especially around the head and wings of the eagle.
- A discernible gap is visible in the joins of the grip to crossguard and especially to the pommel. The quality of the castings varies greatly, often exhibiting pitting and casting seams.

PROOFMARKS

Externally visible proofmarks were not a feature of the blade of original Red Cross Leader's daggers, and the use of the RZM proofmark was not appropriate for the German Red Cross. Consequently Red Cross Leader's daggers encountered bearing a Maker's proofmark on the blade ricasso should be carefully examined, and any dagger bearing the RZM proofmark and any control number should be immediately rejected as a reproduction: as the inappropriate use of the RZM proofmark is a consistent characteristic of Spanish reproduction Red Cross daggers.

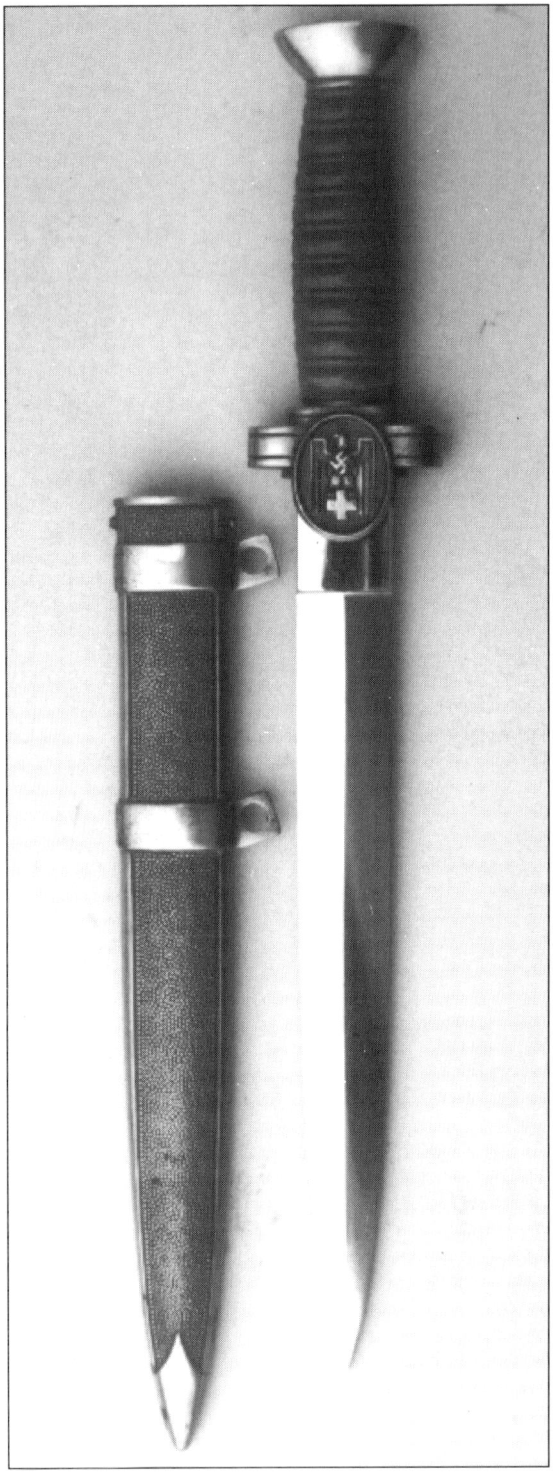

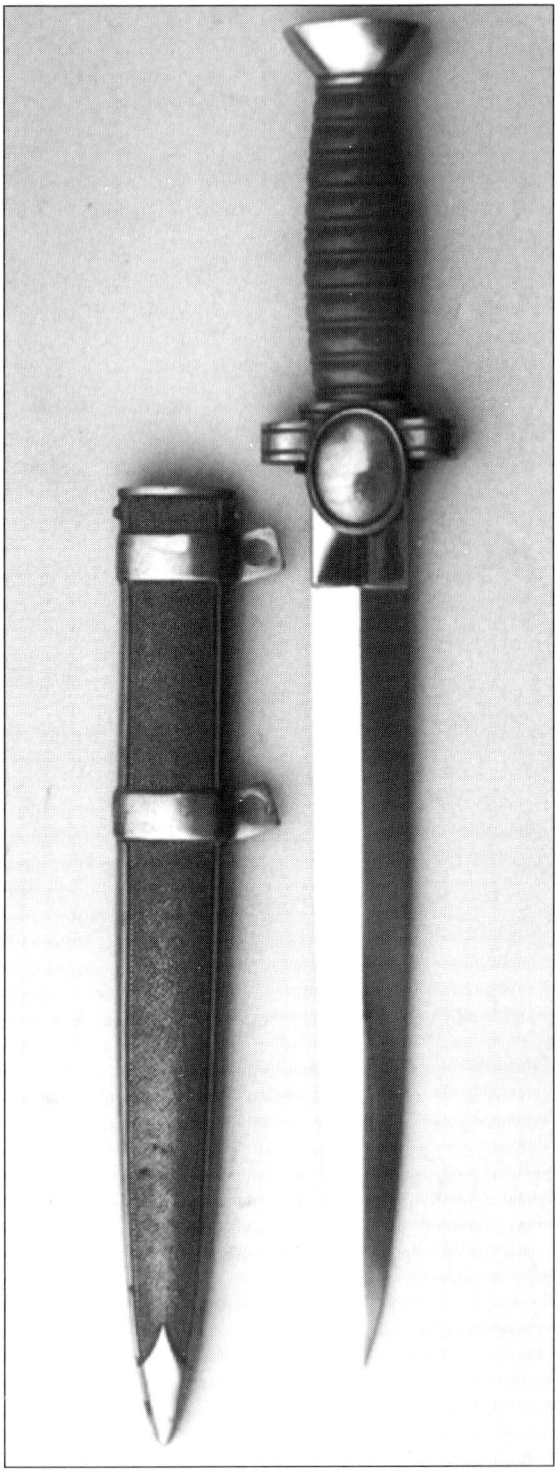

Obverse and reverse views of a genuine German Red Cross Social Welfare Leader's dagger. Note the round scabbard band holes indicative of the Social Welfare section of the DRK instead of the square type found on the regular Red Cross Leader's scabbard. Also of note is the oxidised finish on the pebbled section of the scabbard highlighting the silver plated bands and fittings of the dagger. Also of note is the deep tone of the orange grip which was a feature of many Social Welfare Leader's dagger rather than the deep yellow grip found on the regular Red Cross dagger. Reproduction DRK daggers tend to have light yellow grips and a scabbard with an overall shine.

DRK SUBORDINATE'S HEWER REPRODUCTIONS

RECOGNITION CHECKLIST

BLADE

- Poorly finished blade with inferior quality plating.
- Blade too long by up to 20% more than originals.
- The saw-tooth back edge of the blade on reproductions extends almost to the crossguard, much longer than originals.
- The tang has a very broad flat appearance completely dissimilar to originals.
- DRK hewer blades have been encountered bearing spurious RZM proofmarks.
- The ricasso on reproduction hewers are not as well defined as originals and are up to twice as long.
- The fuller on reproductions is too short terminating almost two inches from the crossguard instead of approximately 3/4 of an inch on originals.
- The saw-tooth back edge of reproductions is executed as a jagged groove where the grooves travel in the same direction whereas on originals the grooves are split and travel in opposing directions simulating an interlocking network of grooves.

SCABBARD

- Many reproductions of the DRK Subordinate's hewer were produced without scabbards, no doubt due to their irregular size.
- Reproduction scabbards have been observed made from sheet steel or aluminium usually having a high gloss cellulose painted finish.
- Scabbard fittings on reproductions are usually cast aluminium or brass.
- Reproduction scabbards often have no liners and where present are usually incorrectly made of tin or wood.
- The upper scabbard fitting is usually devoid of scabbard throat screws and where present they are the incorrect flat headed type.
- The detail on the scabbard fittings is very poorly defined.
- Top and bottom scabbard fittings on reproductions often exhibit areas of pitting, moulding seams and excessive plate lifting.

GRIP

- The use of wooden grip plates whether checkered or plain is inappropriate for this hewer, as they were never used on originals.
- Plain black plastic grips on obverse and reverse sides are incorrect: original plates were plain on the reverse and checkered on the obverse.
- The grip plates secured by a single screw is an incorrect method of attaching the grip plates: there should be one at the top and one at the bottom of the plate with the head of the screw showing on the obverse side.
- Grip plates either wooden or plastic glued into position on the handle are indicative of reproductions.
- Poor definition on the crossguard especially in the area of the Red Cross eagle insignia which loses much of its detail on reproductions.
- The lateral lines on the crossguard are barely discernible on reproductions and at best are very poorly etched.
- The use of incorrect materials such as aluminium and brass to make the crossguard and pommel:

these will exhibit areas of pitting, moulding seams and excessive lifting of the poor quality plating.

➢ The pommel on reproductions is marginally larger than originals and has a somewhat domed appearance.

PROOFMARKS

No proofmark of any description should be outwardly visible on the blade of a DRK Subordinate's hewer. Where any kind of Maker's mark was used on originals it was always applied internally on the tang, and can be either that of Robert Klaas with his two kissing storks logo or P D Lunschloss: the proofmark appearing on the tang is usually "P D L". Reproduction DRK Subordinate's hewers have been encountered without proofmarks, however others have been encountered bearing the RZM proofmark and M7 control number which is totally inappropriate even for original hewers as the DRK did not fall under the jurisdiction of the RZM.

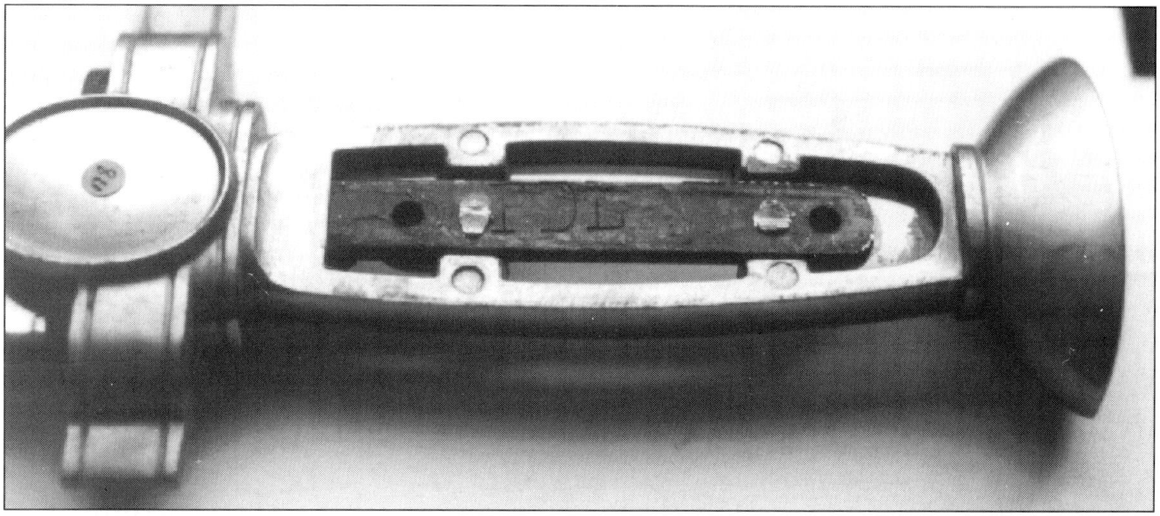

Close-up views of the exposed tangs of two genuine DRK Subordinate's hewers. The example above exhibits the P D L proofmark of P. D. Luneschloss, whilst the bottom tang has the "kissing storks" proofmark of Robert Klaas. These two Solingen firms were the sole manufacturers of the DRK Subordinate's hewer. Other genuine examples will be encountered devoid of any proofmark on the tang, and under no circumstances should a proofmark of any description appear externally on the blade ricasso. Note, the PDL proofmark is applied to the reverse tang and the Klaas proofmark on the obverse tang.

DIPLOMAT AND GOVERNMENT OFFICIAL'S REPRODUCTIONS

The reproduction daggers of both the Diplomats and Government officials have been combined in this chapter for the reproductions of both types of dagger invariably exhibit identical reproduction characteristics although the crossguard eagle faces in different directions for each formation.

Spain and Germany are the main sources of reproduction diplomat daggers. This is one type of dagger which the Spanish have reproduced quite successfully, and in most instances they have been finished to a high standard closely resembling the originals. The Diplomat's dagger requires close examination for as a relatively rare item there is not always an abundance of genuine examples readily available with which to draw comparisons especially at the time of purchasing one of these daggers.

Some relatively early reproduction examples of the Diplomat's dagger such as the type with the pot-bellied eagle grip are readily recognisable, as are the reproductions with the plain and white plastic grips. Excluding these two types of reproductions there are a number of good quality reproduction diplomatic daggers currently on the market which resemble very closely the originals, not only in their outward appearance but also in their construction and material composition.

Spanish reproductions of the Nazi Diplomat's dagger frequently utilise some of the same parts as the Spanish reproduction Army dagger: (this is due to both types of reproduction dagger emanating from the same Maker in Toledo, Spain). The same scabbard and blade are used to the Diplomat's and Army daggers: the Diplomat's dagger merely has different scabbard bands added. Consequently the scabbard on many reproduction Diplomat's daggers exhibit identical characteristics as the reproduction Army scabbard: such as the swirl pattern on the pebbling and the thin metal brazed scabbard liners. ALso in common with the reproduction Army dagger, the blades of this type of reproduction Diplomat's dagger have a matt grey finish instead of a polished sheen. These blades usually bear a spurious RZM proofmark which was not appropriate for any Diplomat or Government official's dagger.

The composition of the grips of reproduction Diplomat's daggers can take several forms: the most common being plain white plastic without any wooden grip liner. Better quality reproductions utilise imitation mother-of-pearl which gives an appearance closer to that of originals, but once again the wooden grip inserts are absent. It is extremely rare to find reproductions with mother-of-pearl and wooden grip liners.

Current Spanish reproductions have a lacquered finish applied to them which tends to give the dagger a dull grey aged appearance. The reverse of the crossguard on this type of reproduction will usually exhibit two distinct marks towards each wing tip. These are sprue marks which are a product of injection moulding and are not to be found on original Diplomat's dagger crossguards.

Over the years several good reproductions have been observed which have been worked upon in an effort to deceive the unwary collector. The "doctoring" process amounted to the hilt, crossguard and scabbard being skillfully polished to remove the grey lacquer and the swirl pattern pebbling so indicative of Spanish reproductions. Removing the white plastic grips and replacing them with mother-of-pearl, the embellishing was completed by the reproduction blade being removed and being replaced with a genuine Army blade. The finished article was very believable specimen of a Diplomat's dagger. The English dealer who had carried out this particular deception was quite proud of his handiwork and admitted that he had carried out several such "modifications", and each case had subsequently sold the dagger as an original item to an unsuspecting collector at a very healthy profit! What he had done in effect was to use his knowledge to rectify the errors in a recognisable reproduction on order to fabricate a fake but almost undetectable Diplomat's dagger. When examining one of these fabrications the only suspicious reproduction characteristic remaining was the faintest shadow of the moulding marks which had not been completely removed.

Furthermore in an effort to eliminate the swirling pattern in the scabbard the pebbling had been heavily buffed in an effort to merge the pattern. This technique has also been observed on reproduction Army scabbard whereby once the pebbling is rounded off it loses much of the discernible pattern which is so readily recognisable on untouched reproduction scabbards. This buffing process usually falls down when the pebbling close to the scabbard bands is examined: for an area either side of the scabbard band is not readily accessible to the buffer, thus causing a slightly raised shadow. This kind of meticulous examination may sound somewhat paranoid, but considering the current market value of a genuine Diplomat's dagger it is well worth the faker's time to take a $100.00 reproduction dagger and expend a considerable amount of effort in order to recoup his investment more than twenty-fold!

Many of the rarer and more prestigious Third Reich reproduction daggers being marketed as genuine such as the Diplomat's dagger and "embellished" reproductions, as in the aforementioned case, are not usually offered openly for sale at Arms Fairs or other public events where they might be scrutinised by a large number of collectors and other dealers who with experiences with genuine diplomatic daggers might detect some slight flaw in their fabrication. Rather they tend to be offered for sale sometimes apparently reluctantly at a dealer's home in a private viewing session on a one to one basis with a collector and the dealer. In this type of setting the unwary collector is especially vulnerable to the experienced dealer who may have innumerable ploys and well practiced stories to sell a phoney dagger ranging from "It's been in my own collection for twenty years" to "I bought it from a little old lady who's husband actually took it from a Diplomat personally in 1945" - none of which offer any solid corroboration for the dagger's authenticity.

The poorer quality Spanish reproductions of the Diplomat's dagger often feature a spurious RZM proofmark, usually accompanied by the M7/36 control number. The use of an RZM proofmark and control number was absolutely inappropriate and was never used on the blade of any genuine Third Reich period Diplomat's or Government official's dagger. The principal Makers' proofmark which will be encountered on reproduction diplomatic daggers are those of Alcoso and Holler. Spanish reproductions from the 60's and 70's used the "F W Holler, Solingen" proofmark, whilst the later and current proofmark is the amended spurious form "F W Holler, Berlin" proofmark adopted since Spain's entry into the EEC in an effort to contravene European copyright laws. Other Maker's proofmarks will be encountered as well as proofmarks on genuine Army blades married to reproduction dagger parts. A consistent feature of reproductions and parts fabrications is the absence of matching assembly numbers on the component parts. Originals invariably bore the parts numbers.

Reproduction "points to observe" is quite lengthy, although it should be borne in mind that these many points apply to a variety of different reproductions and embellishments, and one should not expect to encounter all of the listed characteristics of any single reproduction dagger.

RECOGNITION CHECKLIST

BLADE

- Many reproduction blades have a matt, satin finish often with a grey appearance.
- Maker's proofmarks are etched too lightly.
- The use of RZM proofmark is inappropriate for this type of dagger. This type of proofmark is usually photo-etched.
- Rounded flats on the centre panel of the blades instead of being a clearly defined bevel.
- A thick square tang as opposed to the genuine rounded type.
- Absence of any billet clamp marks.
- A shiny tang without evidence of any firescale invariably found on originals as a result of tempering.
- Blade with flat edges.
- Undersized blade.
- A wide flat tapered tang.
- Very short screw thread on the end of the tang.
- A consistent feature of reproductions and parts fabrication is the absence of matching assembly numbers on the component parts. Originals invariably bore the parts numbers.

SCABBARD

- A swirl pattern in the scabbard pebbling is indicative of Spanish reproductions.
- The hanger rings on each scabbard band are not joined on many reproduction scabbards whereas originals were always joined.
- Scabbard bands made in two parts and brazed into position instead of being sweated into place as originals were.
- The use of wooden or tin scabbard liners usually brazed into position on the scabbard throat.
- The absence of scabbard throat retaining screws is a feature of many reproduction scabbards.
- The scabbard tip being a separate piece and being brazed into position, not a feature of originals.
- Moulding seams on the edge of the scabbard.
- The scabbard bands mounted too low down the scabbard or too close together: the upper scabbard band should be just under the wreathed swastika on originals.
- Scabbard bands too wide or in some cases too narrow.

GRIP

- Plain white plastic grips are a consistent feature of most reproductions: this material was not used to make genuine grips.
- The absence of wooden liner inserts in the grip is an indication of a reproduction, however the presence of wooden liners does not necessarily mean the piece is original for many good quality reproductions do utilise wooden liners.
- A bulging grip often called the "pot belly" grip is a feature of an early reproduction of German manufacture.
- Circular moulding marks on the reverse wing tips of the crossguard are a feature of currently produced Spanish reproductions.
- The ferrule is oversize on some reproductions with the two lateral lines being poorly defined and not very deeply etched. Examples will also be encountered of this type where the lateral decorative lines are not straight.

- ➣ The crossguard and the eagle head pommel should be closely observed for poorly defined detail: also poor quality castings with evidence of pitting as a result of casting and not age.
- ➣ The use of incorrect materials to make the fittings i.e. zinc or aluminium: the use of these materials especially the latter tends to give the dagger a very light feel unlike the weighty feel of originals.
- ➣ The reverse of the crossguard should not have a rough finish, but should have a smooth plate appearance.
- ➣ The unswept wing tips of the crossguard are too pronounced on some reproductions.
- ➣ The beak of the eagle on some reproductions has a flat end instead of a discernible point.
- ➣ The tang retaining nut is of incorrect form and has an ordinary screw groove on Spanish reproductions of the 1970's.
- ➣ The use of simulated mother-of-pearl does not necessarily mean the piece is suspect as this imitation material was also used on originals as a substitute for genuine mother-of-pearl.

PROOFMARKS

The principle proofmarks which will be encountered on reproduction diplomatic daggers are those of: Alcoso, F W Holler and the RZM. The Alcoso proofmark most frequently used on reproduction is the post-1941 type which has the proofmark etched laterally on the blade with the scales and A C S and at its righthand side "Alcoso" in script and "Solingen" in plain print. The F W Holler proofmark will be encountered in two forms: the early type with "F W Holler, Solingen" and the later (and current) type with "F W Holler, Berlin". The RZM proofmark most commonly used on this type of dagger is "RZM M7/36", which was originally attributable to E F Horster of Solingen, but is completely spurious when used in the context of a Diplomat's dagger.

Genuine examples of the Diplomat's dagger will be encountered with plain blades bearing no proofmark whatsoever. This does not necessarily indicate that the piece is a reproduction. The appearance of different Maker's proofmarks on a seemingly genuine blade should not be taken as absolute confirmation that a piece is genuine: for over the years many reproductions have been altered and had a genuine Army blade substituted in order to give a more passable appearance to what is otherwise a reproduction.

* See also page 199 for genuine examples of the Diplomat's and Government Official's daggers.

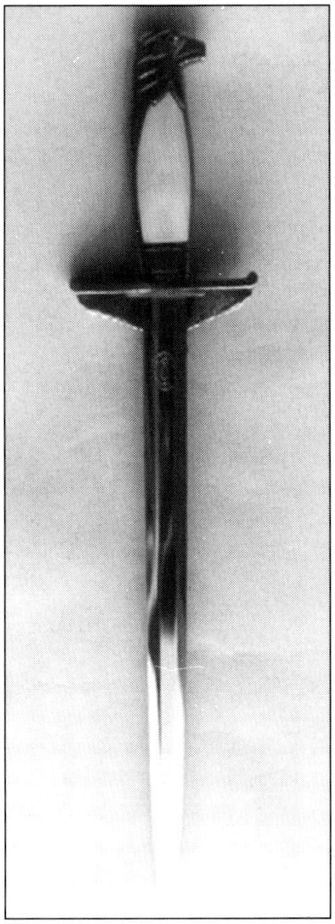
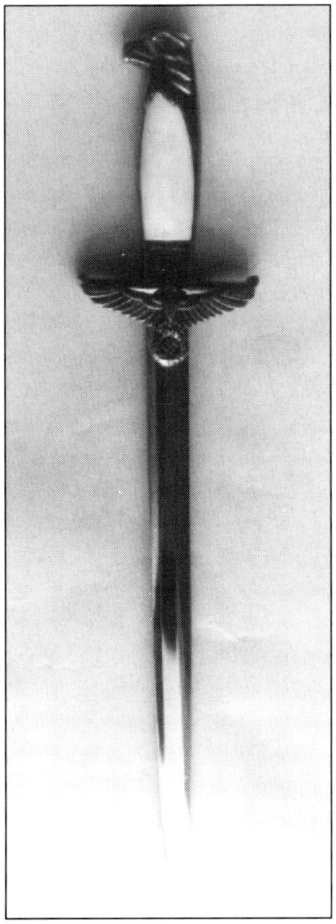
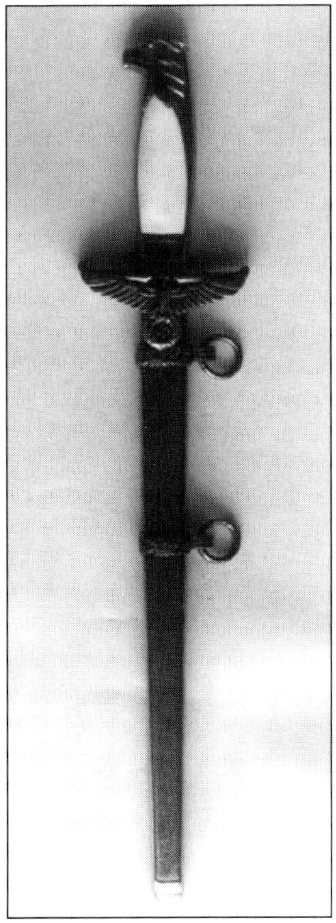
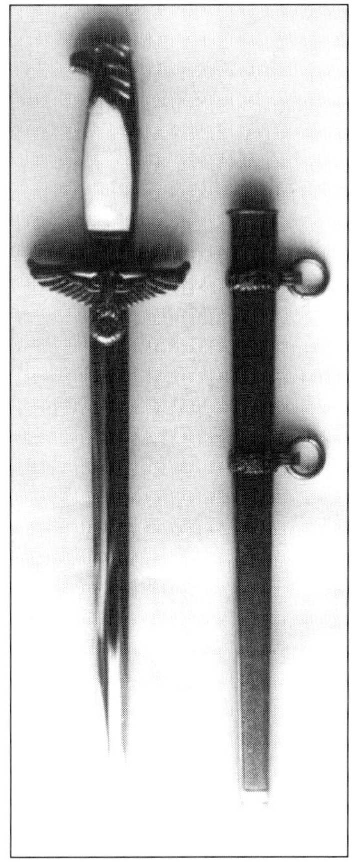

This is the most common type of reproduction Diplomat's dagger on the market today. Whilst this is an excellent display piece it does not stand up to closer inspection. The most obvious fault is the use of white plastic grips instead of mother-of-pearl. The blade is well made with a bright finish, however the Maker's proofmark is the real giveaway, being that of F. W. Holler with the city of manufacture changed from Solingen to Berlin. The grip fittings are quite well defined with good external detail on the crossguard - although the inside has crude casting bubbles, and overall the crossguard is too broad. Also of note are the scabbard bands which are too far apart and the swirl pattern of the scabbard pebbling.

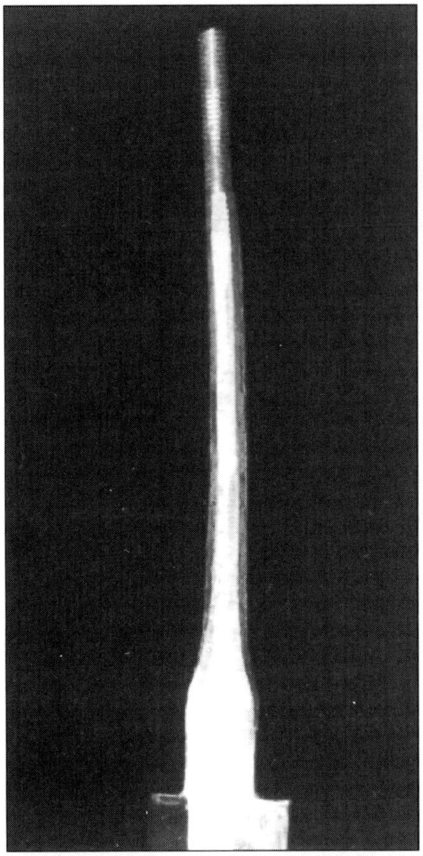
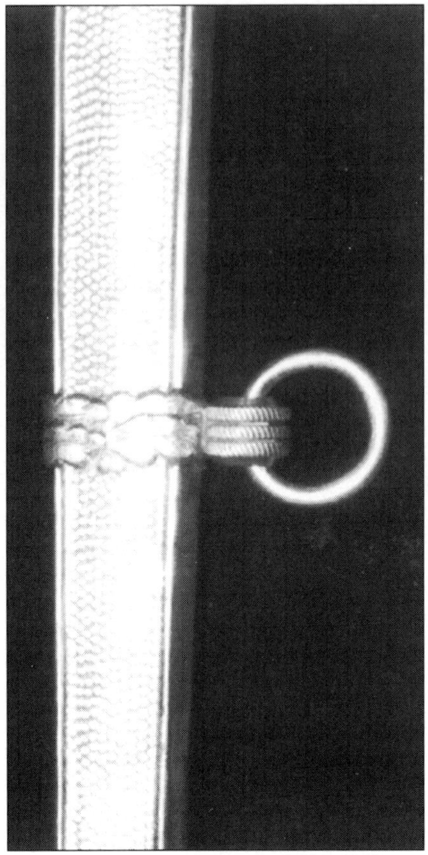
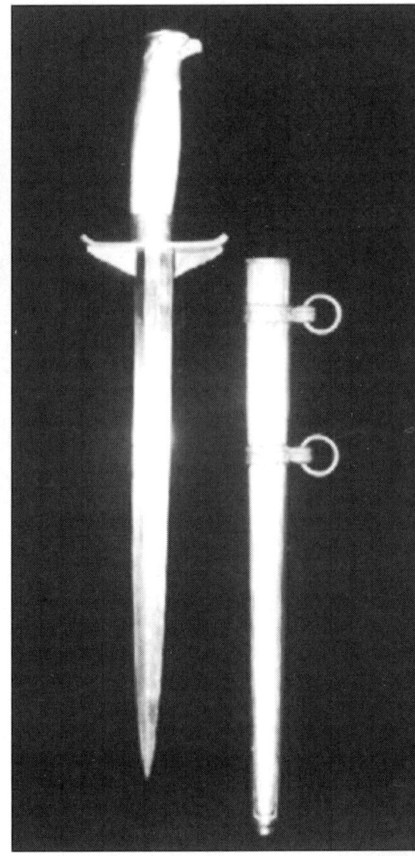
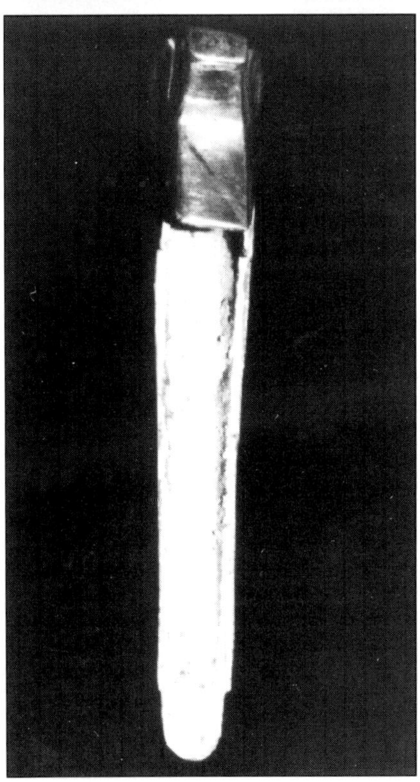
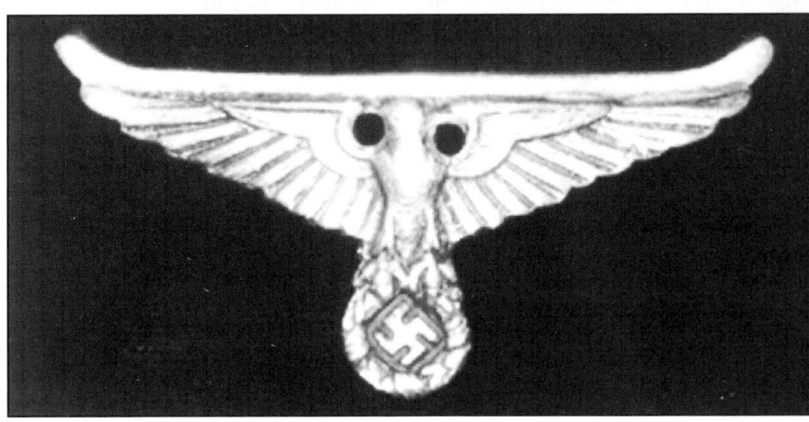

Five different aspects of a reproduction Diplomat's dagger. Many of this dagger's shortcomings only become evident when it is stripped down into its component parts. The blade tang has been crudely filed and is misshapen giving the assembled grip a "stooped" effect. The crossguard detail is very poor having a smooth featureless Eagle's head and torso.

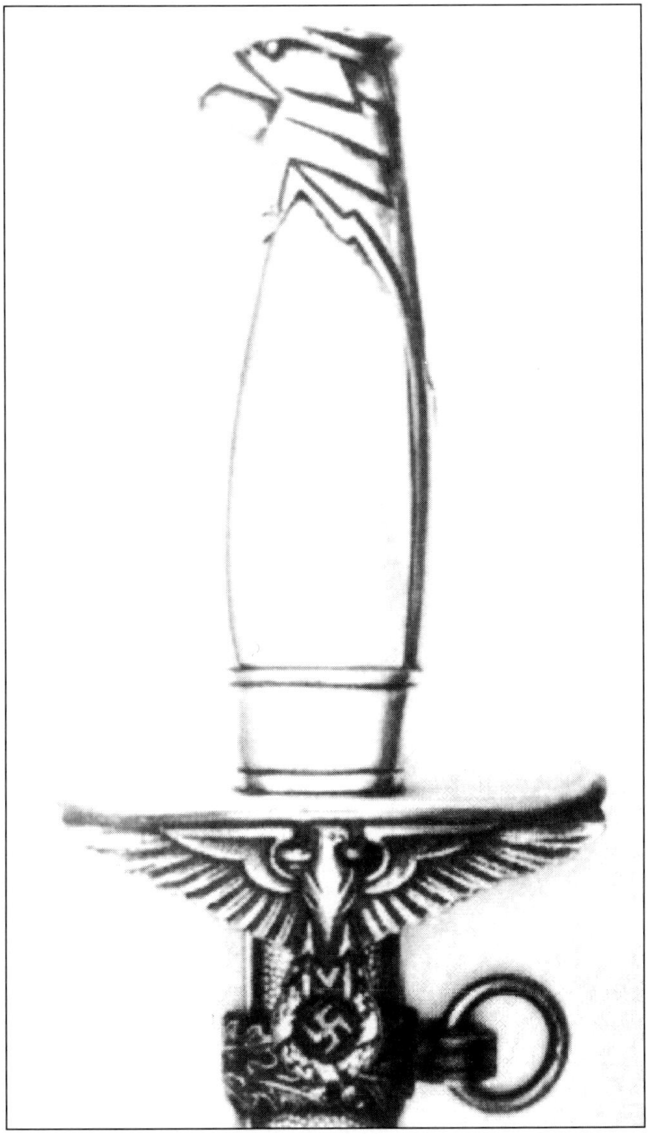

Obverse and reverse sides of a good quality reproduction Diplomat's dagger. This type of reproduction has excellent detail on the grip and scabbard and is only revealed as a reproduction by the "Pot-Bellied" shape of the grip. Apart from this aspect the dagger is difficult to fault having mother-of-pearl grip plates and a good quality blade bearing the Eickhorn squirrel proofmark.

Prototype, Fantasy and One of a Kind Daggers

PROTOTYPE DAGGERS

Prototypes for proposed new patterns of Third Reich daggers were produced between 1933 and 1945, however they are extremely rare and difficult to authenticate. In additions to actual prototype daggers which were manufactured, there were also innumerable designs submitted by a variety of dagger manufacturers and artists - the most prominent of which was Paul Casburg who worked almost exclusively for the firm of Carl Eickhorn.

There is documented evidence of many new daggers being proposed during the 1930's and early 40's including new patterns for the SS, Reichsbahn and Army to mention just three. The latter example was intended to be a dagger specifically for the growing number of Field Marshalls in the German Army. The new dagger for the SS in common with other prototypes was shelved for the duration of World War II, and with the eventual unfavourable outcome for the Germans, these prototypes never went into mass production.

Since the end of World War II reproductions have been made of documented prototypes and in many instances have been passed off on unsuspecting collectors as "the prototype" of that particular dagger. Reproductions of prototypes are collectible and are acceptable in a collection of genuine daggers to illustrate the evolution of the German dagger, however the collector should not be under any illusions when purchasing these daggers that they are anything more than a reproduction of a prototype, and that the amount of money paid for such a dagger should reflect this.

Also there are "prototypes" now in circulation which really should be categorised as fantasy daggers: these pieces are post-war inventions which were never produced in any form during the period of the Third Reich. Many of these fantasy prototypes are produced to an extremely high standard and are sold for outrageous sums of money to the eager collector who believes has discovered a "lost, undocumented prototype". Quite often the collectors who are taken in by these fantasy pieces are advanced collectors with extensive collections of the standard production Third Reich daggers. The rationale for purchasing these pieces is that once a collector has acquired all the documented production daggers, there is nowhere else to go with their collecting hobby but to look for the unusual. This area of collecting is a veritable minefield of prototype, fantasy, presentation and one of a kind reproductions. Unfortunately for the collector, many fantasy pieces have been featured in edged weapon reference books since the 1960's which has given some of these bogus daggers a perceived authenticity they never merited.

FANTASY DAGGERS

The production of fantasy daggers has been a lucrative area for the reproducers for many years. These bogus daggers appear in a number of forms: the most common being variations based on existing documented Third Reich daggers. Frequently they feature modified crossguards, scabbards, pommels, grips etc. - the characteristic most of these features have in common is that they are based around the stiletto style blade of the ubiquitous German Army dagger. The parts used in these fantasy fabrications are usually genuine in the main, but often with intricately redesigned parts: exhibiting formation insignia on crossguards or pommel, or with a separate piece of insignia affixed to the scabbard or grip. In addition to being attributed to various Third Reich organisations or personalities, these daggers are also often passed off as "obscure, undocumented examples" from the Armed Forces of some of Germany's wartime allies i.e. Rumania, Bulgaria, Hungary, Croatia etc. Due to these daggers retaining many familiar characteristics and the fact that they utilise mainly genuine parts, they tend to be more readily accepted by collectors than the blatant fantasy daggers.

These blatant fakes have been designed and manufactured in the post-war era utilising good quality materials with the sole objective of deceiving the unwary collector. Whilst in some instances (for reasons of cost or rarity) a case can be made in favour of reproductions of daggers which actually existed (e.g. to fill a void in one's collection), these fantasy fabrications are solely intended to deceive. Whilst their form does not usually resemble any documented Third Reich period dagger, they do nonetheless invariably feature some familiar characteristic of them connected with the formation they are bogusly being attributed to. A favoured ploy when these daggers are being "unearthed" or "discovered" is the dealer selling the item feigns ignorance of its origins, whilst pointing out some possibly familiar characteristics to the collector. A commonly overheard conversations usually runs like this: "I've just bought this unusual dagger; what do you make of it? I've never seen anything like it before . . ." This disarming tactic lets the dealer off the hook for any subsequent comeback from the collector whilst at the same time arousing his curiosity in inviting his own speculation about the piece - in this way, the unsuspecting collector mentally begins to authenticate and sell the dagger to himself. It never ceases to amaze me that whilst this type of dealer allegedly doesn't know what the piece "really" is, he always knows exactly how much its worth and what he wants for it!

Many fantasy pieces are extremely attractive, beautifully made and exhibit an inventive imagination in their design. This appeal enables this type of dagger to command quite often staggeringly high prices from a besotted collector. Due to the diversity of types and styles of fantasy daggers, it would be impossible to identify them on a dagger by dagger basis; therefore the best advice for the collector considering purchasing one of these items is to apply the same general rules of identification one would use to detect a fake production dagger. This would entail especially scrutinising Maker's proofmarks, the fit of the component parts, etc. However in view of the high standard of finish of many of these pieces, don't allow the quality of the piece to become the main consideration: for with the high values these pieces command, considerable expense has usually gone into their production.

ONE OF A KIND DAGGERS

During the period of the Third Reich one of a kind daggers were produced for presentation to the various Nazi luminaries and Axis heads of state. Reichsmarshall Hermann Goering was without doubt the single most favoured recipient of presentation, one of a kind edged weapons: this was due not only to his prominent position in the Nazi hierarchy, but also because of his well known love of edged weapons and his position as head of the German Hunting Association. There were very few occasions in public or private when Goering was not sporting some form of dagger or sword at his side as an essential accoutrement to his flamboyant sense of dress. Indeed many of the daggers that Goering wore, especially in private at his Carinhall estate, were extremely gaudy, bejeweled examples which would not have looked out of place around the waist of a Middle Eastern potentate.

One of the best known one of a kind presentation daggers designed specifically for Hermann Goering was the Solingen Industrial dagger. This superb piece with a hand forged Damascus steel blade was produced by the Burghers of Solingen in 1944. At this particular time, dagger production had all but ceased in Solingen as a result of Hitler's sidearm order forbidding officers the wearing of dress or ceremonial daggers in favour of a pistol. The Industrial Dagger was never presented to Goering and was indeed ordered to be destroyed just before the end of the war: having its Damascus blade snapped in two. The pieces of the dagger were retrieved and survived the war, as a result of which there have been many reproductions of this dagger produced in the past 30 years.

The Goering Industrial Dagger will be familiar to many collectors and will be encountered in a number of forms with plastic grips ranging in colour from white to yellow and orange. Similarly the fittings and scabbard of these reproductions also vary in quality and type, with some examples being produced in silver and others in gold. The blades encountered will be either artificial Damascus or plain steel.

Many other prominent Nazis were presented with one of a kind daggers: Heinrich Himmler and Viktor Lutz, as Head of the SS and SA respectively, were just two of the many recipients. Examples of many of these extremely rare daggers have been featured in Lt. Colonel Tom Johnson's 6 volume work COLLECTING THE EDGED WEAPONS OF THE THIRD REICH.

It is worth bearing in mind that one of a kind presentation daggers were by definition unique, and that virtually all the documented examples are already in long established private collections or museums. Therefore it is extremely unlikely that genuine one of a kind Third Reich daggers will be found lying on a table at an Arms and Militaria Fair or a Gun Show. It is reasonably safe to assume that any unique dagger offered for sale at these venues is almost certainly bogus, and would require extensive documentation and provenance to prove it otherwise.

This is a fantasy Prototype for a Hitler Youth Leader's dagger for "Gau Winners".

This fantasy illustration is for a Prototype NSFK Honour sword.

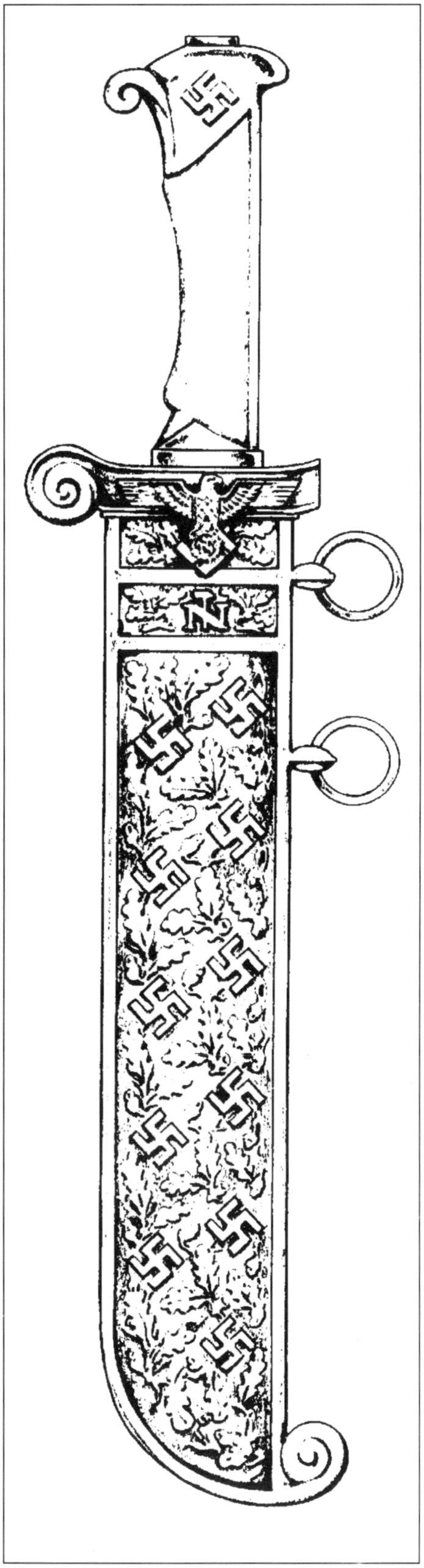
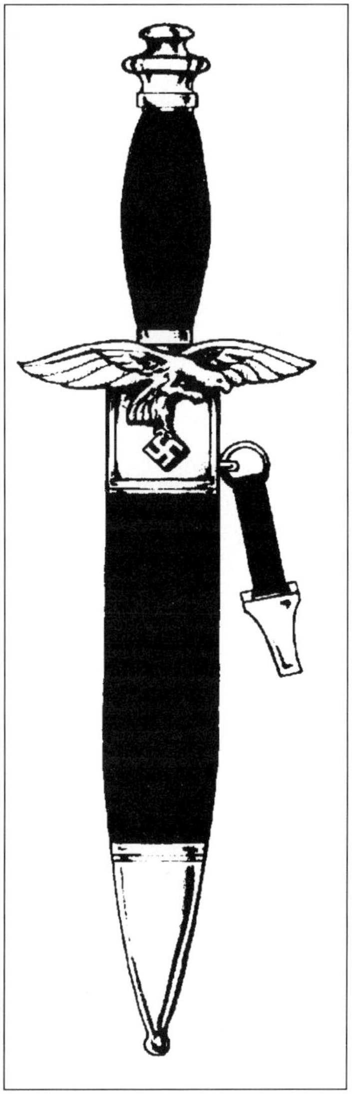
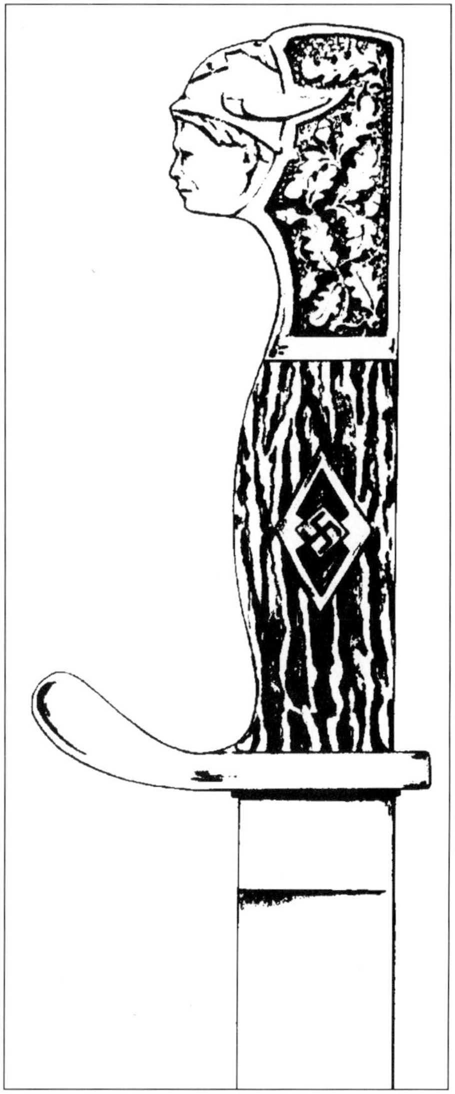

Three fantasy "Prototype" daggers. The oriental looking dagger on the left is supposed to be the "Prototype' of a new dagger for TeNo Leaders. The middle example is a "Prototype" 2nd Pattern DLV/NSFK Flyers knife - this is merely a parts assembly incorporating the crossguard from a 2nd Pattern Luftwaffe dagger, married to the parts of a DLV/NSFK knife. The right hand dagger is a modified dress bayonet embellished to become a "Prototype" Hitler Youth dagger.

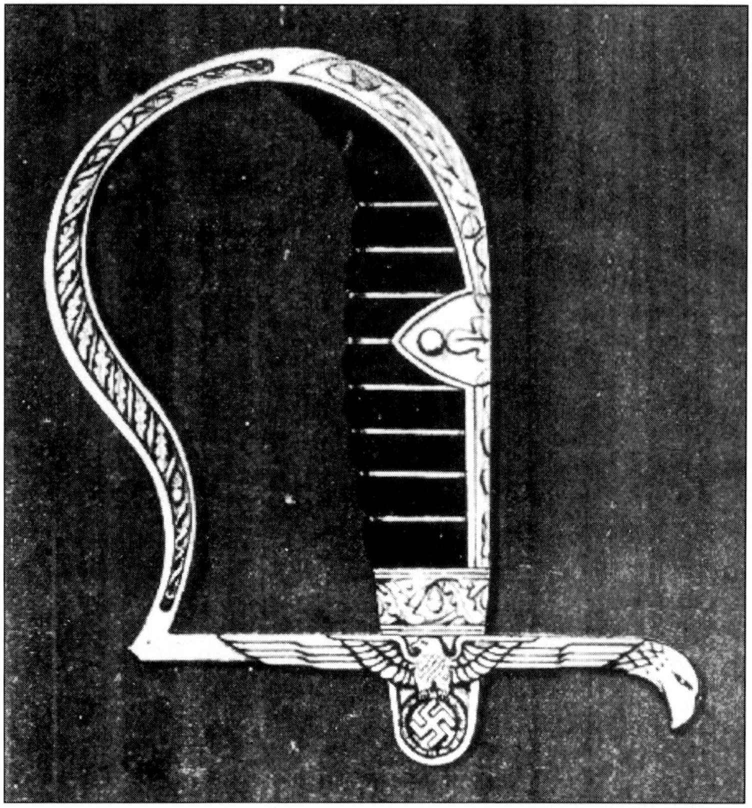

Two examples of fantasy "Prototype" swords of the Third Reich. These swords whilst maintaining the traditional stirrup style hilt of genuine swords have incorporated some variations on familiar Third Reich themes, i.e. the use of the Wehrmacht eagle, German steel helmet and the swastika etc.

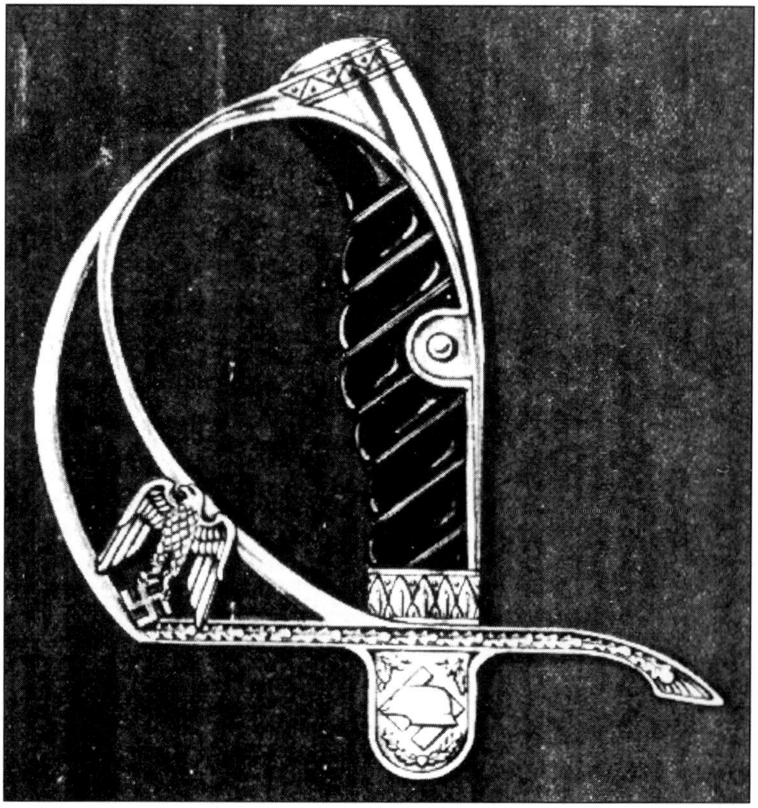

This fantasy SS piece has plastic grips with a swastika emblem inlaid into the obverse side. The obverse blade has a tiger tank and spurious motto photo-etched lightly onto the blade. The reverse blade has an etched dedication invoking the name of Michael Wittmann the famous SS Panzer ace.

This folding knife is marketed as an SS folding utility knife, however in reality this piece is a post-war fantasy. The SS were never issued or awarded any weapon vaguely resembling this fantasy. The eagle and other SS markings are completely spurious.

An SS "Prototype" dagger/dress sidearm. This piece is well made with aluminium crossguard and pommel. The SS runes mounted on the pommel are from the grip of a genuine 1933 pattern SS dagger. The chequered black plastic grips have been secured to the tang with two metal pins. A double edged polished steel blade completes this "Prototype" dagger. The leather scabbard has been custom made to accommodate the "dagger".

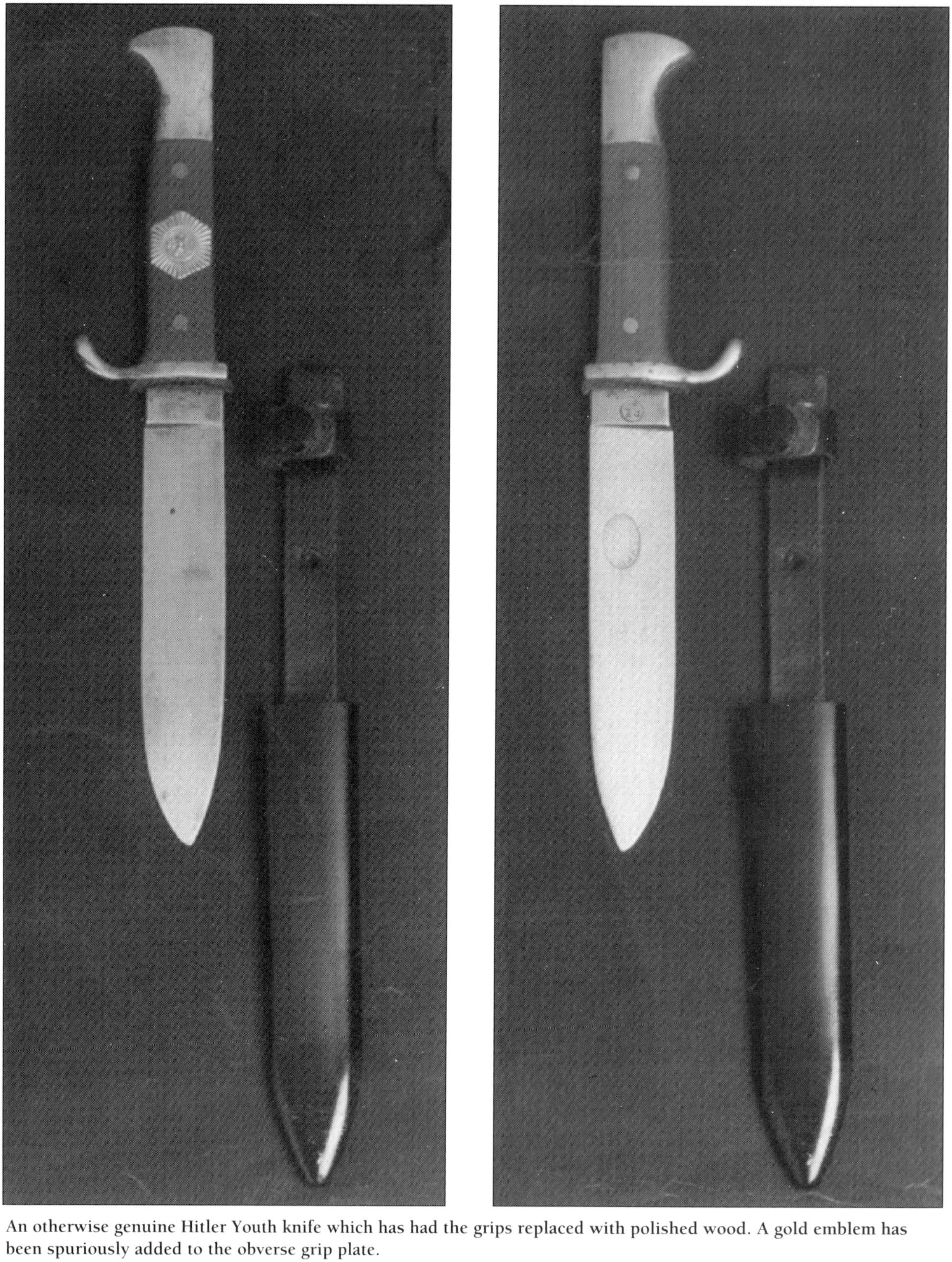

An otherwise genuine Hitler Youth knife which has had the grips replaced with polished wood. A gold emblem has been spuriously added to the obverse grip plate.

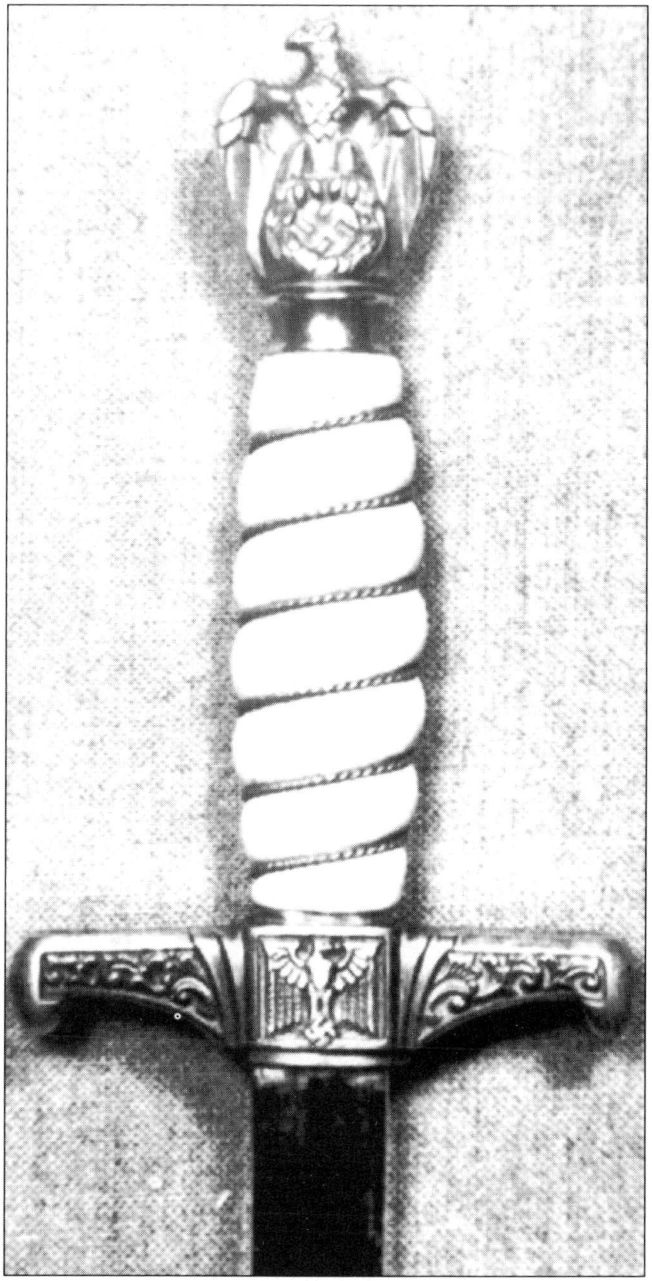

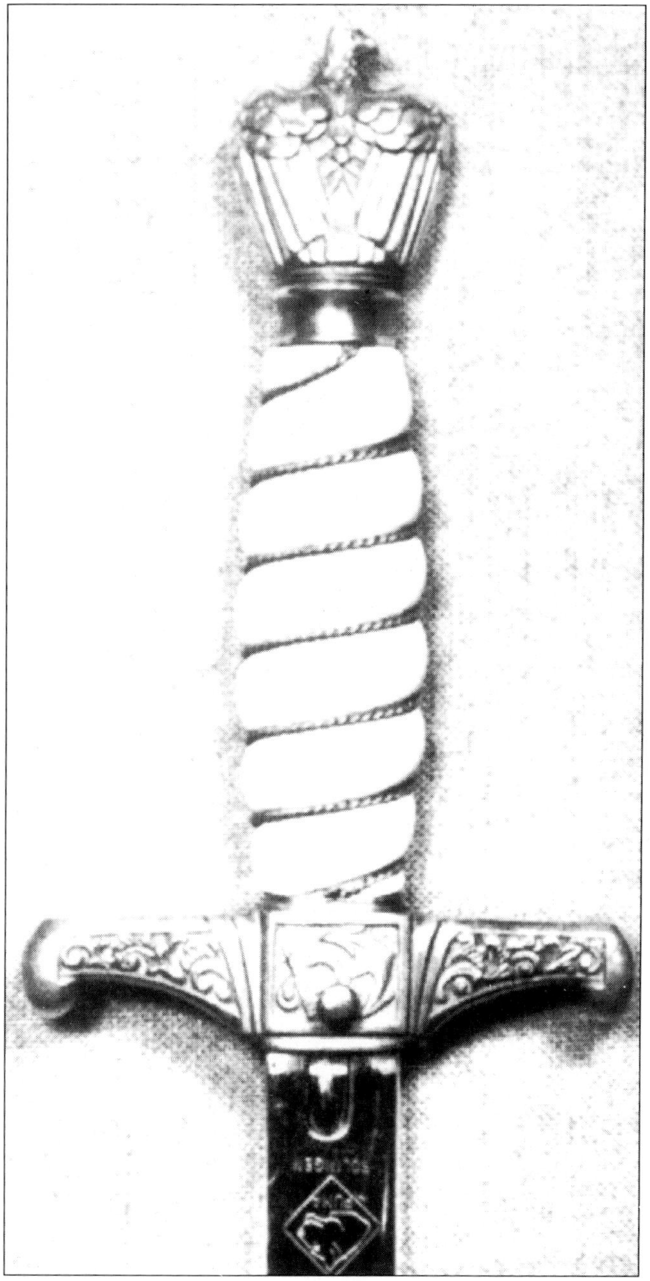

This highly contentious dagger has in the past been variously described as a new Prototype Kriegsmarine Dirk, a Marine Assault dagger, or Prototype Admiral's dagger. Irrespective of its intended use this type of dagger was never an authorised production military dagger during the Third Reich era. Reproductions and parts assembly examples of this dagger have been on the market for 30 years. Note the diamond PUMA proofmark, although other Maker's proofmarks will be encountered on different examples of this dagger.

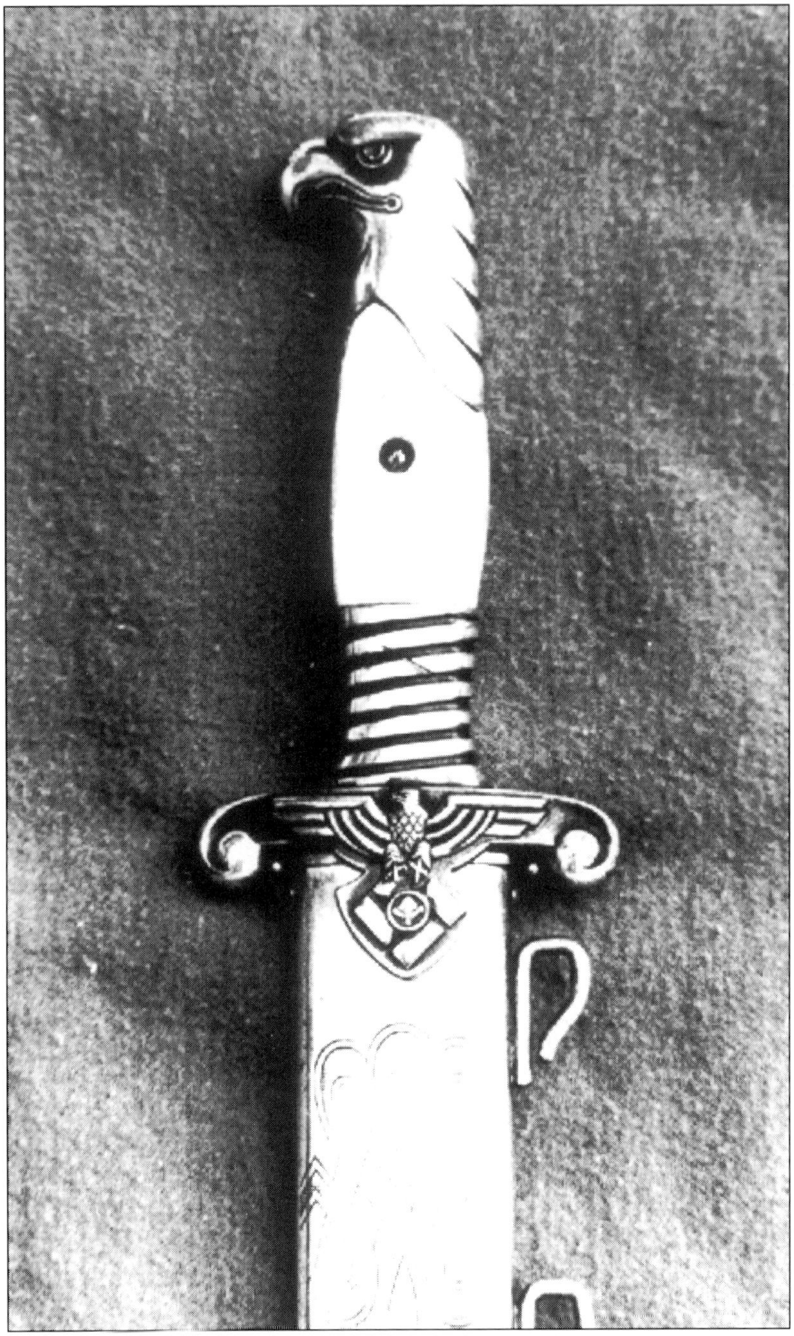

Obverse view of a fantasy RAD Leader's dagger. The alleged "Prototype" is a parts assembly utilising genuine and reproduction parts. The scabbard is that of a genuine RAD Leader's dagger, however the crossguard is completely spurious. At no time during the Third Reich did the RAD use an eagle decoration on the crossguard of either the Subordinate's or Leader's dagger; also the grip plates are held in place by a screw on the obverse grip plate - the opposite side to originals.

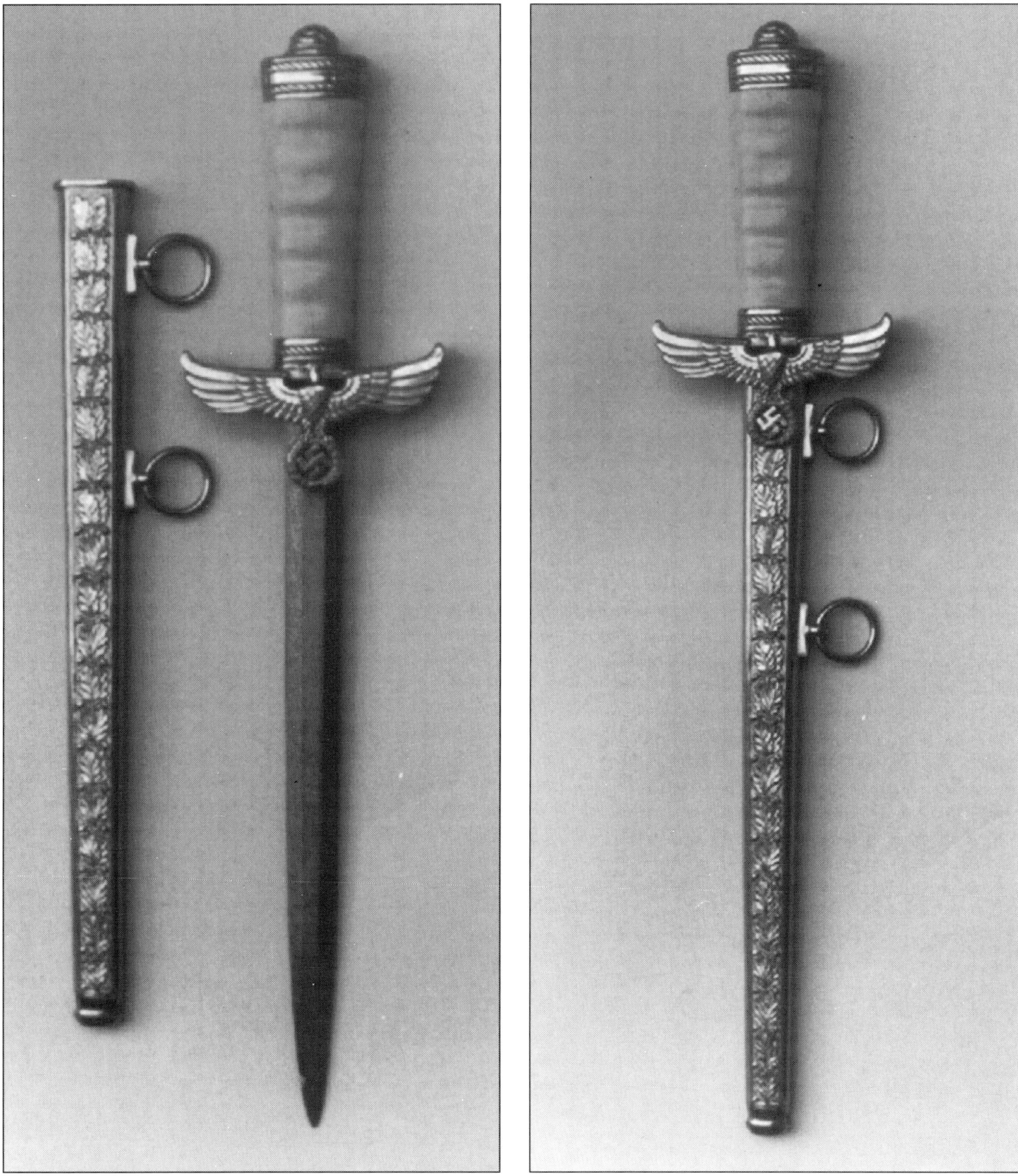

A current Spanish reproduction of the Hermann Goering Industrial dagger. These modern copies of a one of a kind Nazi dagger are available in several qualities and varieties of finish.

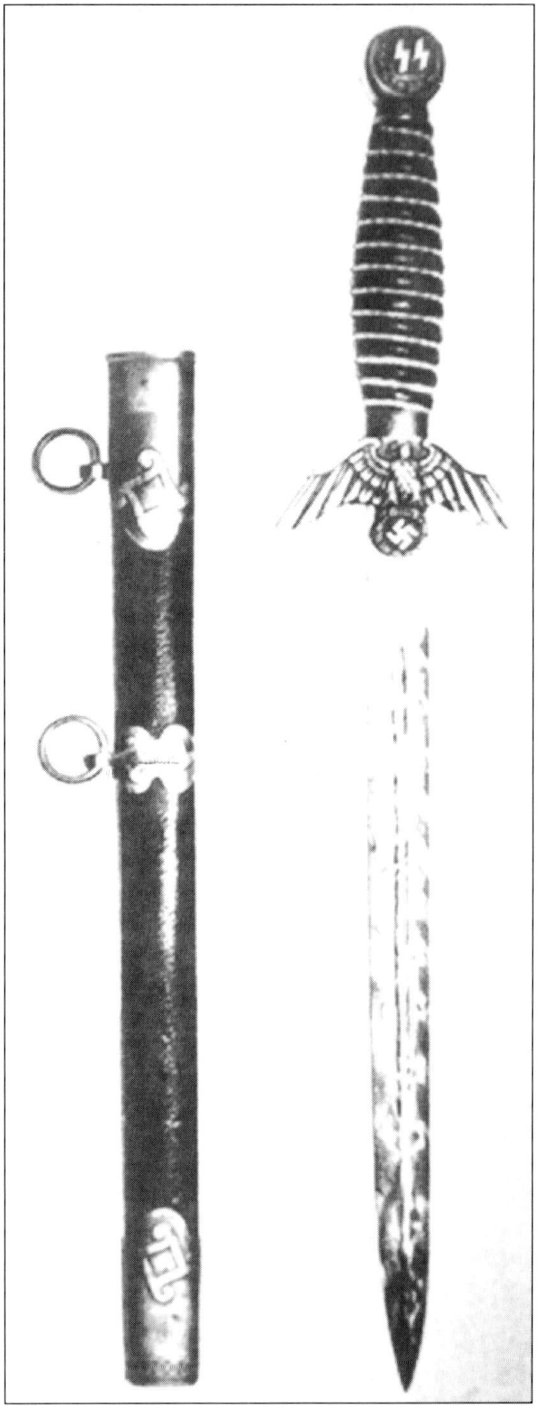

Obverse view of a "Prototype" SS dagger. The scabbard is leather bound with silver fittings decorated with nordic symbols. The dagger has a leather grip bound with silver wire. The pommel is decorated with the SS runes whilst the crossguard bears the swastika emblem. An artificial Damascus blade is featured in this example however they are also made with a plain steel blade.

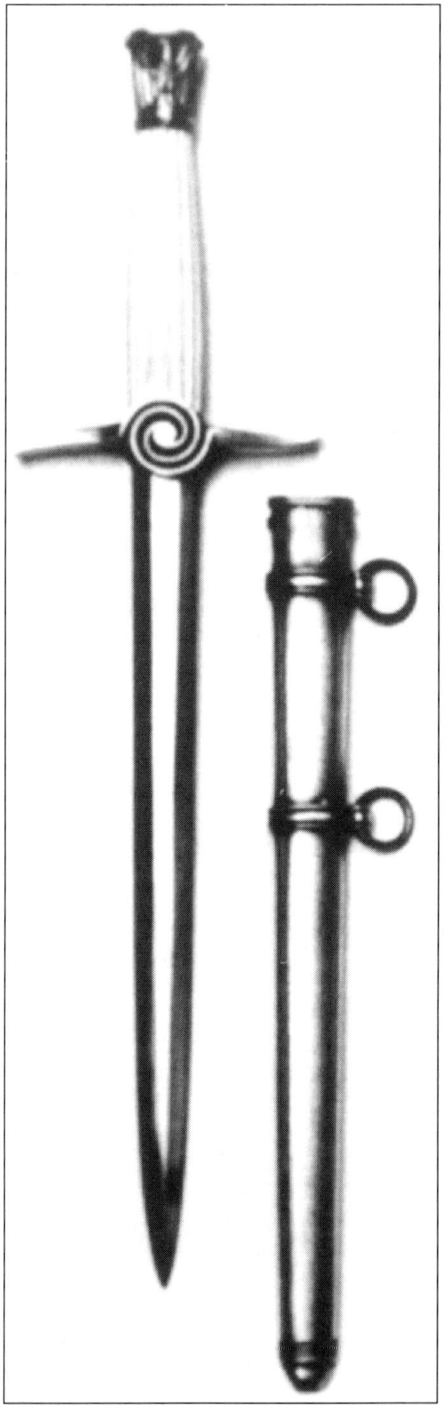

A reproduction of the prototype Army Field Marshal dagger. A breakdown of the component parts of this type of dagger is shown on the opposite page.

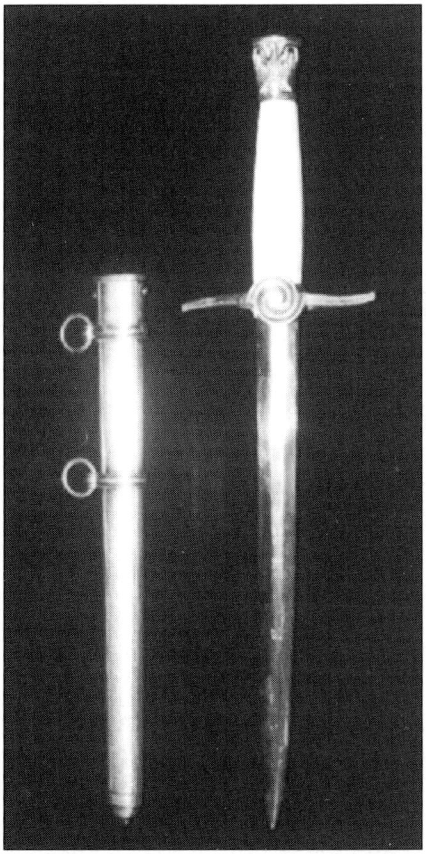
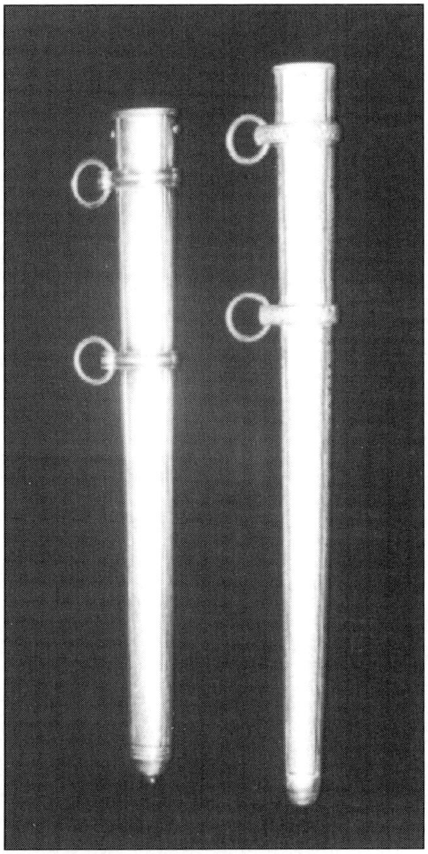
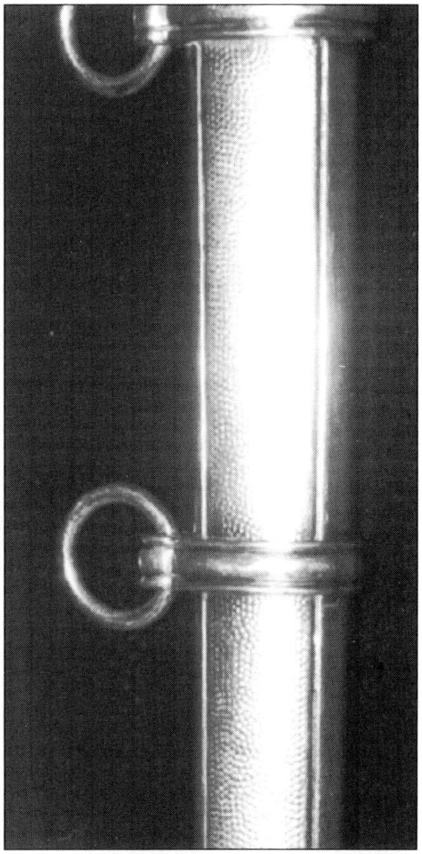

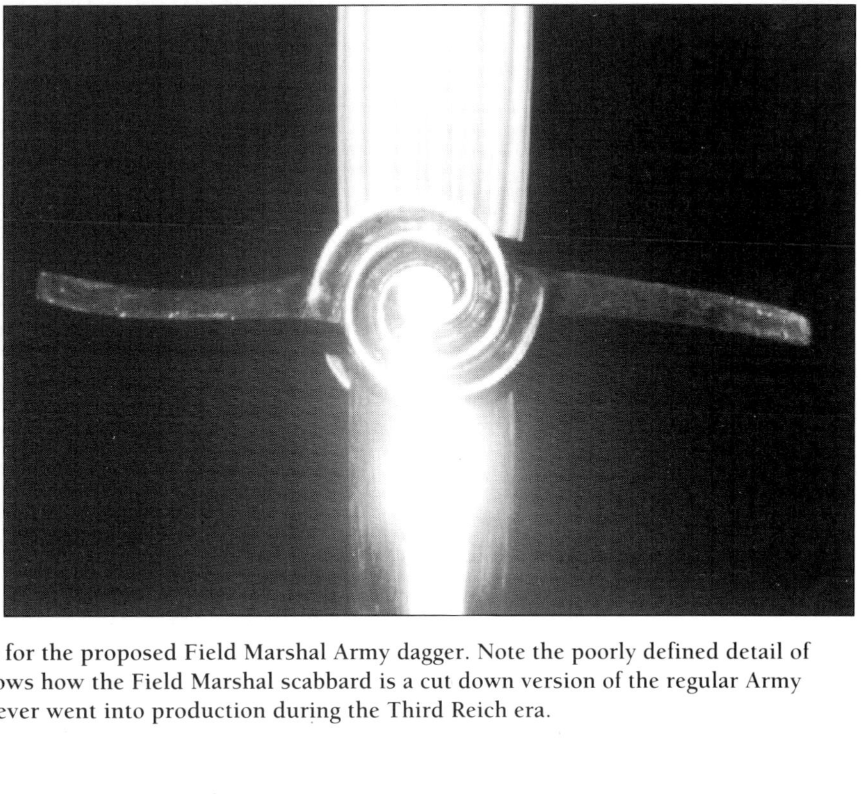

A post-war reproduction of the prototype for the proposed Field Marshal Army dagger. Note the poorly defined detail of the fittings. The scabbard comparison shows how the Field Marshal scabbard is a cut down version of the regular Army dagger scabbard. This proposed dagger never went into production during the Third Reich era.

PARTS ASSEMBLY DAGGERS

Third Reich daggers which have been assembled from various unrelated but otherwise genuine parts are not strictly speaking "reproductions", although it should be mentioned that some parts assembly daggers often do contain reproduction elements. This is especially true where modern reproduction blades are substituted into otherwise genuine daggers as a means of upgrading and increasing their value.

Almost immediately after the end of World War II the surviving German dagger Makers were producing daggers as souvenirs for the victorious Allied troops occupying the Western Zone of Germany. Initially these daggers were indistinguishable from weapons originally produced and assembled during the Third Reich era.

Hitler's sidearm order had halted production of dress daggers more than a year before the end of World War II, leaving the dagger Makers of Solingen with substantial stocks of unassembled dagger parts still in their inventories. The voracious demand for souvenirs of the Nazi years soon depleted these stocks, and with post-war material shortages the dagger Makers were unable to produce the correct type of new parts such as grips without the appropriate raw materials.

These shortages led to many anomalous daggers appearing for sale which although made from genuine parts were not always appropriate for the type of dagger being assembled. This has resulted in the so called "transitional dagger" which in many instances is a dagger made from parts from two different types of daggers with similar characteristics being assembled from a mishmash of parts. A prime example of this is the mixture of DLV dagger and 1st pattern Luftwaffe dagger parts being joined: resulting in a hybrid which is frequently passed off as a "transitional dagger" between the suspension of the DLV dagger and the introduction of the 1st pattern Luftwaffe dagger. This was not the case for although the DLV was in many respects the forerunner of the Luftwaffe, it did nonetheless continue as a separate body ultimately becoming the NSFK. Furthermore the DLV/NSFK adopted a short flyer's knife after the DLV dagger was withdrawn, whilst the Luftwaffe went its own separate way with the 1st pattern Luftwaffe dagger. These hybrid "transitional daggers" invariably command a premium price which they do not justly deserve in view of their antecedents.

There were a multitude of manufacturers in Solingen making the same types of dagger during their heyday in the late 1930's. This led to minor variations in the appearance of crossguards, pommels, etc.; indeed in many instances the differences were so marked that it is quite possible to identify the Maker of a genuine dagger such as the Army dagger merely by observing the characteristics of the crossguard eagle. It is evident from examining numerous examples of common daggers such as the Army that a degree of swapping has occurred not only in the post-war era at the hands of dealers and collectors, but also within the realms of the dagger industry in Solingen. This was no doubt the result of Makers helping one another out with shortages of component parts, as well as the smaller cottage Makers who purchased most of their parts from the larger firms such as Eickhorn and WKC. There are documented instances of Bills of Sale and Invoices for component parts which passed between the various Solingen Makers prior to 1945 which would indicate that this was a legitimate practice; however it does make it difficult for today's collector to now differentiate between a pre-war and post-war substitution of parts.

The parts assembly issue has been further complicated by the similarity of many blades which were and still are interchangeable between different organisations. This has been a particular problem with the Postschutz dagger which at the time it was designed and introduced by Paul Weyersburg in 1939 utilised the pre-existing RLB Leader's blade (already in service for over 3 years).

Another prestigious dagger which causes problems for the collector is the Diplomat's, which has the same stiletto style blade as the infinitely more common Army dagger. This has led to many Diplomat daggers which formerly had pitted or broken blades having replacements of a better example taken from the a genuine Army dagger. The real giveaway clue to this sort of practice is the exclusivity of manufacture of the Diplomat's dagger which was only manufactured by a handful of the better quality Makers such as Eickhorn, and Alcoso; whereas the common Army dagger was manufactured or assembled by virtually every edged weapon Maker in Solingen. Therefore a Diplomat's dagger now exhibiting an obscure or inappropriate Maker's proofmark on the blade would indicate that whilst the other fittings may be genuine, the blade is possibly a post-war replacement taken from an albeit genuine Army dagger (which would certainly diminish its value).

As stocks of certain parts became exhausted and appropriate materials were not available, the Solingen dagger Makers producing for the souvenir market turned to substitute materials. This occurred with the SA dagger, which began to appear with reddish brown plastic grips instead of the correct polished fruitwood grips. At the same time SA daggers were being produced solely for export bearing a squared quadrant proofmark bearing the letters “B A” with one letter in opposing diagonal corners. To comply with export regulations of the 1950's/60's they also bore the “Made in Germany” proofmark on the blade ricasso. These souvenir daggers would appear to have been produced and sold without scabbards, although many have now “acquired” the requisite SA scabbard! These B.A. proofmarked dagger were originally produced with plastic grips, although examples have been encountered which have had the grips replaced with the correct fruitwood type - however these daggers are still nonetheless post-war assemblies.

The most common and basic Nazi edged weapon, the Hitler Youth Knife, also received a new lease of life after the end of World War II. This style of knife had been in existence for many years indeed preceding the Nazis' rise to power, and continues to be popular even to this day. The Hitler Youth Knife was produced post-1945 in a slightly modified form merely being devoid of the HJ diamond insignia; in some instances the black chequered grips were left plain, whilst others had the Boy Scout fleur-de-Lis insignia inlaid or attached to the grip. To comply with anti-Nazi legislation in post-war Germany, Solingen produced Hitler Youth Knives were initially shipped to Spain where they had the HJ diamond insignia added, thus circumventing the legal restrictions. There are a multitude of differently marked Hitler Youth Knives now on the market: some with “Made in Germany”, “Made in Solingen” or with just “Germany” on the ricasso; the RZM proofmark also appears on many HJ Knives produced in the last 20 years. A variety of different post-war Hitler Youth Knives are illustrated in the Hitler Youth section of this book. Whilst post-war assemblies are troublesome to collectors, the most worrying aspect is the up-grading of genuine daggers with post-war produced blades. Reproduction blades are available for virtually every dagger type encompassing military, civil and political daggers. There is a comprehensive range of excellent quality blades emanating from Solingen which start at the bottom of the range with the plain blade ascending through presentation, decorated and Damascus examples. Most of the Spanish reproduction blades are of a laughably inferior quality, however the current crop of german blades are frighteningly accurate exhibiting superb craftsman made quality. These blades provide the most lucrative area of the dagger market for the less scrupulous dealer and collector: for when one of these blades is substituted into a genuine dagger it is extremely difficult for the average collector to detect them.

The most widely misused of these new blades are those designed for the Party form daggers i.e. SS, SA, NSKK and NPEA. The humble but otherwise genuine SA dagger can now have its value increased many fold by the simple expedient of substituting a reproduction blade with the Rohm dedication. The same is true of the SS dagger which is now being fitted with blades bearing Rohm or Himmler dedications. Genuine SS and SA daggers are being further embellished with replacement Damascus and presentation inscribed blades. Examples of all these types of reproduction blades are illustrated in the appropriate sections.

Genuine military daggers are now quite routinely upgrade with good quality modern reproduction blades which feature decorated panels and presentation inscriptions purporting to emanate from such Luftwaffe personalities as Hermann Goering, Werner Moelders, Adolf Galland etc. or formations such as Legion Condor and the most famous Luftwaffe Geschwader. The same is also true of Army dagger blades which now use well known Army personalities and divisions etc. in their bogus inscriptions. The Kriegsmarine dagger likewise has a range of presentation and “Honour” blades currently available with dedications from Raeder or Doenitz. Examples of the current Kriegsmarine “Honour Dagger”blades are illustrated in the Kriegsmarine section. Other Kriegsmarine blades will be encountered with inscriptions for specific ships or even a particular U-Boat: the favourites being Gunther Prien's U-47 and Otto Kretschmer's U-99.

Two parts assembly daggers and a modified bayonet, all three were produced in Germany in the 1960's for an English dealer. All three pieces contain a mixture of genuine and reproduction parts and are finished to an extremely high quality.

DAMASCUS AND DECORATED BLADES

Reproduction Damascus and decorated blades have now become the most profitable area for the less scrupulous dealers and collectors. These type of prestigious blades are now routinely being substituted for plain blades in common but otherwise genuine daggers, greatly increasing their desirability and value.

The quality of reproduction Damascus blades has improved dramatically over the past few years as a direct result of the continual rise in price of Third Reich daggers and the insatiable demand by collectors for more and more prestigious and unusual specimens. There are two main types of Damascus blade: "artificial" and "genuine". These two categories do not relate to authenticity, but reflect the finished quality of the blade and the method of their production. The term "genuine Damascus" when applied to a reproduction blade merely signifies that the blade was produced by the application of traditional techniques of Damast beating and forging, as opposed to the acid bath method used to create "artificial Damascus" blades. These two categories of "artificial" and "genuine" Damascus blade were available to the purchaser during the Third Reich era, and merely reflected the degree of craftsmanship required to create the finished blade.

Similarly these two categories of Damascus blade are now available as post-war reproductions. Frequently collectors are confused when encountering a reproduction Damascus blade precisely because whilst the blade is "genuine" in the sense of *how* it was made, it is nonetheless still a reproduction because of *when* it was made.

Post-war produced "genuine Damascus" blades frequently feature the words "ECHT DAMAST" on the tang or ricasso which indicates the blade has been produced by the "genuine" Damascus forging process. Indeed many of the skilled artisans who produced genuine Damascus blades during the Third Reich era continued with their craft for decades after the end of World War II. These craftsmen have always had pride in their creations and many have signed the blades which have been individually forged with their name or initials: one of the most prolific was Paul Dingler who signed his work with a "PD" proofmark. Essentially these blades have been made from the same materials, by the same process and even by the same craftsmen by both the pre-war and post-war eras.

Included in this section are examples of some of the different styles of Damascus steel blades which were available to the purchaser during the Third Reich period. It should be borne in mind that modern reproductions continue to copy these different styles: the most common being the spidery finish of the maidenhair Damast (top right).

Artificial Damascus blades are the most commonly encountered form of reproduction Damascus blade, however the fact that the same process was used during the Third Reich era does sometimes pose difficulties in detecting their authenticity. The current crop of artificial Damascus blades are produced in Solingen, and exhibit a degree of accuracy and quality of finish which is very difficult to distinguish from artificial Damascus blades manufactured prior to 1945. Due to the process used in their manufacture, the size, weight and finish of these blades are almost identical to pre-war examples, and in many instances are only detectable as reproduction by incorrect positioning or application of Maker's proofmarks, blade dedications (such as the Rohm and Himmler Honour dagger inscriptions) or inappropriate use or positioning of the RZM logo.

Genuine decorated blades were widely available to purchasers of Third Reich daggers between 1933 and 1945. Unfortunately for collectors availability is still not a problem, but the authenticity of current blades is! Reproduction decorated blades appear in a variety of style and patterns mainly to fit military daggers with the stiletto style blade although examples will be encountered on blades of many other Nazi formations. The quality varies widely from the cheap photo-etching to expensively produced etched blue panels. Whilst the first example is invariably applied to Spanish reproduction blades, the latter example has often been applied onto a common but otherwise genuine blade.

Decorating blades by means of photo-etching is not only restricted to daggers; many genuine K98 service bayonets have also been photo-etched since the 60's and 70's with bogus blade and pommel decorations and inscriptions. Most of the decorated bayonet blades are attributed to SS Regiments or Divisions and are completely spurious (ironically these genuine bayonets with spurious etching are now collectors items in their own rights although many collectors still believe them to be 100% genuine-decoration and all). This type of decoration was never a feature of K98 service bayonets in the Third Reich era, although many military dress bayonets were legitimately etched with decorative panels: this being done by a process of acid etching, rather than the more modern technique of photo-etching. This section includes illustrations of authentic decorated blade panels and pommel etching which were available from the Carl Eickhorn Company. Other edged weapon manufacturers also had a range of different blade decorations featuring similar themes to those illustrated.

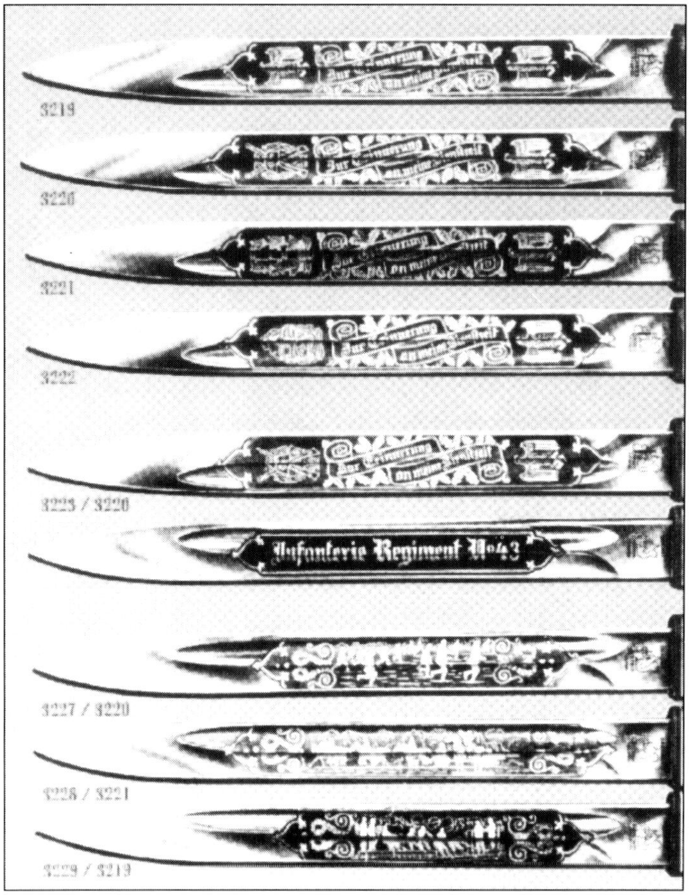

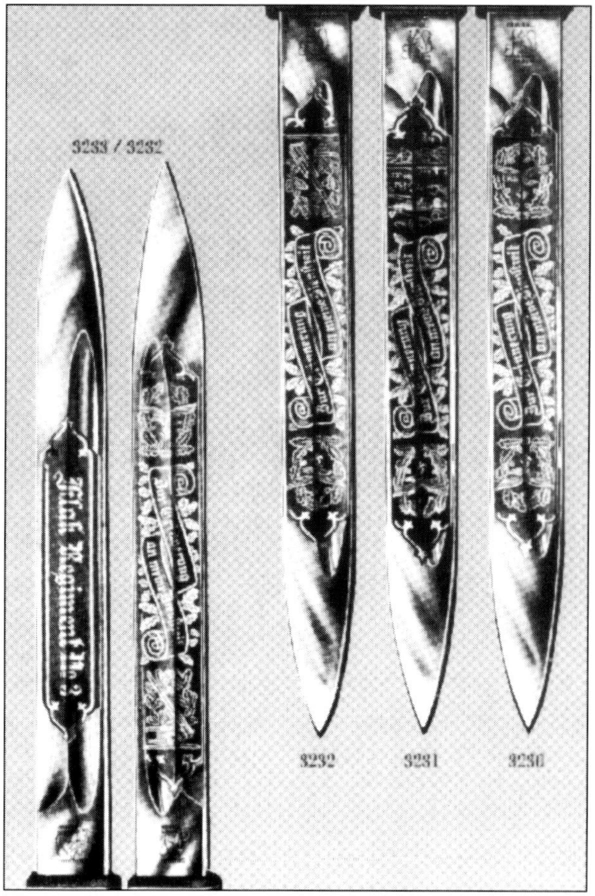

These illustrations show the wide variety of genuine blade decoration available to purchasers during the Third Reich. All these particular styles of blade decoration were offered as optional extras by the firm of Carl Eickhorn of Solingen.

The different types of genuine Damascus blades offered by Carl Eickhorn in the firms 1937 Eickhorn Kundendienst.

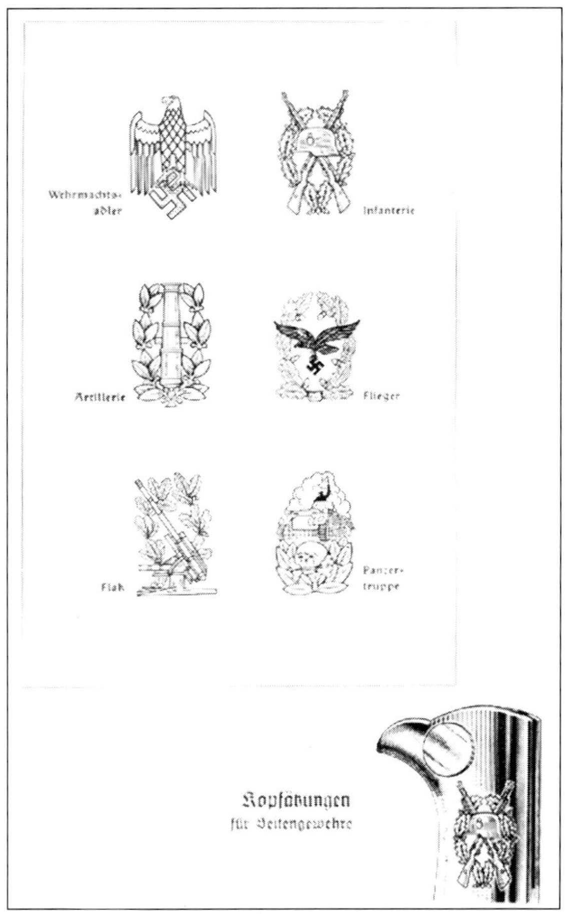

Examples of genuine pommel etching available from Carl Eickhorn's 1937 Kundendienst.

CURRENT REPRODUCTIONS

The dagger market is still awash with reproductions of varying qualities ranging from the long established poorer quality Spanish examples to the top quality German reproduction blades and replacement parts. An English Company, Worldwide Arms of Birmingham, have recently introduced a new range of Third Reich dagger reproductions of a reasonably good quality; included in their range are the three main military types: Army, Navy and Luftwaffe, as well as reproductions of the 1933 pattern SS and SA dagger. This company also produces several reproduction fighting knives including the double-edged Gottlieb Hammesfahr trench knife with grooved wooden grips and steel scabbard and the all steel Demag crank handle bayonet/fighting knife. These fighting knives are extremely convincing and are being offered for sale at between 1/2 and 2/3 the price of genuine examples. The Worldwide Arms reproduction daggers are also well finished and would certainly pose a problem of identification especially to the novice collector, many of whom have already unwittingly purchased these daggers as genuine articles. Unfortunately for collectors these reproductions are not being identified and marketed as reproductions, but are being sold using euphemistic terms such as 1933 "model" of "pattern". These reproductions are not cheap: being sold at more than half the price of a genuine dagger. This relatively higher price for a reproduction is causing many collectors to purchase them believing they have found a genuine bargain. Currently there are several different types of reproduction NPEA dagger appearing on the market evidently from the same source, these include NPEA Student's and Leader's daggers. The different types of daggers all feature the same style of softwood grips which feature a very distinct broad grain running vertically through the wood. Also on the market at the moment is a visually good DRK Subordinate's hewer which looks acceptable until stripped into its component parts.

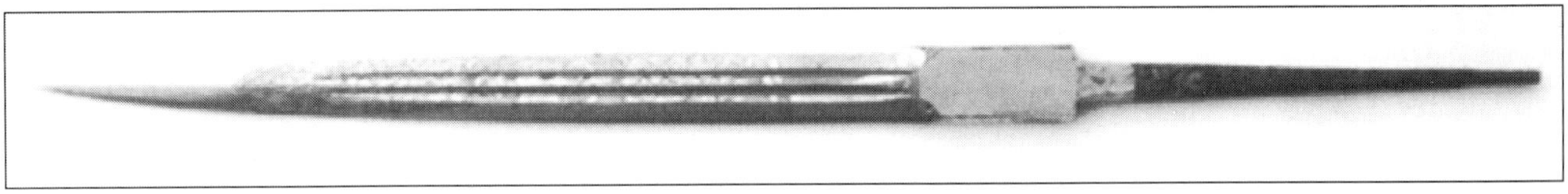

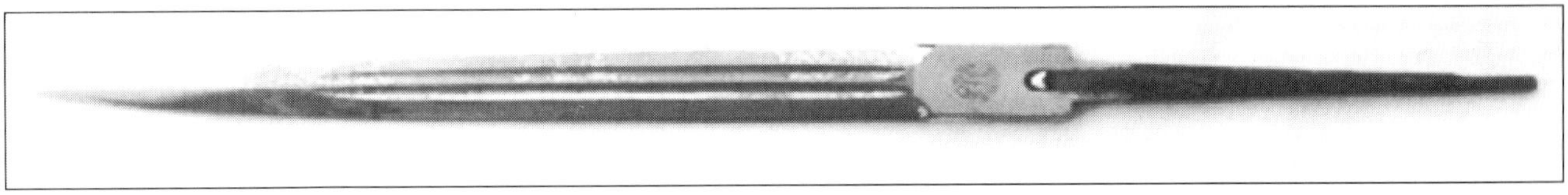

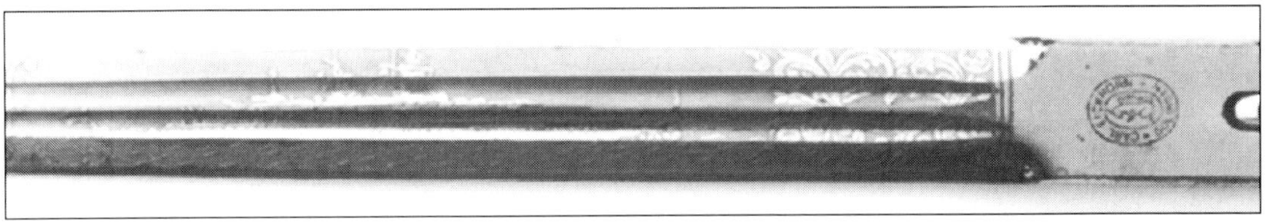

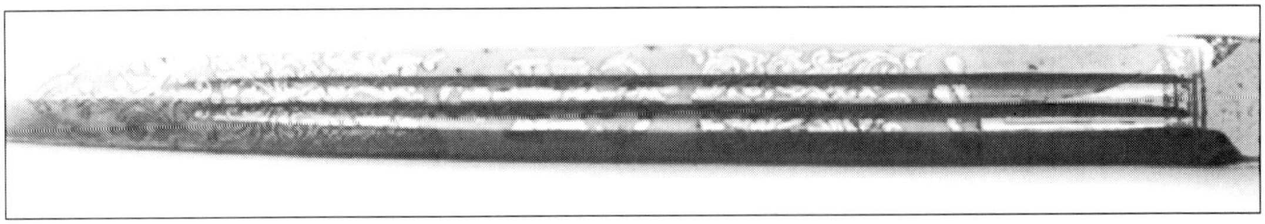

Obverse and reverse sides of a modern reproduction "presentation" Kriegsmarine dagger blade. These blades are available with a variety of blade etchings. This particular blade depicts a pocket battleship in the centre of a floral panel on the obverse side, and a Nazi eagle and swastika superimposed on a fouled anchor on the reverse blade. Also on the reverse side is a depiction of the German Naval Monument at Laboe. The blade ricasso bears an Eickhorn proofmark which is the early small oval type with the squirrel in the middle. These German reproduction blades are exceptionally well made being drop forged and having billet clamp marks and a well fitted and positioned button release spring.

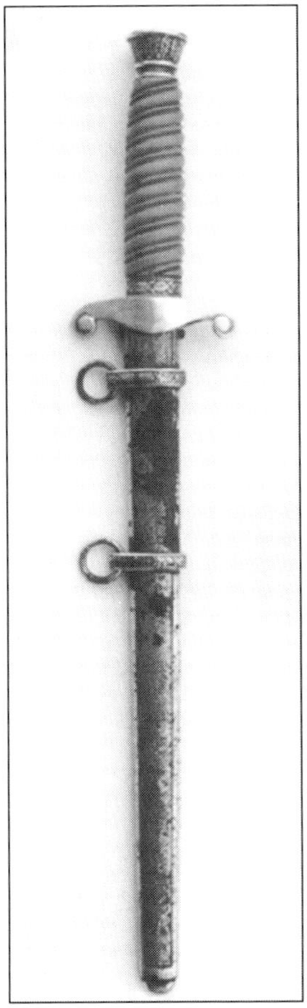

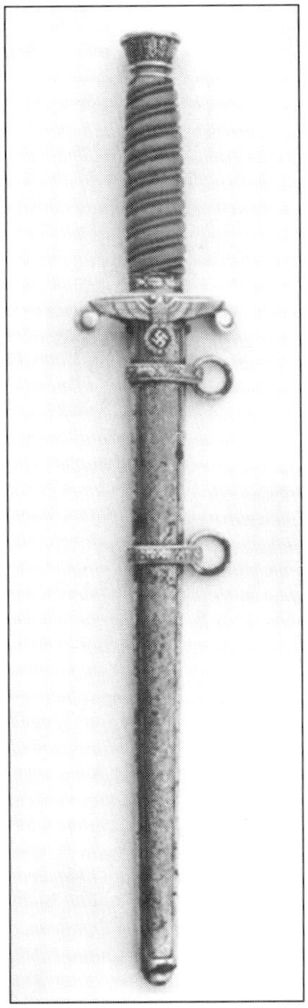

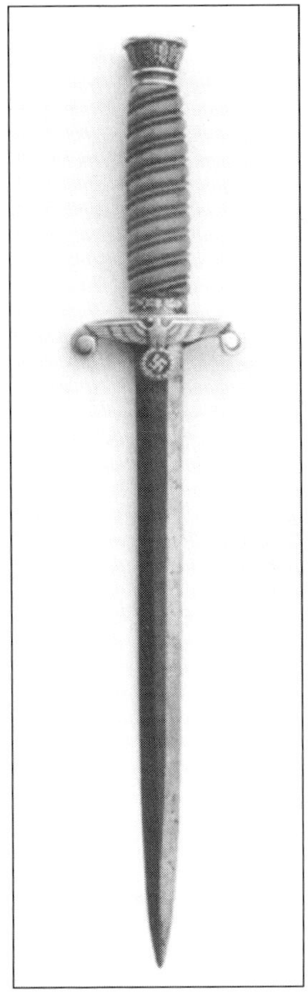

Pictured above left are three views of one of the current reproduction Army daggers. This example purchased from a militaria dealer has been artificially aged and distressed to disguise some of the dagger's reproduction features: mainly the swirling pattern on the scabbard and the matt grey blade, which appears to have been spotted with household bleach to give it a lightly pitted finish. The three scabbards top right show the comparison between genuine and reproduction: the top right example is a reproduction - note how wide apart the scabbard bands are and the very pronounced nature of the scabbard throat screws: the centre and lefthand scabbards are both genuine. Pictured left are close-ups of the obverse and reverse crossguards of a genuine Army dagger (right) and a reproduction (left) - note the pronounced swastika and the large and poorly defined swirls at the end of the crossguard; also note how narrow the rear crossguard is.

Further examples of current reproductions continued on pages 201-208.

WARSAW PACT DAGGERS

Since the dissolution of the Soviet Union and its satellite states and the consequent breakup of the Warsaw Pact, numerous genuine Warsaw Pact daggers have appeared emanating from the old Eastern Bloc. These daggers have no connection with any Third Reich edged weapons, and although they are genuine in their own right have been produced since 1945 for the Armies of Eastern European countries. When these daggers first started appearing in quantity over two years ago, they were relatively inexpensive and a good curiosity buy for the dagger collector. However they are now escalating in price, and parts from these daggers, especially the East German Army dagger have been used in fabricating Third Reich dagger "hybrid" and "prototypes". Also the hanging straps of these daggers which bear a close resemblance to their Third Reich predecessors, will now be routinely found attached to genuine and parts assembly Nazi daggers.

Although these former Communist daggers are genuine, it should be stressed they do not approach the quality of pre-war Solingen made examples. The interest in these daggers has now caused their production to be resumed to fulfil the demand from western European and American collectors in very much the same way that the Solingen Makers continued to produce the souvenir daggers after World War II.

Some East European daggers such as the Polish Naval dagger have had a very consistent design for more than 50 years, and whilst there are plenty of genuine Polish Naval daggers on the market there are now also an equal number of modern reproductions being reproducers by Polish entrepreneurs who also carry an extensive line of Warsaw pact badges and uniforms. Many of these individuals actually market their wares personally at Arms Fairs in Europe and the USA. Much of what comes out of Poland now is reproduction, however it is not always marketed as such; unfortunately collectors have the impression that because these items have come from the former Communist States, that they must be genuine.

Another consequence of the collapse of Communism is the appearance of reconstituted Third Reich dagger accoutrements. This has come about because of the way Germany was partitioned after World War II. The production of Third Reich daggers was carried out mainly in Solingen and associated areas of the Ruhr, which fell within the confines of West Germany. However the dagger Makers did not produce most of the accoutrements for their daggers which had been manufactured mainly in the larger cities in Eastern Germany (such as Berlin, Leipzig, Dresden etc.). For 45 years these cities were in East Germany, consequently there was not the usual trading of these items due to the restricted freedom of commerce imposed by the Communist state. Since 1990 there has been a number of "discoveries" of accoutrements and materials; these materials mainly the fabric used in the manufacture of hanging straps and portepees have been used to manufacture hanging straps for Third Reich daggers using both genuine and reproduction metal fittings. Indeed there has been a veritable flood of some items, such as portepees for the SS sword. These post-war reconstructed items are often impossible to detect when skillfully assembled, however the quality does vary especially when reproduction suspension clasps are used in the fabrication. The one thing all these items have in common is that they are invariable and suspiciously in mint condition.

One final point on the breakup of Eastern Europe: it had always been anticipated that if and when the East opened up, there would be an avalanche of Third Reich daggers looted by the Russians after 1945. This has not materialised mainly for two reasons. Much of the Third Reich war booty was handed in by Eastern veterans because it was made a criminal offense to possess or trade in any Nazi items. Also for many years prior to 1990 astute dealers in the West have been secretly milking what few daggers were still in private hands and bringing them to the West: leaving very few items to be exploited after the collapse of Communism.

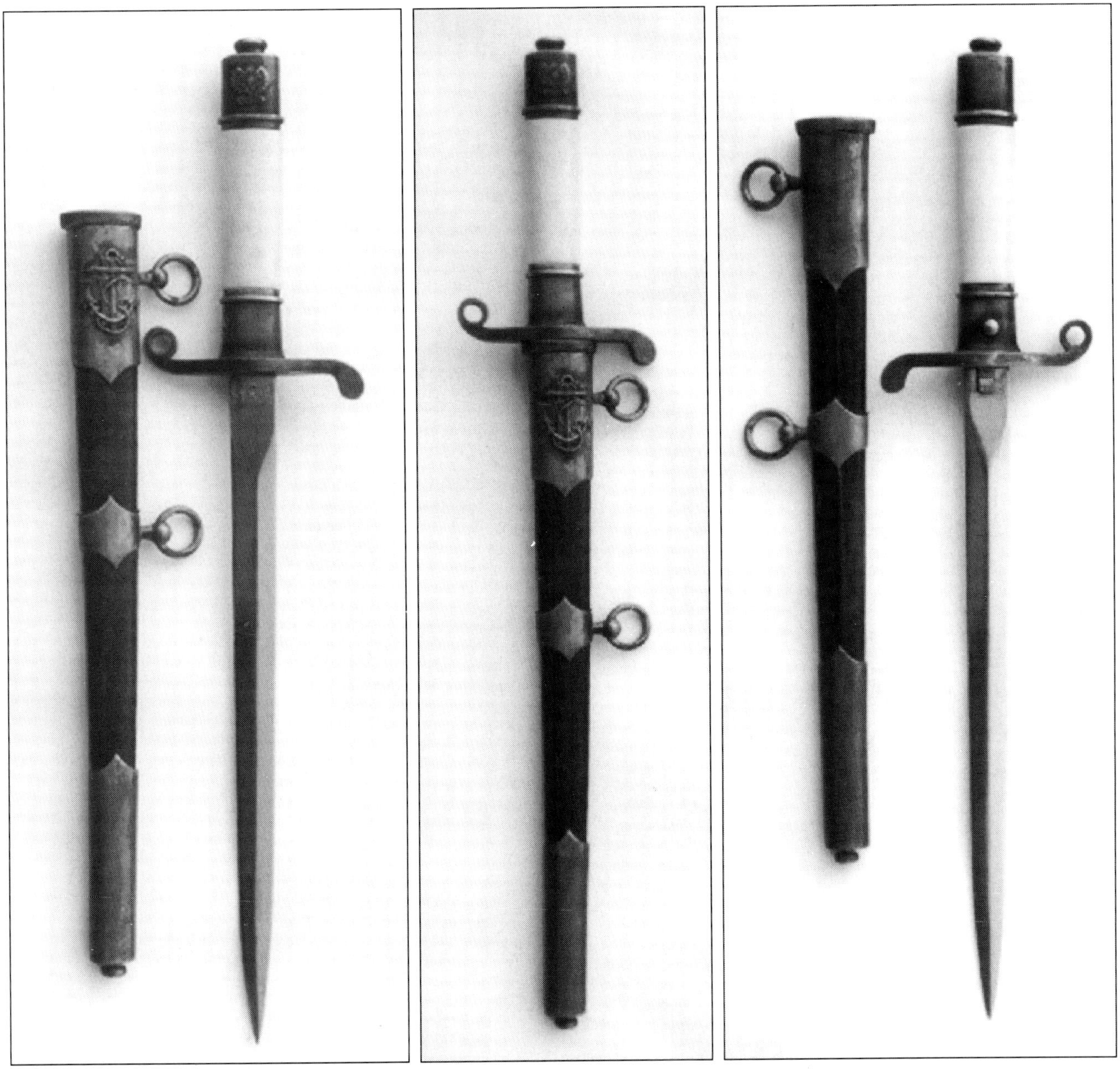

Three different views of a genuine Polish Naval Officer's dagger. This type of dagger is now being extensively reproduced in Poland for export to Western Europe and the USA. The current reproductions take exactly the same form, but have several visible characteristics which distinguish them from genuine Polish daggers. The brass fittings on the dagger and scabbard of current reproductions have an extremely garish yellow finish , and the scabbard binding is plastic rather than the leather of originals. These reproductions are available with numerous types of insignia including Navy, Army, Airforce, Paratroops etc.; the insignia is usually positioned on the top locket of the scabbard. Some examples also have the Polish national colours of red and white in four diagonal quadrants superimposed on the grip.

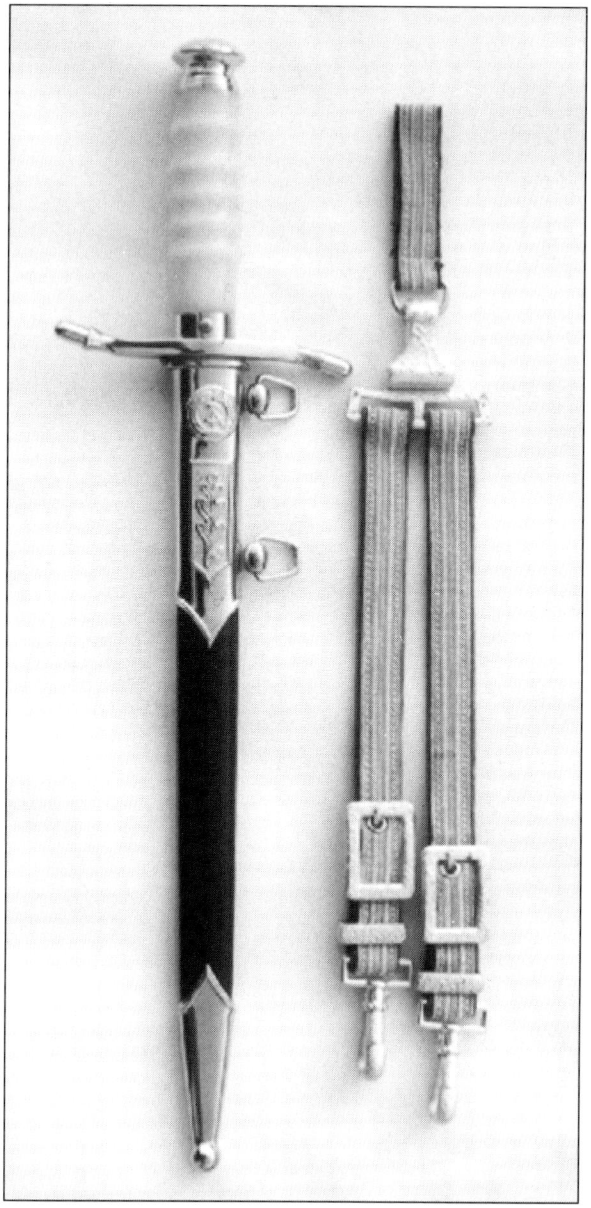

Five different views of a genuine East German Army Officer's dress dagger which came onto the market in quantity following the reunification of Germany. Although they are quite an attractive dagger, they are not made to the same high standard as Third Reich daggers. These daggers were presented in a green cardboard box along with hanging straps and a belt loop. Unfortunately the hanging straps are very similar to those of the Luftwaffe during the Third Reich era, and have been encountered attached to genuine Nazi Luftwaffe daggers. Also the East German General's hanging straps are currently being marketed as Third Reich Luftwaffe General's straps; these straps are attractive and of very good quality with gold fittings on an oakleaf design with red felt backing and gold brocade facings. The East German General's dagger is identical to the ordinary Officer's with the exception of the fittings which are gold for the General's with the East German national insignia on the top of the pommel whereas the lower ranking officer's has a pebbled finish with silver fittings. Also illustrated opposite is the guarantee certificate which came with every genuine dagger. Initially these East German daggers were quite modestly priced, however they are becoming scarcer and consequently are increasing in price.

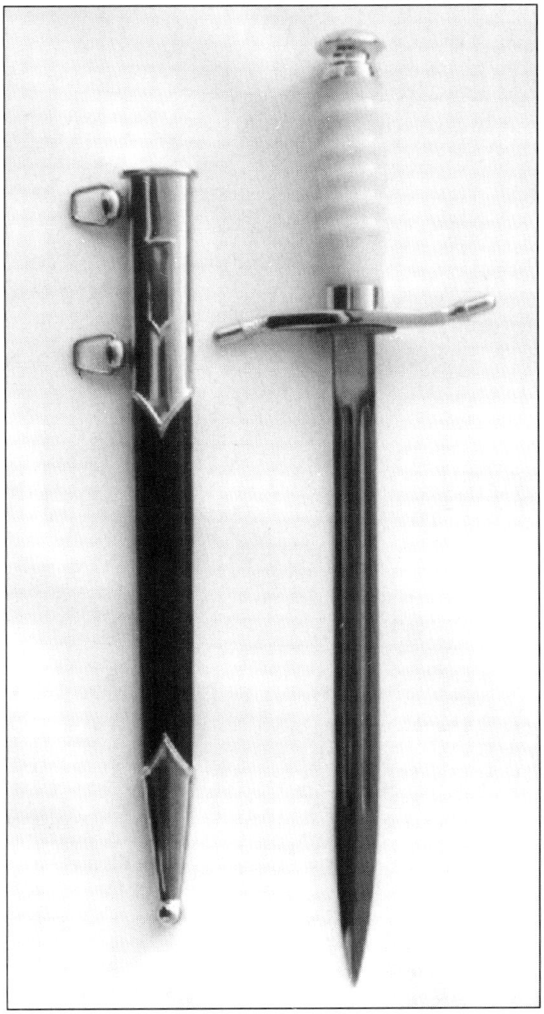

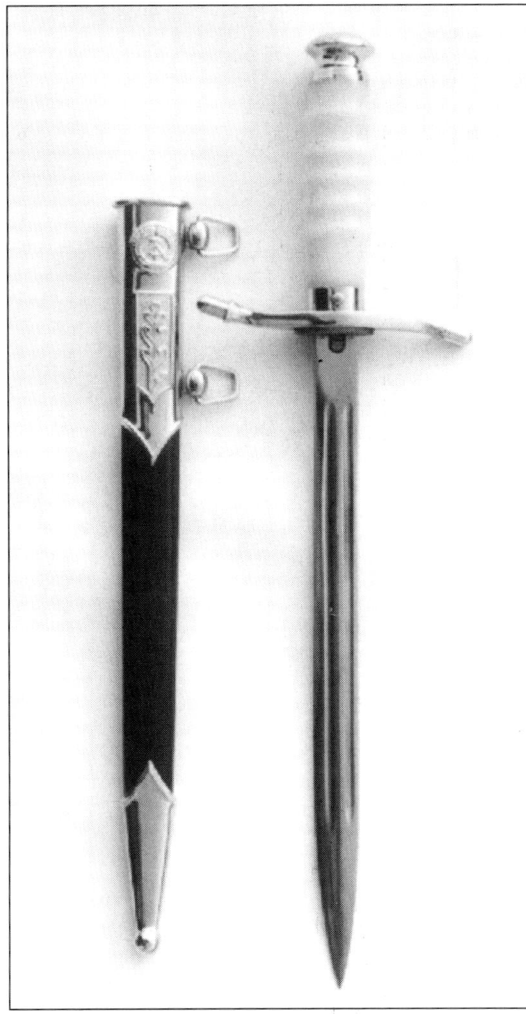

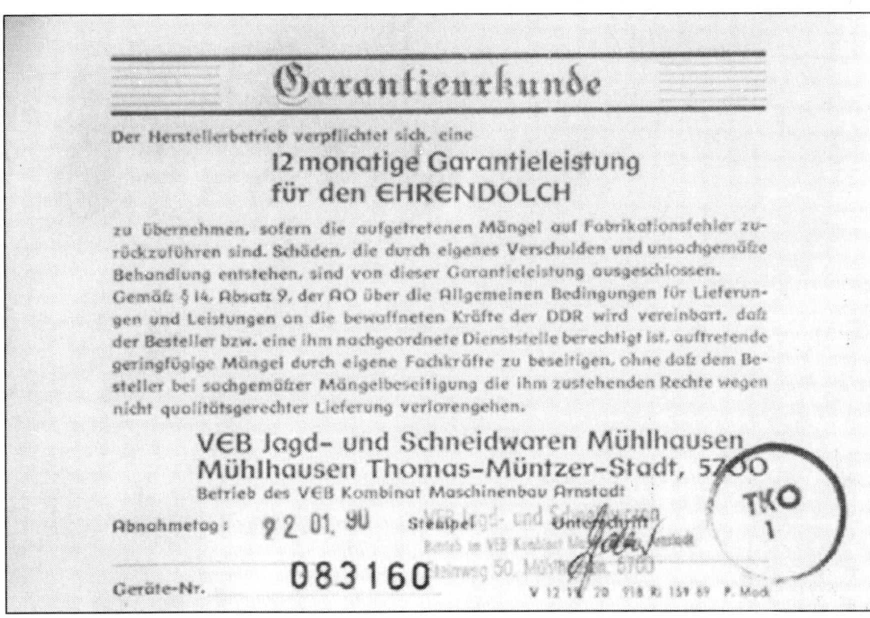

Garantieurkunde

Der Herstellerbetrieb verpflichtet sich, eine

12 monatige Garantieleistung für den EHRENDOLCH

zu übernehmen, sofern die aufgetretenen Mängel auf Fabrikationsfehler zurückzuführen sind. Schäden, die durch eigenes Verschulden und unsachgemäße Behandlung entstehen, sind von dieser Garantieleistung ausgeschlossen.
Gemäß § 14, Absatz 9, der AO über die Allgemeinen Bedingungen für Lieferungen und Leistungen an die bewaffneten Kräfte der DDR wird vereinbart, daß der Besteller bzw. eine ihm nachgeordnete Dienststelle berechtigt ist, auftretende geringfügige Mängel durch eigene Fachkräfte zu beseitigen, ohne daß dem Besteller bei sachgemäßer Mängelbeseitigung die ihm zustehenden Rechte wegen nicht qualitätsgerechter Lieferung verlorengehen.

VEB Jagd- und Schneidwaren Mühlhausen
Mühlhausen Thomas-Müntzer-Stadt, 5700
Betrieb des VEB Kombinat Maschinenbau Arnstadt

Abnahmetag: 92 01. 90 Stempel Unterschrift

TKO 1

Geräte-Nr. 083160

V 12 18 20 918 Ri 159 89 P. Mod.

DAGGER STRIPPING TOOL

In order to quickly and accurately establish the authenticity of any Third Reich dagger, it is essential to strip the dagger down into its component parts. Some daggers such as the three main military types can be almost completely stripped by hand without the aid of any special tool, with the exception of the scabbard slide retaining screws located externally on the neck of the scabbard. However there are several daggers principally the DRK Leader's, Diplomat's and all Party form daggers (i.e. SS, SA, NSKK, NPEA) which require a specialist tool to correctly strip the dagger without inflicting irreparable damage to any of the component parts.

Collectors and dealers can frequently be observed trying to remove stiff tang nuts from SA or SS daggers with a pair of pliers. Whilst this will remove the nut it will also permanently mark the outside edge of the tang nut. A similar operation is also often carried out on scabbard locket or slide screws which are frequently attacked with a household screwdriver or even the edge of a coin, inevitably ruining the original slot in the top of the screw. Far worse damage is caused to more expensive daggers such as the DRK Leader's by the use of inappropriate tools, in the process of disassembling them. The DRK has quite a sophisticated system for securing the grip and pommel to the tang which involves removing an ornate external screw on the top of the pommel which in turn reveals another screw recessed deep inside the pommel which then requires a two pronged tool to engage it for unscrewing. To attempt to strip a dagger such as a DRK Leader's with anything other than the correct tool is risking serious damage to an expensive edged weapon.

Even with the benefit of years of experience, it is never prudent to purchase any dagger without first stripping it: principally to examine the tang. Indeed some daggers such as the DRK Subordinate's do not carry the Maker's proofmark on the blade ricasso, but on the tang. Similarly the tang can reveal many clues to a dagger's origins and authenticity by the presence or absence of billet clamp marks, forging firescale, filing etc.

There is a specialist tool here illustrated which is an essential aid to all dagger collectors. This multi-function tool is capable of stripping all the parts of any Third Reich era dagger quickly, cleanly and without damage to any of the component parts. This particular tool is relatively inexpensive and can be obtained from many reputable dagger dealers. If any collector has difficulty in obtaining one of these stripping tools, please contact the author.

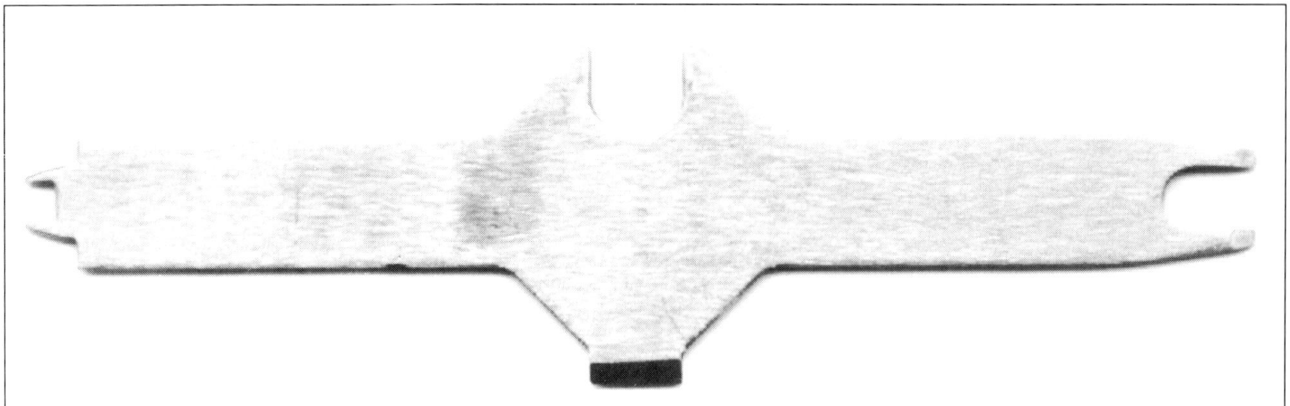

Third Reich dagger stripping tool (not to scale).

Obverse view of a genuine Diplomat's dagger with the correct type of portepee knot and hangers.

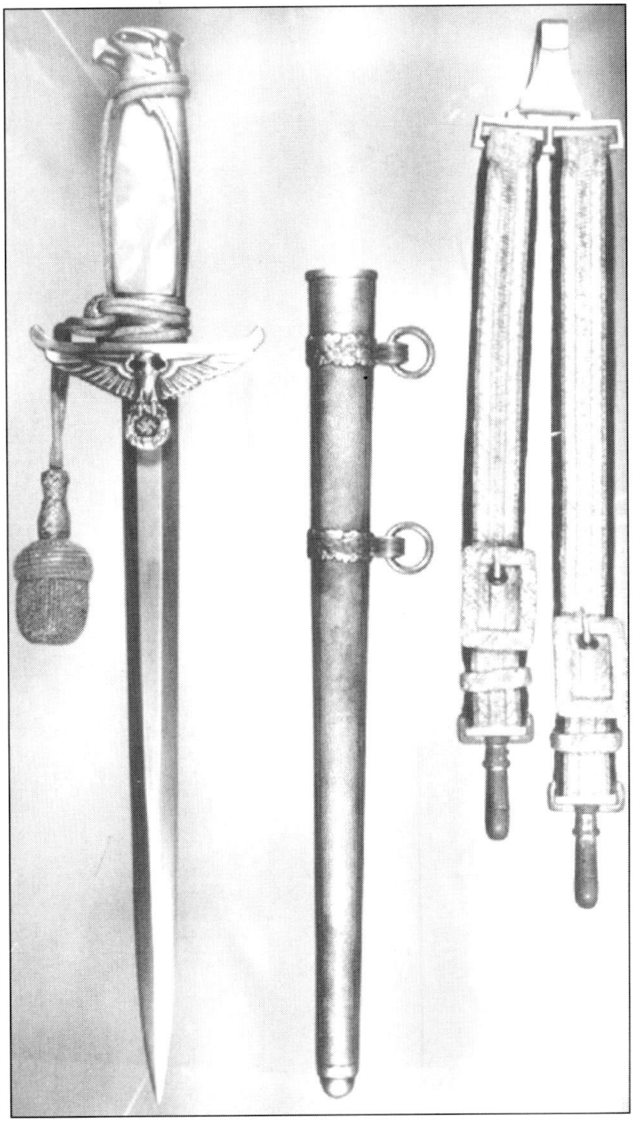

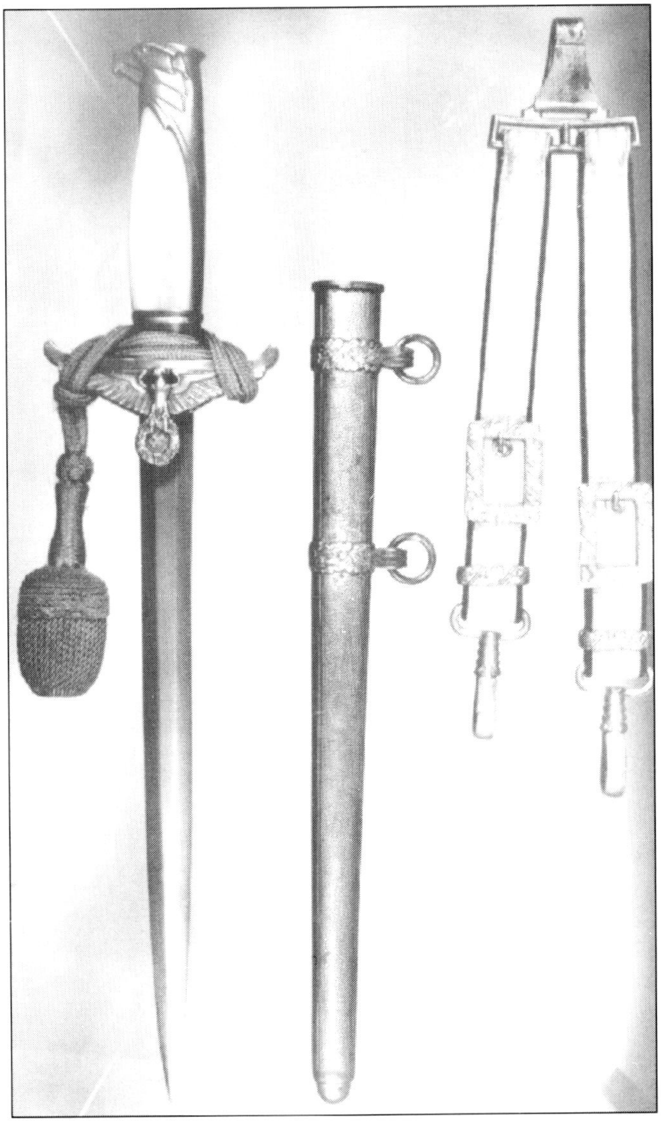

Obverse view of a genuine Government Official's dagger with the correct type of portepee knot and hangers.

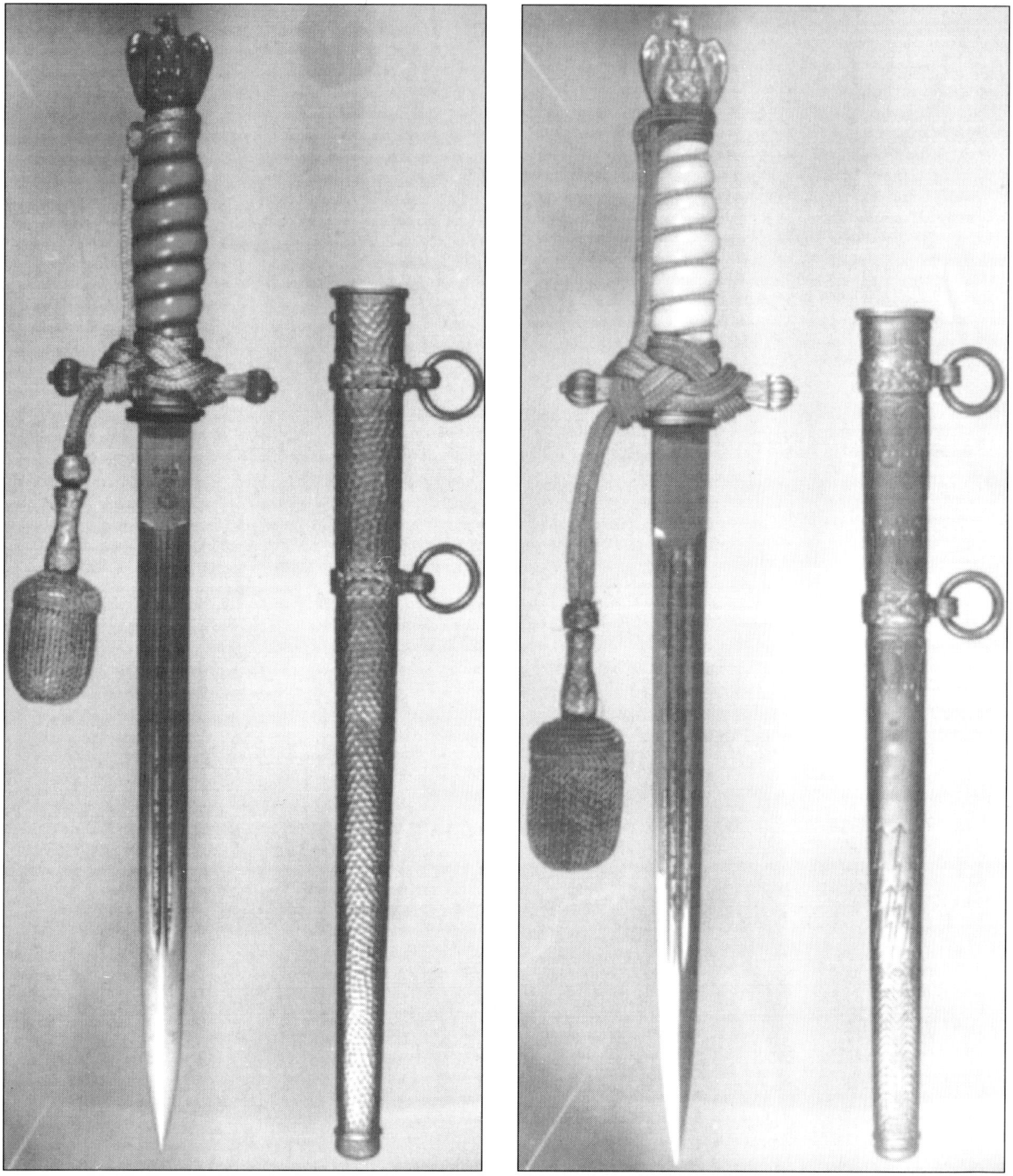

Illustrated above are two different types of genuine Kriegsmarine daggers. On the right is the most common type of naval dirk with white celluloid grip and gilded brass scabbard with the lightning bolt decoration. On the left is a good example of a deluxe pattern Kriegsmarine dirk with a hammered finish to the scabbard; this dagger also has a deep orange tone grip. The combination of hammered scabbard and orange grip is a frequent feature of this type of dagger, whilst the vast majority of genuine Kriegsmarine daggers with lightning bolt scabbards have the plain white celluloid grips.

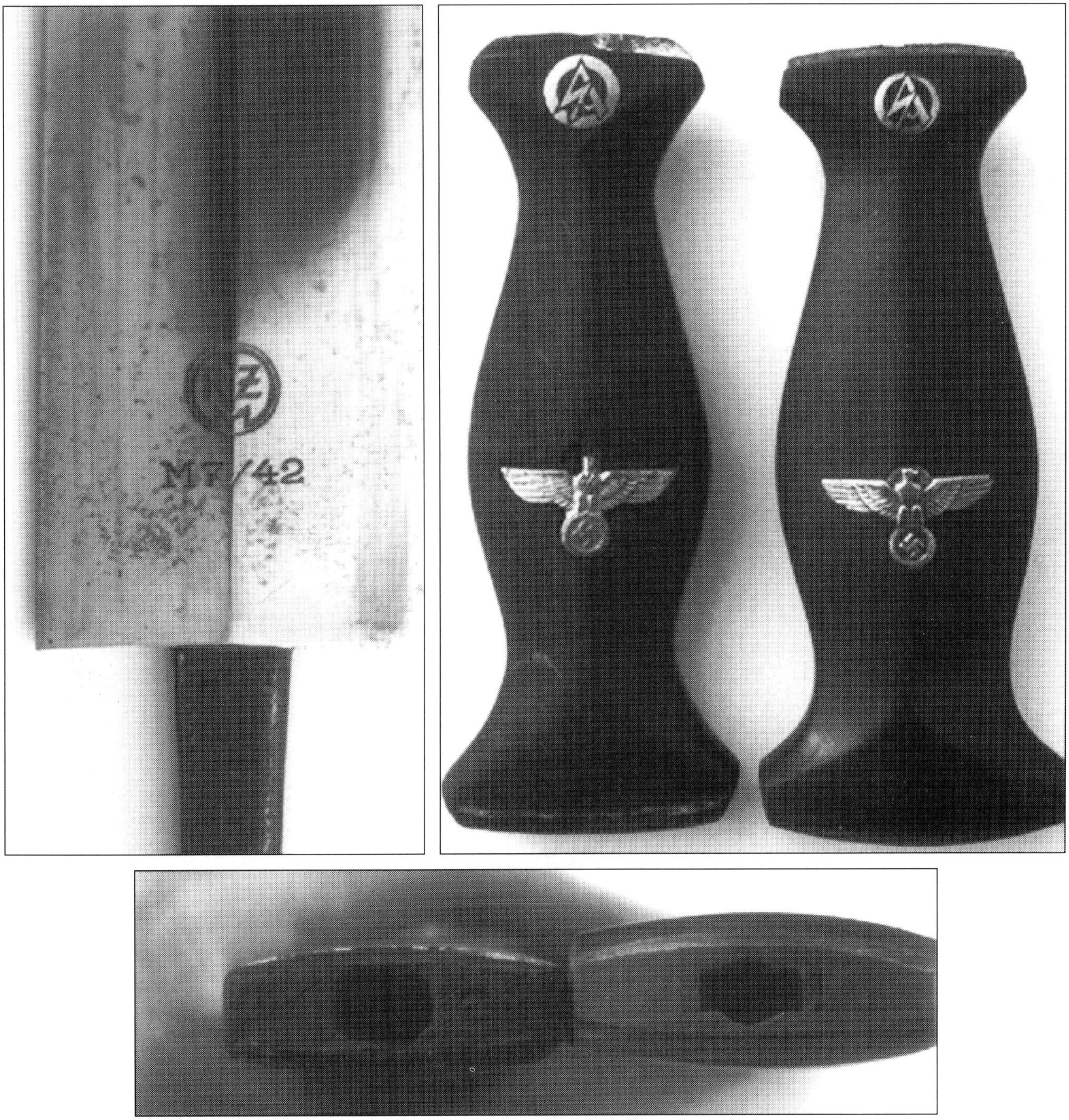

Three different aspects of a currently produced reproduction SA dagger. The two grips illustrated show the marked difference of a genuine SA grip on the right and the reproduction on the left. Note the oversized SA insignia and the badly fitting Nazi eagle insignia. Also of note are the rounded edges at the top and bottom of the reproduction grips which give a very poor crossguard to grip fit. The close up of the tang location hole in the reproduction grip shows how large and crudely formed the reproduction on the left is compared to the genuine example - this is to accommodate the broad tang of the reproduction blade. The close up of the blade ricasso shows the proofmark on this reproduction blade which is an RZM M7/42 control number of WKC which has not been widely used on reproductions until recently. Observe the poor quality of the etching on the control numbers and the hatch mark through the "7", which although of a German style was not normal practice on genuine RZM proofmarks.

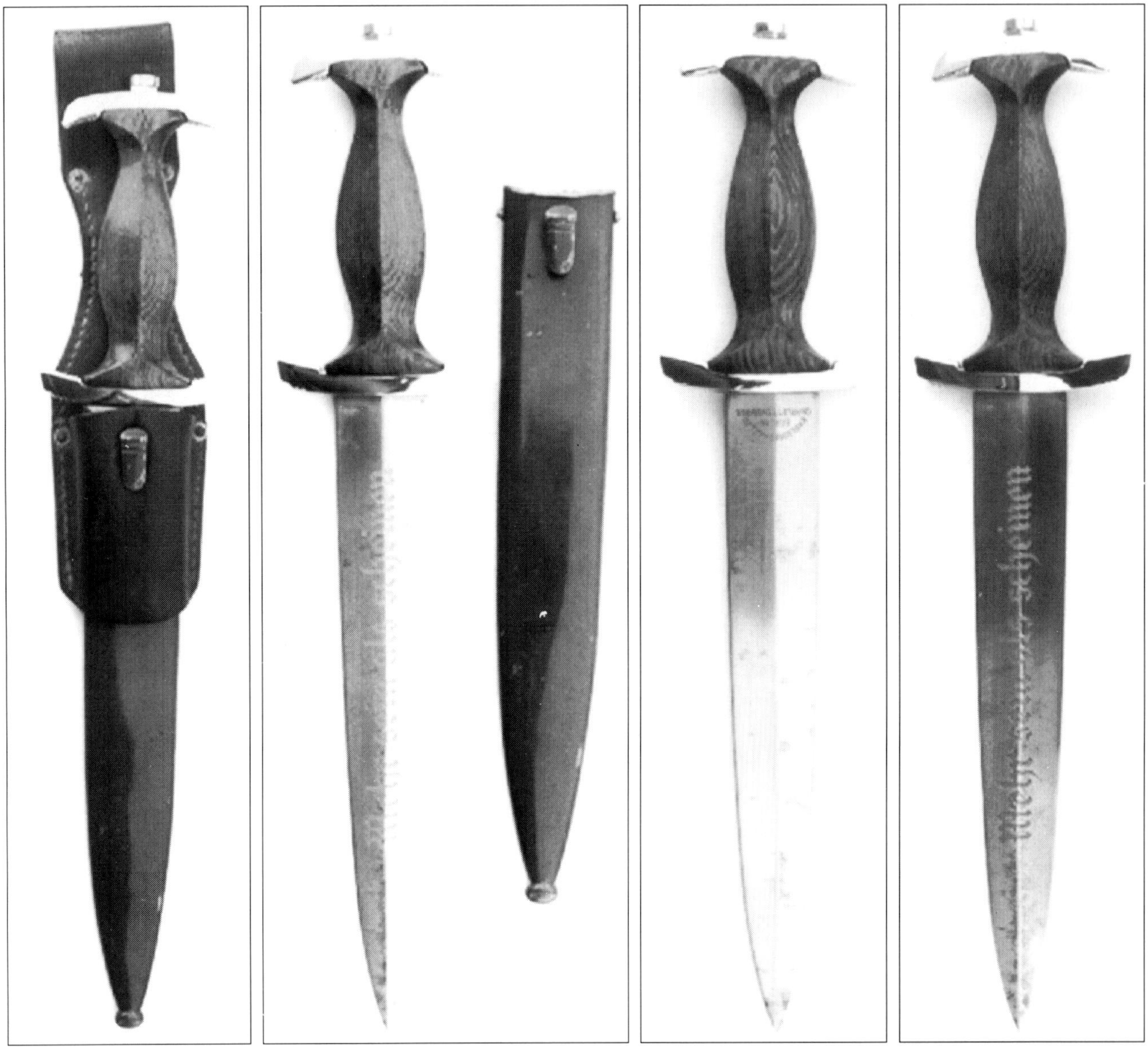

Obverse and reverse sides of the latest reproduction NPEA Student's dagger. The NPEA motto is reasonably well executed but when closely examined exhibits a ragged appearance around the edges of the lettering. The Burgsmüller proofmark is very poorly executed being engraved rather than etched; as can be observed all the letters are of varying sizes and the umlaut is missing from above the Maker's name. The tang of the blade is broad and irregular in shape unlike originals. However it is worth being wary with NPEA daggers because some of these current reproductions with the poor quality blades have had their blades removed and replaced with better quality German reproduction blades allied to the current fittings which then makes a much more passable example of this scarce dagger.

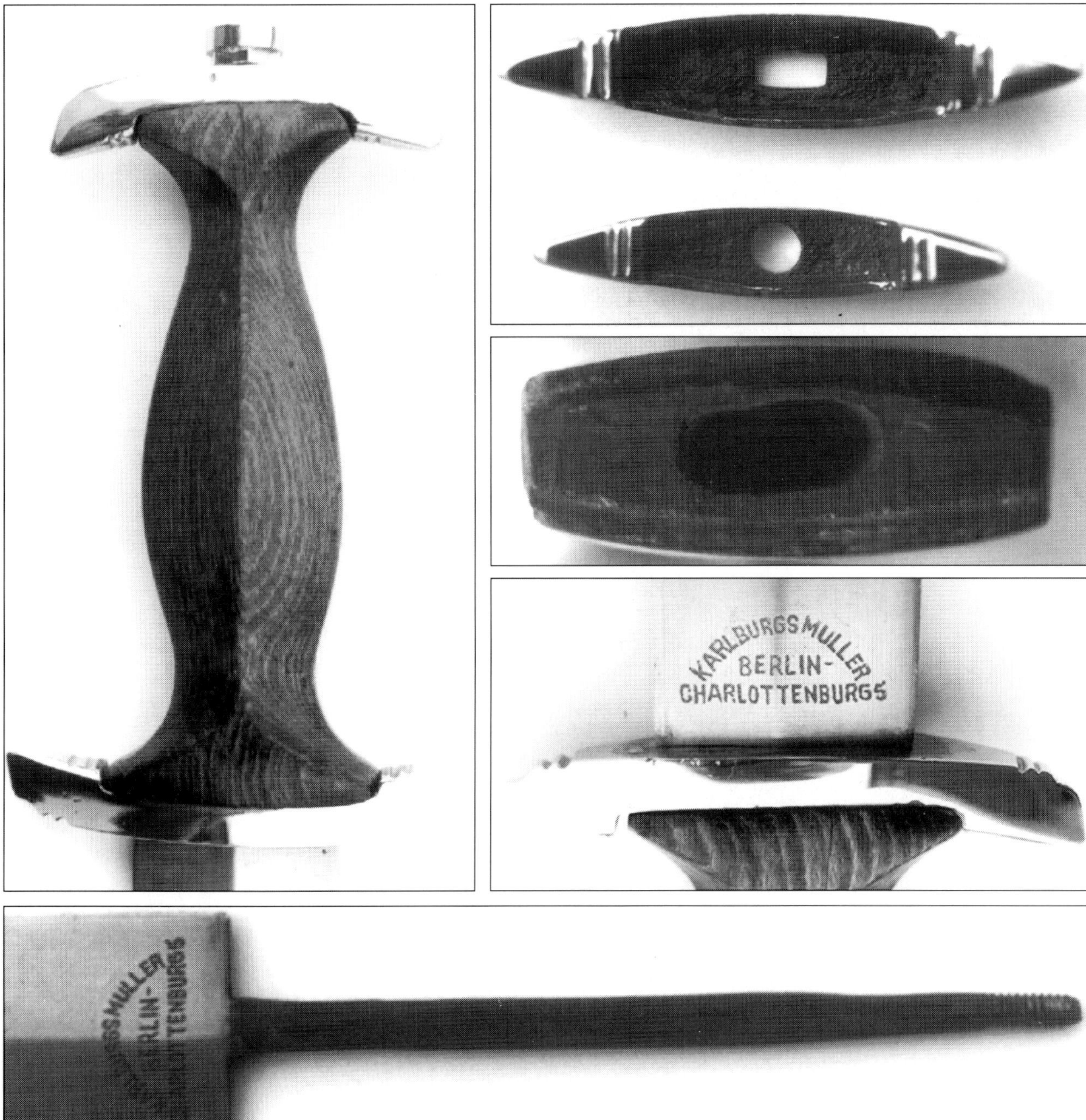

Different grip parts from the currently produced reproduction NPEA dagger. Note the irregular shape of the reproduction grip and the narrowness of its neck which tapers in extremely sharply. Also these reproduction grips are made from a softwood which has a very pronounced grain, unlike the fruitwood grips of originals; they are also heavily stained to give them an aged appearance. The grips have a very pronounced sharp central ridge. The top and bottom crossguard fittings are nickel plated and look quite good until closely examined where they exhibit castings pits, which are even more evident when viewed internally (as pictured above). The tang locating hole in the grip is very wide and irregular in shape to accommodate the broad tang of the reproduction NPEA blade. These reproduction daggers are currently available in two forms: the NPEA Student's dagger using a genuine bayonet frog, and NPEA Leader's dagger which utilises the same type of softwood grip with eagle inlay.

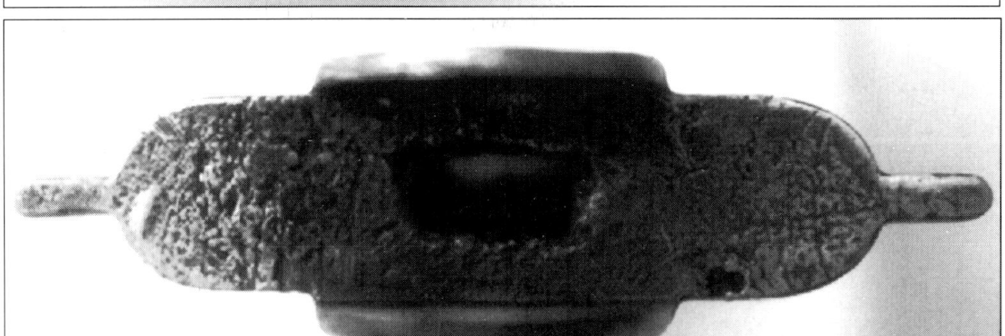

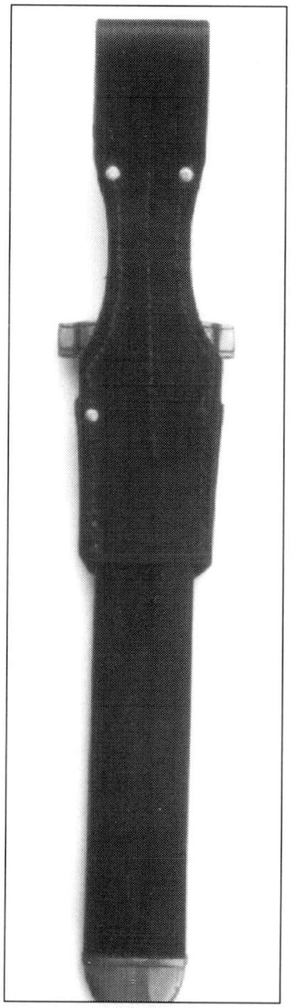
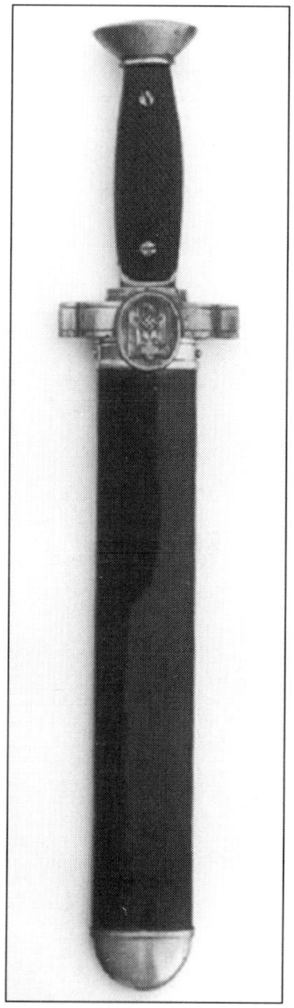
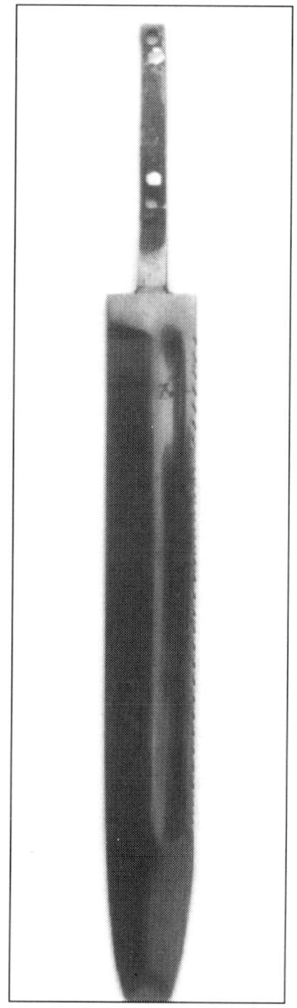
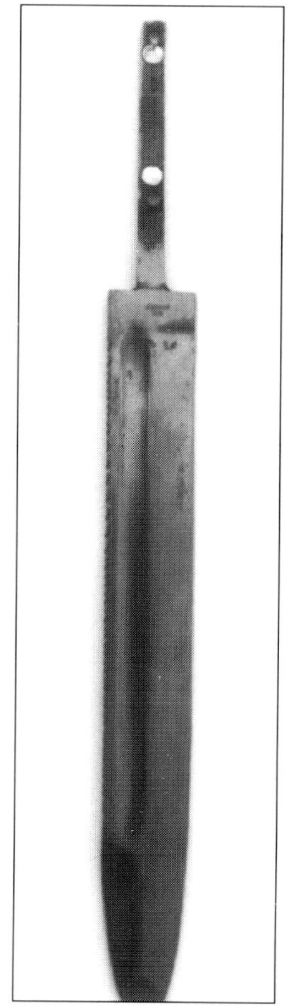
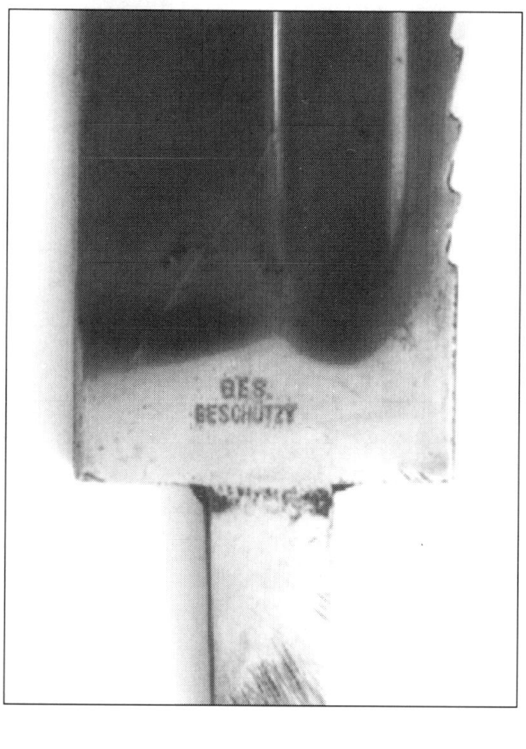

These photographs and close-ups opposite illustrate a currently produced reproduction Red Cross Subordinate's hewer which superficially looks convincing until the hewer is broken down into its component parts. The crossguard exhibits poor detail and extensive pitting from the crude casting of the parts as shown on the photographs opposite. The blade is quite well formed however the tang is very poorly finished with evidence of crude filing to accommodate the badly misshapen tang hole in the crossguard. Also the blade ricasso bears a "Ges Gesch" proofmark which has been crudely engraved - genuine Third Reich period DRK hewers did not normally exhibit any external markings on the blade. The black painted scabbard has alloy fittings top and bottom, however the bottom fitting is just jammed on and has no locating screws. The frog is the only genuine part of this hewer, but is actually a Third Reich period bayonet frog which has been added to disguise the true reproduction nature of the hewer.

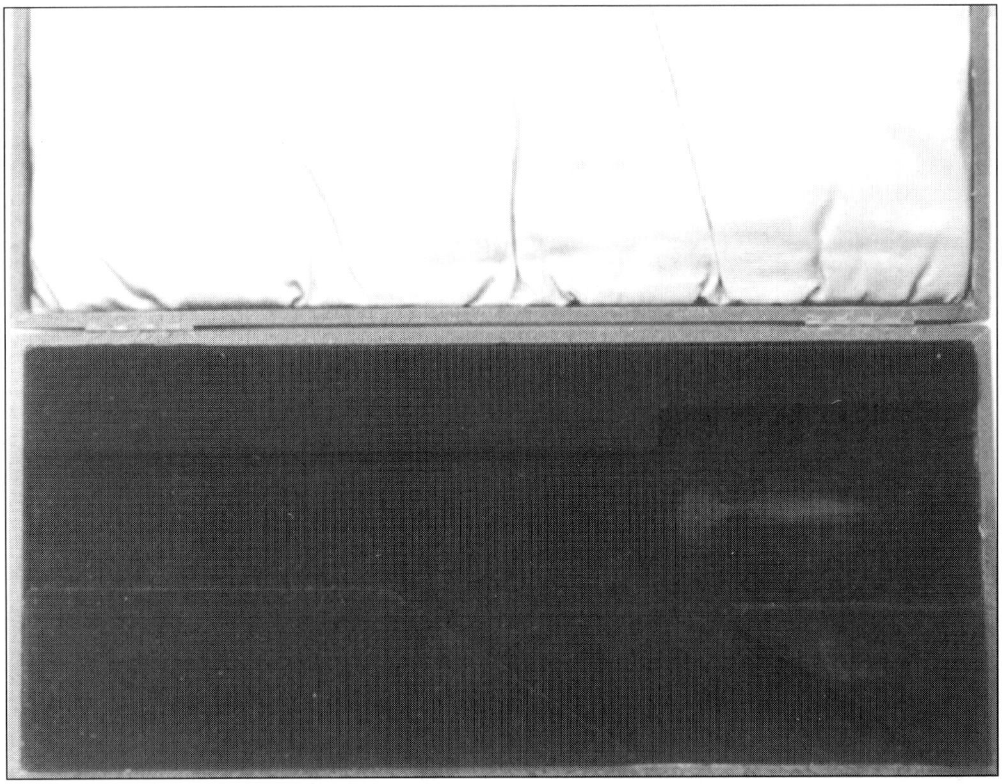

Internal and external views of a modern presentation case designed to accommodate a 1936 pattern chained SS dagger. These black leatherette cases are extremely attractive and well made with a black velvet base and a padded silk lid. The exterior of the case has two silver locking clasps and is decorated with embossed silver SS runes on the lid. Although these cases are a useful display accoutrement, they are not of the Third Reich era; however they are often erroneously used to enhance the value of an otherwise genuine chained SS dagger.

The three hanging knots above graphically illustrate the difficulty in identifying modern reproduction portepee. The example on the top left is a reproduction, whilst the central and righthand knots are examples of different types of genuine Third Reich period portepee. Areas to note on reproductions are: the shank of the knot is somewhat narrower with a more open lattice weave; the bottom of the acorn knot tapers in more sharply; and the top cone horizontal binding is slightly angled on the reproduction and has a more pronounced and exposed tuck where the end of the binding has been pushed under the base of the cone.

On the left are two genuine Third Reich Army daggers: the dagger on the right has a genuine portepee knot, whilst the dagger on the left is wrapped with a reproduction portepee. It is worth bearing in mind that condition is not always a good indicator of originality: for many reproduction knots have been artificially aged, whilst conversely there are still many genuine portepee in mint condition in circulation.

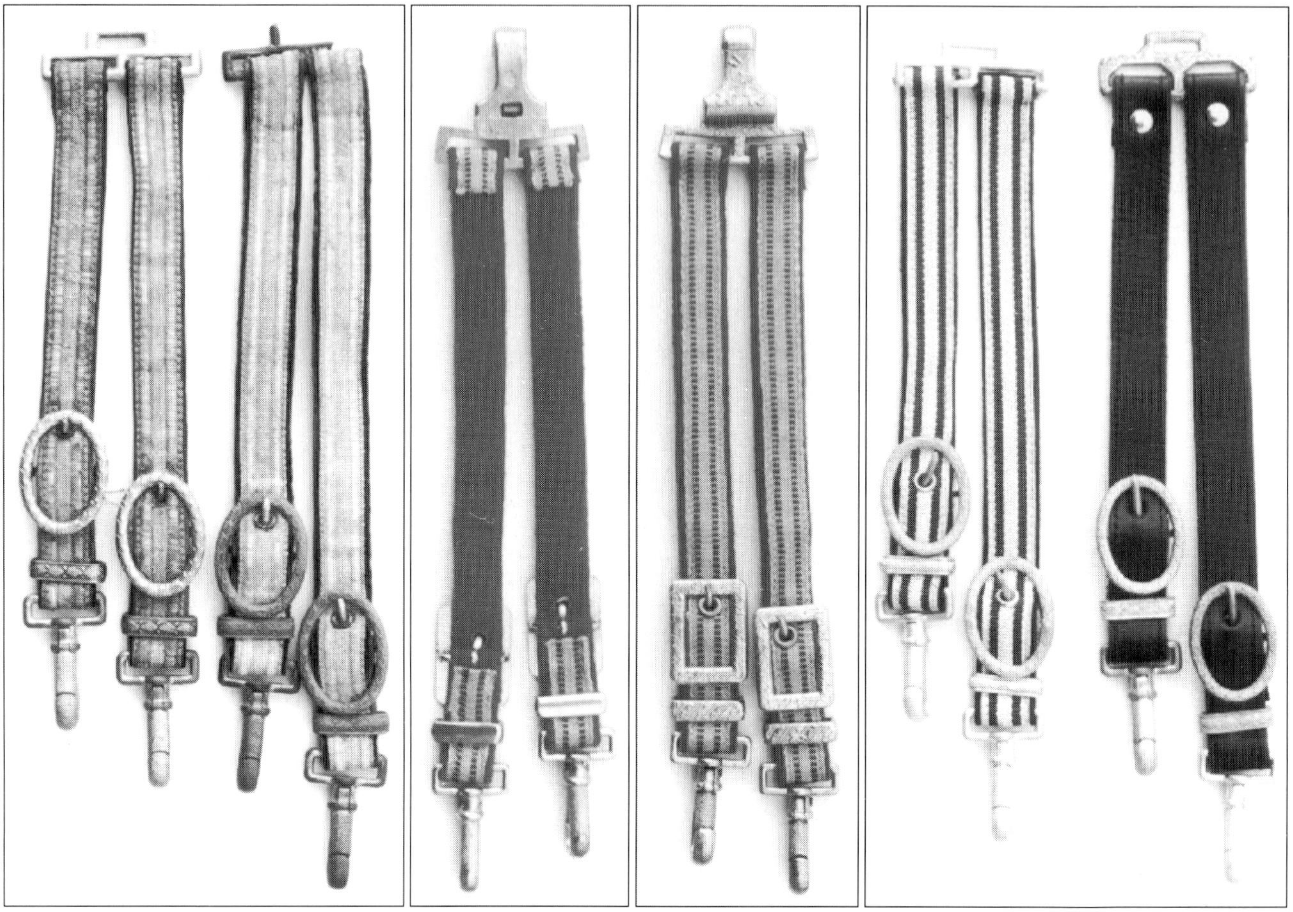

The top left box shows two sets of Army hanging straps: the set on the right being genuine. The reproduction set on the left has been made noticeably shorter - note the poor detail of the oakleaf decoration on the buckles and the plastic appearance of all the fittings which have been made from a very lightweight alloy. The top right box features two reproduction sets of rare Reichsbahn hanging straps: on the left 1938 Bahnschutz Leader's, and on the right Reichsbahn Water Protection Police Leader's. These hanging straps are extremely well made utilising leftover stock of fittings allied to modern fabric or leather. These particular straps bear the Assman proofmark on the reverse of the buckles. Due to many of the good reproduction hanging straps being made utilising leftover stocks of genuine fittings, the types of fittings on the same set of straps are often mismatched as with the Railway Water Protection hangers illustrated here which have regular clasps with a deluxe belt loop. Also when observing all the fittings overall, they often exhibit different types of material composition as well as quality. Additionally some hanging straps feature a combination of genuine and reproduction fittings or modern East German fittings. The narrow teardrop scabbard clasp is the most commonly encountered on reproduction hangers which was sometimes not appropriate for the particular organisation the straps were intended to imitate. All hanging straps now require the same close scrutiny as daggers because artificial ageing can make some of these straps very difficult to identify as reproductions. Unfortunately these good quality reproduction straps are being produced for virtually every type of Third Reich dagger. The obverse and reverse straps in the centre panels are genuine but are modern East German Army General's straps; these well made attractive hangers are now being marketed as Nazi Luftwaffe General's due to the absence of any external East German markings, their red backing and gold square buckles, and the oakleaf decoration on the fittings. These hangers carry a 6 digit production number and the letter "W" within a letter "C" inside the clasps.

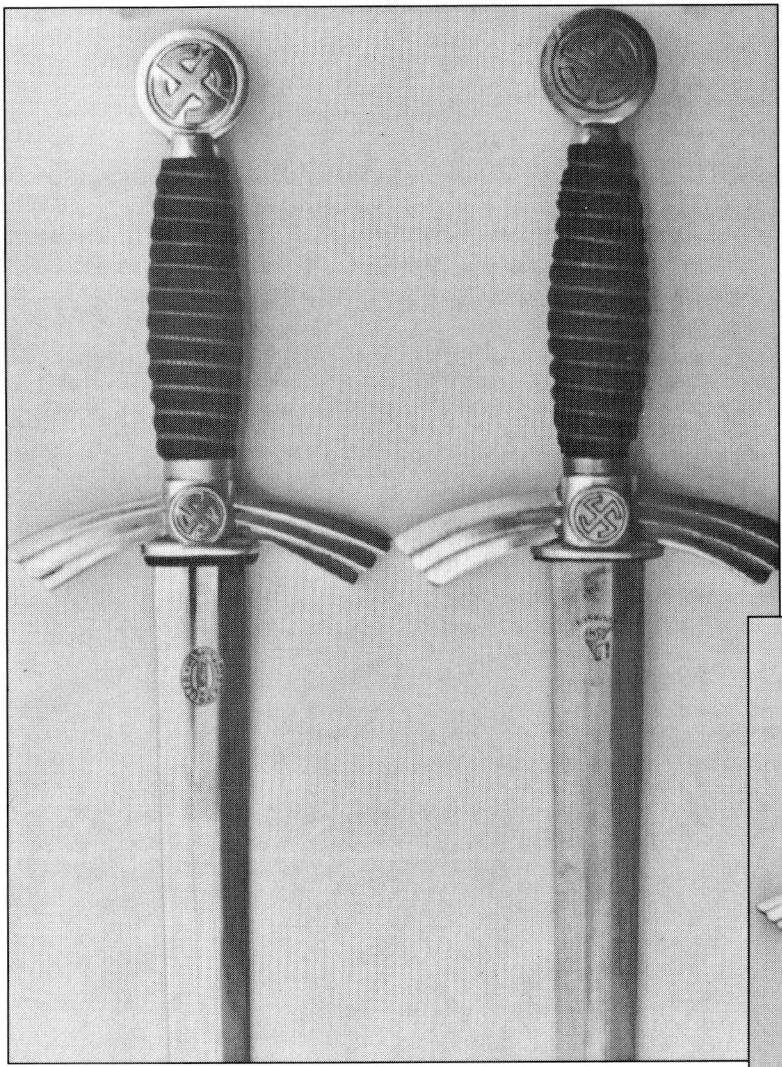

Comparison photograph of the latest reproduction 1st pattern Luftwaffe dagger on the left and a genuine example by SMF on the right. The Maker on the blade of this reproduction is that of F.W. Holler, Solingen. Note the high quality blade on the reproduction which is well formed, has a good finish and is the correct length and proportions. Also observe the thick leather blade washer on the reproduction.

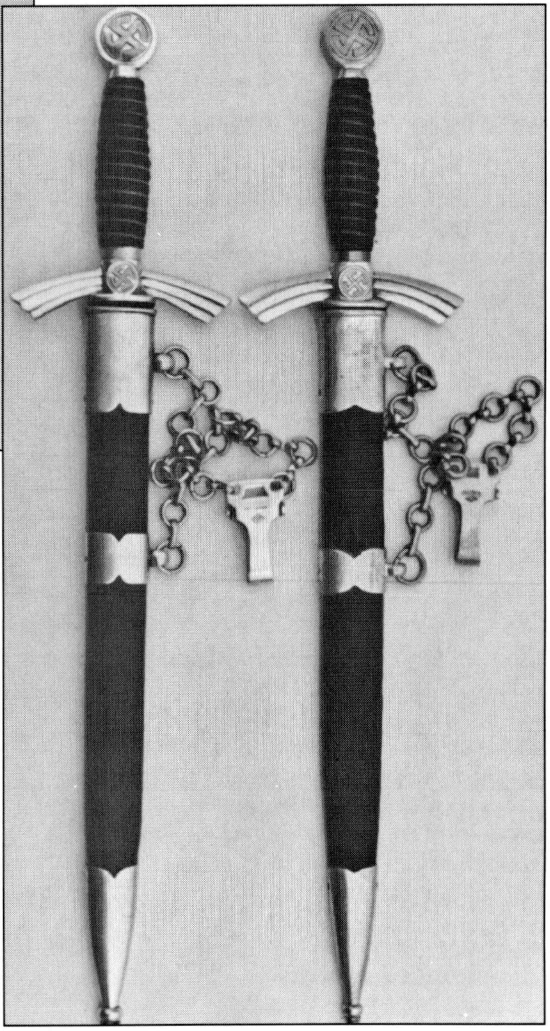

Illustrated on the right are two 1st pattern Luftwaffe daggers. The example on the right of the photo is genuine, whilst the dagger on the left is the latest reproduction of this pattern. This new reproduction is probably the best copy yet made of this dagger: all fittings including hanging chains are of aluminium with good quality blue simulated leather binding on the scabbard and grip. The grip is very well bound with a double strand twisted aluminium wire. The blade washer is made from genuine leather as were originals and only differs marginally in its thickness. The sunwheel swastika insignia on the obverse and reverse pommel and crossguard have a yellow metallic painted finish as opposed to the gilding of originals.

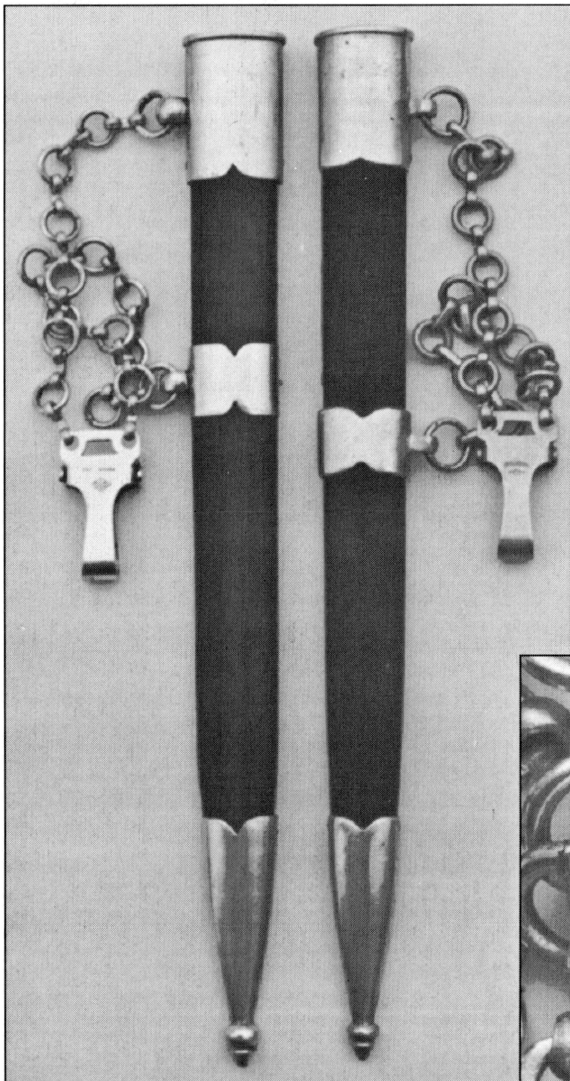

Two 2nd pattern Luftwaffe scabbards - genuine on the right and current reproduction on the left. Note the well formed shape of the reproduction, although the ball ornament on the bottom locket is too bulbous, as are the suspension chain securing loops on the top and middle fittings. Also the centre scabbard fitting is mounted too high up the scabbard. At arm's length the reproduction scabbard is difficult to distinguish from originals, however close examination will reveal a very faint grain in the binding and a noticeable gap where the scabbard covering has been joined. The hanging chains have the normal 6 upper and 8 lower links as found on most originals, however each of the rings has a small gap where they have been joined which is not usually discernible on original chains.

Close-up view of the reverse belt clips and hanging chains of a genuine 1st pattern Luftwaffe dagger on the right and reproduction chains on the left. Note the ragged proofmark within the diamond which is also misshapen compared to the elongated style of the genuine example on the right. Also note the gaps between the suspension rings of the chains.

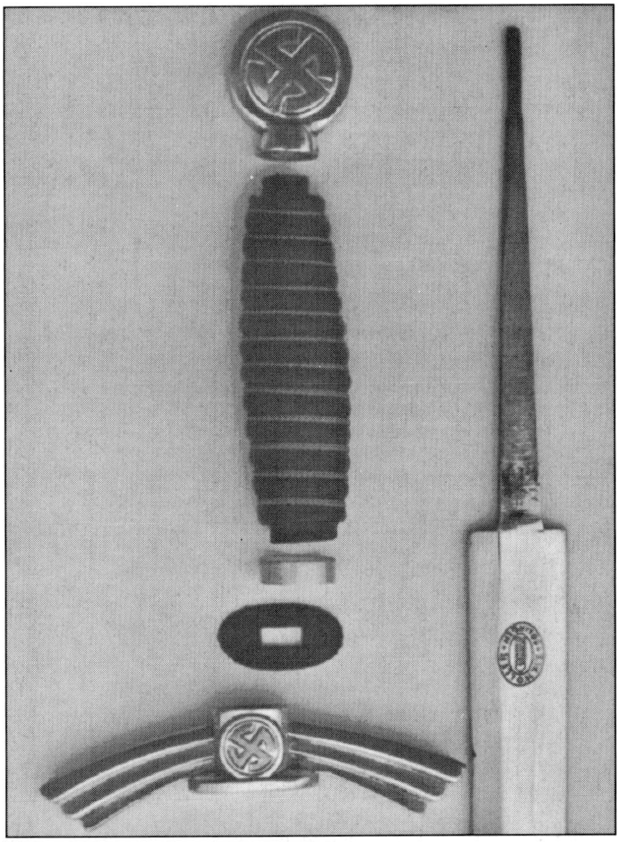

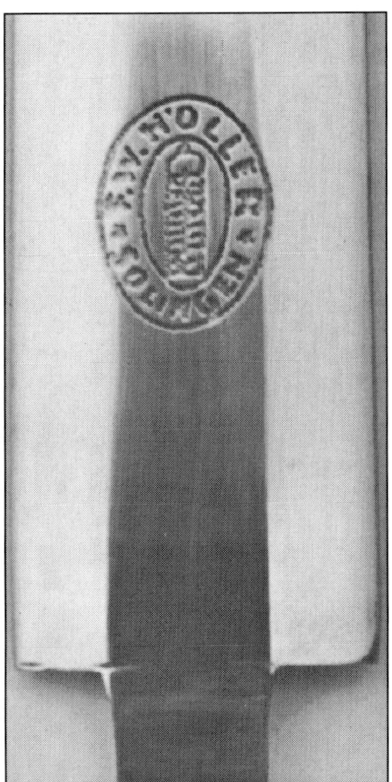

Three different views of the upper blade and grip assembly of the latest reproduction 1st pattern Luftwaffe dagger. All the component parts of the reproduction are the same as a genuine dagger however some shortcomings can be observed. In the comparison above the grip on the right is genuine with the reproduction on the left. Note that the grip is somewhat shorter which probably accounts for the extra thick blade washer, and that the wire binding exits inside the grip through holes at the top and bottom rather than gently recessing into the grip, as on the genuine example on the right. The good quality blade on this reproduction is only let down by the bogus F.W. Holler proofmark which looks acceptable until closely examined: as on the left which shows the irregular shape and size of the letters and the poor definition of the logo.

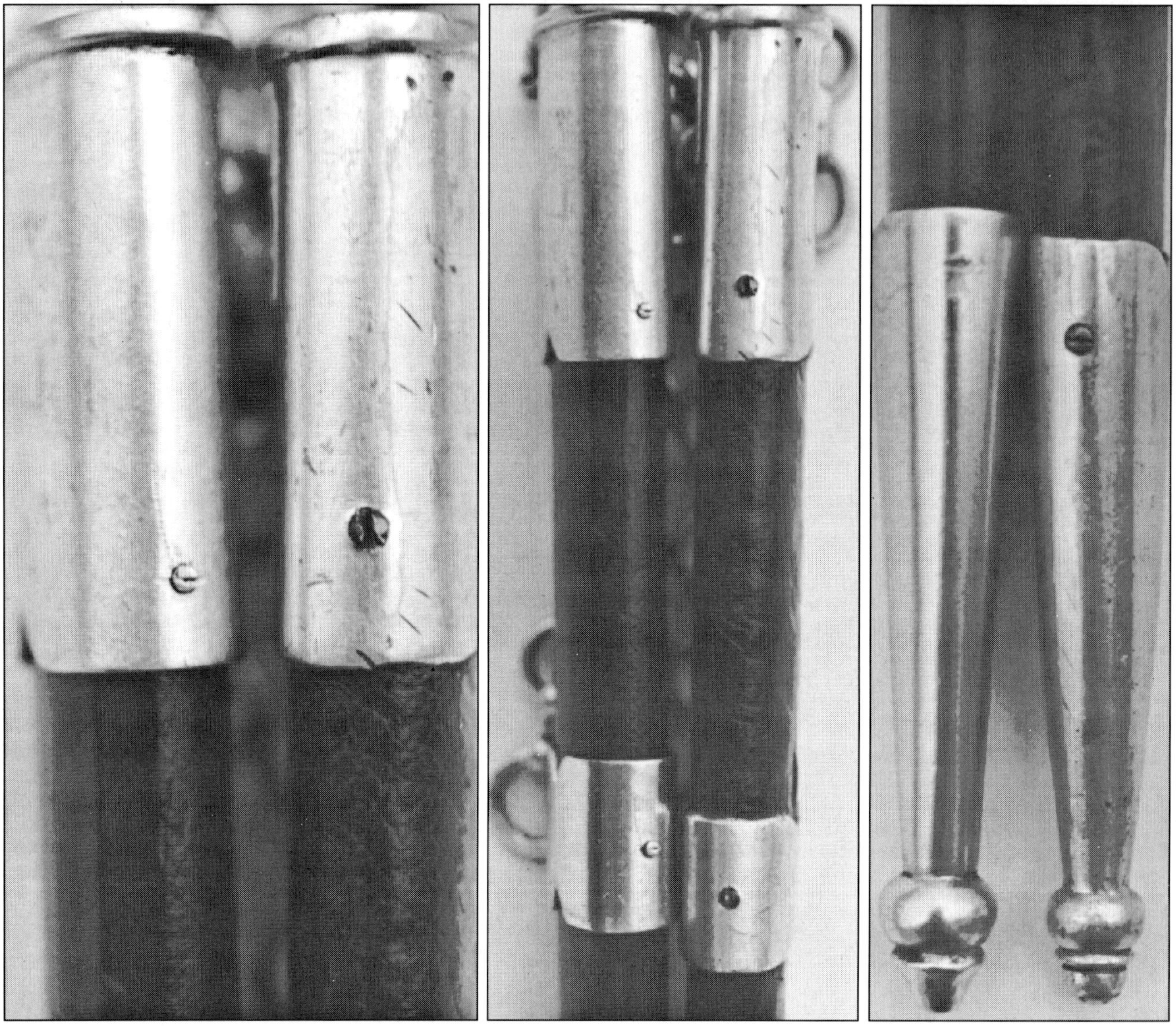

Three close-up comparison views of 1st pattern Luftwaffe scabbards - genuine on the right of each photo and the current reproduction on the left. All three fittings on the reproduction scabbard are held in place by Aluminium pins which have been hammered in and then had a groove cut into them to give them the appearance of retaining screws, however they are not removable. Note the close-up of the scabbard tips on the bottom locket which reveal an oversize spherical decoration compared to the size of the original on the right of the photograph. Also the bottom tip of this fitting only has a single groove instead of the pronounced lip of originals. Visually these reproduction scabbards are extremely good and will undoubtedly find their way into fabrications allied to genuine daggers which have lost their scabbard, as no doubt the suspension chains on these reproductions will also be misused in this way. Earlier reproduction scabbards of this pattern of dagger were quite crudely made and in most instances would not accommodate a genuine dagger which is obviously not the case with this one which has a well formed scabbard throat and is superficially difficult to detect.

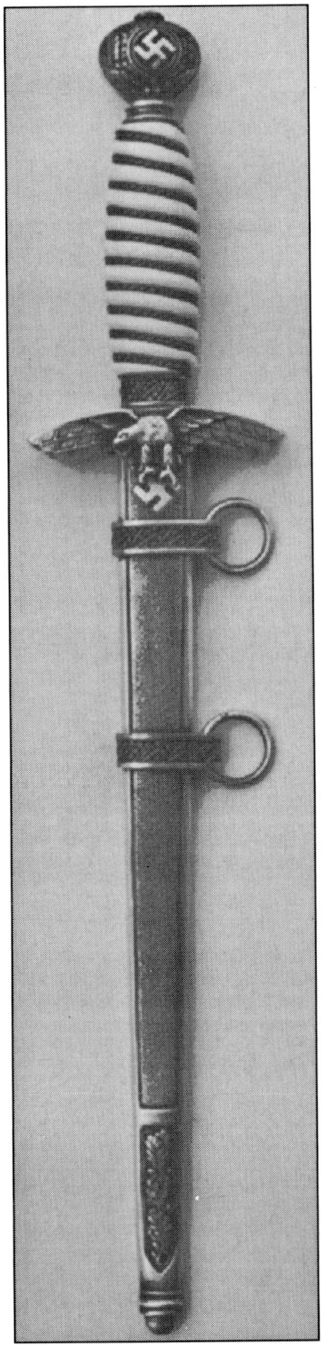 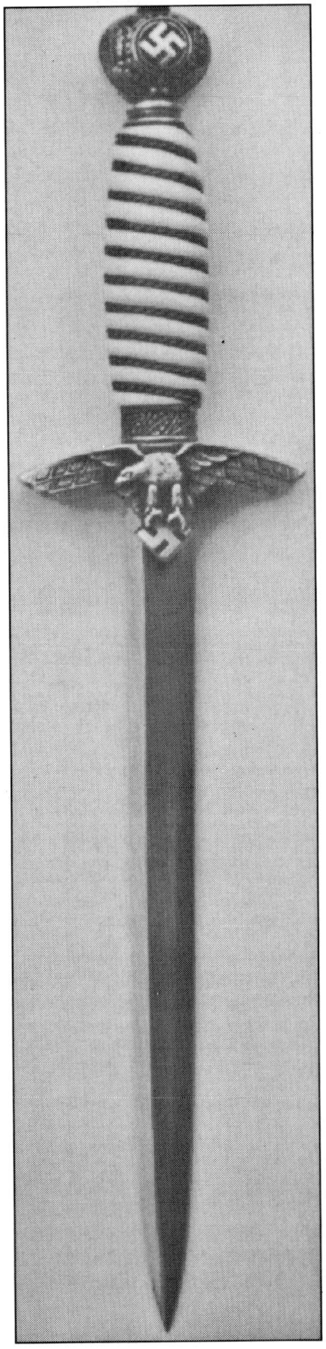 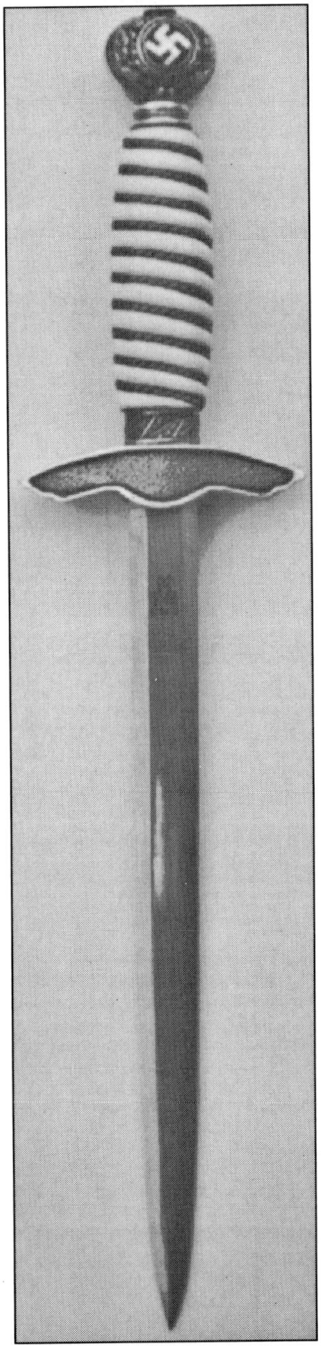 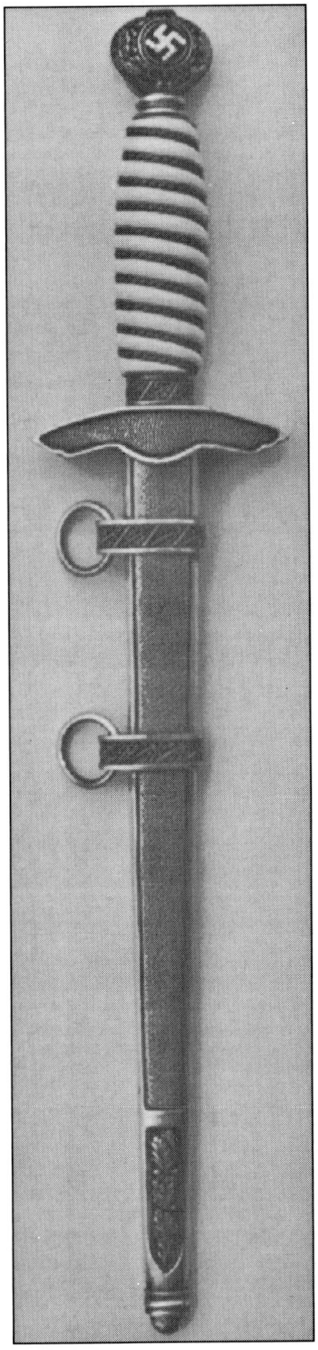

This reproduction of the 2nd pattern Luftwaffe dagger is in some respects one of the better quality reproductions now on the market. The four photos above show the dagger obverse and reverse, both in and out of the scabbard. The detail of the fittings is very crisp, especially the scabbard which is extremely well made with metal internal blade retaining slides. The main point to observe on the scabbard is the oversized hanger rings. The scabbard bands have good detail and only exhibit a minor seam unlike the earlier more obvious reproductions. The top and bottom ends of the grip should be observed as they are somewhat larger than the ferule and pommel base which results in a distinct ridge between the ends of the grip and the fittings. The real give away on these reproductions is the blade which although well made has a central plane which is too wide and bears a bogus Maker's proofmark. The scabbard and grip fittings have had a dark lacquer applied over them to give an aged appearance.

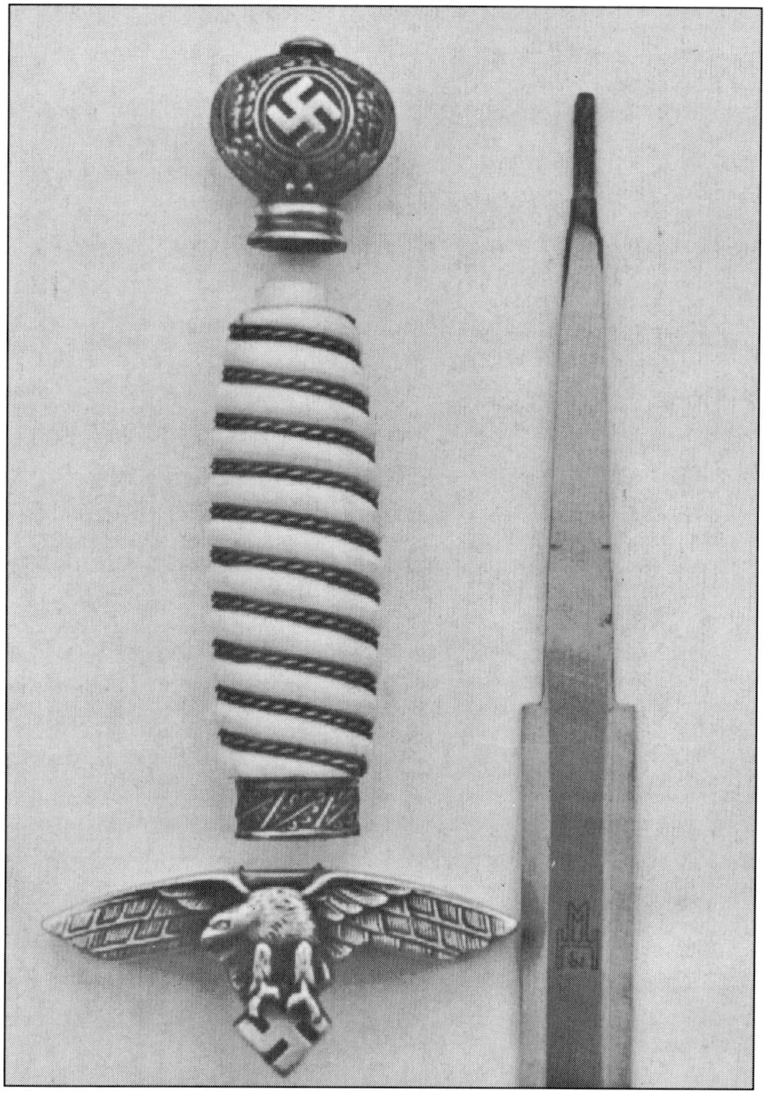

Disassembled views of the current reproduction 2nd pattern Luftwaffe dagger. The grip and fittings are visually very good but exhibit the shortcomings mentioned on the previous page. Note the use of a leather blade washer to enable the poorly made tang to fit inside the grip. The blade is the worst aspect of this particular reproduction, especially the tang which is very crudely formed and has had just rudimentary grinding and heat applied to the tip to allow the end to be threaded. The good quality fittings on this dagger will undoubtedly find their way into fabrications using genuine blades as a substitute for the abysmal specimen in this reproduction.

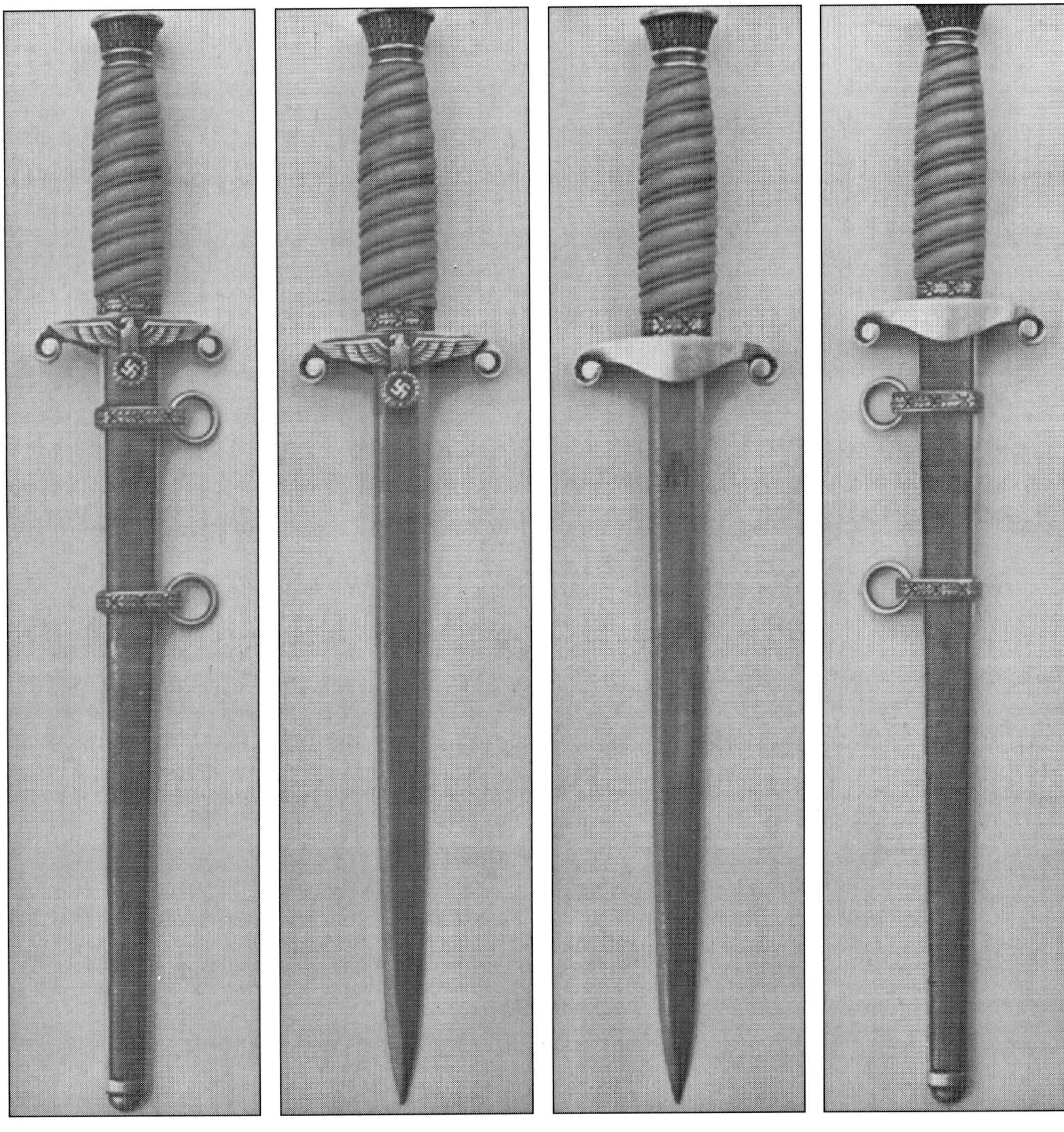

The latest reproduction Army dagger, here illustrated obverse and reverse sides, in and out of scabbard. This reproduction features some modifications to previous examples in that the detail on the scabbard bands, ferrule and pommel is very good and does not exhibit a noticeable degree of moulding seam. The grip is well formed and does not have the sharp ridges found on earlier reproductions. The scabbard has a swirl pattern but less pronounced than previously encountered. The detail of the crossguard eagle is excellent although the reverse is marginally too narrow. The blade is the same as that on the reproduction 2nd pattern Luftwaffe dagger with the M & H proofmark.

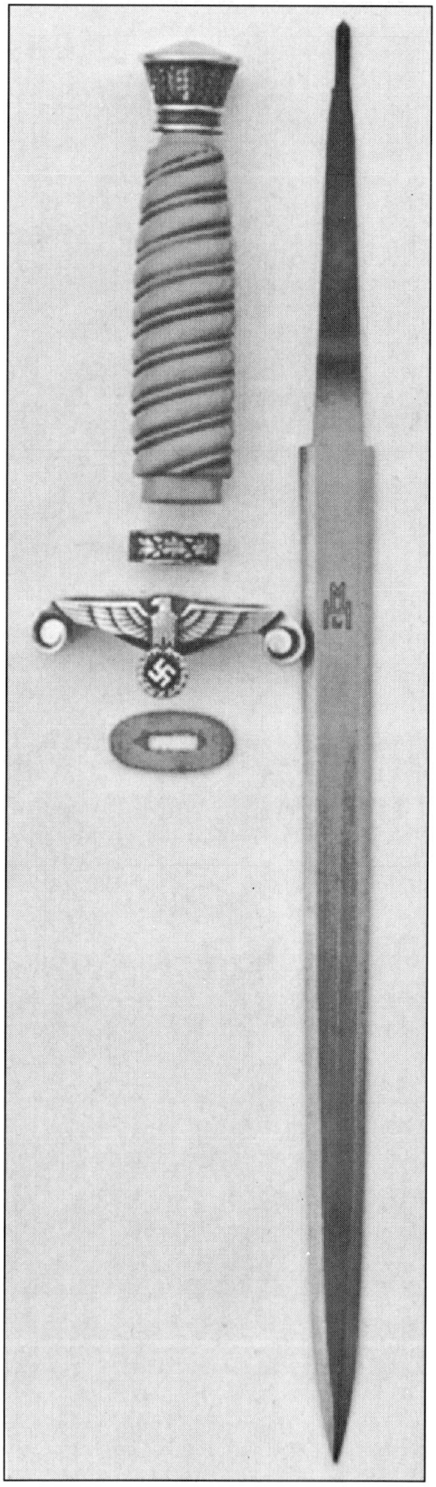

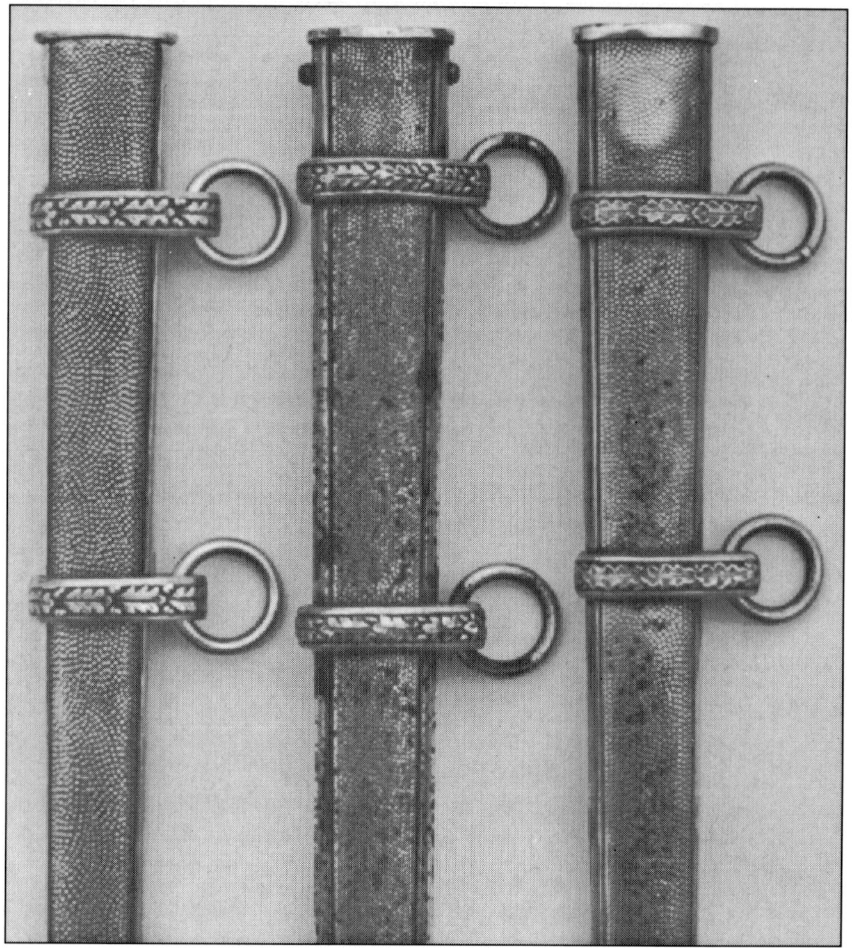

On the left is a disassembled view of the latest reproduction Army dagger: the grip and fittings are as previously described whilst the blade exhibits a crudely formed tang totally dissimilar from Third Reich era blades. Above are pictured three Army dagger scabbards: on the right a genuine example, in the middle a Spanish reproduction scabbard (which has been artificially aged to subdue the swirl pattern), and on the left the latest reproduction Army scabbard for the dagger opposite. Note how the scabbard bands on the latest reproduction are now positioned the same as those on the original, and how the detail of the oakleaf decoration has improved; however although the detail is much crisper it has more the appearance of a Christmas tree than an oakleaf and is running in the opposite direction to that of most genuine Army scabbards. Observe the scabbard throat rim which is much narrower on the reproduction - in fact even narrower than the earlier Spanish reproduction!